Family Resource
Management

MANAGEMENT IN FAMILY LIVING

MANAGEMENT IN FAMILY LIVING

FIFTH EDITION

PAULENA NICKELL

ANN SMITH RICE

SUZANNE P. TUCKER

Colorado State University

John Wiley & Sons, Inc. *New York London Sydney Toronto*

Library of Congress Cataloging in Publication Data:

Nickell, Paulena.
  Management in family living.

  Includes bibliographical references and index.
  1. Home economics.   2. Home.   3. Family.
I. Rice, Ann S., joint author.   II. Tucker,
Suzanne F., joint author.   III. Title.
TX145.N6   1976   640   75-41398
ISBN 0-471-63721-1

Printed in the United States of America

10 9 8 7 6 5 4 3 2

TO

Jean Muir Dorsey

and

The Two Husbands, Both Mike

FOREWORD

This fifth edition of *Management in Family Living* introduces two new authors— Dr. Anne S. Rice, consultant on consumer problems and curriculum development and Mrs. Suzanne Tucker, assistant professor in home and family life. To these two persons should go the credit for the preparation of this manuscript.

Management in Family Living remains a physiological approach to the use of personal and family resources in relation to goals instead of a systems approach. This edition gives the reader a wide range of writing and research into areas affecting the family in its modern environment. It thus will be useful for students studying the interaction of the family on its environment and vice versa. It is written for greater understanding by the student of societal change related to family and personal goals and use of resources.

My gratitude to the two authors for their excellence in preparation.

Long Beach, California

November 1975   Paulena Nickell

PREFACE

During the past decade, changes have occurred in the structure of college courses in management. The focus of management has shifted from care of the home and management of nonhuman resources, to decision making and development of human resources for improving life style and personal fulfillment. Management has emerged as both an art and a science for improving the quality of personal living.

This change happened simultaneously with the refinement of concepts, establishment of precise definition of terms, testing of decision-making models, acceptance of a common theoretical framework for management, and clarification of the management processes and related subsystems. A variety of urgent and provocative societal issues in modern life have mandated these changes. Among these issues are: urgency in the solution of ecological problems and environmental control, importance of individual self fulfillment and renewal, tolerance of a diversity of family forms and life styles, changes in management technology within the living unit, inequality of family income and the plight of poverty in an economy of affluence, and finally, the expansion of alternatives for women which has shifted awareness of roles from principally that of housekeeper to world citizen. Management has achieved status as education for personal fulfillment and control in living for today's families.

The fifth edition is, therefore, a complete revision of the text; it is not just an updating of references and data. The fundamental philosophy that made *Management in Family Living* a persistent choice of colleges throughout the country has been retained and developed into a framework of management as a behavioral, interaction process to achieve life goals. This edition investigates the potential and observed application of management concepts in a diversity of life styles within and outside the nuclear family.

In this edition, chapters six through nineteen of the fourth edition are condensed into three chapters. Seven new chapters are introduced and the remaining five are reoriented to the process of management. The text's *build-a-better-way-of-life* philosophy is directed toward personal fulfillment and effective use of resources without damaging or limiting the quality of resources available to our future society.

In the new edition, the lesser-developed human resources are given special treatment. Strategies for assessing and strengthening these human resources are explored. Value-clarification techniques and decision-making theories are examined in detail. Resources are clearly defined, and techniques for assessing their availability to a family group are explored.

A new chapter on communication reflects the current importance of this interaction process in implementing change in modern society. Communication was considered an influential management concept in the 1964 *Conceptual Framework in Home Management* conference proceedings, and it continues to command a place of importance in management literature. Communication is treated as an essential tool for effective management.

Previous analyses of energy and work simplification are integrated into the chapter called "Managing Home-Related Work," which has applications for all family members, not just the homemaker. This chapter illustrates the interaction of resources and goals in an applied setting.

Environmental resources are also emphasized in the fifth edition of *Management in Family Living*. Environment is defined as both "the combination of external physical conditions" and "the cultural and social conditions that affect the nature and quality of living" of an individual or group. Individual and family interaction with other environmental subsystems are explored in the chapters titled "Managing Environmental Resources" and "Managing Change".

Financial management and the use of wealth as a resource are considered in relation to desired quality of life. Because specific courses in housing, foods, clothing, furnishings, equipment, and family finance are now being offered at most colleges and universities, these resources are applied throughout the book rather than analyzed in individual chapters.

Part IV, "Management in Action," includes three provocative new chapters. "Living in a World of Many People" encompasses such topics as living in a cultural mix, coping with crisis-level change, and finding stability in a technology of change. "Managing Change" presents case vignettes and readings as excercises in decision making and identifies crucial issues that threaten society if change is not managed effectively.

A glossary of concise definitions of concepts used frequently in the text is included to help the reader understand the meaning of words in the context of management.

In summary, the overall objectives of the authors in revising *Management in Family Living* are:

- utilizing a behavioral, interaction approach—one of personal interdependency rather than home management,

- viewing management as four interacting processes,

- emphasizing human and environmental resources,

- recognizing the relationship between personal management and world ecology—social and biological,

- stressing change as a function of management,

- humanizing management by treating it as a practical system for goal-attainment,

- rendering management relevant to male and female college students by treating management as the administrative branch of personal living,

- heightening the interest of readers through controversy and a sense of inquiry, by raising questions rather than providing "pat" answers,

- assuring a broad application of the book by avoiding typical white, Anglo-Saxon, middle-class family orientation as the only possible life style, and

- producing a practical, college management text that portrays clearly the major management concepts and the framework they form and helps students apply these concepts to their personal and professional lives.

The fifth edition of *Management in Family Living* is, by design, a comprehensive but readable college-level management text, unencumbered by excessive references to research. Yet, it is strongly based on research and incorporates the research findings from many fields of study into its practical, humanistic approach to management as an avenue to a better way of life.

DR. ANN S. RICE
DR. SUZANNE TUCKER
AUGUST 1975

CONTENTS

FOREWORD

PART I CONCEPTS OF MANAGEMENT

1 FAMILY LIFE IN A CHANGING WORLD   3

2 NATURE AND ROLE OF MANAGEMENT   31

3 MOTIVATIONS FOR MANAGEMENT   57

4 DECISION MAKING   85

5 IDENTIFYING RESOURCES   109

6 ASSESSING RESOURCES   137

PART II MANAGING HUMAN RESOURCES

7 DEVELOPING HUMAN RESOURCES   157

8 STRENGTHENING COMMUNICATION   195

9 MANAGING TIME   219

10 MANAGING HOME-RELATED WORK   241

PART III MANAGING ECONOMIC RESOURCES

11 MANAGING INCOME AND CREDIT   273

12 WEALTH AS A RESOURCE   325

PART IV   MANAGEMENT IN ACTION

13   MANAGING ENVIRONMENTAL RESOURCES   367

14   LIVING IN A WORLD OF MANY PEOPLE   399

15   MANAGING CHANGE   421

GLOSSARY   457

INDEX   467

MANAGEMENT IN FAMILY LIVING

Part I

CONCEPTS OF
MANAGEMENT

1

FAMILY LIFE IN A CHANGING WORLD

What do people want from life? How do they go about differentiating between the important and the unimportant? Once people recognize priorities in their lives, how do they achieve what they desire? Are the answers to these questions consistent throughout life?

Determining individual answers to these and similar questions can provide direction to life in this changing world. Change occurs through the application of natural and human forces. Floods, wind storms, and earthquakes are examples of natural forces; while mobility, population growth, and technology are examples of human forces. If people know and understand what they want from life, they can make adjustments to accommodate even the changes they cannot control.

For example, a person may decide that a comfortable living unit, close friends, family contacts, religious service, or learning are important. If a change—of job, health, income, or location—happens to such a person, he or she might reevaluate these priorities but would be guided by the knowledge of what is important in making the needed change. Policy decisions or guidelines for the allocation of resources are among the techniques used to establish or demonstrate prioritities in life.

Hill referred to the establishment of family policies as an influential factor in attaining a successful family life. His research brought about the discovery that families having consistent policies about the use of money, time, and other resources, are more successful in adjusting to change than those who do not have such policies.[1] Examples of policy decisions could include when family members should use a credit card or pay cash for a purchase, children's bedtimes, or whether or not household items should be shared with those outside the immediate family. These general decisions guide family members in making individual actions consistent with family priorities.

Change then occurs in each person's or family's life. Knowledge of the concepts of management can be applied to any goal, life style, small group or

3

social class—to direct change toward a more satisfying life. Management involves making things happen in personal, family, or community life.

Quality of Life

Feelings of happiness or satisfaction with material and nonmaterial accomplishments are termed *quality of life.*[2] Measures of change in quality of life within society have been attempted but have been only partial indicators of material and nonmaterial accomplishments.

The Gross National Product (GNP) is one of the frequently cited yet incomplete measures of material progress. GNP is a summary of the monetary value of goods and services produced primarily through gainful employment. The negative effects on quality of life caused by environmental pollution, unemployment, or underemployment are missing from this measure. Included in GNP is the money spent to solve past mistakes, as in the case of curtailing water pollution. These expenses may prevent further deterioration of the water, but will probably not advance the quality of life. Other spending may inhibit quality of life but is included in GNP calculations.

Also omitted from GNP are most contributions of those performing work for no pay. Household members' use of time in home-related work affects people's feelings of satisfaction, as does volunteer work or personal care time. Economists who have calculated the market value of household work of all family members estimate that the value of this work would increase GNP by approximately one-fourth to one-third.[3] These services do not involve money exchanges and, therefore, are currently omitted from GNP calculations.[4]

Nonmaterial accomplishments are more difficult to measure because characteristics like changes in feelings of human dignity are specific to a given time, person, and place. In a volume titled *Indicators of Social Change,* the need for measuring society's successes and failures in nonmaterial accomplishments is explored. Changes in environmental quality, family structure, and consumer practices are examples of some of the proposed indicators of social change.[5] Both measures of material and nonmaterial accomplishment are incomplete; but they do indicate trends that affect quality of life for individuals and families.

Although no one set of national goals for quality of life meets all person's needs, social service professions are recognizing the importance of the concept of quality of life. Objectives for one such agency, the Cooperative Extension Service, are included in a report, "A People and a Spirit," and are listed as follows:

1.   Enhance the quality of individual and family decisions and provide the skills to carry them out.

2. Help people learn to use community services and take part in developing them.

3. Improve the social, economic, and geographic mobility of the individual.[6]

These goals describe skills that people may need to achieve what they want but do not describe specific qualities of life.

In trying to improve quality of life, people attempt to control themselves and their surroundings. People who once might have adopted new tools, substances, or methods without a second thought are now asking themselves if these changes improve, inhibit, or maintain quality of life. There are no easy answers to such questions. While most people agree that quality of life is desirable, definitions of specific qualities and ways to reach them differ, as illustrated by the following life styles.

LIFE STYLES

Through the selection and implementation of a life style, people demonstrate qualities of life—what they want, expect, and consider reasonable in their lives. A life style includes the roles and role combinations an individual accepts—consumer, citizen, employee, parent, and spouse are examples. These roles aid individuals in defining relationships and in adjusting selected roles to those of other people or groups. If these role combinations become a pattern shared by groups of people, they are termed a *life style*. According to Feldman and Thiebar, life style also involves a central life focus such as rearing children, employment, or community involvement.[7]

Families are considered, by some persons, to be the dominant life style in society,[8] while others contend that family membership as a life style may be a thing of the past.[9] In discussing family life, authors even differ in their definitions of the term "family." The Bureau of the Census' definition is often used:

The term 'family'. . . refers to a group of two persons or more related by blood, marriage, or adoption and residing together; all such persons are considered as members of one family.[10]

A very broad definition of a family is a group of two or more persons who are economically and emotionally interdependent. Others define the term as a nuclear family—a man and woman joined in marriage, and their children.[11] Perhaps authors choose their definitions from possible life styles.

Family Life Styles

The nuclear family is a frequently discussed "life style" interpreted as a social norm. In this family form, individuals interact with each other in relationships such as husband-wife, father-mother, son-mother, or brother-brother, as well as relating to groups or persons outside the family. Murdock considers the socialization of children to be the central focus in this family norm.[12]

There may be more than one life style within the nuclear family. If a woman combines employment with home-related roles, as approximately two-fifths of the married women do,[13] her life style and that of her family differs from a similar family in which the woman is a full-time homemaker. If an employed woman considers her family roles to be more important than her career roles, her family's life style as well as her own could differ from that of the family whose individual careers are as important or more important than family life.

The reversal of roles—husbands as homemakers and wives as breadwinners—is another alternative within the family. The above examples illustrate ways in which changes in the roles of one or more family members can alter a family's life style.

The number of people in the family and their individual resources affect and are affected by life style decisions. The role combinations of a childless family for example, differ from those of families with children. An increase in the number of childless families is revealed in the following statistics:

About one out of four married couples with husband under 35 years old in March 1972 had no own children under 18 years old present in their home.[14]

In contrast, the 1960 Census figure was 18 percent. For these childless families, socialization of children would be replaced by other central concerns, such as community services or career development.

Single parent families account for about 11 percent of all households and numbered close to 7.5 million in the mid-seventies. Most of these families were headed by women.[15] The life style of these families was changed through death, divorce, adoption, or the birth of a child to an unmarried woman. People who retire or become disabled may also select new role combinations because of changes in time demands, financial resources, or physical abilities. A person's or family's life style may change with time, and not all changes are completely controlled by the individual.

Interactions between grandchildren, parents, and other relatives are a part of life style that can also influence an individual's perception of quality of life. Researchers have observed the contact between relatives outside the nuclear family. According to Turner:

. . . an abundance of evidence has recently been assembled to show that kinship remains a factor in the lives of most American families at all socio-economic levels and that relations among kin have more than a token significance.[16]

Hill's study of three-generational families in the Minneapolis-St. Paul area disclosed that more help was given to and received from family than to or from any other source.[17] Some nuclear families may not be as isolated and independent as was once assumed.

Alternate Life Styles

The divorce rate has been perhaps illegitimately used to illustrate widespread dissatisfaction with current family life styles. The often-mentioned statistic—one divorce for every four marriages—is misleading. According to Scanzoni, this statistic compares the annual number of marriages to the number of divorces granted in that year.

Scanzoni suggested an alternate comparison of the number of divorces to every 1000 married women—approximately one percent in 1967. While this percentage seems small, 523,000 divorces were granted during that year alone.[18] The remarriage rate among divorced persons is higher than the marriage rate among single persons.[19] Could this comparison of marriage rates mean that divorced people are more disillusioned with their marriage partners or specific situations in their marriages than they are with marriage in general?

Life style selection can also occur outside the previously mentioned family forms. Among alternate life styles are communal groups, singleness, group marriage, homosexual relationships, or cohabitation without marriage. Each of these alternatives has more than one life style possibility. Communes for example, can be oriented toward religious values, "dropping out" of society, creation of a new social order, or other goals. These groups may or may not involve nuclear families, the presence of children, or sexual monogamy. There may or may not be a pooling of individual resources for the group's welfare, and the size and degree of permanence of such groups varies.

Some of the above life styles may seem unusual to people who have been members of nuclear families, but communal living, polygamy, and other alternatives have existed in society for many years.[20] Although accurate national statistics indicating the number of people choosing alternate life styles or their relative success are unavailable, it is important to remember that such alternatives do exist, regardless of whether or not the reader considers them desirable.

This discussion of life styles is a brief analysis, but it illustrates some trends in role selection within and outside the family. The purpose of the discussion is to indicate the diversity in life styles and to serve as a background for the study of managerial situations and problems that individuals and families encounter in working toward specific qualities of life.

Family Functions and Management

What do families do—what functions do they serve—for individuals, for the family group, and for society? Researchers and theorists have outlined purposes or *functions* of families that have an impact on management. Some or all of the functions described below may be applied to alternate as well as traditional life styles. The ways in which these functions are performed, as well as the priorities placed upon them, reflect the specific life style of the group.

FAMILY FUNCTIONS FOR INDIVIDUALS

Families provide individuals with experiences that can aid in personality development. Accepting roles, learning tasks, and receiving support and security from other family members are among the activities that can influence personality development. Home managers who select experiences appropriate for the individual's abilities are considering this family function.

Current analyses of the relative success with which families perform this function include the questioning of what are or should be appropriate male and female roles. People are asking if personality development applies to adults as well as to children, to the aged as well as to young adults. Do parents, for example, learn from their children's communication or from changes in household responsibilities? While families are not the sole influence in personality development, the daily contact between family members has its impact on individual personality and on quality of life.

FUNCTIONS FOR THE FAMILY AS A GROUP

Families also serve functions for the family group. Bell and Vogel isolated four such functions: task performance, leadership, integration and solidarity, and pattern maintenance.[21] Task performance varies with the commitment of individuals within the family. If family members can understand that domestic responsibilities relate to family or personal goals, they will be more committed to performing such tasks. Individuals who appreciate and respect family membership will be more cooperative in task performance than those who are only partially committed. According to Bell and Vogel, sharing tasks can also increase the bonds between family members and, hence, enhance feelings of group unity.[22]

Roles of Family Members

There has been a decline in the size of families. Birth rates and expectations for family size have decreased.[23] Sex role specialization becomes difficult to maintain as family size decreases. Research indicates that employment and leisure are of primary importance to American men, and marriage and parenthood are generally secondary but supportive roles. Typically, a man who is a good provider is considered a valuable family member; but young men report more active family roles than those of previous generations.[24]

In a study of time used for household work, men averaged 1.6 hours daily, whether or not their wife was employed. As in previous studies, the tasks performed by males followed a sexual division of labor. Husbands generally did yard work, household maintenance, and helped other family members with record keeping, shopping, and entertaining children. Husbands of employed homemakers who had small babies provided considerably more help than did other husbands. The amount of time men used for home-related work appeared to also vary with the number of hours they were employed.[25]

The participation of women in the labor force was mentioned earlier in this chapter. Increasing numbers of young married women, including those with preschool children, have been adding part time or full time work roles to their home related roles. Females in the above study did most of the home-related work regardless of whether or not they were employed. The daily averages ranged from four or five hours for employed women without children to 12 hours for unemployed women with seven or more children, one of which was under one year of age.[25] Should roles be clearly defined according to one's sex? Although authors may be advocating shared task performance, research indicates that this sharing is not typical, at least for the families in the Cornell University study.[26]

Leadership

Leadership, the process of influencing others by ideas, is an important resource for management.[27,28] Although one or more family members may finalize decisions, these people may be influenced or led by others in the household. Leadership, as discussed by Bell and Vogel, should involve a consideration of individual needs, interests, and goals as well as those of the group as a whole. There can be any number of leaders providing direction toward family goals, and leadership can change with the specific decision as well as gradually over a period of time.

Employed family members have been observed to have slightly more influence in decision making than those who were unemployed. Perhaps, as Blood and Wolfe suggested, the relative influence of family members may be decided by the resources they provide to the family.[29] *Democratic decision making,* in which each person affected by an action has a voice in making the decision, is an idealistic form of leadership. In practice there is a plurality of power divisions among family members with the norm being slightly in favor of males (see Chapter 4).

The development of group unity is implied in the above discussion. Without some degree of unity and common interests (*integration* and *solidarity*), family groups would not be able to function. Families differ in the kinds and degrees of unity and solidarity they work toward. Some families share numerous interests—working together, leisure time, community activities, and household management. Other families would find this pattern of total sharing restrictive and would develop strong interpresonal bonds through some shared activities as well as through individual interests.

Pattern Maintenance

This function provides a sense of direction to a family's life through application of values and general standards of behavior. Family members hold individual values and standards, but through pattern maintenance there can be continuity of tradition. Family celebrations—using special holiday foods, decorations, activities, or clothing—demonstrate a family's efforts to maintain patterns and to transmit them to those outside the group. Bell and Vogel stated that a family's value system is more specific than that of society. Because of the small size of a family group, flexibility is possible in implementing these specific values.[30]

FUNCTIONS FOR SOCIETY

There is a suggestion that changes in American families constitute part of a differentiation process as society moves into more specialized subsystems. The loss of many family functions in so-called "advanced societies" is inevitable. The state, the church, large industrial developments, voluntary associations, and educational institutions take over functions formerly assumed by the family. In this process of change, the family becomes more specialized.[31]

Economic Functions

Families are economic as well as socializing units. As an economic unit, a family is composed of individuals with mutual rights and responsibilities as well as relationships. Related members often live together in a common home and share in the returns of their labors and in the consumption of common goods.

Families perform certain economic functions and bestow certain economic rights to family members that may otherwise be unavailable to individuals. The adult members of a family are legally responsible for the support of children not yet of earning age. A husband is legally responsible for his wife's debts unless public action is taken by one or the other to disclaim such debts.

Family status also transfers to all family members *homestead rights* in property owned and occupied as a home, protecting the homestead against creditors. So strong are the marriage bonds in the eyes of the courts, that in some states having community property laws, all property acquired after marriage (except that received as a gift, by inheritance or will) by either husband or wife becomes community property. In such situations, upon the death of either the husband or wife, one half of all the community property, regardless of will, may belong to the surviving spouse.

While society attempts to equalize opportunities, the laws of inheritance allow families to give advantage to their children and heirs. In the absence of a will, state laws will transfer the properties to family members according to the provision of the state of residence. The economic view of the family accounts for the use of "household" or "consumer unit" as the reference unit in many economic surveys and parallels earlier references to the family as a "producing unit."

The economic significance of the family arises not only from the tasks the members perform for and with one another but from the rights and obligations that the family relationship entails. The economic functions range from self support and support of children until they are able to support themselves, to parental responsibility for teaching their children the attitudes and values necessary to make economic decisions and to build personalities capable of adequately meeting the complexities of modern life.

The family is a consuming unit and, as such, has the responsibility to define the family's role and function in the economy and to improve the welfare of the group. These economic functions and the laws that support them tend to favor marriage and nuclear family life styles.

Implications for Management

In the following chart, Liston outlines 10 family functions related to society, including the economic function. Also listed are examples of decisions that families could consider in interacting with external environments that accompany each function. Decisions like those outlined below can cause changes in life styles and produce consequences for people outside the family group.

SOCIAL FUNCTIONS	EXAMPLES OF MANAGERIAL DECISIONS
1. Replacement:	
Perpetuation of family and contribution to nation's population at an appropriate rate.	How many children are appropriate? Should the family adopt rather than have children of their own?
2. Protection:	
Provision of minimum essentials of food, clothing, shelter, and so on.	What goods and services should be provided to protect the health and safety of each family member?
3. Status:	
Ascribed position in society in terms of kinship, nativity, citizenship, socio-economic level, and so on.	How may family members be helped to achieve a sense of belonging, "being," and responding in relation to their respective status positions?
4. Affection:	
Provision of appropriate kinds and amounts of emotional nurturance for each family member— an essential for growth and development.	In what ways may the "art of loving" be achieved among family members and in other relationships?
5. Economic Behavior:	
Give-and-take within the family and with other social institutions that provide goods and services for consumption (i.e., with business enterprises, governments, voluntary groups, relatives, neighbors, and friends).	Who should be the main earners of money income? What goods and services needed by the family should be attained by do-it-yourself processes (i.e., by household production for no pay)? What goods and services should be demanded in the market? Who should make decisions about uses of resources (i.e., money, property, human attributes, community opportunities, time, space, and so on)?

SOCIAL FUNCTIONS	EXAMPLES OF MANAGERIAL DECISIONS

6. Political-Legal Behavior:

Give-and-take with governmental and legal systems (local, state, and national) via utilization of rights and opportunities and fulfillment of responsibilities.

What can be done to motivate and facilitate family members' active participation in civic affairs?

7. Religious Orientation:

Identification with a selected system of religious beliefs and spiritual orientation toward life.

How should family members support their church in human effort as well as in financial contribution?
How can family members be helped to crystallize their personal value systems?

8. Recreation:

Achievement of physical and mental health and satisfying interpersonal relationships through leisure and play.

How may a balance of work and leisure be achieved by family members?
What leisure activities are appropriate?

9. Socialization:

Helping members acquire basic personal disciplines, necessary interaction skills, essential role competences, appropriate attitudes and aspirations, and personalized value orientations that are consistent with their present and anticipated environments.

What can be done to help family members develop consumer competence? How may value and goal conflicts among family members be mediated?

In what ways may the family help its members prepare for the rapidly changing environments of the future?

SOCIAL FUNCTIONS	EXAMPLES OF MANAGERIAL DECISIONS
10. Adaptation:	
Harmonizing home conditions and behaviors of members with changes in various types of environments (physical, biological, technical, economic, political-legal, social, psycho-social, and emotional).	What can be done to cope positively with chronic sickness or disability within the family group? How may personal stress be minimized when families move from one community to another of a quite different type? What adjustments in family member roles seem most appropriate when the wife takes paid employment?[32]

FUNCTIONING IN A CHANGING WORLD

Changes in these larger systems influence the quality of life in households. Families are now more interdependent and less self-sufficient than when each household produced and consumed the majority of its own food, clothing, housing, furniture, and related services.

Industrialization and changes in the economy provide families with an unprecedented selection of goods and services. Political units—on local, regional, national, and international levels—make decisions that influence individual and group life. Community standards and religious and educational organizations have formulated patterns of acceptable behavior that also influence personal and family life.

Industrialization and the trend toward a service economy have produced three major changes for individuals and families. First, people have left their living units to work or prepare for work. Second, industrialization has brought about urbanization of our population and has increased family mobility. Third, industrialization has expanded the kinds and volumes of goods and services available in daily life. Families, once primary units of production, have become primary units of consumption.

Dispersion of Family Members

Family members once shared work on small farms or in businesses. The hours of work may have been long, but the entire family shared in the production process. Now wage earners may not spend as many hours earning a living as they did before 1940, but this time is normally spent away from the living unit.[33] The young, the elderly, and in more than half of all families, wives are dependent on others for an income. The wage earner's occupation, in large part, determines the status of dependent family members.[34] In turn, young family members learn many job-related skills away from the living unit—in schools, in other formal experiences, or in informal activities with peer groups. This dispersion of family members makes time for developing interpersonal relationships in the family group difficult to arrange.

Companionship among family members is now more related to leisure than to work. Governmental agencies have responded to this change by developing recreational facilities—parks with play equipment for children and adults, camp sites, lakes for boating, and swimming pools. Business and industry have produced leisure equipment for household use; snow mobiles, camping gear, and the familiar "camper" trucks are examples. The availability of such equipment and facilities has promoted joint family activities.

Quantity and quality of resources will affect the usability of the specific recreational equipment or facilities. Gasoline is needed to use some of the above equipment or to reach some facilities. Time is needed to prepare, to use and to maintain equipment for leisure activities, and space is needed to store it. If family interactions are important, the specific group will find alternate resources or activities to replace or will more carefully use the scarcer ones to reach their goals.

Population Distribution and Mobility

Families have been attracted to the availability of employment in urban areas. Currently, nearly 7 out of every 10 families are living in metropolitan areas.[35] In 1970, 63 million people were living outside and 140 million within metropolitan areas. However, three-fourths of the population increase in metropolitan areas is due to an increased birth rate and one-fourth is due to migration.[36] Within metropolitan areas, suburbs have been rapidly increasing in population, in contrast to the almost stable size of central cities. This trend is a distinct change from the 1920's when one-half of the population lived in rural areas.

In commenting on the relationship between population distribution and quality of life, Beale writes:

Up to this time, the larger the proportion of Americans who live in metropolitan-size communities—the larger the proportion who live with ready access to college education or medical facilities; the lower the proportion who live in substandard housing or with poverty-level incomes; and the higher the proportion of women who find opportunities for employment outside the home at better than low-skilled jobs and subsistence wages. On the other hand, the greater the metropolitan concentration, the greater the percentage of the population engaged in or victimized by crimes, either of violence or against property; the greater the proportion of youth susceptible to drug use; the greater exposure to air pollution; and the less the likelihood of owning one's home. In short, there are trade-offs, and it is in large part a matter of personal judgment as to what the net effects of population distribution patterns are on quality of life.[37]

Toffler reports that during one year—March 1967 to 1968—36,600,000 Americans over one year of age changed residences.[38] The Census data illustrates trends in the frequency and distance of family moves. Since 1948, approximately 20 percent of the population moves to another living unit in a year's time.[39] Of this group, two-thirds move only short distances, usually remaining within the same community or county. In fact, 50 percent of all moves are of less than five miles. Families usually move to adjust to new requirements for space, location, design of living unit, occupational demands, or related needs and desires.

Most of those who marry change residences either at the time of marriage or within a year after marriage. The mobility rate decreases gradually from an 88 percent maximum for family heads between 14 and 24 years of age, to 22 percent for family heads 65 years old or over.

Families as Consumers and Producers

As mentioned previously, families have become consumers rather than only material producers. Products can be purchased in a form ready for immediate use or partially prepared for convenient completion. Services available to families are also increasing. Fuchs determined that more than one-half of the employed persons were in the service sector of the economy.[40] Meal preparation and service, laundry, financial management, education, and child care are examples of services that can be delegated to nonfamily professionals.

In this affluent society, women have become chiefly responsible for family consumption. Knowledge of materials, construction, intended and alternate uses, care and price in relation to quality can help consumers to select goods that will meet household needs. Similar considerations in the selection of services also affect the quality of life. As Theodore W. Schultz points out, the information about goods and services available to households may be incomplete for making effective purchase decisions.[41]

Today's youth are also active consumers. Teenage consumers spend an estimated $30 billion annually.[42] The experiences these young consumers gain in using money, in part, influence their feelings about quality of life and provide a basis for future decision making.

Not all production has left the living unit. As consumers, family members transport goods or travel to services, store items so they can be used, complete preparation, and maintain goods. Some home production may be continued because of the feelings of satisfaction derived from "do-it-yourself" projects, feelings of shared productivity among family members, the quality or uniqueness of results, or the economy of such home production.

Although the majority of families enjoy the choices of affluence, low income consumers spend the majority of their funds for necessities of food, housing, and clothing. Families with subsistence incomes have limited alternatives and lack sufficient incomes to accommodate errors in consumer decision making.[43]

Low income families, according to Richards, "tend to include more nonwhites, fewer earners, more families with female heads, larger families, and more old or young persons."[44] Although the percentage of unemployment is higher among persons with low income than among the total population, more than half of those below poverty lines are working.[45] These families are aware of the "standard package" of durable goods owned or desired by many consumers but often have insufficient incomes for such purchases. Poverty then, not only involves a lack of income but a lack of hope for future improvement.

To meet the needs of low income families, governmental agencies have developed several programs. These programs on local, state, or national levels provide money to those not in the labor force, help workers prepare for and seek employment, and provide goods and services directly to the poor.[46]

Table 1.1 illustrates family income trends between 1947 and 1973. There has been an increasing number of families in the three highest income classifications. By 1971 half of all families received $10,000 or more. During that year, the poverty level for a four-person family was $4137. Although family size is not included in the table, 10 percent of all families or 25.6 million people fell below the low income level.[47] Size of household income is a partial component of quality of life but does not describe effectiveness in the use of this income or feelings of satisfaction or dissatisfaction with the results of financial management.

As other authors have noted, affluent consumers may believe that they are not "as well off" as the statistics indicate. Services once available to middle income families are now too expensive for those persons with a $50,000 annual income. Some resources—like those of space and lumber—have decreased in relation to demand, causing increases in land and building costs. Costs of goods and services have also increased because of rising wages—construction, household help, and catering are examples. Some goods and services are more often used by middle income consumers than they were in

Table 1.1 Dollar Cut-Off Levels for Each Fifth and Top Five Percent of Families: 1947 to 1973 (in constant 1973 dollars). An increasing distance in dollar income between those in upper- and lower-income categories is illustrated.

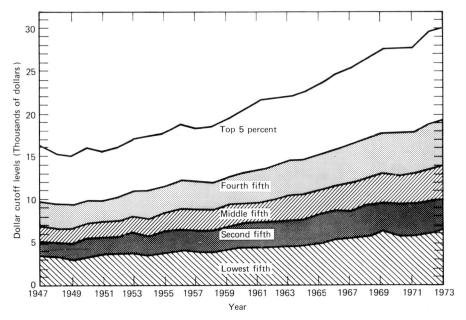

SOURCE: U.S. Bureau of the Census, *Current Population Reports,* Series P-60, No. 97, "Money Income in 1973 of Families and Persons in the United States," U.S. Government Printing Office, Washington, D.C., (1975).

the past—airplane tickets, television sets, and household appliances are examples of the more readily available goods and services.

In discussing the cost of goods and services in relation to income, Kristol stated that working class families who have recently crossed the poverty line may be satisfied with affluence. Mass production has allowed these families to purchase items that would have previously been unaffordable. He believed that dissatisfaction comes from those who have above-average incomes. These consumers may find it difficult to markedly advance their standards of living due to competition in the marketplace for scarce goods or services.[48]

ANTICIPATING CHANGE

Changes within and outside a family group affect the quality of life. Families who can anticipate change can plan adjustments in their way of life. The family life cycle describes alterations in resources and demands on resources across the life of a modal or typical family. Knowledge of the family life cycle facilitates long range planning and improvements in quality of life.

Families with Children

Nuclear families pass through a cycle that begins with the marriage of two young persons, grows with the coming of children, and then returns to a two-person group.

A view of the family's life cycle, from its beginning to its end, assuming there are no breaks, reveals definite and discernible stages. These stages tend to overlap, yet each has its own clearly defined situations and problems. In the earlier stages, only the two persons starting the new home are concerned. For the family with children, the needs of the growing children and the family's place in the community are of paramount importance. During these stages, family demands often compete with the adults' personal desires and, thus, cause conflicts or frustrations. If the adults have developed a philosophy that gives direction to the life of the family as a whole, adjustments can be made with less strain, and conflicts can be more easily resolved. This is particularly true if parents keep abreast of the pressures their children face from outside social contacts.

The family life cycle may be divided into three major stages, usually called the beginning family, the expanding family, and the contracting family.[49] To these three stages Bigelow[50] adds eight substages, four of which represent stages of schooling, as follows:

FAMILY STAGE	SUBSTAGE
I. Beginning	1. Period of establishment
II. Expanding	2. Childbearing and preschool
	3. Elementary school
	4. High school
	5. College
III. Contracting	6. Vocational adjustment of children
	7. Financial recovery
	8. Retirement

Most families with children go through all these substages. If college is omitted, a family goes directly from the high school substage to the period of vocational adjustment. When there are a number of children there may, of course, be more than one child in college at the same time.

Three Major Stages in the Life Cycle

Stage I—The beginning family.   The first substage of the family life cycle is the period of *establishment*. It begins with marriage and continues until the first child is born. This stage is often called the "getting acquainted" stage, when the two partners in the marriage venture are learning to know each other. It begins during courtship and may extend into marriage for a shorter or longer period, depending upon the personalities of the two people. The kind of relationships that the husband and wife establish at this time will influence the quality of their future relations. The long-term goals they formulate now will influence their way of living and the manner in which they use their resource of time, material goods, skills, energy, and income throughout their married life.

Stage II—The expanding family.   The expanding family covers a longer pe-riod than the beginning family and includes a number of substages. It begins with the birth of the first child and ends when the last child leaves home. The first substage is designated as *child-bearing and preschool* and is also marked by the accumulation of goods. During this time parents find it necessary to make adjustments in their relations to each other and to their children as they are born. The changes in this substage follow at a rapid pace as the parents quickly take on new and different responsibilities.

The *elementary* school period begins a series of overlapping experiences that cover the time when the children are 6 to 12 years of age. This is when children begin their formal education and make their first independent contacts with the outside world. During this period, parents are primarily concerned with the educational and health needs of the children, with es-tablishing an environment in which the children will have a feeling of belong-ing, with providing nutritious food, suitable clothing, and adequate housing for personal development, as well as social and community contacts outside the home. At this time it is important for children to be included in the family management, where many decisions can be discussed in a friendly at-mosphere at the level of the child's understanding. Family budgeting, ways the family can best entertain friends, and the use of the car or cars are examples of problems that can be shared by parents and children.

The *high-school* period in the family cycle includes the time when the children are 12 to 18 years of age—the teen-age period. The parents are now occupied with helping the children through high school, vocational, or trade school, and assisting them in solving their personality, social, recreational, and vocational problems, to aid them in becoming independent and self-reliant in-dividuals.

The *college* phase covers the time when children are in college. The chief parental duties are helping to select a college and to finance education. This is the time when many families, especially those with more than one child in college, find it necessary to draw on their savings to finance a part of college expenses. The parents' assistance may also be needed by their children to solve social problems that may arise before, and sometimes after, the children's own marriages.

Stage III—The contracting family. The period of *vocational adjustment*, sometimes called the *launching* period, begins when the first child leaves home as a young adult and ends when the last child leaves home for a life of his or her own. It is marked by a young person's departure for marriage or full-time employment. It is a period of uncertainty and adjustment for parents and children. The parents' financial assistance may be needed for a new vocational venture, a wedding, travel, or many other activities. The family circle is widened to include new relatives through marriage as well as grandchildren, and new lines of communication must be established. Parents begin to take on a new role as grandparents.

The period of *financial recovery* begins after the children leave home and become self supporting. Current expenses drop rapidly. Debts that have accumulated over the busy years are paid, and saving for the future takes a large share of the income. Generally the parents are young enough to retain active interests of their own. Some may have time and money to travel. It is desirable for both husband and wife to develop interests that will be satisfying during the period of retirement. Many women need to *recover or rediscover* an absorbing interest beyond the children who are now busy with their own homes and families. Of course, many have followed their interests on a part- or full-time basis along with their marriage. For the large group of homemakers who had no profession before marriage, the community in which they live offers many opportunities for interesting and creative experiences. Many types of employment are available to a woman seeking financial opportunities.

The period of *financial recovery* calls for social and vocational adjustments in anticipation of retirement. If people are to have a feeling of adequacy and independence in their later years, they must plan for it before those years arrive. During the time of rediscovery, creative avocational experiences and talents can be developed that will be useful when strength, health, and mental and physical abilities call for restricted activity. Fortunately, interest and judgment are two characteristics that often increase rather than decrease with age. By alternating the use of the mind, as in reading or watching the best of television, with some physical activity, one can retain or develop a feeling of fulfillment and adequacy despite one's age.

The last substage is the time of *retirement*. The wants of individuals during this stage usually grow less intense, and the need for care and protection increases. It is the period of adjustment to physical changes, to changes in environmental conditions, to changes in human relations, and often to changes in income. For those who can make the necessary adjustments and who have health and strength, human relations will continue to be satisfying even though the physical setting of the home may change. This is the period when avocational arts are important to the family and to the aging person.

Childless Families

The family life cycle described previously refers to families of two parents and a near-average number of children. Deviate families have been viewed so inconsequentially that they are barely mentioned in family literature. It is often assumed that median is typical, and that the typical American family consists of husband, wife, and two children. Conversely, it is still true that the largest percentage of families in this country (about 40 percent at the present time) is composed of only two persons—husband and wife. The usual assumption is that two-person families are confined to the newly married, and at the other end of the age-scale, to those whose children have left home. This, too, is a myth. Even when young wives and women over 49 are excluded, between 15 and 20 percent of all women who ever marry typically remain childless. The percentage varies conversely with birth rate trends and is at the upper end of the range now when birth rates are at the lowest point they have been in years.

Relatively little is known about childless families and their life cycle. Until 1960, even the Census data did not distinguish truly childless families (those in which no children had ever been born or adopted) from families in which there were no children under the age of 18 living at home at the time of the census. In 1958, at the annual meeting of the Population Association of America, Grabill and Glick presented a report on background demographic variations of women without children and stated that to their knowledge, their report was the first publication dealing only with Census data on women without children.[51]

In 1964, Rice developed an economic life cycle of childless families based on unpublished national Census data and two of the annual Surveys of Consumer Finances conducted by the Survey Research Center at the University of Michigan, from national samples.[52] Using four life cycle stages of childless couples based on the number of years since marriage, Rice isolated the following demographic conditions and economic patterns of childless families, using the median characteristics of 950 childless families and comparing them with 5150 parent families.

Stage I: First Five Years of Marriage

Couples who remain childless throughout their married life tend to marry at a later age than those who have children, and the childless husband and wife are also nearer the same age. Typical childless husbands were 1.6 years older than their wives and 3.8 years older than husbands who will have children. The median age at first marriage of childless husbands was 26.5 and 24.9 for wives. The older age at marriage may be an important factor contributing to the percentage of families remaining childless throughout the family life cycle. There was little difference in religious preference between childless and parent couples, except for the fact that a significantly higher percentage of childless families reported "no religion."

Most childless couples begin housekeeping in a rented, urban apartment, and they move frequently; 58 percent lived in their present residence less than a year. By the end of Stage I, 24 percent owned their own homes, a significantly lower percentage than for parent families (38 percent).

The gross family income was higher than parents' in this stage because 85 percent of childless wives were gainfully employed, adding about 31 percent of gross family income. Almost 90 percent of these childless families had some liquid assets and close to 10 percent had $5000 or more. Median amount held was $775. In spite of high liquid assets, 62 percent had installment debt, the median amount being 15.4 percent of disposable income.

Childless couples travel more in Stage 1 than at any other, buy more furniture, and have a higher installment debt ratio than at any other period. In spite of high liquid assets, a large percentage of wives working, and no dependents, they believe in life insurance (71 percent had policies and 27 percent took out a new policy during this stage).

Stage II: The Second Five Years of Marriage

Nearly 90 percent of childless couples move in Stage II, but nearly half stay within the county. By the end of the stage, 60 percent have bought a home and 35 percent have mortgages, still less than parent families.

Incomes generally remain high in this stage; 65 percent of the wives work, contributing nearly 42 percent of the family income; 90 percent have liquid assets and the median more than triples—to $2850. Twenty percent have liquid assets of $5000 or more.

Median outlay on furniture and household appliances is less than in Stage I and 35 percent paid cash for all such purchases; 60 percent had some installment debt, the median amount being 13.3 percent of disposable income. A smaller percentage of childless families in Stage II own cars; 50 percent took at least one vacation trip per year traveling about 875 miles, but spending $100 less per year than in Stage I.

They continue to buy life insurance; 85 percent have such policies in Stage II and 10 percent buy a new policy during this stage. Automobile purchases, furniture, and household appliance purchases drop slightly from Stage I in spite of the fact that liquid assets more than triple.

Stage III: The Second Decade of Marriage

At the beginning of Stage III, when the head of the childless family is 36.5 years old and his wife 34.9, the family income reaches its peak. The median income of the wife has by this time passed its peak, and she contributes about 29 percent of the family income; but 71 percent of the wives continue to work.

Families are more stable in this decade. The median number of years in the same house is five, and only six percent moved out of the state during each five year period. A larger number of childless families owned their own homes in this stage than in any other period and significantly more than parent families. Almost 80 percent owned their homes by the end of the stage. Those who rent (18 percent) pay more for rent than in previous stages.

Liquid assets peak ($3750) with 92 percent having some assets by this time. The percentage with installment debt drops to 34, but the ratio of debt to income remains the same (13.3 percent). Fifty percent of the childless couples pay cash for their furniture purchases during the second decade of marriage, and only five percent finance their durable purchases.

The percentage of these families taking vacations every year drops to 42, but the median amount spent by vacationers nearly doubles, and they travel farther (1300 miles) from home. More childless couples own cars in Stage III than at any other time; 47 percent bought a car in the year of the study.

Life insurance premiums rise during this stage but 3.4 percent drop their insurance. Still, 12 percent purchased a new life insurance policy in the year of the study.

Stage IV: Married Twenty Years or More

By this time parent families have usually launched at least one child into marriage and are just reaching the peak of their family incomes. Childless families passed their peak income in Stage III and begin the gradual descent to retirement during Stage IV. Part of the decline in the childless couples' income is due to the relatively small percentage of childless wives who work during this stage. The percentage of working wives drops from 71 in Stage III to less than half in Stage IV. The median income of wives who work also drops in this stage and they contribute less than 30 percent of the family income. About 30 percent of childless wives continue working after the husband retires.

By this time, 78 percent of the childless families own their own homes, almost the exact percentage of those who owned their homes in Stage III. The median childless family in this stage has lived in its present house for 7 to 10 years, 64 percent have lived in the same house for 6 years, and only 6 percent lived out of the state five years earlier. Equity in owned homes is highest during this stage, as would be expected from the longer period of ownership; only 22 percent have home mortgage debts. About 20 percent of childless families rent during the stage.

Liquid assets equal approximately one-half the gross family income and 90 percent have some such assets. Only 25 percent have installment debt, lower than at any other stage; and the debt/income ratio is 10.6. About 62 percent pay cash for all their furniture and household appliance purchases; and they spend almost as much in this stage as in the prior stage, about $270 per year. Ten percent bought all their household durables on credit.

Fewer families in Stage IV take vacation trips than at any other stage of the life cycle, 27.5 percent; but those who do spend more than at any other stage of marriage ($480 per year) and travel further from home (1333 miles). Less than 22 percent of childless families married 20 years or more bought a car in the year of the study, compared with at least 40 percent in each of the other stages.

In comparing all childless families with all parent families in this representative national sample, Rice observed that the educational attainment of childless wives was significantly higher than that of parent wives, and also higher than that of their own or the husband's parent. This finding supports the long-held belief that there is an inverse relationship between educational attainment of wives and their fertility.

Childless families are more mobile than parent families, buy their houses at a later stage in the family cycle, prefer urban communities, and are more likely to be living in rented apartments. They buy fewer cars and a larger percentage do not have a car—perhaps because more of them live in urban areas where public transportation is likely to supply their transportation needs. Childless couples travel more during the early years of their marriage and less than parent families during the later years of marriage.

Childless families use credit less frequently, but when credit is used, greater amounts are financed, and they invest more in speculative forms of assets than do parent families. A smaller percentage of childless families have life insurance and the premiums are lower indicating less coverage; but the percentage with such insurance is higher than might be expected (73). One final conclusion of this study was that childless husbands were more willing to remarry than were childless wives.

These economic characteristics are indicative of the life styles of childless families and provide a background setting for later discussions of management practices and problems of one type of family that cannot progress through the usual stages of the family life cycle because they do not have children. The life cycles of single-parent families, families of larger than average size, those with disabilities, or families whose children are vastly different in age will also differ from the norm.

Summary

This chapter has examined some of the major trends that affect family management. Issues regarding the stability of the family as a social and economic unit were discussed. Life styles of the typical family with children were examined in relation to management. Alternate forms of life styles and those of childless families were explored.

By discussing the quality of life and the pluralistic forms of life style, the chapter demonstrates varied approaches to improving quality of living and the function of management in achieving desired quality of life. The following chapters explore managerial concepts that individuals and families can use to improve the specific qualities of life they consider important.

References

1. Bloom, M. T., "What Makes a Successful Family," *Readers Digest,* *102:*63 (May 1973), pp. 121–124.

2. James, R. D., "Measuring the Quality of Life," *The Wall Street Journal,* (May 18, 1972), p. 18.

3. Gauger, W. H., "The Potential Contribution to the GNP of Valuing Household Work," unpublished speech to AHEA annual meeting, (1973), p. 14.

4. Schultz, T. W., "Woman's New Economic Commandments," pp. 79–88, in *Families of the Future,* Iowa State University Press, Ames, Iowa (1972).

5. Sheldon, E. B. and Moore, W. E., *Indicators of Social Change,* Russell Sage Foundation, New York, (1968).

6. "A People and A Spirit," Cooperative Extension Service, Washington, D.C., (1968).

7. Feldman, S. D., and Thielbar, G. W. (eds.), *Life Styles: Diversity in American Society,* Little, Brown and Company, (1972).

8. Scanzoni, J., *Sexual Bargaining,* Prentice–Hall, Englewood Cliffs, N.J., (1972).

9. Velie, L., "The Myth of the Vanishing Family," *Readers Digest, 102:*610 (February 1973), pp. 111–115.

10. U.S. Bureau of the Census, "Household and Family Characteristics: March 1972," *Current Population Reports,* Series P 20, No. 246, Washington, D.C., (1973).

11. Murdock, G. P., *Social Structure,* Free Press, New York, (1965), p. 1.

12. *Ibid.*

13. U.S. Bureau of the Census, *Statistical Abstract of the United States 1971,* U.S. Government Printing Office, (1972).

14.   U.S. Bureau of the Census, "Household and Family Characteristics: March 1972," *Current Population Reports,* Series P 20, No. 246, Washington, D.C., (1973), p. 3.

15.   U.S. Bureau of the Census, "Household and Families by Types: March 1972," *Current Population Reports,* Series P 20, No. 237, Washington, D.C., (1972).

16.   Turner, R. H., *Family Interaction,* Wiley, New York, (1970), p. 410.

17.   Hill, R., Foote, N., Aldous, J., Carlson, R., and Macdonald, R., *Family Development in Three Generations,* Schenkman, Cambridge, Mass., (1970).

18.   Scanzoni, J., *op. cit.,* pp. 8–9.

19.   Plateris, A. A., "Increases in Divorces, United States, 1970," U.S. Public Health Services, Series 21, No. 20, (1970), p. 10.

20.   Downing, J., "The Tribal Family and the Society of Awakening," pp. 119–135, in Otto, Herbert A. (ed.), *The Family in Search of a Future,* Appelton-Century-Crofts, New York, (1970).

21.   Bell, N. W. and Vogel, E. F., *A Modern Introduction to the Family,* Free Press, New York, (1968), pp. 21–30.

22.   *Ibid.,* p. 23.

23.   U.S. Bureau of the Census, "Birth Expectations and Fertility: June 1972," *Current Population Reports,* Series P 20, No. 240, (September 1972), p. 1.

24.   Brenton, M., *The American Male,* Fawcett, Greenwich, Conn., (1966).

25.   "Time Used by Husbands for Household Work," *Family Economics Review,* (June 1970), pp. 8–11.

26.   Walker, K. E., "Homemaking Still Takes Time," *Journal of Home Economics, 61:*6 (1969), pp. 621–624.

27.   Bell, N. W. and Vogel, E. F., *op. cit.,* p. 23.

28. Liston, M. I., "Managerial Functioning," p. 64, in *Behavioral Aspects of Management,* Proceedings of the Western Regional College Teachers Home Management Family Economics, Salt Lake City, Utah, (1971).

29. Blood, R. O. and Wolfe, D. M., *Husbands and Wives: The Dynamics of Married Living,* Free Press, Glencoe, Ill., (1960).

30. Bell, N. W. and Vogel, E. F., *op. cit.,* p. 28.

31. Parsons, T., "The Stability of the American Family System," in Bell, N. W., and Vogel, E. F., *op. cit.,* Chapter 7.

32. Liston, M. I., *op. cit.,* pp. 65–67.

33. U.S. Bureau of the Census, "Household and Family Characteristics: March 1972," *Current Population Reports,* Series P 20, No. 246, (1973), p. 1.

34. Winch, R. F., *The Modern Family,* Holt, Rinehart and Winston, New York, (1963), p. 111.

35. Taeuber, C., "Some Current Population Trends," *Family Economics Review,* (March 1972), p. 1.

36. *Ibid.,* p. 6.

37. Beale, C. L., "Implications of Population Trends for Quality of Life," *Family Economics Review,* (March 1973), p. 6.

38. Toffler, A., *Future Shock,* Random House, New York, (1970), p. 78.

39. U.S. Bureau of the Census, "Mobility of the Population of the United States: March 1970 to March 1971," *Current Population Reports,* Series P 20, No. 235, Washington, D.C., (1972), p. 1.

40. Fuchs, V. R., *The Service Economy,* National Bureau of Economic Research, New York, (1968).

41. Schultz, T. W., "Woman's New Economic Commandments," p. 88, in *Families of the Future,* Iowa State University, Ames, Iowa, (1972).

42. Troelstrup, A. W., *The Consumer in American Society,* McGraw-Hill, New York, (1970).

43. Peterson, E., "Consumer Problems of Low-Income Families," in *Working With Low-Income Families,* American Home Economics Association, Washington, D.C., (1965), pp. 140–145.

44. Richards, L. G., "Consumer Practices of the Poor," in Irelan, L. M. (ed.), *Low-Income Life Styles,* U.S. Department of Health, Education and Welfare, Welfare Administration Pub. 14, (1966), p. 69.

45. Miller, H. P., *Rich Man, Poor Man,* Thomas Y. Crowell, New York, (1971), p. 131.

46. *Ibid.,* p. 109.

47. U.S. Bureau of the Census, "Characteristics of the Low-Income Population, 1971," *Current Population Reports,* Series P 60, No. 86, (1972), p. 2.

48. Kristol, I., "The Frustrations of Affluence," *The Wall Street Journal,* (July 20, 1973), p. 8.

49. For purposes of organization, The Family Life Conference held in Washington, D.C. in May 1948, considered the cycle as divided into three parts: Stage 1, The Beginning Family; Stage 2, The Expanding Family; and Stage 3, The Contracting Family.

50. Bigelow, H. F., "What Are Usual Family Patterns?" *Journal of Home Economics, 42,*1, (January 1950), pp. 27–29.

51. Grabill, W. H. and Glick, P. C., "Demographic and Social Aspects of Childlessness: Census Data," *Milbank Memorial Fund Quarterly, 37,* (1959), pp. 60–86.

52. Rice, A. S., *An Economic Life Cycle of Childless Families,* unpublished doctoral dissertation, Florida State University, Tallahassee, Fla. (1964).

2

NATURE AND ROLE OF MANAGEMENT

Management is planned activity directed toward the realization of values and the satisfaction of wants. It is the accomplishment of desired ends. It makes use of the findings of science and of knowledge concerning all aspects of life—economic, social, psychological, physical, spiritual, and technical. Personal or family management is the harnessing of this knowledge to selection and application of resources to meet demands of living situations, to solve problems, and to resolve conflicts. It involves the weighing of values and the making of decisions.

Everyone learns to manage the resources at his disposal. Some learn to manage well, others not so well; but all manage with some degree of competence. The more skilled a person becomes in the process of management, the greater the possible control over life and, consequently, the greater the quality of living.

In a modern technological environment, where situations are complex and highly flexible, where many choices occur daily, and where values are changing rapidly, people must depend on reasoned ways of accomplishing results. Fixed rules and set ways of behavior are not possible. Habitual ways of doing things quickly become obsolete. Under these circumstances each individual is forced to choose the *means* and the *methods* for goal attainment.

Management is not only a means to accomplish desired outcomes *through* people, as is most often the case in business and industry; it is also a means to accomplish desired outcomes *within* people. Personal management is a means for human development, self actualization, and renewal. Liston defines renewal in people as:

helping them to help themselves, as individuals or as members of groups, to achieve a more creative and relevant sense of being and becoming. It also means helping them to value participative managerial competency as an important dimension of self-esteem and as a means of releasing their personal potentials and of growing closer to self–actualization. Renewal in people means freeing them from the chains of obsolete tradition and minimizing their fears of being manipulated by the more powerful.[1]

Unfortunately the non–business use of management has been linked so often to home management and to middle-class standards for homekeeping that any other approach is slowly and reluctantly understood. Many people have associated personal management so closely with the mechanics of homekeeping that they believe personal management classes are suitable only for women and then only if these women expect to stay at home, care for the house, cater to physical wants of family members, and do little else.

Contrary to this belief, personal management is the key to successful and satisfying living and is a strong tool for regenerating society and bringing about a more harmonious world population. Management is far from "how to clean the parlor" or "organize the linens." Most modern houses don't even have parlors. Instead they have "living" rooms and "family" rooms, and the linens may be of disposable paper that requires more resource use in selection than in care.

Personal management is dynamic. It involves decision making that leads to action directed toward change. It is *making* things happen rather than *letting* things happen. It is a system for controlling the quality of living, and it is as practical for men as it is for women, for children as for adults, for individuals or for families or any other form of group living.

Nature of Personal Management

In this book, management is approached as a *behavioral interaction process* to achieve goals through the practical use of available resources. Management is necessarily a behavioral means of accomplishing ends because it has to be used to function. It requires force—mental work and physical power of people—to keep it functioning.

Management is a behavioral process that recognizes the actions and reactions of persons in living situations as they discover and use their resources to achieve something they want. It consists of all the behavioral processes experienced by people as they identify and cope with problems of setting goals, establishing and testing values and norms, identifying roles, solving conflicts, establishing power-authority lines within the family and influence patterns outside the family, perpetuating themselves, and communicating with others in the solution of all these problems in their own particular situations. These situations occur wherever the people who use them are found—in school, in business, in churches, in government, in homes, in cars, and on the street. Application of management differs with each person's resources, goals, and modes of expression. Management means different things to different people and is executed in varying qualities by each person or group.

In addition to being behavioral, management is also an *interaction* process. Decision making, division of labor, socialization, role-identity and conflict-harmonization all require interaction with other individuals. To reach decisions or even to gain information, family members must interact in some manner with other members of the family and often with members of the larger community. Neither harmony nor conflict can occur without interaction. For this reason communication, the medium of interaction, is crucial to harmony in living and the development of constructive change. Even when residing alone, an individual does not exist in a vacuum but interacts with others.

Management is a *process*—a series of specific functions that brings about desired results. The process provides an organized means to achieve what an individual wants. It is founded on principles tested over time and in differing circumstances by people with varied interests, needs, and resources. The process may be utilized by individuals to achieve individual goals or by a group of people living together in a household. The use made of a family's resources and the extent to which the family's goals are realized depends, in large measure, on the managerial interest, ability, and leadership of each family member and his or her ability to motivate each member of the group. However, the *process* remains relatively stable. It can be relied upon to work not only in time of ease and plenty but in crisis situations and times of scarce resources.

The elements of the managerial process include planning, organizing, implementing, and evaluating the use of new and currently available resources to achieve established goals.

WHY MANAGE?

Human needs and desires change through time; and through research, progress is made. New tools, new substances, and new sources of power are discovered and created; and new methods are devised to meet changes in human needs and wants. In turn, new desires arise. In this process people gain knowledge and increase control of natural and technological environments, but human environments sometimes become difficult to control.

The impact of these changes on the human being and social institutions gives rise to conflicts because individuals tend to accept new procedures, new equipment, and new products in their technological environment more readily than they accept change in personal life. In adjusting to the new, social and cultural changes lag behind technological change. This differential pace results in a constant effort to alter personal life to keep up with technological change. It sometimes results in altering technological developments to suit personal preferences.

People differ in their perceptions of which aspects of their lives are manageable. Some believe their lives are completely controlled by outside forces. Political structures, religious leaders, peer pressures, or cultural expectations are among these forces. Others believe that some or all aspects of their lives are manageable. They believe that they can cause things to happen and that they are responsible for what happens to them. These are the individuals and families who consider management as a way of life.

Management is the channeling of effort in a given direction. It is the natural outgrowth of human associations in the living environment. As soon as the family is established and persons begin working together for common purposes, needs arise to develop a plan of action, to delegate responsibility, and to organize and control the use of available human and environmental resources. Evaluation is needed to bring actions in harmony with objectives.

WHAT TO MANAGE

Whether functioning as an individual or as a family, people manage *resources*, assets that can be used to reach goals. Assets consist of any worthwhile possession, personal quality or trait of value, or characteristic of the environment that has use. The resources individuals and families have at their disposal consist of the tools, financial assets, capabilities, and the ways and means they possess. These resources are used in countless ways to achieve what is important to each person and to the family as a group. Assuming that decisions have been made concerning what is important to work for, the question of which resources are available must then be considered.

For simplicity, resources may be classified into three categories: human, economic, and environmental according to the interdisciplinary framework presented in Chapter 6.

Human Resources

These assets are instrumental traits or qualities within people. In spite of the attention given to resources in management literature, in practice, the extent to which most people tap their potential human resources is far short of their capabilities. The gap between actual and potential human resource development is sufficient to cause concern within the society. The quality of living in this nation and the world would increase significantly if ways could be found to motivate acceleration in the development of human potential. To accomplish this end, human resources need to be analyzed further. Human resources may be cognitive, affective, psychomotor, or temporal.

Cognitive human resources are mental traits or characteristics of an individual that relate to knowledge acquired by reasoning and perception, such as intelligence, knowledge, understanding, adaptability, resourcefulness, and self control. Knowledge—awareness, understanding, or specific information about something gained through study or experience—is a typical cognitive resource. Cognitive resources are valuable because they affect the quantity and quality of other resources needed to achieve group goals.

Affective human resources are traits and feelings pertaining to or resulting from emotions, such as interests, attitudes, motivation, enthusiasm, faith, and tolerance. Affective resources are attitudinal characteristics. Interest is a typical affective resource. Interest—an attitude of curiosity or an urge to do something—represents absorption in ideas, activities, or things. When a person is interested in something, his attention is held to it for longer periods of time than would otherwise occur. Affective resources are important because they influence activity in predisposed directions and they affect perseverance with tasks.

Psychomotor human resources are those that combine muscular activity with associated mental processes. They are those assets that include both ability and proficiency in carrying out activities involving some physical exertion, such as communicative skills, manners, work habits, and the senses of sight, smell, taste, and touch. Managerial skills combine many psychomotor resources such as posture, consumer skills, home-related work skills, and motion-mindedness. *Skill* is the ability and the proficiency to do something. Skill is an expertise and dexterity in carrying out an act to achieve dependable, consistent results. Most skills fit into the category of psychomotor human resources. Because *energy* is the power to carry on both physical and mental activities, it is also classed as a psychomotor human resource. The capacity for action and use of energy are crucial to management.

Temporal resources are considered as human resources because the classification includes not only the minutes, hours, days, weeks, and years of clock time but also psychological time—an individual's characteristic methods of assimilating, using, and perceiving the passage of time. *Time* is the duration of the interval when activities occur. There are three important and distinctly different types of time: (1) *Scientific* "clock" time is based on the regular movements of the earth in relation to the sun, and counted as 24 hours per day, seven days per week, and so on. (2) *Biological time* or the cyclical occurrence of certain bodily functions is the internal clock within a person that indicates when it is "time" to get up in the morning, to be hungry, or to become sleepy. (3) *Psychological time* is the awareness of the passage of time. To some persons, "just a moment" may mean a few seconds of clock time. To others who are keenly interested in an activity, "in a minute" may mean several hours. This is the kind of time that makes clock time seem to pass more slowly on some occasions and more swiftly on others. Clock time has the unique characteristic of being the one resource constant in amount for all persons. Biological and psychological time vary from person to person and even differ within a person from one period of life to another.

Human resources are highly important to the family. Not only are they the means of accomplishing desired ends, but in using them well the group acts together in such a way that common goals seem more real and attainable and the quality of interpersonal relations can be lifted.

Economic Resources

Economic resources may be divided into four categories: money income, elastic income, wealth, and fringe benefits. Many of the economic resources are sought as goals because of their instrumental worth in achieving comfort and esteem.

Money income is defined as gross receipts or monetary gains to all family members derived from labor or capital. It represents purchasing power and includes the frequency and pattern of such flow to the family within a given time period. Wages, commissions, tips and bonuses, capital gains, dividends, interest, and retirement receipts are examples of money income. Monetary gifts and inheritance are also money income.

Elastic income is credit—purchasing power extended through deferred payment. Credit should be considered in this context because it expands purchasing power and increases capital opportunities. This concept of elasticity in income is growing in importance because of its increased, almost universal use in the U.S. and many other parts of the world. Elastic income is based on a unique combination of other resources—character, capacity, and collateral provided by money and wealth—considered in light of current and future purchasing power in the economic environment. Elastic income is a resource that offers both a threat and a benefit to families and individuals who wield power over its use.

Wealth is the ownership of real property, income-producing assets, durables, and personal possessions of all family members as well as the family's characteristic *pattern* of holdings. Wealth includes savings accounts, stocks and bonds, jewelry, clothing, household furnishings, dwellings, and land.

Fringe benefits are those nonmoney assets that are derived as a consequence of employment and for which the employer pays at least a portion of the cost. Fringe benefits expand purchasing power by conserving money needed for life and hospitalization insurance, cost of illnesses, or savings for retirement.

Environmental Resources

Environment is the combination of external physical conditions that affect and influence quality of life, including natural tangible surroundings and less tangible environmental resources. Environment may also be defined as a complex of social and cultural conditions affecting the nature of an individual or group.[2] Some environmental resources are ardently sought as goals in today's dichotomy of scarcity and plenty.

Physical environmental resources include natural, tangible surroundings such as earth, rain, minerals, and other natural resources that can be perceived by the sense of touch. Elements of the environment and climate that are less tangible but can be measured, such as air, light, sound, humidity, space, and temperature are examples of less tangible, physical surroundings.

Social environmental resources consist of the social organizations, economic institutions, political structures and systems, and community facilities and services that influence values, standards, norms, habits, mores, customs, goals, and behavior. Business and industrial establishments not only make goods and services available to implement living but also furnish employment that supports wealth. Community facilities, especially those that are free, are sometimes overlooked as family resources but may contribute immeasurably to quality of living when used.

The amounts and quality of resources that every individual or family has at its disposal are unique. People are not always aware of the total supply of resources at their command. Some resources remain undeveloped until they are recognized and exercised. Valuable resources may either be wasted or not fully used because of lack of understanding of their availability or use to achieve goals.[3] Other resources are untapped because the individual lacks interest or motivation to uncover and expand them as resources.[4]

Failure to use intellectual abilities or factual knowledge to meet living problems greatly reduces a person's potential satisfaction and requires an abuse of other resources to secure the same quality of life. A careful inventory of all available and potential resources is essential if management is to achieve the highest level of goal attainment. Management plays the integrating role as these resources—limited or abundant—are used daily in personal and family life.

The Management Process

A *process* is, by definition, a system of production operations. A process is composed of a series of actions or functions to bring about an end result. The management process consists of a series of four progressive and interde-

Figure 2.1   The Management Wheel. Management is a wheel of activities, each involving decision making and each utilizing a different combination of resources to satisfy wants.

pendent managerial activities often called sub-systems or functions of management:

- *planning* to achieve goals

- *organizing* for performance

- *implementing* the plan

- *evaluating* the results in light of goals sought.

Not all authors give the managerial activities the same names, but there is general agreement that these activities must be carried out in the management process regardless of what resource or combination of resources is utilized. Each of these sub-systems requires and is diffused with decision making, a mental activity that is considered the core of management as illustrated in Figure 2.1.

The purpose of management is to bring about change. The quantity, quality, and "mix" of resources that are managed will change with each goal, each person, and each situation in which the individual or group functions. The process of managing and its sub-system of activities remains relatively constant, in spite of the fact that portions of one sub-system may not be utilized or may be combined or overlapped with the other sub-systems in a unique way. The process is constant, but the results of management are as varied as the goals and resources of the persons applying the process to their lives.

PLANNING

Planning is devising a scheme for reaching goals. It includes setting and clarifying goals, establishing priorities among goals, establishing standards for measuring goal attainment, and determining the activities needed to reach the goals.[5] It includes a wide range of decisions dealing with family activities, resources, and changing family wants.

Goals make planning purposeful and, if understood by those involved in management, are the basis of sound planning. They guide the person or family in deciding what and how work or activities should be done and provide direction for utilizing resources throughout the management process.[6]

Planning involves decision making—identifying the problem to be solved or the goal to be achieved, obtaining information, formulating possible courses of action, considering consequences of each alternative, and selecting the course of action that seems most productive. Planners search for alternatives that will satisfy the needs of the individual or family concerned. When, as in a family, more than one person is involved in planning, effective communication becomes essential in coordinating activities.

An awareness of the relative priorities of specific goals and activities can aid planners to assign resources and to achieve flexibility in management. Because it is usually not feasible for all personal or family wants to be achieved, the Cooperative Extension Service has suggested the following categories of priorities in goals and activities:

- list what has to be done,

- list what ought to be done,

- list what one wants to do, and

- list also what should be left undone.[7]

Such lists, mental or written, can help planners consider the relative importance of goals and activities. Effectiveness of planning is dependent upon the realism of the plan in light of resources.

Plans vary in the amount of time needed to achieve goals. Daily activities are considered short term in nature; the purchase of a living unit would, in most instances, be considered an intermediate goal requiring months or several years for completion; and improvement in quality of life usually requires long-range planning across a life time. The varied time requirements of plans must be coordinated if all goals are to be achieved.

If management is to achieve maximum satisfaction of living for a group, planning will be a group process. All persons who are affected by decisions and involved in group action need to be included in the planning and decision making process. People are generally more willing to exert effort for group benefit if they have had choices in determining direction of action.

ORGANIZING

The numerous plans made in living units call for a variety of activities across time, and if these activities are to be carried out effectively, some form of organization is essential. Organization is the logical arrangement of activities within a plan. It consists of dividing responsibilities among group members and delegating authority, as well as scheduling and synchronizing activities.

In dividing responsibilities, a manager may select one person or a small group to complete a task or activity because that person or group is best able to produce the desired results. The manager may believe that the person or group has more available time, skills, or abilities than other members of the group. This method of assigning tasks is termed "job or *task-centered organization.*"[8]

"*Person-centered organization*" emphasizes new learning possibilities for the worker in task completion. A preschool child, for example, might make cookies to learn about food preparation or to experience satisfaction in a creative activity. In such a situation, the results—the appearance of the cookies—would not be as important as learning to use kitchen equipment, following a recipe, and measuring ingredients. The appearance of the cookies would be more important if they were to be sold to earn money for vacation spending.

Research in industry and education has demonstrated that workers and students alike perform best in a combined job and person-centered style of organization. In such circumstances, people know what needs to be done and are aware of the learning resulting from their experiences.

Several levels of complexity of organizational make-up are mentioned by Baker:

A level is one person organizing a task. Sometimes this is called work-simpli-fying. Another level is one person arranging his own efforts for the completion of several tasks he needs to do into a sequence or pattern. A mother employed outside her home is likely to be organized at this level. A third level is more complicated. It requires that the manager arrange the efforts of others who are doing the work into a pattern so that one or more tasks can be completed.[9]

Parents who include their growing children in various homemaking tasks are organizing at the third level, but should be cautioned that the mere perfor-mance of assigned duties by children does not necessarily teach them to manage their time or to organize and synchronize their activities.

IMPLEMENTING

Implementing is putting the plan into action—the "doing" process of manage-ment. It is the accomplishment of goals through control of action, the evalua-tion of progress toward goals, and the adjustment of plans to meet changing resources and needs.

Implementing involves careful observations of performance to be certain that action is moving in the desired direction. These observations may concern the costs in resources of time, money, or effort; or they may concern satisfac-tions derived from the work or activity. Satisfaction can be so important in family living that a plan may be completely changed if one or more family members have negative feelings or are likely to be harmed in some way by the activities. Also, during implementing a goal may prove to be unwanted even though it had once seemed desirable because prediction is not always accurate.

Implementing, thus calls for flexibility in thinking, rather than a rigid pat-tern of action. It may sometimes require that group welfare be emphasized above personal desires.

Self descipline and supervision are skills that managers utilize in imple-menting plans. A person working with little or no cooperation may find self control to be important in accomplishing desired results. A manager who is overseeing the goal-directed activity of others is involved in *supervision*. Knowledge of what is to be done must be transmitted; methods and instruc-tions for doing a task must be understood; and individuals for doing a task and individuals must be energized into constructive action to achieve goals.

Direction and guidance are two aspects of supervision that parallel "task" and "person centered" organization. The difference between the two lies in the fact that, in *direction,* the emphasis is placed upon the process itself, because clear and adequate instructions must be transmitted to assure understanding of the work method. In *guidance* however, interest is focused on what is happening to the individual carrying out the process. In situations involving human relations or learning methods of work, guidance may predominate because the growth and welfare of the learner may be more important than the accomplished work.

When speed in achievement or the quality of the end product is important and personal learning is not so vital, direction can be geared toward obtaining desired results. Clear-cut instructions can often be the best source of the learner's confidence. Where safety is involved, accuracy of instructions is essential.

EVALUATING

Evaluating is the assessment of progress in the management sub-systems and in goal attainment. The impact of management on quality of living across time and consideration of possible improvement in the management processes are functions of evaluation. Overlapping the action stage of implementing with evaluation can reduce problems and improve the implementation of a plan.

Evaluating, as a distinct phase of management, goes beyond checking; it analyzes results and judges effectiveness. It attempts to discover reasons why outcomes vary from the projected or desired goal. It is a broader, longer view that analyzes impacts of action on the total pattern of living. Evaluators see beyond momentary mistakes, confusions, or needed changes, to the degree of accomplishment. Checking on management effectiveness or efficiency requires analysis, honesty, objectivity and a sound basis for judgement. In managing family living, the measure by which relative success or failure of a plan can be evaluated is the extent to which it has advanced the family's goals. The more definite and clear-cut the goals, the more accurate evaluation can be.

INTERDEPENDENCY OF THE MANAGEMENT SUB-SYSTEMS

For clarity of concepts, this analysis of activities of the four sub-systems of the management process has portrayed each sub-system as a separate series of activities. In application, however, it is more typical to find the sub-systems overlapping.[10]

The terms nominal, ordinal, interval, and ratio have been used in statistics to illustrate levels of research and appropriate tests to determine significant differences.[11] The same terms are applied in Figure 2.2 in a four-level model to integrate planning and organizing activities of management.

In the illustration, the lowest level of planning is the *nominal level* where selecting of activities is achieved through listing, by name only, the items to

Figure 2.2 A Planning Model. The Planning Model describes four levels of planning in everyday living. More complex situations require higher levels of planning to affect change. The nominal level is the simplest and perhaps the most frequently used. The ordinal level includes sequencing; the interval level includes selecting, sequencing, and scheduling; while the highest form of planning adds synchronizing to the first three levels.

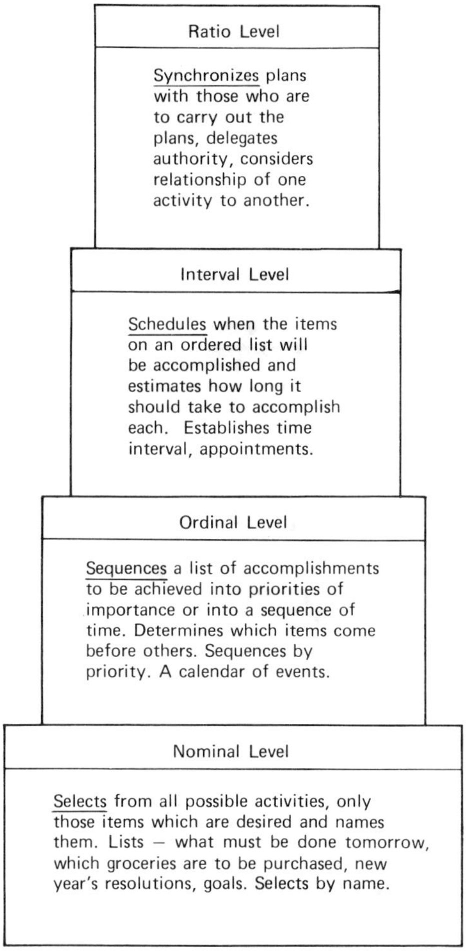

Ratio Level

Synchronizes plans with those who are to carry out the plans, delegates authority, considers relationship of one activity to another.

Interval Level

Schedules when the items on an ordered list will be accomplished and estimates how long it should take to accomplish each. Establishes time interval, appointments.

Ordinal Level

Sequences a list of accomplishments to be achieved into priorities of importance or into a sequence of time. Determines which items come before others. Sequences by priority. A calendar of events.

Nominal Level

Selects from all possible activities, only those items which are desired and names them. Lists — what must be done tomorrow, which groceries are to be purchased, new year's resolutions, goals. Selects by name.

be accomplished. This is the level utilized in New Year's resolutions and grocery lists. No attempt is made to put the items in any particular order, to assign priorities, or establish time estimates. It is not always necessary for the list to be written since a mental note of items may be sufficient for some activities.

The *ordinal level* is a higher order of sequencing. At this level of planning, the list of accomplishments to be achieved is put into order of priorities of importance. This stage requires a higher degree of management since decisions are necessary to predict consequences of doing one job before another. The series of projects is assigned an order or importance without definite time limits. This type of planning is typical for most people until a deadline or time limitation becomes apparent.

Students often use the nominal (listing) level of planning when they know two reference papers are to be handed in by the end of the term. Although the papers are kept in mind and their importance judged against current activities, there is no real pressure to place the list in order of priorities unless the professor calls for a temporary bibliography and outline or a conference to discuss the project plans. In that case, some preliminary decisions must be made on the paper's topic followed by locating several useful references on the subject prior to the conference. When tasks must be accomplished in a particular order, the ordinal level of planning has been reached and organization begins.

The interval level is the first level of planning to fully utilize the organization process of management. At this stage it is necessary to decide when the items on an ordered list will be accomplished and to estimate how long it should take to complete each item on the list.[12] Both of these steps are organizational. The interval level refines the selecting and sequencing stages of planning and interweaves the organizing of materials into a *schedule*. Scheduling of doctor's appointments allowing from 15 minutes to an hour per patient (depending upon the illness) is a simple illustration of this stage in the management process. When a working wife plans her day by leaving home an hour early to do the laundry on the way to work, arranges to have lunch in town so she can pick up a few items from the department store on her lunch hour, and leaves a note telling her husband she will be home later than usual so she can do the grocery shopping on the way home from work, she is scheduling the events of the day. This degree of planning and organizing is typical of interval-level scheduling.

For short periods, such as a day or less, total time usage may be scheduled while leaving some short periods of time unscheduled as a buffer against interruptions and unexpected events. For longer periods of time, only definite activities and inflexible events will probably be sequenced in the initial plan. More detailed planning may be necessary nearer to the day of activity.

The ratio level of organizing requires that plans be synchronized with those who are to carry out the plans. Authority can be delegated to others and consideration given to the relationship of one happening to another. After goals have been established, achievement of the ratio level of organization may proceed according to a plan such as the one that follows:

1.   List the inflexible, essential items first, then add the flexible items to be included.

2. Estimate the time needed to accomplish each event.

3. Reconcile the time available with the total time needed to accomplish all items on the list.

4. Order—place in a sequence of time—the items that have to be accomplished, then those that should be accomplished; then, if time permits, include those items desired to be accomplished and delete those to be omitted.

5. Write the plan on paper. This may be done in a very simple or a highly complex form, depending on the need.

6. Coordinate the plan with other persons involved in achievement of the established goals.

If it is to be workable, the ratio level of synchronizing the organization activities of management must:

• be flexible. Leave some unassigned time for each person.

• consider personal needs, likes, and ideosyncracies. Disliked jobs can be split up and done in "doses," dovetailed with pleasant jobs, or done at a time when they are less distasteful.

• allow time for individuals to be alone.

• be realistic in amount of work that can be accomplished in the available time.

• combine as many tasks as possible into simultaneous action if efficiency is a goal or a requisite to goal attainment.

• consider needed rest and warming-up periods.

Conceptual Framework of the Management Process

Concepts are the elements of thought essential to the structure of a discipline. If concepts are to be lasting, they must be broad in application but specific in meaning. All the concepts in the diagrammatic model of the management process illustrated below are stated as nouns (to simplify identification and definition) except the four key sub-systems of management and decision-making, the heart of the management process. In Figure 2.3, these are shown in the gerund form (a verbal form ending in "ing" which is used as a noun while conveying the meaning of the verb) because of their action-orientation.

The interrelatedness of concepts is illustrated by connecting lines operating like connective tissues between the bones of the human skeletal framework. These relationships are more flexible than rigid lines indicate, in order to allow for change of focus of the framework.

An individual, living within a family group in a societal environment, is influenced to varying degrees by the group and the societal environment of extended family structure, peer associates, and the customs, habits, and norms of the community in which the person lives. In turn, he reciprocates by influencing each of the societal groups to which he belongs.

As a result of these social influences, the individual and his immediate family form a hierarchy of values that are generalized concepts of what is desirable and important to the holder. The activities of daily living present situations, problems, conflicts, and opportunities calling for the establishment of goals—objectives toward which endeavor is directed—and standards—acknowledged criteria for qualitative or quantitative comparison to measure goal attainment. Values appear in triangular form to symbolize a ranking of value components into a hierarchy. Goals and standards are symbolized by diamonds that indicate a decision function in flow charting.

Resources are inputs in the process of management. Human, evironmental, and economic resources are stored in an available bank of readiness to be selected and utilized in various combinations through the management process. Information and creative thought increase the power of resource inputs in gratification of goals and the creation of desirable quality of living.

Decisions are necessary to determine which resources will be used and to solve problems or resolve situations leading to the desired quality of life. The procedures of decision making permeate the four management sub-systems—planning, organizing, implementing, and evaluating. Decision making is not diagrammed in the flow chart because it is an essential part of each of the other processes. Decisions relate to value formation, to goal determination, to development of standards, and to selection of resources. In fact, each line that connects one concept to another may be thought of as decision making.

Through the management sub–systems, illustrated as defined processes by the hexagon, goods and services are produced and consumed or saved for later use. New resources may be produced or the usefulness of old resources may be increased through planning, organizing, implementing, and evaluating.

Change is the result of the management process. Change is directly related to quality of living. If the quality of life produced is satisfactory, new

Figure 2.3 Flow Chart Model of the Management Process.

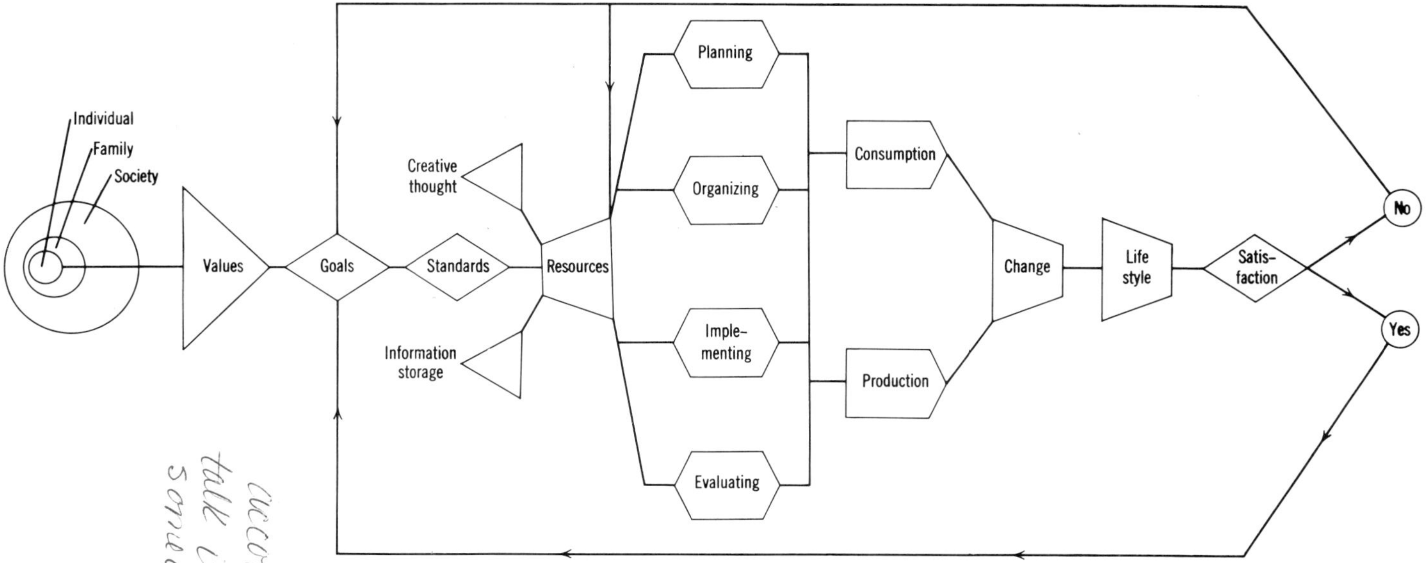

accountability –
talk it over w/
someone

goals may be established and the process of management begun again. If the changes produce dissatisfaction with quality of living, the situation can be reevaluated, alternate goals and resources selected, and action redirected through the appropriate management sub–systems.

The purpose of management is to control change. The product of management is quality of living. Management occurs on many levels, some more effective than others. Management depends on the quality and number of resources that are available and purposefully developed. It also depends on the quality of planning, organizing, implementing, and evaluating that transfers resources into services for other family members: nutritious and appetizing meals, companionship, or socialization of children. These may be thought of as either goods or services that are produced or consumed by family members in the course of everyday living.

The quality of management can be improved through practice, and research indicates that this quality may also be improved through education in management. It is, therefore, crucial to the potential quality of life in this nation and the world that education and effort be directed toward improving the quality of individual and family management.

INTERRELATEDNESS OF THE MANAGEMENT FUNCTIONS

In the management model, the four sub-systems are indicated as separate entities. In reality, one of the management functions cannot operate without interacting in some degree with the other three functions. Hence, the effectiveness of each management process is dependent upon the quality and appropriateness of the other functions in terms of the desired change. Figure 2.4 illustrates the interrelatedness of the management functions of planning, organizing, implementing, and evaluating.

This overlapping of processes may be examined in the example of an automobile purchase. Planning and evaluating overlap when the Moore family asks themselves if they really need another car. Plans have been made for a summer vacation before Melody, their oldest daughter, starts fall classes at a nearby junior college. They wonder if all these goals are feasible.

After deciding that a used car will serve their purposes, they consider what features are needed and what "extras" would be useful in the car. The Moores overlap planning and organizing at this stage by assigning information-gathering to various family members. Insurance and licensing costs are estimated, various lending agencies are consulted, available used cars are considered after looking at private and dealers' ads in the local paper. The automobiles are evaluated in comparison to wanted and needed features and to available money. Some implementing has occurred with the organizing process.

Figure 2.4   Interrelatedness of the Management Functions.

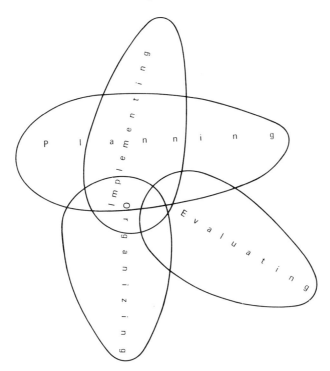

Once the car has been selected, implementing continues with the purchase of needed insurance and licenses. The Moores have learned to check bills of sale and have made all of the legal arrangements for transfer of title.

Although they are concerned with personal development, supervision in this situation is primarily job-centered—they are concerned about results. Use and care of the automobile were considered in organizing, but they are especially important with implementing. Has the mechanic made the requested repairs before the time of sale?

Evaluation occurred throughout the process, but the Moores make a practice of evaluating their management and goal attainment after purchasing, too. The parents decided to purchase the car from a nearby dealer because a warranty was provided. If later they learn that the coverage under the warranty is minimal, then the Moores will need to reevaluate their purchase and will probably conclude that the planning-organizing stage of information-gathering needs to be strengthened. For future purchases, warranties will need to be added to the list of features; make, and model of the car, insurance and licensing costs, and methods of payment if the family expects to receive satisfaction from the purchase.

The short-term goal of owning an additional car has been reached, and the management processes as well as the product have been evaluated. But what is the long-term impact on quality of life? Automobiles please their owners but increase the pollution in the air, the congestion of traffic, and the difficulty of parking, and, therefore, can reduce the owners' long-run satisfaction.

HABITS AND MANAGEMENT

Habits—actions repeated frequently enough to become automatic—can be resources for management. They free a person's thoughts while performing activities, and they provide patterns for living in times of change. The more routine tasks that can be committed to habit, the freer that person's mind is for making fresh decisions. A manager does not need to consider how to perform routine tasks related to care of self or care of the living unit, as long as such habits serve the purposes for which they were originally designated.[13]

If habits are not serving their original purposes; if purposes, resources, or other circumstances have changed; then habits may need to be evaluated and changes programmed.

QUALITY OF MANAGEMENT

Whenever action is planned and controlled, managment occurs. However, the quality of management varies widely. The crucial question is, "*Which* factors more directly affect the quality of management?" Just as psychologists often study abnormal people in an attempt to better understand qualities of normality, analysis of mismanagement may reveal factors that contribute to successful management.[14] Observations from work with families lead to some possible reasons why some people use their resources with unsatisfactory results.

1. Family goals may be hazy, indefinite, or so weak that they fail to motivate careful use of resources. Or the compulsion of one group member may be so intense that the use of the entire family's resources may be swayed by that person.

2. Family members may not completely understand the meaning of management. They may be unaware of the purposive activities of the process. Those who do not understand may resist planning because

they say it gives them a "confined feeling." "I'd rather do what I want to do when I want to, and have what I want when I want it!" is a familiar reaction to attempted improvement in management.

3. Family members simply may be unaware of all available resources, especially the valuable human resources, and may not get full use from them.

4. People are inclined to seek formulas to use resources they know about, particularly money and time, rather than guidelines that can be adapted to their particular situation. If such a formula is found, tried, and is ineffective, the feeling is that management is somehow at fault.

5. People may not realize the need to evaluate their experiences and the results of their activities in relation to their goals. They may not recognize the use of evaluation for future improvement.

6. The inability to distinguish "essentials" from "niceties" and to establish priorities can be a basic problem of many less effective managers.

Such lack of understanding and awareness may illustrate a failure to realize what management is and its relation to quality of living. Motivation to succeed may be inactive or absent and a "get by" attitude is easily developed if people are unaware of personal or family goals.

DANGERS IN OVERMANAGEMENT

There are certain dangers inherent in the management process. These dangers are of real importance, as they strongly affect other members of the family and may be felt outside the family group.

The person who has unusual managerial ability easily conceives purposes and plans more rapidly than they can be carried out by himself or others. It is often hard for this individual to realize the time needed for each person to do his share of group activity, and as a result he or she can become impatient with the delay in results. In the home, an impatient manager is apt to say, "It takes much less time to do it myself than to have the children do it." Such a remark indicates that the parent may have lost sight of the educational value the child would derive in learning to do tasks, or the satisfaction the child would receive from sharing in the activities of the family.

An overzealous parent may expect a child to assume managerial responsibilities beyond his abilities or interest. A protective parent, however, may not expect a child to carry responsibilities compatible with his abilities. In either extreme, the child can miss valuable experiences.

A group member who is achievement oriented in planning and thinking can develop a nagging habit or "drive." It is difficult for members of the group who are timed differently to reconcile the temperament of others with their own. Synchronizing the different tempos of people is a challenge for any manager. Failure to recognize individual differences can retard achievement of group goals. The person who drives others of slower tempo too rapidly makes planning and organizing an *end* instead of a *means* to an end.

The overenergetic man or woman who is constantly bustling, is usually unhappy unless everyone else is also bustling. Such people may not be as effective as they may seem. Successful management is not obvious. It allows some freedom of action to all members of the group, but it does require that each member become accountable for his actions toward group goals.

A danger that frequently arises in connection with time and energy management is that the energies of some or all of a family may be strained in order that one member may take on other responsibilities. The overloading of those who are already carrying heavy responsibilities can cause worry, fatigue, illness, friction, emotional upsets, and unhappy relationships.

Overexertion, which may result from trying to live up to a plan or finish some task that takes more time than calculated, should also be avoided. The person who habitually works on nerve or who borrows from the next day's store of energy in order to accomplish work planned for today usually ends the day thoroughly exhausted and unable to carry his or her full share of responsibility the next day. Overwork can occur if a student crams for an exam and is left drained of energy and unprepared for the next day's workload.

Overmanagement has a way of taking the delight of spontaniety out of life and may curtail creativity and innovative spirits. The homemaker who is so meticulous in the care of the house that anyone entering the home is reluctant to sit down defeats the goal of creating a warm and welcome home. The successful manager is the person who can plan, organize, implement, and evaluate goal-related activities.

THE CHALLENGE OF MANAGEMENT

Management in family living is effective to the degree that it results in the accomplishment of work that must be carried forward, brings satisfaction from the use of money and abilities, and releases time and energy for recreational activities and self discovery. It also improves the choice and use made of goods and services, influences the establishment of reasonable standards, and improves quality of living not only for the individual and his family, but for the on-going population of the world. It integrates human values into living as changed conditions affect daily life. Such management is constructive and satisfying to individuals and to society.

People learn to manage by analyzing situations, by studying human nature, by being aware of what is involved in improving management practices, by checking personal qualities against the qualities that lead to satisfaction in living, and by enriching experiences with new points of view. Self satisfaction may be a deadly threat to development. Blindly following the path of least resistance, doggedly doing things the "way mother did them," or traditionally following the performance of others hinders progress and personal growth.

Personal and family management is successful when it places individual development ahead of organization and makes the process of management the means to the end—to provide satisfying human experiences: present and future. Pat solutions or patterns of action will not fit each need. Each person and each living unit has its own needs and requires a plan of its own. The persons who are effective in management are those who shape their plans to fit theirs and their family's needs and desires. When this is done, management becomes a growing, vital part of the living experience.

Summary

Management is a means of achieving goals through the use of resources. The management process is a valuable aid to the improvement of life.

The interrelated activities or sub-systems of the management process described in this chapter include: planning to achieve goals, organizing for performance, implementing the plan, and evaluating the results in light of goals sought.

Management improves quality of life when it places importance on personal or group goals and recognizes the management functions as *means* rather then *ends* in themselves. Providing order and direction to life requires each person and each family to consider their own needs and desires rather than looking for a set of universal rules for management. When all motivations are considered, management becomes a growing and vital part of personal development and family achievement of a satisfying quality of living.

References

1. Liston, M. I., "Managerial Functioning," in *Behavioral Aspects of Management,* Proceedings of a conference for Western Regional Teachers of Home Management-Family Economics, Salt Lake City, Utah, (1971), pp. 57–70.

2. Steidl, R. E., "An Ecological Approach to the Study of Family Management Behavior," *The Family: Focus on Management,* American Home Economics Association, Washington, D. C., (1970), p. 26.

3. Gross, I., Crandall, E. and Knoll, M., *Management in Modern Families,* Appleton-Century-Crofts, New York, (1973), pp. 152–153.

4. Schlater, J. D., "The Management Process and Its Core Concepts," *Journal of Home Economics,* 59, 2(February 1967), p. 98.

5. Maloch, F. and Deacon, R. E., "Proposed Framework for Home Management," *Journal of Home Economics,* 58, 1(January 1966), p. 32.

6. Young, R., "Goals and Goal Setting," *American Institute of Planners' Journal,* 32, 2(1966), pp. 76–85.

7. Using Your Time to Gain Satisfaction, unpublished Home and Family Program, Cooperative Extension Service, Colorado State University, Fort Collins, Colo.

8. Nichols, A., *Person-Centered and Task-Centered Styles of Organization,* unpublished doctoral dissertation, Michigan State University, East Lansing, Mich. (1964).

9. Baker, G., *Management in Families: Process of Managing,* Michigan State Univerisity Cooperative Extension Service, Extension Bulletin 455, (January 1965), p. 8.

10. Johnson, R. A., Kast, F. E., and Rosenzweig, J. E., *The Theory and Management of Systems,* McGraw-Hill, New York, (1967), pp. 14–18.

11. Van Dalen, D. B. and Meyer, W. J., *Understanding Educational Research,* McGraw-Hill, New York, (1966), pp. 317–318.

12.   Davis, R. C., *The Fundamentals of Top Management,* Prentice–Hall, Englewood Cliffs, N.J., (1951), p. 648.

13.   Moore, B. M., "Time Tension and Mental Health," *Journal of Home Economics,* 49, 10(December 1957), pp. 759–763.

14.   Terry, G. R., and Irwin, R. D., *Principles of Management,* Homewood, Ill. (1964) p. 4.

3

MOTIVATIONS FOR MANAGEMENT

Why do some people climb mountains while others would not climb a six-foot ladder? Why do people spend time or money in differing activities? Why is it that children in the same family can develop such unique and differing personalities?

An understanding of human motivations can provide some answers to these and other questions about individual or family differences. *Motivations* are reasons for actions or influences that can alter an individual's behavior. The specific motivations to be discussed in this chapter include:

- *needs* and *values*—general reasons why people manage

- *goals*—what people attempt to accomplish

- *standards*—measures of quality, quantity, and method of goal attainment.

The differences between these motivations and their relationships to each other are discussed in this section of Chapter 3.

Why People Manage

Values and needs are more general and less visible forms of motivation than are goals and standards. Values or needs like freedom, love, or self-actualization, because they are abstract, are more difficult to measure than concrete progress toward a goal of college graduation or concern for neatness in a living unit. These more general concepts, however, form the basis for setting goals and standards.

NEEDS

In attempting to describe steps in the development of a healthy personality, Maslow outlined the concept of human needs.[1] A basic assumption here is that healthy people seek self-improvement. This assumption includes the recognition that such improvement requires effort—it is not always easy.

The framework of levels of human needs (Figure 3-1) is illustrated in a ladder-like arrangement. People progress from one level to another much like climbing a ladder; the end result is full development of human potential. As with the ladder, people who have partially satisfied a level of need may find that they continue to work on that need while extending themselves to meet those of higher levels. Maslow suggested that these classifications of human needs apply to people throughout the world—not just to one or a few cultures.[2]

Levels of Needs

Needs illustrate some of the similarities in human motivation. *Physiological needs* are important to maintaining life and are more specific than are the higher level needs. If a person is starving, lacking shelter, or in serious need of sleep, he or she is motivated to fulfill this need. If food is desperately needed, a person may be unconcerned about the quality of food or how it is to be served so long as food is present. A person who is in a very warm or very cold classroom may observe that the need for physical comfort influences the ability to learn.

Safety needs include freedom from fear, threat, danger, or deprivation. Parents who threaten misbehaving children with punishment are appealing to this level of need. The physiological and safety needs are very basic to living. Some psychologists have expressed concern, however, that some individuals never progress beyond these two most elemental levels.[3]

Social needs relate to social interaction, such as acceptance, love, and belonging. People have an affinity for companionship, for caring, and being cared for. *Esteem needs* include self respect, recognition, and status. In some situations, people consider esteem a higher level need than self-actualization. A person who senses a need to be respected in an occupational group or in a community may, for example, work toward personal growth as a means of recognition.

The realization of one's human potential is termed *self-actualization.*[4] According to Maslow, few people become completely self-actualized. Creativity, self discipline, unity of personality, and openness to experience are characteristics of healthy people who are working toward self-actualization.[5]

The concept of human needs can be applied to self motivation and to motivation of others. It is apparent from the above description, that human needs provide motivation for management. If, for example, a person feels that

Figure 3.1   Levels of Human Needs.

his or her safety needs are being met, an opportunity for additional safety will probably not change behavior. Because a sequence of needs exists, an appeal to higher level needs like esteem or self-actualization may be inappropriate for a person who is struggling to merely sustain life. Because people's needs change, motivations once considered extremely important may later be irrelevant.

Relation to Values

The relationship between needs and values is hazy. Maslow used the two terms interchangeably; however, he notes that cultural background affects the formation of some specific values, while needs are not limited to one culture.[6] It is possible that needs are either more general values, or that they are an alternate form of human motivation. Values can help in deciding how needs are to be met.

Needs are universal, biologically-based motivations that can be considered different from values.[7] People sense voids—or needs—in life and are motivated to seek these missing elements. Values are individual, socially-based motivations. A specific quantity of food, shelter, or water will satisfy physiological needs; but if health is a personal value, more individualized nutritional requirements may be developed. Religious values might also influence the selections of food or beverage to meet physiological needs.

Values can parallel needs or be in conflict with needs. The person who values health is probably also working toward physiological and safety needs. Progress in satisfying human needs can conflict with values, as in the case of a health-oriented person who is also seeking social acceptance. Being part of a crowd may include drinking, smoking, or using drugs—activities that conflict with the person's definition of health. In conflicts between values and needs, the latter will have a higher priority in many, but not all, cases. If a value is of extreme importance, it might outweigh needs.

It seems that knowledge of human needs can help people to determine priorities and analyze interrelationships among values. Values, in turn, individualize the more specifically defined needs.

VALUES

Values give meaning to life, and they answer the question of why people make specific selections from alternative courses of action. In common use, value means the worth or merit of an item or idea, as exemplified by the following phrases—the "retail value is . . . ," "that idea has value," or "he made a valuable contribution." The meaning of the term as used in management theory is more precise, in that values are the reasons for an item's worth or for an idea's merit. According to Kluckhohn, a *value* is "a conception, explicit or implicit, distinctive of an individual or characteristic of a group, of the desirable which influences the selection from the available modes, means, and ends of action."[8] Values are all inclusive, deeply internalized, personal feelings that direct action. Values are desirable to the person who holds them. Since values cannot be seen, they must be recognized in behavior. Examples of values include freedom, love, honesty, leisure, knowledge, convenience, comfort, economy, efficiency, and prestige.

Characteristics of Values

Kluckholn's definition of values implies some characteristics that are helpful in distinguishing values from other forms of motivation. The term "conception" denotes the general nature of values. Because values are so general, they can be demonstrated in a number of ways in varied activities. A person who values knowledge can demonstrate the value through formal coursework, reading, travel, or social interaction.

The word "desirable" reinforces the general nature of values, but it also implies additional characteristics. Values are intense personal feelings about behavior and expectations of life. Values are more general, more influential, and more permanent than desires or wishes. Values have both factual and emotional components, making them broader than either attitudes or beliefs. Because values are intense feelings, people can become emotionally charged when discussing how life should be or when resolving value conflicts.

This general nature of values also implies a pattern of consistent behavior. Patterns of similar choices over a period of time more accurately reflect values than do one-time activities. How a person spends money or time in one day can be based on whim, impulse, or desire; continuous patterns of resource use, however, reflect values.

The term value also has a positive or true meaning to the person who holds the value. Some values and the consequent ways of demonstrating them in daily interaction may seem inappropriate to a certain person, family, or culture; but are the values themselves "bad"? In evaluating a family's living unit as "ugly" or a person's behavior as "dishonest", the observer is using his or her values to assess the decisions of others. Although the negative of honesty is dishonesty, can dishonesty be considered a concept of the desirable? In such situations, it is possible that the priorities of the decision maker differ from those of the observer. Aesthetics or beauty might not be as important to the family as economy, comfort, or convenience. Does this placing of aesthetics in lower priority mean that the family prefers ugliness—a "bad" value?

Because values are reasons for action—because they describe why people behave as they do—they are seldom fully achieved. Consider love or happiness; if these are important, a person will demonstrate the value in a number of ways. If the person senses that progress has been made toward becoming more loving or more happy, he or she will seek additional ways to demonstrate the value.

Values can be verbalized and held at a conscious level—*explicit*—or held subconsciously and recognized only in behavior—*implicit*. People may articulate certain values, but their actions contradict those statements. Such actions can be prompted by more important values that have not been consciously recognized. *Clarification of values* involves conscious awareness and crystalizes meaning and importance and can lead to more consistent behavior and to increased satisfaction with the results of management.

Values can be held on a personal, family, or cultural level. Sharing them

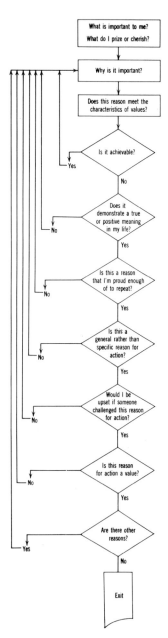

Figure 3.2   Identifying Personal Values. Analyzing reasons for behavior patterns can lead to clarification of values. By examining the above chart, a person might identify travel, marriage, or savings as important patterns in life. These are general yet they are achievable terms. Answering why these prized aspects of life are important might clarify attitudes, beliefs, goals, or desires that also need to be analyzed to realize values. The process takes effort, but bringing knowledge of values to a conscious level helps people direct their lives.

among family members or within a community or nation can produce feelings of unity of purpose. Older family members transmit their meaning of values to younger people in the group; similar learning occurs through the mass media and community membership. The process of learning about values is gradual; although values can and do change, they are relatively stable.

Because of the general nature of values, their meaning is personal. An individual interpretation of freedom might be seen as the absence of all responsibilities. Others define freedom as doing what they want when they want to do it. Both these definitions might be considered devoid of responsible and mature understanding by another individual. As people increase their recognition of values, they question and individualize meaning. This questioning, defining, and sorting of priorities is part of life-long personality development.

The last part of Kluckholn's definition states that values can influence behavior when more than one course of action is available. Through decision making, people demonstrate what they consider to be good, important, or desirable. In this selecting process, people encounter conflicts—differences between the current situation and expectations. These conflicts can be internal, or they can be conflicts in meaning or priorities of values with other people. An example of an internal value conflict is found in the person who values friendship and honesty and wonders if tact is contrary to the value of honesty. An interpersonal value conflict occurs if one family member is highly motivated toward personal achievement while others are motivated toward family unity. Because people are motivated toward consistent behavior, they attempt to reconcile differences among values and between values and actions. Value conflicts motivate people to further sort priorities—friendship may have either more or less importance than honesty. Conflicts with other peoples' values can be resolved by accepting interpersonal differences, by rearranging group or individual priorities, or by redefining values.

Value Patterns

Choice making within a family occurs in a given society and in a given cultural and historic period. The influence of an outside person or group on a family member depends on the individual family member and on the power of those attempting to influence. Value patterns and the related philosophy a family develops help decide the nature and effect of outside influences. No one can totally free himself from social dictates, and some people are even dominated by them. Value patterns of the social group bring pressures that cannot be easily avoided. Nevertheless, evaluations are made first as an individual, then as a member of a family, of a community, and, finally, as a member of all mankind.

People in a given culture tend to hold similar basic values that become criteria for choice, even though the importance placed on specific values may vary. Value patterns are also related to time and situation. For example, in the western United States, the prevailing manner of living is informal; in New England, the mode is more formal.

Each family may want to work out its own set of values or *value system* suitable and believable to all family members. If such agreement is not attempted, values may be conflicting or unclear, and this can hinder the family or its members in choice making. The development of a common value pattern is not an easy task. Results of one research study indicate that a small number of common values are held by all family members. There also appears to be a greater likelihood of shared values in small rather than in large families.[9] There is also an alternative, more general way of describing value patterns.

A *value orientation* provides an overview of a philosophy of life. This orientation has a number of dimensions that describe man's general view of nature, man's relationship to nature, and man's relationship to other persons.[10] A person or family who believes that people control the environment will be motivated differently than will people who believe that man works cooperatively with nature. Another example of differences in value orientation is found in people who emphasize tradition or worship of ancestors, in contrast to those who emphasize current situations or a future orientation. These generalized value orientations can be passed from generation to generation. In a study of three-generational families, Hill found much agreement in value orientations across the three generations.[11]

Classification of Values

Although values may be classified in various ways, for the purposes of this discussion they will be considered as intrinsic and instrumental. An *intrinsic value* is one that is important and desirable simply for its own sake. In reviewing the first two chapters, the reader should notice that one life style or one set of goals was not advocated as "best" for all people. This reasoning is based on a predominant value in home management—human dignity,[12] the optimum development of the individual,[13] or individuality. This value—however it is labeled—involves respect of personal uniqueness and for that of others. Also involved is the creation of household and community atmospheres that foster personal growth. Human dignity, aesthetics, or love with their many facets are intrinsic values that have merit in themselves.

An *instrumental value* is a means of attaining higher level values. Efficiency and order have been categorized by McKee as two of the instrumental values in home management.[14] These values are sought as means rather than as ends. Efficiency, for example, can improve the quality of results of an activity and can free resources for other uses. Instrumental values like economy or convenience can be viewed as steps toward or tools for demonstrating other values. Order in a household can help to demonstrate love; shared activities can lead to personal growth. Recognition of such priorities and interactions between values can help individuals and families to sort priorities among other motivations and among possible actions.

Some values possess both intrinsic and instrumental worth. In some measure they are means to other values. Comfort, health, ambition, love, knowledge, play, art, and religion can be both intrinsic and instrumental. Values are interdependent, intimately related, and provide guidance in individual and family behavior.

To illustrate this interdependent and intimate relationship between values of intrinsic and instrumental worth, consider the example of a young person who is highly sensitive to the expression of beauty in the forms of poetry, music, and sculpture, but who is especially talented in painting. In deciding to paint a picture, he may be motivated by values other than that of beauty. If he needs more money to live on and if the sale of the picture will bring him the needed cash, he may be motivated by economic necessity. To the extent that he is using his talent to earn a living, the value he finds in painting becomes his means to an end. However, he finds intrinsic value in the desire to create a thing of beauty for itself alone. He may be motivated by still other values such as gratification of ambition, pride in skill, and fine workmanship.

Value patterns can develop into a ranking or hierarchial arrangement. Intrinsic values are described by Gross, Crandall, and Knoll as more important than the changeable instrumental values because of their relative permanence.[15] Values of extreme importance are applied to many aspects of life while others may be demonstrated in only a few situations. This ranking or hierarchy of values develops as value conflicts are resolved. It also guides people toward consistency in decision making.

Identifying Personal Values

Values are influential in determining quality of life; so individuals and families may want to direct their effort toward identifying and clarifying these motivations for management. Patterns of attitudes, beliefs, interests, activities, and goals are reflections of values that are sometimes called value indicators.

To identify personal values, individuals and families can ask themselves about the reasons behind these indicators. The diagram in Figure 3.2 indicates some sample questions that readers might apply to identify their values. If, for example, a family observes that they plan at least one group vacation a year—in spite of financial difficulties or potential time conflicts with individual activities—this recurring goal or pattern of activities could be considered a value indicator. In analysis, the family might identify more than one reason for action—family unity, leisure, or happiness are three such possibilities. Other clues are found in behavior that disappoints or ideas that upset a person or group. Determining the basic reasons for being disappointed or upset can produce broader understanding of personal values.

What People Work For

Goals are the ends that individuals or families are willing to work for. They are more definite than values because they can be accomplished. They are tangible things: objects, ends, or purposes. Many goals develop from desires, philosophies, attitudes, and values. Most people seek happiness and a satisfying pattern of personal living. Many goals are formed in the expectation that reaching them will bring a satisfying life. Some of these goals may be specific while others may be more general; consequently some may be more or less motivating than others.

Goal setting is a continual process. Throughout life each family is constantly weighing values and changing attitudes about attainment and acquisition. As a result action may be directed toward seeking new methods of reaching established goals. Goals are related to both standards and values. Standards help to measure progress toward goals and to decide how the goals are to be reached. A well-understood pattern of values helps individuals and families to define their goals and decide the things of greatest importance to them.

PRIORITIES AND TIMING OF GOALS

Priorities of goals were discussed in Chapter 2. The reader will remember that goals can be considered as those that "must" be done, that "ought" to be done, that people "want" to do, or as activities or items that were once important but can now be forgotten. Priorities in goals are influenced by values and standards.

The three most familiar types of goals according to the time needed to achieve them are: (a) long-term or ultimate goals; (b) intermediate or short-term goals; and (c) means-ends goals, leading to other goals.[16]

The *long-term goals* are considered fairly permanent. They are sought over long periods of time and, consequently, are omnipresent. They have real meaning to a family group. Although they may be the first goals a family formulates, they are usually the last a family realizes. A young family that plans for early retirement of the breadwinner or breadwinners is working toward a long-range goal. Because they initiate and influence many of the intermediate goals, long-range goals are of great importance.

Families often set *intermediate* or *short-term goals* as ways of achieving long-term goals. Intermediate goals are more definite than long-term goals, and it is easier to form a clear-cut picture of them. The young family with a long-term goal of early retirement may save a given amount of money each year toward the longer range goal. They may visit various places on vacations to determine where they would like to retire. These intermediate range goals frequently involve making decisions or selections, sometimes unconsciously, from among several alternatives because it seems that they will prove the best means to achieve certain long-term goals.[17]

Means-end goals are less complex. They are the decisions made or the steps taken to attain other goals. There are many means-end goals that are ends in themselves and that are reached with a small number of activities; for example, whipping up an eggnog to whet the appetite of a small child, writing a check to pay a bill, or cutting flowers for the living room. These means-ends goals are sometimes also described as short-range or immediate goals because of the limited amount of time involved in reaching them.

When a person wishes to keep a living unit looking attractive, he or she sets an intermediate goal. To achieve this goal the person sweeps, dusts, cleans the floors, arranges the furniture, and so on. By combining these frequent means-end activities, he or she attains the intermediate goal.

Intermediate range goals, sought over periods of months or years, are more complex. Their realization requires many activities and a number of decisions: the purchase of major household goods, educational plans, or annual vacations are examples.

The time element in goal attainment resembles the flow of traffic on a freeway: cars weaving from one lane of traffic to another, competing with other cars to reach their destinations, some turning off here and some there, and others turning on to take their places. Like traffic controllers, people seek a balance in the time element for goal attainment. Limiting considerations to only short-range or means-end goals inhibits an overview of them and can produce continual feelings of crisis. Considering only long-range goals inhibits feelings of progress and can lead to lowered motivation. Goals are usually interrelated, interdependent, and carried on concurrently as part of daily living. They play an important part in life and are dynamic because they motivate thought and action for both individuals and family members.

Gardner cautions people to be aware of goals and not to get so involved in procedures for reaching a goal that the goal itself is overlooked.[18] Gardner is speaking of *goal-mindedness*, or what Edwards calls goal-oriented behavior.[19] A person who rapidly associates ideas and who quickly and skillfully perceives and fashions goal patterns is *goal minded*.[20] People with this ability can keep long-range goals in focus as they pursue daily activities that involve immediate or intermediate range goals.

People who successfully combine multiple roles—employee, family member, and community participant—have perceptions that extend beyond daily routines or frustrations; goal-mindedness is involved in such perceptions as is a realistic view of personal abilities and potential. Goal-mindedness provides a perspective for allocating resources among competing goals.

Changing Goals

Some goals are reached daily and others are added to the family's goal-complex. Others may be discarded because the cost in resources required to reach them seems unreasonable. The interests and activities of family members lead them to new goals, some of which may become long-term in importance. For instance, a mother's interest in the education of her children may mean that she will assume leadership in a parent-teacher organization or become a member of the local school board. An interest in antique furniture may motivate a person to refinish enough pieces to furnish a room. Children's activities in scouting or sports may help shape new ideas for them that will involve their parents' goals as well. Many goals change gradually as families pass through their life cycles. For example, parents whose children have left home may turn from the desire for home ownership to that of renting a smaller house or an apartment.

A serious accident or illness, death, divorce, unemployment, crop failures, or declining markets may bring sudden changes in family life. Any one of these events may shatter financial plans, change hopes for children, or lead to loss of position or home. All of these occurrences require a reappraisal of family goals and the patterns of values for each family member, with the result that many changes may be necessary in the family's way of life.

Goals involving shared effort are the source of common interest. From time to time, personal and family long-term and immediate goals should be carefully analyzed in relation to resources. Each person has competing wants from which selections must be made. Deciding which goals are most desirable, acceptable, and attainable and which appear vital to all members of the family takes time, thought, and often many discussions. When both personal and family goals are agreed on, integrated, and cooperatively decided, fewer disappointments are suffered, less conflicts are experienced, and more goals are realized.

To be real, goals need to become dynamic parts of life. To make them a part of daily routine requires conviction and effort. There is little magic in integrating long-term goals into daily living; stumbling blocks arise to make adjustments necessary. At times, the goals wished for may be impossible to attain. When this happens, the goals are either revised or new goals are set, and ways of attaining them are found.

Although the goals of each family differ in many ways from those of other families and methods of attainment vary greatly, families may find a number of major goals worth seeking. Immediate and intermediate goals often cluster around such long-range goals as:

1.   Establishing values that give meaning to personal and family living.

2.   Developing satisfying interpersonal relations that recognize human differences.

3.   Helping each member of the family to develop physically, mentally, socially, and spiritually.

4.   Creating an environment that stimulates individual and family participation in local and national affairs.

5.   Improving management of family resources to ensure attainment of goals.

The family that decides which goals are most important and desirable, and then works toward their achievement, is likely to get what it wants from life.

The Concept of Standards

Values have been defined as measures of worth. *Standards* are a set of criteria stemming from value patterns, determining the amount and kind of interest in an item or activity, and the satisfaction received. As judgments are made, standards serve as a measure or criterion for measurement of objects, ways of implementing goals, and ways of living. They are what individuals and families will accept as adequate and worthwhile.

In some ways, standards act as limits on individual and family behavior. They compel action toward an item or achievement because satisfaction or worth is expected from the item or accomplishment. Other possible possessions, goals, or activities will be avoided because of personal or group standards. Standards overtly show how much importance is placed on items and courses of action. For the individual, standards act as self-imposed or socially inflicted demands.

In a family, standards act as demands by the group or by a part of it or from outside by some segment of the social group. They are dynamic because they stimulate an individual or group to action.

Cooper says: "We set a standard for each kind of activity determined, intrinsically, by what we think will provide maximum satisfaction for it, and extrinsically, by what we believe will make the maximum contribution to the realization of our life plans."[21] A simple illustration of the demands standards make on people as individuals or as a family, which may affect the use of resources, is the type of table service used. Standards of service vary—some are elaborate, some are simple. In one family, all meals are served on the dining-room table; in another, all meals are served in the kitchen; and in still another, food may be put out in its original package—a loaf of bread in the wrapper, jelly or peanut butter in a jar, and milk in a carton. Some families use one standard of service when guests are present, but another for family members only. Each family chooses its table service in light of its own standards, values, and goals, not those of others. The exceptions are families that avidly follow the style or dictates of the social group, and these families could even be demonstrating conformity as a value.

An example of how social group pressures influence standards is that of two teen-age sisters who insisted that their father allow them to carry a surfboard on top of the family car, although neither they nor any member of the family knew how to surf. Displaying the board impressed their friends and gave the girls a feeling of social acceptance.

SOURCES OF STANDARDS

What are the origins of standards? Their sources can be traced to a culture or social groups, to scientific findings, or to the background of the person or group holding the standards.

Conventional standards originate in a cultural or social group. Based on repeated experiences of people within that group, certain measures of values and goals are established. The reader should note that there are differences between conventional standards and customs or habitual courses of action. A custom is a tradition handed down from the past in which usage or practice tends to regulate social behavior. Placing salads to the left of the plate in a table service is a matter of custom. Conventional standards, however, can be traced to values. Iced tea glasses are placed on underliners because people need a convenient place for a spoon rest or to protect the table and table cloth from the moisture of melting ice. Similarly, placing the knife to the right and the fork to the left of a plate is a matter of standard, because it is also associated with the value of comfort or convenience. In cutting food, the right hand uses the knife nearest it, and the left hand uses the fork nearest it.

Conventional standards sometimes become law. For safety purposes, people are restricted in driving and parking automobiles to a specific side of a street or highway. For the financial security of children, parents are expected to pay some of the cost of child-rearing, even after a divorce. Standards of morality are based in multiple values, but like all conventional standards, they are individually interpreted.

Scientific standards are based on fact or research data. Walker stated that scientific standards involve specific quantities—such as the quantities of specific nutrients included in nutritional standards relating to health.[22] Research has also been applied to safety in housing; standards regarding wiring, air conditioning, or strength needed in materials for construction are examples of some of these safety standards. As new research methods are developed or as more accurate measures are found, scientific standards change, as has been the case in nutritional research.

Personal or *family standards* are those that originate with an individual or a small group. These measures of acceptability can change with the people in a situation. A family may accept a standard of shared morning or evening meals to demonstrate the value of family unity. If important individual activities are later scheduled at the same hour, the family will need to evaluate the importance of this standard in relation to the new situation. Personal standards regarding dress or care of a living unit reflect the values that person holds.

CLASSIFICATION OF STANDARDS

Standards may be classified in a number of ways. In this discussion, however, they will be classified as to: (a) content; (b) fixedness or flexibility; and (c) quality. These classes are not mutually exclusive, and some overlapping will be found. For example, quality may operate along with either content or with restrictiveness or flexibility. The line of demarcation between classes is difficult to draw because, in this complex world, people are motivated from many sides. The classes are sufficiently distinct, however, to merit separate investigation.

Content is a tangible classification of standards. It is usually recognized objectively usually in material form, although it may also be realized mentally. Content standards describe what it is that people are working toward. One's overall standard of living is partially a content standard but should be distinguished from actual current level of living. *Standard of living* is the composite of all the goods and services and the pattern of consuming considered essential by a person or group. Level of consumption by scale of living (or level of living) was defined by Kyrk and Hoyt as descriptive of the inventory of actual commodities and services that people prize and measure and that flow through and are used by the consuming unit.[23] One's standard of living is usually higher than achieved level of living because the standard measures the content and quality of acceptable living over a period of time. Level of living is what is actually being consumed and experienced at the time.

Industrialization has made a wide variety of goods and services available from which choices are made. For example, a microwave oven can be accessible to those who can afford and who desire it. The decision to buy or not to buy may depend on how strongly other goods and services are wanted and the purposes the microwave oven is expected to serve for a family. The goods and services finally chosen comprise the standard of tangible objects and services— one's standard of content for living.

Since family resources can be limited and must be allocated among many needs and wants, awareness of a standard in terms of content can be an asset in determining what is important. Families who struggle to give each family member what he wants and also to remain financially solvent voice this dilemma of choice.

Fixedness or *flexibility* shows degree, varying from rigid, through less rigid, to flexible. Restrictiveness of standards varies in place and time. The difference in the standard of a wife's behavior toward her husband in a Far Eastern country or in the United States and the behavior of children in the pioneer days or today are examples of variation of rigidness in place and time.

Rigid standards may be associated with social or religious rites and are, therefore, imposed on a family by an outside group. Theoretical perfectionism arises when a compelling personal attitude imposes rigid standards—for example, the urge to keep a perfectly ordered house.

If this expression of rigidity originates with the social group, deviation or complete change may be difficult in the face of disapproval. For example, a group of employees may believe that people who work together should rent or own local living units that reflect the individual's status within the firm. Neither a new employee nor his or her family knows of this standard. The duplex rented by the family is suitable for their life style but is located in another community. The employee, however, is rated above average in all aspects of his performance at work. Other employees may associate with the person at work but may choose not to associate socially with the person or his family because of violation of their rigid standard.

Flexible standards allow people to adjust procedures or conduct to existing situations. Acceptance of flexible standards gives greater freedom of choice, and life is likely to be more relaxed, relations less strained, and anxieties less apparent. Adjusting housekeeping standards to changing conditions in family life illustrates the worth of flexible standards. For example, the way people do or do not dust may sometimes depend on circumstances. When people have the time, they may do a very thorough job, dusting in every crack and corner; when less time is available, they may clean only the places that show dust badly; and when no time is available, they may pull the draperies so the dust is not as noticeable.

People may have rigid standards in some aspects of their lives and homes and flexible standards in others because of values and the situations people encounter. For instance, a woman or man who is style conscious and must dress impeccably and in high fashion in public, maintains a rigid standard in public life. But if the same person is satisfied to dress less well, even carelessly, at home, he or she maintains a flexible standard in private.

Because friends and neighbors can observe standards, moving from rigid to flexible ones is not always easy. If people strongly believe in the need to change standards and feel that the changes are suited to personal and family needs, there is no reason to be embarrassed if others do not immediately accept such changes. When resources such as time and energy are limited, rigid standards may be inhibitive while flexible standards may allow greater freedom of action.

Quality is usually what we mean when we refer to the standards of another person, or of ourselves, or of a community. Quality refers to the character or essence of something evaluated subjectively and is usually expressed in terms of degree or range.

We evaluate, by some psychic measure, the quality of behavior, procedures, objects, or someone's thinking. We might say that a person who stands to greet others entering a room and who exhibits exceptionally refined manners holds high standards in comparison to others. This distinction in quality between high and low or between good and bad is relative, unless the contrast is quite sharp, as in the distinction between beauty and ugliness. Objective indicators have been developed for measuring some qualities—as in the case of gasoline octane ratings, safety glass in cars, or food grades. Consumers make subjective judgments about the qualities they want and then select a product based on the information available.

The standard of living of an individual, a family, a community, or a nation is a measure of desired quality. Whereas the scale or level of living indicates content, the standard of living is a mental image. Included in a standard of living are the desired goods and services and the satisfaction expected from them. The satisfaction derived is, thus, a measure of quality. As characterized by Bonde, standard of living's importance is . . .

a dynamic force directing the choices made in the use of resources. It is that which determines the system of priorities relating to what one is willing to give up and to what one will fight to retain under most difficult circum-

stances. . . It is that which makes of one's many diverse decisions an organic whole which is recognizable yet incapable of measurement in economic terms.[24]

The standard of living is usually held at a cultural or socio-economic group level but is interpreted at an individual or household level. People regard the things of life and the satisfactions derived from them in relation to what is important, what is valued, and what is affordable.

Standards can be viewed as general criteria for evaluating quality of life or can be more specifically applied to goal attainment. Standards applied to life without specific mention of goals can be considered as specifications for values.[25] Like construction specifications, life standards describe preferred qualities and quantities in life and influence goal setting. In the following section of the chapter, standards will be applied in a second way—as measures for goal attainment. Both general and specific applications of standards have importance in motivating managerial behavior.

Translating Motivations into Life Experience

Each person has some philosophy of life that guides individual or group behavior, although he may not think of it as a philosophy. Values and needs form the basis of this philosophy, and goals and standards translate the philosophy of life into daily activities. A philosophy is gradually developed and changes with needs, demands, knowledge, and experience. This section of the chapter is related to activating a philosophy of life.

INTERACTION BETWEEN MOTIVATIONS

Values and needs are basic reasons for action. Goals describe what people want to do or be; standards serve as measures for goals and values. Figure 3.3 illustrates this relationship between values, goals, and standards. Note that the same value can lead to a number of goals, each with a unique set of standards. People can also work toward the same goal for a variety of value-related reasons. Making similar analyses for personal goals helps to translate personal value patterns into action and provides a feeling for values at work in human behavior.

The chart is intended to illustrate some possible combinations of goals, values, and standards—not to indicate "best" ones. If the reader disagrees with some of the goals or standards, asking about reasons for the disagreement should lead to further knowledge of personal motivations.

Figure 3.3   Motivations for Management

Values that influence behavior: Why?	Goals that demonstrate the value: What?	Standards that measure goal attainment: How well? How much? How?
Ambition	to advance professionally	—learning from others on the job —advancing within the company in the next two years —earning $_____ by age 40 —local recognition of my capabilities —professional reading
	to become an active community member	—serving on the local museum board —membership in the church choir —voting at all state and federal elections after gaining sufficient information to make a decision —feeling that I've made the community a little more pleasant to live in
Health	to lose or gain weight	—losing (or gaining) 10 lbs. by _____ date —joining a community-sponsored exercise club —eating three, small but nutritious meals a day —snacking on low calorie food —getting 6 hours of sleep a night
	to keep my living unit clean	—picking up clutter at the end of each day —keeping the kitchen and bathroom spotless —reducing problems with alergies to dust —exercising while cleaning
Love	to retain close family ties	—frequent telephone or written contact with relatives outside the community —comfortable family communication —vacationing with extended family every two years
	to participate in community affairs	—see achievement—or —participating in town meetings —attending city government meetings when important issues are being decided —registering to vote —taking people without transportation to the polling place —active party membership

Figure 3.3 (Continued)

Values that influence behavior: Why?	Goals that demonstrate the value: What?	Standards that measure goal attainment: How well? How much? How?
Play or leisure	improve skill in a favorite sport (swimming, skiing or basketball)	—taking lessons from a professional —frequent practice —feeling comfortable with my form
Knowledge	to improve my reading skills	—daily practice —taking a reading course and improving reading speed by 200 words per minute —learning more from the reading

	to graduate from college	—by _____
		      (date)
		—in _____
		      (subject matter)
		—with _____
		      (grade point average)
		—keeping current in homework
		—participating in professional student organizations

	to learn more about my job	—participate in on-the-job training —learn from other employees —feel more confident with the work I do —ask questions when I don't understand an assignment

Progress toward Goals

Some standards in the chart are intentionally vague. It is possible to develop more specific standards directly related to measuring goal attainment by establishing procedures for reaching goals and in performance or desired results. Procedural standards for a goal of moving to another community or living unit could answer a number of questions: who will do the packing, how will items be packed, what will be moved and what will be disposed of, will a firm be hired to move the items, will a truck be rented, or can transportation be borrowed, who will unpack, and other matters of procedure. *Procedural standards* regarding how a goal is to be implemented reflect values and help to progress toward goals.

Performance standards used in assessing goal attainment describe the quality or quantity of desired results. These standards can be expressed in exact terms or in a range of acceptable limits. For the goal of moving, a cost or time limit could be set for completing the move. Expectations regarding results of the move are also forms of standards—such as additional space for hobbies or entertaining, or the success of adjustment to a new community or neighborhood. Ideas useful to develop performance standards are explored as follows.

Performance standards can be applied to purchases of goods and services and to changes desired in behavior. In applying performance standards to the purchase of a small electrical appliance, a consumer could include the following: expectations regarding needed preparation before use, convenience, cleanability, appropriateness of size, cost of operation, and cost of maintenance, storage, or disposal. Considering, before purchase, what a person or group wants a product to do can assure consumers of greater satisfaction than when standards are discovered after an expensive purchase is made.

Similarly, people can set performance standards for behavioral goals. Mager states that these standards should be developed only for vague and important goals.[26] His belief is based on the effort required to define desired quantity and quality of results. Terms like "improve", "active", and "low calorie" are among the vague descriptions in figure 3.3. Developing functional definitions for these terms in the specific situation helps people to recognize the nature of the specific behavioral change they desire.

Starting with a goal of improving housekeeping skills, losing weight, or developing reading abilities, a number of alternate standards can be developed. If a person wants to lose weight, knowledge of current weight is essential to measuring progress toward the goal. Deciding to lose weight without deciding how much to lose makes measuring progress quite difficult. Setting standards for the amount of loss and setting a time deadline can help people to recognize progress and to identify when the goal has been met. The standards should be realistic in relation to other goals and in relation to resources if they are to be an asset to management. The important issue is to develop standards that are meaningful in content or quantity and quality for the person or group setting and implementing the goal.

Developing performance and procedural standards can direct group or individual effort toward the desired quality of life. Clearly developed standards can be an asset to management, especially in group activity. In such activity, one person may implement a group goal, or the entire group may implement a goal developed by one member. Without a clear understanding of what should result or how implementation is to occur, satisfaction can be minimized, and resources can be misallocated. Such results may not be influential in minor decisions or less important goals; but even in these cases, group unity can be affected. Once clearly defined standards have been developed, there may be a temptation to retain them in spite of intervening circumstances. Evaluation of the appropriateness of goals and standards in view of situational changes is an important aspect of goal attainment.

Evaluating Standards

Gross and Crandall formulated a number of suggestions for evaluating standards.[27] They asked the reader to first consider the cost of holding a standard. In terms of resource use and the effect on people, is the standard worth the cost? Another suggestion is to determine the reason for the standard and to evaluate whether the standard is still serving that purpose. An older homemaker who does laundry early each day may discover that her laundry standard originated when her children were small and the volume of laundry was great. Now that she has determined the reason for the standard, she can decide if habit is involved or if other reasons have evolved for holding the same standard. Gross and Crandall's final guideline is to determine the relationship between the standard and priorities in values. If the relationship to values is direct, the standard may be more influential than if the relationship is indirect. These guidelines can be useful in evaluating the reality and appropriateness of standards for goal attainment.

MOTIVATING OTHERS

People in leadership positions can also apply the concepts in this chapter to their work with others. A household, business, or community leader can provide conditions that facilitate or limit an individual's ability to meet needs, demonstrate values, reach goals, and understand group standards.

Research by Herzberg and Myers indicates that supervisors in business not only provide motivation for workers but also satisfy basic maintenance needs.[28] *Maintenance needs*, comparable to Maslow's physiological, safety, love and esteem needs, are met through income, physical setting, social interaction, fairness and other aspects of a job. The conclusion is that people will be dissatisfied if the maintenance needs are not met.

Motivational needs, related to self-actualization, are met in the work itself. People, according to both Herzberg and Myers, need work that is challenging and meaningful.[29] Matching personal motivations and resources to the activities people are assigned is an important aspect of this approach to motivation. Do people also need this kind of challenge if they are to be involved in homes or in communities?

If one person in a household is consistently assigned only unchallenging tasks, like taking out the garbage, will he or she be motivated to be more involved in that task or in the household group? Household or community leaders might unconsciously assign one person undesirable or boring activities because the person seems so willing to help. Unless the person's identity with the group is quite strong, it is possible that he or she might lose interest in the group because of lack of challenge. Too much of a challenge for the person's abilities can also frustrate involvement. Family and community leaders who are alert to individual motivations will plan activities and tasks suitable and challenging to the individual.

Some household and community tasks may not be extremely challenging, but if these activities are rotated among group members or combined with challenging ones, motivation can be maintained or increased. People will be more willing to be involved in less challenging tasks if they understand the relationship of these tasks to personal or family goals.

Summary

This chapter has illustrated the importance of clarifying personal and family motivations in achieving desired qualities of life. People who are consciously aware of needs, values, goals, and standards in their lives can determine the order and direction of their management. Needs and values have been described as basic reasons for action, while goals have been described as what people are working toward. Standards have been pictured as value-based criteria against which goals are selected and clarified. Although, for discussion purposes, the motivations have been clearly separated, they are interwoven in a personal or family philosophy of life.

References

1. Maslow, H. A., "Psychological Data and Value Theory," in Maslow, H. A. (ed.), *New Knowledge In Human Values,* Harper and Row, New York, (1959), pp. 119–136.

2. *Ibid.*

3. Dyer, W. G., "Basic Needs as Motivators of Behavior," in *Behavioral Aspects of Management,* Proceedings of the Western Regional College Teachers of Home Management-Family Economics, Salt Lake City, Utah, (1971), p. 33.

4. Maslow, H. A., *Motivation and Personality,* Harper and Row, New York, (1954).

5. Maslow, H. A., *op. cit.,* pp. 126–127.

6. *Ibid.,* pp. 122–123.

7. Kluckholn, C., et al., "Values and Value Orientation in the Theory of Action," in Parsons, T. and Shills, E. (eds.), *Toward a General Theory of Action,* Harvard University Press, Cambridge, Mass., (1954), pp. 425–430.

8. *Ibid.,* p. 395.

9. Schlater, J. D., *Investigating Values Underlying Family Decisions,* Michigan Agricultural Experiment Station Research Bulletin No. 23, (May 1969).

10. Kluckholn, F. R. and Strodtbeck, F. L., *Variations in Value Orientation,* Row, Peterson and Co., Evanston, Ill., (1961).

11. Hill, R., Foote, N., Aldous, J., Carlson, R., and MacDonald, R., *Family Development in Three Generations,* Schenkman, (1970), p. 44.

12. Richardson, G., "Are There Universal Values? An Interview with Dorthy Lee," *Penny's Forum,* (Spring-Summer 1972), pp. 22–23.

13. McKee, W. W., "Values in Home Management," Proceedings of Conference on Values and Decision-Making in Home Management, Michigan State University, Mich. (1955).

14. *Ibid.*

15. Gross, I. H., Crandall, E. W., and Knoll, M. M., *Management for Modern Families,* Appleton-Century-Crofts, New York, (1973), p. 120.

16. Jones, M. H., and Irwin, Richard D., *Executive Decision-Making,* Homewood, Ill., (1957), pp. 7–18.

17. *Ibid.*, p. 14.

18. Gardner, J. W., *Self-Renewal,* Harper and Row, New York, (1965), p. 47.

19. Edwards, K. P., "A Theoretical Approach to Goal-Oriented Family Behavior," *Journal of Home Economics, 62:*9 (November 1970), pp. 652–655.

20. Cooper, J. D., *The Art of Decision-Making,* Doubleday, New York, (1961).

21. *Ibid.*

22. Walker, F. S., "Standards in a Managerial Context," in *Actualizing Concepts in Home Management,* American Home Economics Association, Washington, D.C., (1974), p. 13.

23. Kyrk, H., *Theory of Consumption,* Houghton Mifflin, Boston, Mass. (1923), p. 174; Hoyt, E., *Consumption in Our Society,* McGraw-Hill, New York, (1938), p. 265.

24. Guthmann, H. G., Browne, W., and Bonde, R. L., *The Individual, Marriage, and the Family,* William C. Browne, Dubuque, Iowa, (1962), p. 152.

25. Gross, I. H., Crandall, E. W., and Knoll, M. M., *op. cit.,* p. 114.

26. Mager, R. F., *Goal Analysis,* Fearon, Belmont, California, (1972).

27. Gross, I. H. and Crandall, E. W., *Management for Modern Families,* Appleton-Century-Crofts, New York, (1963), pp. 40–43.

28.   Herzberg, F., "One More Time: How Do You Motivate Employees?" *Harvard Business Review, 46:*1 (January-February 1968), pp. 53–62; Myers, M. S., "Who Are Your Motivated Workers?" *Harvard Business Review, 42:*1 (January-February 1964), pp. 73–88.

29.   *Ibid.*

4

DECISION MAKING

Individuals and families face unsolved problems, unresolved conflicts, opportunities to accept or reject, and new self-imposed directions. Issues and alternatives for resolving such conflicts are explored in this chapter.

Decision making is the action taken in selecting from various courses of action. People facing only one alternative or perceiving only one course of action are not experiencing decision making. For example, a student seeking parttime employment may be offered one particular job. If the student believes that he has no alternative—that he must accept this job—he has not made a decision. If the student believes that he can either accept or reject the job, he has a choice between alternatives. This second example is one of decision making.

Opinions differ as to whether or not actions selected at the subconscious level are classified as decision making. While decision making can be carried out—in part or totally—at the subconscious level, there are advantages to conscious, deliberate thinking. Decisions, even the minor ones, form patterns of living that affect quality of life. Conscious evaluation of routine actions can help to identify previously unrecognized choices, to consider long-range consequences for the decision maker and others affected by the decision, and to assure that planned actions are in line with personal or group priorities. Conscious deliberation can also facilitate successful decision making by alerting decision makers to events outside their control that could influence the results of decision making. Such knowledge can lead to realistic selection from possible courses of action.

What, then, is the relationship of decision making to management? Theorists offer at least three answers to this question: decision making is synonymous with management; it is one step or process in management; or decision making occurs throughout each of the management processes. All three explanations indicate that decision making is influential in management, and the reader may want to consider which of the above options he favors.

Decision making, according to these authors, occurs throughout the processes of management described in Chapter Two. People decide on goals, standards, resource allocation, sequences of action, or needed changes in

85

view of the important values in their lives. These managerial decisions are interrelated because of their focus on goal attainment. Hence, knowledge and skills in decision making, affect goal attainment and influence quality of life.

Components of Decision Making

The components or steps in decision making do not always occur in a step-like order. These components should be considered as the building materials of decision making. The order in which the materials are to be used and their specific purposes have been outlined by experts, but individuals or groups using the steps may omit some, overlap others, or alter the sequence of use. Decision making steps, like the use of building materials, can reflect the environment in which they are used as well as the personalities of the participants.

The number of steps or phases proposed by writers varies, but all have elements in common with the three steps suggested by John Dewey: 1) what is the problem 2) what are the alternatives 3) which alternative is best?[1] The steps, phases, or components to be explored in this section of the chapter include:

1. Identifying the problem

2. Obtaining information and formulating possible courses of action

3. Considering the consequences of each alternative

4. Selecting a course of action.

Brim points out that;

. . . the conception of phases is suitable for use in analyses of decisions ranging in scope from solving a mathematical or chess puzzle to the choice of a college or a husband or a wife. In fact it is just this type of formal analysis of the basic phases of the process that permits one to see the similar nature of all decision problems.[2]

IDENTIFYING THE PROBLEM

The first component in decision making is the recognition that a problem or need to decide exists and that definition of the problem or need is important. Symptoms of a more pervasive problem may first alert a decision maker to a need for change. Obvious symptoms can divert attention from a deeper problem; attacking symptoms instead of analyzing the total situation can lead to inappropriate conclusions and the creation of larger future problems.

Families, as compared to other groups, may be faced with unique challenges in problem identification. Because family members change across time, families may wonder if behavioral changes are due to normal development or if a serious problem exists.[3] A child who misbehaves may merely be testing family standards, may be in need of positive parental attention, or may be responding to actions of other family members or friends. The family members' definitions of the problem are influenced by their childhood experiences and contact with the child. Family members who have interacted with the same child under a variety of circumstances may have individual perceptions about the cause or causes of the problem. Neighbors, friends, or professionals working with such a family might identify the problem differently than would family members. To find the essential factor or factors in such a situation is not always easy and may require time, skills in observation, and perseverance. At this stage in the solution of a problem, two resources can be helpful: first, a desire to find causes of the problem; and second, an unprejudiced view of the circumstances within the situation.

The family's value system influences identification of a problem. A family that values independence may not consider arguments among family members as a threat to the family, while another family oriented toward conformity might be horrified at the thought of an argument. Individual differences are also apparent.[4] People differ, for example, in their preferences for identifying broad problem areas (creative model) or narrowing in on specific situations (analytical model). Clinical evidence has shown that recognition of problems is influenced by the degree to which the problems involve unconscious components of personality. A person's defense against a situation may be to deny the existence of any problem or to inappropriately define the problem. Age differences also seem to be a factor of concern with problem definition.

OBTAINING INFORMATION AND FORMULATING COURSES OF ACTION

Once the problem or situation calling for change has been identified, information is gathered to formulate possible courses of action. Past information can be utilized or synthesized to produce new ideas. This synthesis or imagination has been considered to be a part of creativity.[5] Individuals may not be aware of the importance of this substage because of the volume of information received in daily interaction and stored for later use.

The amount and quality of resources devoted to information gathering and to creative thinking, at this stage, may vary with the importance of the decision and with alternate demands on these resources. How much information to gather and how long to wait for all possible information to be accumulated has sparked controversy among professionals and families.

Individuals and families need to consider costs of information gathering in relation to its benefits. A person might evaluate time, effort, gasoline, or other transportation costs in relation to information learned, money saved, feelings of satisfaction, or quality of results in comparative grocery shopping and purchasing sale items. A family might share information gathering about an upcoming vacation among family members to help each person learn as well as to provide the family with information for decision making. The cost-benefit analyses in such situations might not be figured only in terms of monetary equivalents.

According to Weick,[6] family members may have unequal access to relevant information. A person who cares for an elderly family member will, for example, have more access to information about the elderly person's health and behavior than will out-of-town family members. The person or group with primary information is often relied upon to share that data with others involved in decision making. Biases, personal goals, and trust in others can influence the accuracy and selectivity of presentations of such information. Advertising, other media presentations, neighbors, salespeople, and, infrequently, experts are among the sources of information used in consumer decision making. To assure acceptable alternatives, the reliability of sources of information may need to be evaluated.

In some decision making situations, people are faced with information that is inconsistent or dissonant with action being proposed or being implemented. In attempting to achieve consistency, it is possible to emphasize the positive features of the selected alternative or the negative features of rejected choices. If the information is of extreme importance and if the original choice can be revised, the previously rejected alternative may be reconsidered. Festinger[7] described experiments testing this theory of *cognitive dissonance* with groups of children and adults. His conclusion was that people do attempt to reduce dissonance by varying mechanisms.

Decision makers are often faced with inconsistent information during and after decision making. Recognizing that psychological adaptation to these inconsistencies is a normal adjustment helps in understanding personal or others' behavior. A person who has decided to loose weight will encounter little dissonance in avoiding dessert if he is highly motivated to reach the goal. If he just learned that fresh strawberry pie was in season and ordered a large slice of the pie with whipped cream, his own behavior would be inconsistent with his goal, triggering feelings of dissonance and motivating adaptation. Information that is inconsistent with a person's view of life creates internal conflict and motivates changes in behavior or attitudes.

CONSIDERING ALTERNATIVES

Five or six concepts at one time are the upper limit in most people's thinking.[8] Davis found that homemakers considered only two alternatives in a decision making situation.[9] More recently, Lancaster reported that homemakers she studied considered two or three alternatives in decision making.[10] How many alternatives should be considered in decision making?

Considering the effects of decision making requires a certain amount of abstract thinking. Because people differ in abilities to visualize outcomes and consequences of action, not all people will use such thinking. Some people evaluate alternatives in pairs, mentally experimenting—rejecting impractical ones, and adding another set of alternatives.[11] This technique is especially appealing if a person can test and perhaps later reverse the decision. A student, for example, can experience a variety of jobs, through volunteer activities or part-time work, while still in school. It is not as easy, however, to decide after having a child that the person does not like being a parent. Consideration of consequences before acting in important decisions can help in adjusting to negative aspects of the selected alternative or in minimizing any less desirable consequences.

SELECTING A COURSE OF ACTION

Little is known about selecting alternatives; however, this phase or component is influential because of its effects on life style. Some alternatives are unconsciously eliminated in the earlier phases because of lack of suitability. Such prescreening allows decision makers to more carefully screen the remaining alternatives.

Research indicates that people seek a reasonable alternative but don't often bother trying to find a "best" alternative. Optimum decision making is the seeking of one "best" alternative. Because people do not recognize all possible alternatives, may not have access to complete information, and do not have complete control over all factors affecting the outcome of a decision, optimal decision making may be unrealistic. By limiting the scope of a problem in decision making, people may seek a limited range of alternatives and then decide on one or a combination of alternatives that is reasonable in the current situation. Finding an alternative that should lead to some improvement without seeking a universally "best" approach is identified by Simon as satisficing.[12]

Heuristic decision making is the use of general principles or operational maxims to select a reasonable alternative when faced with incomplete information.[13] These principles or ethical guidelines are based on experiences of people who have made similar decisions or experienced similar problems in the past. Utilizing these heuristics, decision makers plan for a resonable but not necessarily a best alternative. Generalizations like, "keep lines of communication open within a family," "the customer is always right," or "no more than 25 percent of annual income should be spent on housing," are examples of heuristics. These guidelines are not always followed, but can alert people to important considerations in selecting an alternative.

Accepting responsibility for the decision and evaluating outcomes are two additional components sometimes included within decision making. Evaluation is an asset throughout decision making whether or not it is listed as a step or component, because it can correct errors in judgment and improve the overall effectiveness of decision making.

These decision making components, labeled as a *normative model* in chart

Chart 4.1   Decision Making Components: A Normative Model. The normative model is illustrated as a process used to limit the selection from alternatives based on understanding of past experiences, the present situation, and future expectations. This arrangement of decision making components is a general one that applies human resources to the selection of a course of action.

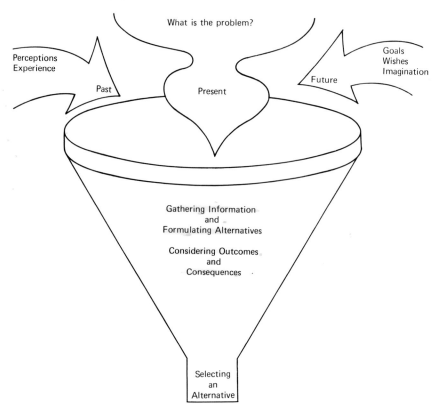

4.1, describe how people make decisions. In reality, some of the above components or phases are emphasized, reordered, overlapped, or omitted in some decisions. The uses of these components can vary with the content of the decision, the personalities of decision makers, and the environment in which decision making occurs. Note the varied emphases of components in the models that follow.

Models for Decision Making

Decision making models are simplifications of life situations used to teach or to analyze how people make decisions. Several such models are discussed in this section of the chapter. Because the approaches to modeling are theoretical in nature, the reader will discover that human decisions combine features from the various models. The models presented are classified by the content of the decision, the situation, the decision style which is based primarily on personality, and the relationship between decisions.

CONTENT

Decision making has been analyzed according to emphasis on content or kind of decision making. *Social decisions* focus on value or role conflict. *Economic decisions* focus on multiple goal selection in relation to resource scarceties. *Technical decisions* are directed primarily at implementing decisions and relate to the attainment of a specific goal. Two additional classifications—legal and political decisions—are more public than the other three. *Legal decisions* made by various levels of government affect personal and family decisions— as in the case of zoning regulations or safety standards for consumer goods. *Political decisions* emphasize how to decide—establishing the power structure within a household, community, or nation.[14]

Social Decisions

These decisions are seldom made, but they have a major influence on quality of life. They focus on *role selection* or *value clarification*.[15] Because people occupy several roles, acceptance of additional or deletion of roles may cause conflicts. Others' expectations can also conflict with the decision maker's views of the responsibilities within the role or priorities among roles.

Career decisions can involve value and role conflicts. The decision is not frequently made, so past experience may be limited to observations of other people in career roles. A person concerned about other people may want to teach or work in a community service agency, yet a concern for financial security might motivate the person to consider a higher paying career. A person who values aesthetics might consider interior design or costume design as a career, yet the work might have more pressures attached to it or longer work hours than desired by a person who wants to also have time for family life. Value and role conflicts are present in social decisions.

Personal values guide decision makers who encounter conflicts. In a one-parent family, the adult family member may consider remarriage. If she or he experienced companionship and security in the previous marriage, the adult might consider remarrying a logical possibility. The family, however, may be well adjusted to its current life style; and marriage would bring about some changes. The person might wonder how the children's happiness would be affected by remarriage and how the other adult would act as a parent. If, in this case, the other adult has not been previously married and has not had much contact with children, past experience has limited application to the decision. Seeking expert advice or opinions of others who have been successful in similar decisions could alert the person to some previously unrecognized considerations. An awareness of personal values and a recognition of conflicts is the starting point in social decision making. Social decision making is a more personal and more subjective approach to decision making than are some of the alternate models.

Using previously identified components of decision making and existing hypotheses, Keenan[16] formulated a model for making social decisions. Because role selection and value conflicts can be complex, the first phase in this model is to identify conflicts and their causes. The second phase focuses on mediating or settling differences between values. The third component is a precise analysis of policies, of amount of change, of procedures, or of alternatives for effecting the resolution of values (See Figure 4.2).

Rigid models of present and proposed roles and values should be evaluated if the decision maker is to reduce conflict in social decision making. Because values are the focus, Price believed that rigid adherence to previously determined goals could inhibit satisfactory resolution of social decisions.[17] Although people sometimes seek "right" or "correct" alternatives in decision making, such evaluations in social decision making can only be made in terms

Figure 4.2 Social Decisions.

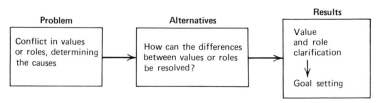

Problem	Alternatives	Results
Conflict in values or roles, determining the causes	How can the differences between values or roles be resolved?	Value and role clarification ↓ Goal setting

of the decision maker's values and the absence of, or change in the degree of, strain resulting from the decision.

Economic Decisions

Economic models, once thought to be the only model for decision making, emphasize the selective use of resources to reach multiple goals. These models usually attempt to maximize satisfaction and minimize resource use. Because individuals and families have finite resources and multiple goals, interests, and needs, an awareness of economic models has been stressed in management.

Three resources—time, energy, and money—have received primary attention in economic decision making. These three resources have been emphasized because they can be used to reach a variety of goals, because they can be objectively measured, and because people have recognized limits in personal or household access to these resources. Limitations in other resources—such as space in a living unit or community and fuel supplies could also motivate economic decisions.

In making economic decisions, people compare costs in resource use to benefits in satisfaction or in resource gain. Theoretically, people are aware of their goals and select an alternative or combine alternatives that entail the least cost and the greatest benefit in relation to goals. This action is called *maximizing utility*—getting the most return with the least investment. In actuality, decision makers may not be clearly aware of the specific goals and may alter goals because of the decision making experience.

According to Diesing, there are varying degrees of precision in comparing costs of economic decision making. *Utility,* or the usefulness of alternatives, can be compared in terms of simple preferences, in costs of means, and in costs of both means and ends. Such costs are compared against an objective scale—usually time or money.[18]

Specific economic decision models have been developed for varying completeness of information and degrees of risk. Although early models in-

Figure 4.3   Economic Decision Making.

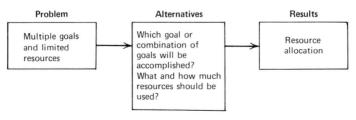

cluded the assumption that decision makers have complete access to information, this is not usually the case. In purchasing a needed item, a consumer might not be aware of the sale planned for the following week, the availability of replacement parts, or other information that could affect overall satisfaction with the decision.

Information gathering can be either a costly or a cost-saving process for economic decision makers. Resources used in decision making combined with the costs of putting the decision into action are both analyzed by those concerned about careful use of resources for goal attainment. Because people are exposed to vast quantities of information in daily interactions, past experience can decrease the cost of data collection. The usefulness of this stored information, however, should be evaluated in relation to the current situation.

Because people cannot completely or habitually do not predict the future, there may be some feeling of uncertainty in economic or other models for decision making. The uncertainty can be related to the outcomes of the decision or the consequences following the decision. A person can use the Weather Bureau's estimate of a 60 percent chance of rain to decide what to do or wear on a given day. This prediction relates to the outcome—will it rain or won't it? The consequences are more personal in this case—will the person get soaked if he walks to work; will the fishing be good if it rains; or will the guests be uncomfortable if the party is held indoors and it doesn't rain?

In dealing with personal or household decisions, estimates of risk may not be numerically computed or the risks may go unrecognized. As researchers learn more about life, people may be able to more precisely predict outcomes, as in the case of genetics. Although decisions regarding family planning are classified as social or socioeconomic, people have expressed anxiety at the risk of children being born with physical or mental defects. Scientists can now determine the likelihood of a couple's having a child with genetic defects from family and personal health histories of the couple.[19] This application of research findings via genetic counseling provides people with more objective views of the degree of risk and also alerts them to potential consequences.

Anxiety develops when people recognize uncertainty in their decision making. Information gathering can help decision makers to reduce such anxiety. In consumer economic decisions, brand loyalty, personal advice from product users, warranties, or free samples are some of the anxiety-reducing sources. Research indicated that the sources of information selected by consumers vary more with the type of purchase than with the characteristics of the decision makers, although both have their influence.[20]

People differ in how much and in what kinds of risk they are willing to take in decision making. Research in laboratory settings in a number of countries shows that individuals advocate greater risk in group than in individual decision making. Clark[21] questions whether findings would be similar if groups with common goals were studied in their natural environments. Do family members making group decisions advocate greater degrees of risk than they might in private?

In decision making, people also differ in whether or not and in how they protect themselves from the consequences of undesirable events or outcomes. A person who purchases life or health insurance may not be planning to die or get sick but recognizes the possibility of either event. Wearing safety glasses or using seat belts in a car are two other examples of recognition of and preparation for undesirable events. The challenge in such situations is to recognize these undesirable consequences and to protect against the major, undesirable events, while retaining sufficient resources to attain goals.

In comparing economic and social decision making, note that economic decisions contain clearer initial definitions of problems, goals, and resources than do social decisions. Resource measurement is carefully carried out, and procedural models can be useful in retaining objectivity in the allocation of resources in economic decisions. Social decisions, with their emphasis on values, are not as oriented toward efficiency in goal attainment as are the economic ones. Economic decisions may proceed from social decisions.

Technical Decisions

Technical decisions relate to the attainment of one specific goal or implementation of previously-made economic and social decisions. Deciding on a method of financial record keeping could be classifed as a technical decision. Diesing[22] states that with repetition technical decisions become *techniques*. Keenan proposes that technical decisions have "right answers," while this is not usually the case in economic or social decisions.[23] As with economic decisions, people can select an effective means for goal attainment or seek the most effective alternative to implement a goal. These "how to" decisions diagrammed in Figure 4.4 may not seem extremely important but set the tone of daily living and can affect the quality of results of more pervasive decisions.

In theory, the content of decisions can influence the processes used in decision making. Recognition that values, resource allocation, or the attainment of one specific goal is being emphasized should help people in making

Figure 4.4   Technical Decision Making.

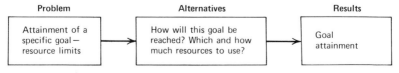

Problem	Alternatives	Results
Attainment of a specific goal — resource limits	How will this goal be reached? Which and how much resources to use?	Goal attainment

effective decisions. Do individuals and families emphasize differing decision making components according to these models? Should they? What would the consequences be if a person or group treated a social decision as an economic or a technical one?

SITUATION

It is possible for people to base decisions on their personality, on an objective analysis of the situation, or on a combination of both. Decisions formulated from the personality of the decision maker are labeled as *irrational.* These decisions are emotionally based, as in the case of an impulsive purchase of bakery goods. There is nothing inherently wrong with irrational decisions; but selecting a course of action because of urges, compulsions, or whims provides the decision maker with a narrow view of the situation.

Decisions viewed with detachment—as if the decision maker was an impartial observer—are called *rational decisions.* Back proposed that these decisions should be in a middle range of importance in order to be objectively based.[24] Mathematical models devised to promote rational analyses of decisions could be applied to a number of economic or technical decisions. These models alert decision makers to the importance of the varied components— emphasizing short and long-range consequences—and provide an overview of the situation.

For decisions of considerable importance, like the social decision previously described, Back[25] proposed an existential, experience-based, *nonrational model.* In such situations, neither straightforward, objective analyses nor personality would provide the desired basis for decision making. Intuitive thinking and knowledge that other workable alternatives exist can create doubts in the minds of those making nonrational decisions. Because there is not a straightforward procedure for deciding, personal growth can occur with these unique, nonrepetitive decisions.

Early economic theory assumed that people were rational in their thinking. While it might be desirable to move toward rationality in economic or technical decisions, is complete rationality possible or desirable in all decision making? Readers who might be tempted to classify themselves as being irrational, rational, or nonrational in their thinking, should remember that emphasis varies with the situation. People may also combine elements of rationality with irrationality or nonrationality in a single decision.

DECISION STYLE

Decision making procedures or steps can vary with personality as well as with the situation. The components or phases outlined earlier in the chapter can be arranged in numerous ways or *decision making styles.* Using hypothetical situations, Bustrillos analyzed the decision making styles of noncollege educated homemakers according to mode, time reference, and decision rule.

Mode is the way of verbalizing a problem and has at least three dimensions. A *hypothetical mode* is conditional, verbalizing doubt; i.e., "We could . . ." or "If . . ." A *factual mode* describes an individual's perception of facts and uses past experience; i.e., "It costs too much to . . ." An *action-suggestive mode* proposes solutions with little or no analysis of the problem; i.e., "She should . . ." Bustrillos reported that combinations of modes were frequently used, with the hypothetical mode used least often.[26] Bustrillos and, in a later study of college educated homemakers, Rivenes both identified the factual mode as most frequently used.[27]

Time reference is the relationship of the decision to *future* consequences, to the immediacy of the *present*, or to the tradition or experiences of the *past* in evaluating alternatives. Both Rivenes and Bustrillos observed the present time reference most frequently, although the orientation varied somewhat with the specific decision.[28] Homemakers in these studies were inclined to emphasize aspects of their current circumstances or feelings, more than emphasizing the possible consequences or previous experiences.

Decision rule is the guideline for making a choice. It has at least three emphases: preference ranking, objective elimination, and immediate closure. *Preference ranking* is the scaling of alternatives from "best" to "worst" based on personal preference rather than on situational analysis. *Objective elimination* takes the situation into account and suggests varied options for each situation. *Immediate closure* is the verbalizing of one alternative although rapid mental evaluation of other alternatives can occur. In Bustrillos' study, approximately half of the respondents ranked alternatives according to personal preference, while Rivenes' respondents used objective elimination more often.

A *decision style* is a combination of the three components of mode, time reference, and decision rule. A large number of decision styles were reported by Bustrillos. They varied with the homemaker and with the specific problem. The most frequently used style was a factual mode, a present time reference, and preference ranking.[29] This research illustrates the flexibility needed in dealing with others who are making decisions. The uses of decision making componenets or phases are as varied as are people and the situations they encounter.

Personality in relation to decision making processes has been studied by Price[30] who identified major differences in decision making styles between self-actualized or person-centered and nonself-actualized or task-centered individuals. Problem identification and analysis were carried out more quickly by those who were self-actualized. Information was likely to be sought within the nuclear family by the behavioral-centered group, while others used extended family and people outside the family as sources of information. Price also observed a trend toward risk-taking among the self-actualized, while others took fewer risks. The emphasis in the behavioral-centered families was placed on the effects of decision making on the people in the situation. The task-centered families emphasized goal attainment and group acceptance. If this categorization of self-actualization is an accurate measure of mental health, it appears that the uses of decision making components vary with the mental health of decision makers.

A decision style is an individual's way of combining and emphasizing the components of decision making for personal uses. Style as studied by Bustrillos is a reflection of the problem identification, time reference, and way of selecting an alternative. Price studied style in terms of the uses of decision making components and the emphasis on goal attainment or on the effects of decision making on people in the group.

A decision-making style could also be thought of as a reflection of a person's values. People who value leisure will orient their uses of resources toward restive activities and streamline other aspects of life considered necessary but not as important as leisure. Minimal amounts of clothing and furniture that could be easily packed and moved might be selected. Household work might be minimized to allow time for leisurely activities. This dimension of decision making style is related to priorities among decisions and the content of decisions, in contrast to the emphasis on how decision making components are used. It is possible to consider a decision making style as a human resource used to reach goals.

RELATIONSHIPS BETWEEN DECISIONS

Decisions made at one time affect and are influenced by other decisions, although these relationships are not always apparent when a decision is made. A person approaching retirement decides, for example, to change to a new form of group health insurance that will cover the family after retirement. The decision maker knows that dropping the first policy means limited coverage during a 10 month probationary period. The risk in this decision does not seem serious because the family has had no claims against health insurance policies during the previous decade. If within two months, another family member becomes ill and spends three weeks in a nearby hospital, the risk has changed. Later decisions could deal with sources and methods of payment for the unexpected expenses and adaptations in the living unit that could shorten the time of recuperation of the stricken family member at home. This example illustrates that decisions are interrelated.

Plonk[31] developed and tested a model to illustrate relationships between decisions. Crucial decisions that necessitate related decisions are called *central* or strategic decisions. Social decisions can fit within this class, as might some socioeconomic and economic decisions. *Satellite* decisions are supplementary and follow central ones. The central-satellite decision relationship includes one major decision with related ones proceeding from it in a radial linkage.

If a central decision is made to move to a mobile home, related decisions might include the desired size and arrangement of the unit, selection of a location, or planning the method of financing. These and other satellite decisions affect feelings of satisfaction with the original decision. The central decision also forms the boundary for these later ones.

An alternate linkage is a *series*—with a chain of decisions, each proceeding from the others. The decision regarding payment of hospital expenses in the retirement planning situation followed the initial decision to seek an alternative form of group health insurance, so the linkage is a series one. These chains or series can occur alone or as part of a central-satellite complex. Decision making is a dynamic process because decisions are often interrelated and interdependent.

Family Decision Making

Because of their long-term, daily interactions, families' decision making can be unique in comparison with that of other groups or individuals, as pointed out earlier in this chapter. The key to individual decision making is in the awareness and evaluation of alternatives. In group decision making, an added consideration is found in interpersonal influences and communication.

DECISION STRATEGIES

Family decision making can occur in an atmosphere of competition or interpersonal conflict or in an atmosphere of cooperation. Davis[32] states that family members do not always agree on decision making roles, procedures, and strategies, or on who is to implement the decision. A *conflict strategy* could include lack of trust in competitors, diverse goals, or selective presentation of information to add support to the favored alternative. A potential problem can exist in the long-range consequences of a conflict strategy if other family members recognize the biased sharing of information. The other family members may then lack confidence in the person's contributions.

A *cooperative strategy* involves trust, open communication, and common goals. This strategy is more easily achieved in situations of shared decision making, in which each person affected by a decision has influence in the outcomes of choices made.

Resources—A Special Case

Is family decision making easier or more difficult when income is limited? People with marginal incomes have fewer decisions to make because most of their income, if not all of it, is being used for necessities. Alternatives like postponing purchases to take advantage of sales or buying in quantity are not practical because needs are immediate and little or no money may be available in savings for such purchases.[33] Similarly, purchasing high-quality goods that have a long life will not be possible if money is not available for these items. Limitations in monetary resources can lead to fewer decisions but can also produce much anxiety. People with discretionary income may encounter more decisions and may have more alternatives available to them. These factors make decision making a complex process, but the consequences of an inappropriate decision may not be as serious for those with an adequate income.

Physical Setting

The physical setting for family decision making also influences the interaction within a family. Noise from a television set, radio, or interruptions from telephone calls or visitors can alter the quality of communication. Furniture can be too comfortable or uncomfortable for the attention necessary for effective decision making. Even seating and lighting arrangements can affect decision making when people are not able to see others' nonverbal cues.

Family Composition

Because families are groups of people with differing ages and experiences and with common goals, the composition of a family may also influence the use of decision-making components. Young family members can learn about decision making from the guidance and sharing in group decision making. Exposure to varied ideas causes these young decision makers to consider others' points of view and promotes creative thinking. Tallman[34] suggests flexibility in the family decision-making structure to allow all able family members to contribute ideas. This contribution may vary with the specific decision. A four-year-old child, for example, may have influence in deciding on weekend activities but may not be consulted in relation to long-range financial plans.

The varied ages and attention spans within a family can influence the group's time span for concentrated decision making. The person with the shortest attention span may limit the quality of interaction when his attention span has been exceeded.

Age has other influences on decision making. As people age they process information in larger bits. While children or young adults may recognize and retain small bits of data, older persons tend to identify concepts or seek principles in information processing.[35] An extended family is presented with unique assets and limitations in decision making because of the range in age of family members. People who are over the age of 60 have a broadened experience base from which to draw but a shorter short-term retention in comparison to people in their 20's. Older persons generally adapt to these changes by slowing their pace and increasing their accuracy.[36] While these age differences are useful in balancing perceptions and in achieving accurate solutions to problems, it can be initially frustrating to recognize that everyone's pace is not the same and that there are differing perceptions of a decision making situation.

The number of family members also has an impact on family decision making. Each additional member has personal goals, individual commitments outside the family group, unique personality, and, as they grow older, human resources that can be shared with others in the household. This addition of family members places more demands on resources, alerts the group to more or differing alternatives, and provides more human resources to implement decisions.

According to Tallman,[37] some form of centralized authority or leadership is needed to coordinate members' activities, to promote sharing of ideas, and to encourage evaluation of decision making. This leadership, if effective, will not threaten the self concepts of other family members. The reader may want to question whether authority should rest with one person or whether it can be changed, depending on the specific decision and the situation.

WHO MAKES FAMILY DECISIONS?

People who have been concerned with family decision making have theorized and researched the issues of who makes family decisions, who has more influence, and how these influences change throughout the life cycle. This section will describe concepts and research findings related to the issue of power in family decision making.

Power is the potential influence that one person or group has over another.[38] A person may be powerful in decision making because others fear him, because his is the traditional role of power, or because others respect the abilities of that individual. If, for one reason or another, the family agrees that a person should hold certain power, that family member is experiencing *authority*.

Power may or may not be shared in family decision making. *Dominance* is a classification used if one person or part of a group has more influence than others in a group. A dominant individual may or may not consider the ideas of others in decision making. A man who appears quite dominant in decision making may take cues from his wife's conversations that lead him to select a given alternative. Although he is dominant in the selecting of an alternative, his wife has influence on the outcome of the decision. A number of decision making studies evaluate influence in the final selection of alternatives without regard for the relative influence of family members during the decision making process.

Equalitarian decision making[39] is the term used to describe shared power. One form of equalitarian power, *syncratic decision making*, is the resolution of each decision as a group. A couple who cooperatively decide about household finances or what food to prepare demonstrate this form of shared power. Syncratic decision making is a time-consuming process but helps family members to verbalize what is important to them and to explore individual standards and resources.

Autonomic decision making[40] is the delegating of decisions to individual family members. A family member who has knowledge and experience or traditional responsibility for certain aspects of family life makes decisions about those aspects of life. A person who is competent in financial matters may specialize in family monetary decision making; another family member may emphasize the interpersonal decisions for the group. Autonomic decision making is the sharing of power through specialization. The risk in such a situation is that knowledgeable members can leave a family without others being adequately informed about the decisions or that the family member with the expertise may be temporarily gone from the group when his knowledge and experience is needed. Changes in the specific division of power can occur and may necessitate learning by those who are assuming new powers.

Cross-cultural research has illustrated the need to consider the cultural aspects of power as well as the resources of families in decision making.[41] In a study of families in three societies, Straus[42] observed social class differences in family decision making. In an experimental situation, working-class families were less successful in decision making than were middle-class families. Differences were noted in information sharing and creativity in problem solving. Fewer social-class differences were observed, however, in urban families.

Generally the research has been related to the relative influence of husbands and wives, but teenagers and young children also have influence in decision making.[43] This sharing of decision making among all family members is referred to as *democratic decision making*. Some form of shared authority is mentioned in a number of research studies.[44] The relative importance of these separate areas of authority has not been completely explored.

The relative education of a husband and wife and a wife's employment outside the home appear to relate to the distribution of power in family decision making.[45] Those with contacts outside the home may have more opportunities to develop interpersonal skills and, therefore, have more influence in decision making.

Recognition of who makes final decisions and the influence of other family members in these decisions can be an asset to professionals working with families. If a professional is attempting to improve the financial management within a family, knowledge of power in relation to the monetary decisions can help the professional in deciding with whom he or she should be communicating.

Is there a best form of power in family decision making? There are advantages in having some form of shared decision making because family members are more willing to implement decisions if they have some say in the process. More importantly, people need to consider their individual preferences. Johannis indicated, and Gross, Crandall, and Knoll agreed, that family members need to establish some pattern of influence that is agreeable to those in the family.[46]

Summary

The decision making components, sometimes called the normative model for decison making, do not always occur in a rigid, step-like structure. The content of a decision, the situation, and the personality of decision makers influence the arrangement of and the emphases within components. Family decision making is somewhat unique because of the long-term, day-to-day interaction of family members. The uses of the decision making components are affected by the attitudes of individuals, the composition and resources of the group, the physical setting, and the power structure of the family. Conscious awareness and evaluation of the impact of decision making on quality of life can motivate people to increase the effectiveness of their decision making and, thereby, achieve a higher degree of satisfaction from life.

References

1. Dewey, J. *How We Think,* D. C. Heath, New York, (1910), p. 8.

2. Brim, O. C., Glass, D. C., Lavin, D. E., and Goodman, N., *Personality and Decision Processes,* Stanford University Press, Stanford, Calif., (1962), pp. 10–11.

3. Weick, K. E., "Group Processsess, Family Processes, and Problem Solving," in Aldous, J., Condon, T., Hill, R., Straus, M., and Tallman, I., *Family Problem Solving,* Dryden, Hinsdale, Ill., (1971), p. 10.

4. Brim, *op. cit.,* p. 12.

5. Overstreet, H. A., *The Mature Mind,* W. W. Norton, New York, (1949), p. 64.

6. Weick, *op. cit.,* pp. 6–7.

7. Festinger, L., "Cognitive Dissonance," *Scientific American, 207* (1962), pp. 93–102.

8. Johnson, D. M., *The Psychology of Thought and Judgment,* Harper and Row, New York, (1955), p. 82.

9. Davis, M. J., "Decision-Making in Relation to the Performance of Household Activities in New York State Homes," unpublished doctoral dissertation, Cornell University, Ithaca, N.Y., (1957).

10. Lancaster, R. R., "Case Studies of the Decision-Making of Ten Non-College Educated Homemakers," unpublished master's thesis, University of Kansas, Lawrence, Kan., (1966).

11. *Ibid.,* p. 43.

12. Simon, H. A., *Models of Man: Social and Rational,* Wiley, New York, (1957), pp. 241–260.

13. Miller, D. W. and Starr, M. K., *The Structure of Human Decisions,* Prentice-Hall, Englewood Cliffs, N.J., (1967), pp. 50–51.

14. Diesing, P., *Reason in Society: Five Types of Decisions and Their Social Conditions,* University of Illinois, Urbana, Ill., (1962).

15. *Ibid.*, pp. 97–98.

16. Keenan, M. K., *"Models for Decision-Making,"* Department of Home Economics, California State University, Long Beach, Calif., (1969), pp. 12–14.

17. Price, D., "Social Decision Making," in *The Family: Focus on Management,* American Home Economics Association, Washington, D.C., (1970), pp. 14–22.

18. Diesing, P., *op. cit.,* pp. 48–56.

19. Augenstein, L. G., "Social Responsibility," *Journal of Home Economics, 59,* 3 (October 1967), pp. 629–635.

20. Taylor, J. W., "The Role of Risk in Consumer Behavior," *Journal of Marketing, 38* (April 1974), pp. 54–60.

21. Clark, R. D., "Risk Taking in Groups: a Social Psychological Analysis," *Journal of Risk and Insurance, 41*:1 (March 1974), pp. 75–92.

22. Diesing, P., *op. cit.,* p. 9.

23. Keenan, M. K., *op. cit.,* p. 6.

24. Back, K. W., "Decisions Under Uncertainty—Rational, Irrational and Non-rational," *American Behavioral Scientist, 4:*6 (February 1961), pp. 14–19.

25. *Ibid.*

26. Bustrillos, N., "Decision-Making Styles of Selected Mexican Homemakers," unpublished doctoral dissertation, Michigan State University, East Lansing, Mich. (1963), p. 81.

27. *Ibid.*, and Rivenes, D. N., "A Study of Decision-making Style," upublished master's thesis, Pennsylvania State University, University Park, Penn., (1964), p. 51.

28. *Ibid.*

29. Bustrillos, *op. cit.,* p. 125.

30.   Price, D. Z., "Relationship of Decision Style and Self-Actualization," *Home Economics Research Journal, 2:*1 (September 1973), pp. 12–20.

31.   Plonk, M. A., "Exploring Interrelationships in a Central-Satellite Decision Complex," *Journal of Home Economics, 60:*10 (December 1968), pp. 789–792.

32.   Davis, H. L., "Family Decision Making as Conflict Management," *Advances in Consumer Research, 1* (1974), pp. 532–535.

33.   Meyers, T., "The Extra Cost of Being Poor," *Journal of Home Economics, 62:*6 (June 1970), 379–384.

34.   Tallman, I., "The Family as a Small Problem Solving Group," *Journal of Marriage and the Family, 32* (February 1970), p. 96.

35.   Birren, J. E., "Age and Decision Strategies," in A. T. Welford and J. E. Birren (eds.), *Decision Making and Age,* S. Karger, New York, (1969), pp. 23–36.

36.   Welford, A. T., "Age and Skill: Motor, Intellectual and Social," in A. T. Welford and J. E. Birren (eds.), *op. cit.*

37.   Tallman, *op. cit.,* p. 96.

38.   Blood, R. O. and Wolfe, D. M., *Husbands and Wives: The Dynamics of Married Living,* Free Press, Glencoe, Ill., (1960), p. 11.

39.   Herbst, P. G., "Conceptual Framework for Studying the Family," in O. A. Oeser and S. B. Hammond (eds.), *Social Structure and Personality in a City,* Macmillan, New York, (1954), pp. 133–134.

40.   *Ibid.*

41.   Rodman H., "Marital Power in France, Greece, Yugoslavia, and in the United States: a Cross-National Discussion," *Journal of Marriage and the Family, 29* (1967), pp. 320–324.

42.   Straus, M. A., "Communication, Creativity, and Problem-solving Ability of Middle- and Working-class Families in Three Societies," *American Journal of Sociology, 73* (January 1968), pp. 417–430.

43. Zunich M., "Teenage Influence on Personal and Family Purchases," *Journal of Home Economics, 58*:6 (June 1966), p. 483.

44. Kendel, D. B. and Lesser, G. S., "Marital Decision Making in American and Danish Urban Families—A Research Note," *Journal of Marriage and the Family, 34* (February 1972), pp. 134–138; Honey, R., Britton, V., and Hotchkiss, A. S., *Decision-Making in the Use of Family Financial Resources,* Pennsylvania Agricultural Experiment Station Bulletin 643, (1959), pp. 5–6.

45. Kendel, *op. cit.;* Blood and Wolfe, *op. cit.*

46. Johannis, T. G., "Participation by Fathers, Mothers and Teenage Sons and Daughters in Selected Family Economic Activity," *The Coordinator, 6* (1957), p. 16: Gross, I. H., Crandall, E. W., and Knoll, M. M., *Management for Modern Families,* Appleton-Century-Crofts, New York, (1973), p. 54.

5

IDENTIFYING RESOURCES

Resources have received so little attention in popular literature that most people find it difficult to define the term *resources* and are even less likely to be able to identify usable resources. Before they can be used to an advantage, resources need to be recognized and a system of assessing and evaluating them needs to be established.

Definition

Goals are what people want. Resources are what people use to reach their goals, the means they work with to maintain control over their lives. Resources are the tools and talents with which people build their life styles and attain their goals.

By definition, resources are *assets* that can be *used* to accomplish *goals*. The three italicized words in this definition, "assets," "used," and "goals," play an important role in the identification of resources and, thereby, merit closer examination.

RESOURCES ARE ASSETS

Assets are usually considered in monetary terms, such as money, savings, income, or personal property that has exchange value. These are economic resources that families manage to achieve their individual and collective goals. The term "asset" technically is used in the plural in wealth accounting and refers to any item that can be turned into cash to pay liabilities. All useful or valuable items that are owned are considered as components of wealth. Therefore, in addition to money, wealth includes property, possessions, and anything that has the potential of creating more wealth.

Resources is a more inclusive term that denotes any possession on hand or in reserve and available for use—a term that includes actual and potential wealth. Assets, used in an economic sense, include the value of tangible things such as cash and inventory (possessions), as well as the value of less tangibles, such as credit and good will.

However, families have resources other than economic assets. When defining resources, the term "asset" means not only valuable possessions, but personal qualities or traits of individuals, characteristics of the environment, and commonly held community and national resources that can be used in reaching goals.

Human capital has been said to be the most valuable asset that any organization possesses.[1] This is especially true of individuals and families. Human capital refers to the personal characteristics, capabilities, talents, skills, traits, and physical appearances of the people in an organization. The ability to deal promptly and effectively with problems, decision-making style, knowledge, judgement, understanding, creativity, ambition, interests, attitudes, loyalty, motivation, and skills are often more important to the achievement of goals than money or wealth.

Community facilities—parks, shopping centers, roads, and fire protection—are assets that are held in trust with the citizens of a community. National and world resources are important assets that affect the lives of every individual and family. Scarcities of oil and other natural resources have focused primary attention upon national assets such as the supply of petroleum to run cars and energy to light houses and supply the factories that make the products that support the nation's way of life.

Environmental quality is an issue of vital concern in fast–growing communities throughout the world. As civilization begins to encroach upon the physical environment that sustains life, environmental resources become increasingly important. Scarcity and encroachment tend to emphasize the prominence of environmental resources.

Thus, it is apparent that when resources are defined as assets, the reader must think not only of money and houses, cars and appliances—economic resources—but human potential, personal characteristics, community facilities, environmental qualities, and natural resources as well.

RESOURCES HAVE USES

Use of resources is, however, as crucial as the assets themselves in determining the quality of life that people can and do achieve. It is not always what a person has but what he or she does with it that counts most in the long run. High motivation can cause people to exceed all predictions for success in school or work just as low motivation can lead many to fail or barely pass subjects they could easily master.

In describing the human potentiality concept, Otto pointed out that the average human being functions at a very small fraction of his potential.[2] This American psychologist and marriage counselor estimates that we are currently operating at only four percent of human capacity. Also, according to Otto, that capacity has been decreasing since the turn of the century when James estimated that the average healthy human being was functioning at ten percent of capacity.[3] Margaret Mead's estimate of six percent in 1964 further strengthens Otto's belief in the declining use that average healthy people make of their capabilities— their human resources.[4]

In discussing utility of resources, Gross, Crandall, and Knoll suggest that resources are recognized *as such* only after uses are found for them and recount as an example the definition at the turn of the century of uranium as a useless white metal.[5] However, these authors also consider as resources those which are held in reserve. The present authors agree with this approach to resources, for it is within this untapped reserve of resources that a better way of life can be found by people who are willing to develop and use their resources to a fuller extent. The definition of resources as assets that can be used in goal attainment does not necessitate use before consideration as resources.

Some resources are consumed through use; others are increased by use. Human resources—capabilities, skills, knowledge, and talents—are examples of the latter. With consumable resources, there is still the question of whether to delay use for attainment of long-range goals or to use them for short-term gratification.

RESOURCES ACHIEVE GOALS

Goals are the third concept inherent in the definition of resources. Goals are ends toward which effort is directed—winning a track meet, learning to rope a calf, finishing college, or getting a job. Although a goal is loosely defined as "whatever is desired by the person or group seeking it," in reality, there are restrictions on the goals that are achievable with available resources. There are also restrictions on personal goals that are attainable without harming or threatening the rights of others.

Wants are usually more temporary wishes or cravings. Temporary outbursts of anger associated with a desire to do harm to the person who caused the anger are usually not translated into goals. Rational people learn to control such violent wishes because they serve only momentarily as mental retaliation. Such wishes would be considered as goals only if they were lasting and recurrent. Goals are usually more lasting, may be consciously planned, and are usually more realistic than wants. They should reflect the positive wishes of all those whose resources are utilized and who will be affected by goal attainment. The habitual burglar who premeditates theft has a very real goal that violates the rights of others and is therefore, harmful. However, achievement of even a harmful goal requires the use of resources.

It is easy for a childless couple with current goals of higher education to look wishfully at a congenial family with children playing together on a camp-out; but to set adoption or the birth of a child as an immediate goal would logically entail more deliberation of consequences on education, economics, and pattern of living for the couple. However, individuals are not free to pursue all the goals they may desire. Laws prohibit a person's pursuing goals that are in conflict with the rights of others. The reader may logically ask, "Can goals be harmful?" Such a question may help in differentiating wants and wishes from goals.

CONSTRAINTS

A potential resource that is a liability instead of an asset is a *constraint* on goal attainment and is therefore, not operating as a resource.[6] Underdeveloped resources may function as constraints, but they need only to be consciously assessed and constructively developed to become resources. Webster's definition of a resource as a supply of something to take care of a need or a means of accomplishing something emphasizes the goal-oriented aspect of this definition.[7]

Goals are often related to self actualization and renewal. They may be consciously identified, such as a college education, or they may be subconsciously held, such as an inquisitive probing for truth. Goals may be individually recognized and pursued, or culturally mediated by family, peers, or society.

If resources are the tools and talents with which people attain their personal and group goals, these assets become constraints when they are not developed for use. Just as clothes hanging unworn in a closet take up valuable space, personal talents that are underdeveloped preempt the dreamer's time with unfulfilled accomplishments.

If satisfaction is to be achieved from resource use, a variety of alternative resources will need to be recognized, considered, and used effectively in the pursuit of consciously chosen goals.

Characteristics of Resources

Most economic resources, with the exception of credit, can be recognized by sight. Money, houses, vacuum cleaners, food, and cars are easily identified by sight. However, since less tangible and human resources are not seen, some other way of recognizing and assessing them is needed. A list of at least four of their characteristics may help in the identification of resources: utility in goal satisfaction, accessibility to the user, interchangeability, and manageability.

UTILITY

In goal satisfaction, utility is one of the most undisputed characteristics of resources. It means value, worth, applicability, and productiveness for a purpose. Utility is often in the eyes of the beholder and may vary from person to person and from time to time.

The utility of a resource is determined by the user's knowledge because it depends upon his awareness of the potential that resources possess for goal satisfaction. Attitude also affects the utility of resources. Some people prefer to develop their "fix-it" and "do-it-yourself" talents instead of hiring repairs to a home or buying ready-made clothing. A wife who takes pride in making her husband's ties will use her time, knowledge of construction techniques, skill in operating the machine, and tools such as a sewing machine, scissors, and iron to make the tie. Unless the tie is made from scraps left from another garment, she will require about the same amount of transportation to shop for fabric as would be needed for buying a ready-made tie. However, in making a tie she may use less of the family money resource than if she purchased it ready made. When money is available, but garments are made at home by preference, this attitude places a higher utility value on talents than on money. When garments are made only if funds are insufficient to buy ready-made garments, money has a higher utility value than talents, skills, time, and creativity.

There are times when the desired product or standards regarding the product will determine the utility of a resource. Some people prefer to bake bread or to grow their own vegetables than to buy them in the market, not because of scarcity of one resource or another, but because they prefer the taste of home-produced food or because the practice is more compatible with their cultural patterns.

For many years economists have recognized various kinds of utility: time, place, form, and diminishing utility.[8] The concept of utility is subjective and, consequently, not measurable in exact quantities. It is impossible to tell how much utility two different people gain when drinking a glass of milk. It may be equal or unequal. We do know, however, that when several glasses of milk are consecutively consumed, the last glass will give less enjoyment than the first. Each glass of milk, consumed immediately after the one before, produces less enjoyment and therefore, is said to have *diminishing utility* over glasses of milk previously consumed. Even if milk were free, the law of diminishing utility would set a maximum on the amount of milk that a family would drink in a given day.[9]

If John is offered a job in another city, the job has utility and will produce money resources only if John is willing to live in or near that city. This is an example of *place utility* of resources relating to wage-earning skills. An owned home may be useful as a resource as long as a person is living in it, but if employment causes a move to another area, the utility of the house is lessened and may even become a liability if it cannot be sold or turned into income-producing property.

Time utility refers to the availability of a resource at the time it is needed, when it has the most want-satisfying power. The time utility of resources can be illustrated by knowledge of certain facts in relation to income taxes. If the knowledge or supporting records are not available at the time that the tax forms are being filed, the utility of such knowledge has been reduced or negated because of this time factor. A resource loses value or utility when the need for it is gone. If you need transportation to the airport to catch a plane at a specified time, the offer of a ride the next day will provide little service. Therefore the utility life-span of a resource may be determined by a number of factors including goals, knowledge of the user, and time or place of use, in addition to needs and wants.

Conscious evaluation of the utility of resources available to each individual and to the family as a unit can enhance the worth of resources possessed and can lead to greater satisfaction from resources held in reserve.

ACCESSIBILITY

The second characteristic of all resources is accessibility. Assets must exist on hand or in reserve if they are to be considered as resources for goal attainment. For an asset to be used, it must be within the user's grasp. A neighbor's savings will do little good in time of an emergency unless the neighbor offers a loan or gift.

Resources exist and are accessible in varying quantities or qualities. Some have elastic limits and can be stretched by conscious development. Some assets take longer to cultivate than others, such as knowledge; and in the process of development, they are accessible in varying amounts and qualities. Some assets, like physical health, require daily maintenance. Some resources require mobility to be accessible. A car is accessible only if it is in the place where it is needed. If a person flies to Miami for a vacation, a car left in Colorado is not accessible during the vacation.

Some resources demand self discipline and a conscious change of attitude to develop them. For instance, a person studying for a test, learning to play an instrument, or managing money on a reduced income. Because human resources are so important to the management of other resources, some strategies for consciously developing and increasing the supply and quality of human resources are explored in Chapter Seven.

Some resources exist and are, therefore, accessible but defy measurement; the quantity and quality of others can be measured easily by existing standards. This difference in measureability is due to the varied forms that resources take. Some resources, such as material possessions or even rain, can be seen and their worth estimated. With others, such as interpersonal skills, communication, or talents, only indexes of the resources are apparent as evidence of their existence and accessibility.

The quality and quantity of accessible resources differ among persons and families. This is why some authors have considered scarcity or the limited nature of certain resources as characteristic of all resources. Bratton cited time and money as examples of limited resources and explained that continued use of them, for one purpose, will deplete their limited supply. She considered skills and knowledge as being "bounded" by time and limited in degree of availability.[10] However, it appears to the authors that utility and accessibility, manageability, and interchangeability are more salient characteristics of all resources than scarcity or the limited nature of some resources.

In actuality, resources such as time, solar energy, and many environmental and community resources are not finite but are generally available to everyone, within geographical limits. Although Sheboygan, Wisconsin does not have the same community resources as Milwaukee, the community resources of Sheboygan are equally available to all citizens of Sheboygan who have the money, time, and inclination to use them.

Solar energy is more available at higher altitudes and in more sunny locations than it is at sea level or in overcast climates. However, solar energy is equally accessible to all residents of one geographical area. Use made of the resource will differ from one family to another. In today's economy, overabundance of products may motivate more of decision making and choice in management than may scarcity.

Resources are valuable when available for use, but they are often desired most by those who possess them in lesser degrees. The old adage that "possession is nine-tenths of the law" is a reminder of possession and accessibility as characteristics of all resources.

INTERCHANGEABILITY

A third characteristic of resources is interchangeability. All resources are interrelated to the extent that one may be substituted for or interchanged with another in the quest for goals. When a person lacks the money he needs to buy the level of living he desires, he may be motivated to develop other resources that can be sold to earn money. Catering skills or the ability to write salable magazine articles may be undeveloped until a person desires something that cannot be afforded from current income.

Equal substitution is not a requirement of resources, for it would be impossible to equate time with money or money with knowledge. Instead of buying a new chair when the old one needs recovering, one may be reupholstered through the use of a sewing machine, fabric, thread, notions, time, knowledge, and energy of the person willing to accomplish the task. Less money resource may be required and the opportunity to develop and practice a creative, leisure–time skill may be provided. But the initial cost of the sewing machine may be more expensive than a new chair or a professional job of upholstery, unless the machine and upholstery equipment are used for other construction.

A variety of resources may be substituted for commercially manufactured products and professional services. Raw materials from which home-produced items are made must be secured with time and usually money, transportation, and fuel. Quality of the finished home-produced item will depend on the skills, knowledge, and inclination, as well as the time of the operator. Attitude and appreciation also affect quality.

The relationship between resources varies with time and place, and especially with age. The multiple effects of resources can be observed by introducing a single material good, such as a television, into family life, or a motor cycle into the life of a teenager. With a new television, the homemaker may get more rest because he or she watches television in the evenings instead of performing household chores; hobbies, such as knitting may be pursued and can be done at the same time as watching television. Meals may be moved to a more convenient time and place to allow family members to see news reports, or children to watch their favorite programs. Less time may be allocated by all family members for outside recreation and reading. Less money may be spent on outside entertainment as the cost of the television may have come from the recreation budget.

Mundel's classes of change in work simplification may also help to explain the effect of substitution and multiple effect of resources. According to Mundel, each level of change causes changes in motions and, consequently resources in each of the levels below.[11]

A Class 5 change (substitution in raw materials) brings about changes in each of the four classes below it. A substitution of polyester fiber for linen in clothing (a change in raw materials) alters the appearance of the finished garment by making it crease resistant and pliable and by adding comfort for active movement. It also changes the production sequence in manufacturing the product because the technique and source of supplies required to produce

Table 5.1   Mundel's Classes of Change.

Class of change	Description	Examples
Highest 5	Change in: Raw material	1. Polyester instead of cotton garments 2. Paper instead of linen napkins 3. Plastic instead of damask table cloth
4	Change in: Finished product	1. Snowmobile instead of sled 2. Square instead of round biscuits 3. Formica instead of wooden table
3	Change in: Production sequence	1. Taking all equipment for table setting to table at one time 2. Making a cake by one-bowl instead of traditional method 3. Completely making one side of bed before moving to other side
2	Change in: Tools, equipment and work areas	1. Using a tray to carry dishes, silver and glasses to table 2. Using electric mixer instead of wire whip or spoon to beat egg whites 3. Storing saucepans near sink instead of under the range
Lowest 1	Change in: Body positions and motions	1. Polishing car with two hands instead of one 2. Sitting instead of standing when ironing 3. Using rhythmic motions in sweeping

polyester yarns is vastly different from that for linen yarns. Polyester yarns are most often knitted, while linen is usually woven. Because of the stretchability of polyesters, garments made from them are manufactured differently from linen garments. The tools, patterns, notions, and work areas needed to construct polyester garments differ from that used in linen construction. Thread for stitching polyester is usually made of polyester also, so the stretching of the garment will not cause the thread used for seams to break. Seam tapes used on polyesters must be stretchable. Interlocked machine stitches must also stretch to produce best results. Therefore, a change in the machine is implied. A change in knowledge, skills, time, and energy of the worker is also necessitated, all because of a change in this raw material for clothing.

Many additional interchanges in resources are set in motion. Use of oil in the manufacture of the polyester yarn reduces the supply of fuel resources for transportation, but saves on electrical energy resources needed for pressing linen between wearings. Polyesters do not require ironing. Because of their convenience, the widespread use of polyester clothing has had a major effect on the dry cleaning and related service industries. Thus, Mundel's Classes of Change in work simplification illustrates the interrelatedness of resources and demonstrates how an interchange of one resource may bring change throughout the total process of resource management.

Exchange of one resource for another entails both costs and risks. In today's youth cult, hitchhiking has been substituted for travel by bus, plane, or train in many areas of this country and in Europe. It is considered by some not only as a way of substituting time for money, but as a way of living with the elements, experiencing the environment, and sharing more of the culture of people from different areas. However, in the following letter to Ann Landers, the consequences were more severe than the cost of an alternate form of transportation.

DEAR ANN: I beg of you, don't stop warning girls about the dangers of hitch-hiking. I know you've printed several letters in your column on this subject, but mine might make a stronger impression than most because I can tell them firsthand what it's like to be raped.

It was midnight. Not much traffic. The car was new. The man looked middle-aged and respectable. Two minutes after I got into his car I knew I was in for it. I was hoping he'd slow down just enough for me to open the door and jump out, but he never did. Before I knew it, we were parked on a side road and his hands were around my throat. "I can kill you in 10 seconds," he said calmly, "or you can be a good girl and cooperate."

I tried to scream but my throat was dry. I had no voice. His hands were powerful. He was like a jungle animal the way he moved. He dragged me out of the car and threw me to the ground. I was no match for him. Besides, he looked crazy. I was afraid if I fought him, he'd choke me to death. So I cooperated.

When he finished with me, he carried me back to the car, drove onto the highway and shoved me out on the grading. I was in a state of shock but I remember thanking God for sparing my life.

A middle-aged couple picked me up within a few minutes. They drove me straight to the emergency room of a hospital. The doctor said I was a very lucky girl. All I had was three broken ribs and a sprained neck. I could have ended up like a dozen of other girls I've read about in the newspapers—raped and murdered.

The bus fare to the place I was going would have cost me $4.50. How's that for an O. Henry ending?

—Exhibit A

Dear A: Thank you for telling your story. The best part of it is that you lived to write the letter.[12]

Resources are interchangeable, not only because they may be substituted one for another, but because resources have alternate uses. Energy may be used for a wide assortment of activities to accomplish a variety of purposes. Instead of spending a small amount of money each day for a package of cigarettes, the money may be saved. At the end of two years, the amount saved could buy a ski outfit of boots, skiis, poles, and ski clothes. Instead of using an hour of time every night watching television, that time could be used to study a foreign language. Time spent at the rate of an hour a day studying Spanish could make it possible, within a year, to communicate satisfactorily with Mexican business people and understand the customs during a trip to that country. Small amounts of time may not be saved but can be used for alternate activites—to accomplish more easily a large task or to sharpen intellectual skills.

Although it is possible to emphasize the use of one resource for a period of time, such as studying for a major examination or looking for a new job, a balance of resources is needed to achieve maximum satisfaction with one's way of life. Time, energy, space, air, and sound are resources that are *interdependent*—interwoven into the use of almost all other resources. The ongoing nature of time and energy and the fact that it is almost impossible to utilize one without the other attest to the interrelatedness of these resources and the relationship between them and other resources. The presence of energy is essential to the utilization of time. Creative activities, such as painting and sketching, require time and energy. Surfing takes energy, equipment, and time, as well as skill and knowledge. Interdependence is a dimension that strengthens the interchangeable nature of resources.

According to Paolucci and O'Brien, few resources are used in their original form. One resource is constantly being converted into another.[13] Conversion usually requires postponing the benefits from the resource transformation. When money is used to build a home which, in turn, creates space for family interaction, there is a time-lag between the investment of money, time, and energy into planning the house and the final "key-turning." It is this time delay in converting one resource into another that distinguishes conversion from substitution.

Resources may also be created by investing time, money, and energy in human capital—education and purposeful development of specific instrumental abilities. Managerial knowledge and skills, consumer technology, ability to make home repairs, proficiency in producing goods and services for family consumption, and capacity to set attainable goals in harmony with personal and cultural goals are instrumental abilities that may be considered human capital. Human capital is a necessary factor in management.[14]

Interchangeability of resources is exhibited through substitution, alternate usage, exchange, multiple effect, interdependence, conversion, and creation. Can you think of any other ways resources are interchangeable? Are knowledge and skills or attitudes interdependent on any other resources?

MANAGEABILITY

The fourth characteristic of resources is manageability. All resources are to some degree manageable. Although they may not be completely controllable, it is possible to exert *limited control* over all of them. It may not be possible to add a foot to body height through management, but it is possible to add some height through improved health and posture development. Within the present technology, people cannot exert complete control over the weather or other environmental factors; but society has made great strides in that direction. Air conditioning and heating make the air within homes, offices, and automobiles more comfortable. Smog devices on automobiles and filters on airborne waste emissions of industry can decrease eye irritation from polluted air.

Resource manageability makes it possible to *focus* on development of one resource at a particular time, as in the case of an injured athlete learning to walk again after a severe accident. The capabilities of a homemaker can be refocused from care of the home to earning income outside the home when inflation threatens to curtail standards to which a family had become accustomed.

Manageability of resources also makes it possible to *predict*, with some degree of accuracy, the outcomes of resource use, as in the case of the weather, so that precautions may be taken against windstorms, hurricanes, and severe snowstorms. It is possible to extend life span through discovery of cures for communicable diseases and preventative medicine; it is also possible to protect against the loss of other resources available to the family as a consequence of the death of a breadwinner.

Resource manageability means that *goals may be achieved through conscious choice and application* of resources in the management processes. A time plan can maximize time available for social interaction and civic service. It is possible to organize use of space within the limits of one's apartment to achieve a more convenient arrangement for indoor gardening. It is also possible to implement a food service career by managing knowledge and skills in that direction. It is possible to limit use of environmental resources to assure that life will be worth living ten, twenty, or a hundred years from now.

Factors Affecting the Use of Resources

Among the most prominent factors affecting the use of resources are motivation; the quality, quantity and mix of resources available; life cycle and family composition; education and goals; communication within the group; and customs, habits and life style patterns preestablished by the group.

MOTIVATION

Motivation is a prime factor in resource use because it is an internal attitude. It is the way people use what they have that is important in meeting and establishing life's goals. Motivation directs or limits the quantity, quality, and mix of resources that a person is willing to use in goal attainment.

Motivation is a result of combined forces, some of which are recognized as resources. For example, it is thought that people who live in tropical climates generally have less ambition (motivation) than those who live in cooler climates. According to this theory, environmental resources act as a depressant on resource allocation. But examples of outstanding accomplishments by people living in the tropics indicate that something more than climate is responsible for achievement—perhaps motivation. Surely education increases motivation by exposing people to alternative possibilities and, likewise, toward complete understanding of resource management. Those who criticize low income families for their lack of motivation have failed to acknowledge that motivation is also a resource, one that is developed through education, exposure to alternatives, and training in acceptance of responsibility for one's own destiny.

CAPACITY

The ability to receive, hold, and absorb information and ideas is called capacity. Human capacity sets limits on the use of resources; but, as has been pointed out earlier in the chapter, most people's capacity so far exceeds their attainment, that the big task of management is to expose underachievers to alternatives and to motivate them to increase output.

PHILOSOPHY

Philosophy is closely associated with a person's standard of living. It is expressed through the system of values by which people live; and it is exposed in the things people have. Patterns of individual and group behavior—especially patterns of resource use focused on satisfying desires—are compositely called one's standard of living.[15] People whose dominant manner of living focuses on improvement or maintenance of health often have strong beliefs against eating food with chemical additives or those that have been sprayed with pesticides. These dominant values become meshed into that group's life style and are, thus, indicators of why people "spend" their resources as they do.

Values such as frugality or luxury and comfort, asceticism or self-indulgence, and the stability or flexibility of expenditures are reflections of a group's philosophies regarding the use of resources to achieve, what is to them, a satisfying life system.

Cole described a standard as a mental, physical, written, graphic, or other kind of representation of desirable qualities that is used as a basis to compare like products or procedures for identification or measurement of satisfaction, to which products and services are often made to conform.[16] In today's consumer-oriented world, there are many different kinds of standards that direct resource use. For example, standards are used in food processing and preparation as a measure of product acceptability.

Whether standards are specific, as those relating to foods, or general, as in standards of living, they reflect what people believe are desirable qualities or minimum acceptable characteristics of what they want. And they determine the resources that will be utilized to achieve goals. When standards of living are defined in terms of quantity and quality of goods and services desired, they strongly affect resource choices.[17] It is because standards are attitudinal and reflect people's life philosophy, that they are such a strong force in determining which resources will be used in what quantities for attainment of specific goals.

Sometimes the prevailing concerns of a society, culture, or nation will strongly effect the resource allocation of individuals and families. During an energy crisis, the controversy between environmental preservation versus satisfaction of current demands, forces choices among resources. At such a time, some individuals broaden their philosophies of living to include the ecological framework of the total life-support system. In such an atmosphere, people are faced with consideration of energy costs of consumption choices and the achievement of goals without destroying the world in which their children and grandchildren will be living. For example, Americans must become "waste watchers" if the ten or more pounds of waste that is produced daily per capita as a by-product of this technological age is not to bury the civilization beneath it.[18] People face some crucial decisions about resource use to break the bonds that hold them "energy slaves," using thirty-three percent of the world's energy, while only six percent of the world's population lives within the country's boundaries.[19]

FAMILY HERITAGE

Family heritage is an influential factor in transmitting values and establishing approved ways of satisfying wants. Heritage and subcultures limit or expand the traditional use of resources. Oriental families devote considerable time and effort to honoring the oldest family member because their culture encourages respect for the elderly. Management patterns are influenced by the aged. Time is set aside by each family member to spend with the elderly. Their judgment is sought, and resources are devoted to their comfort and honor.

A Japanese father who had been in the U.S. studying while his wife and son remained in Japan spoke of his need to return to his family before his son learned to talk. He explained that in traditional Japanese families, men and women do not communicate openly, and men use a different language from that of the women. The father was concerned that while he had been in the U.S., his son lacked a male voice to imitate. In his family, men hold a dominant position in family management and control the manner in which resources are used.

In certain Latin American countries, formal education of women is not highly prized. Consequently, little effort, time, or money is devoted to the education of women except to prepare them for their role as wife and manager of the home. Only in recent years have some American families considered the cost of education for women worth sacrificing resources needed for other purposes.

Heritage is legacy and tradition passed down from one generation to another. It is the status or lot acquired by a person by birth—rank or position in the family and in the social environment. Status and tradition within a group determine not only who will control the resources—who will make the decisions—but also the quantity and quality of the group's resources that will be devoted to each person.

RESOURCE QUALITY, QUANTITY, AND COMBINATIONS

During the early married years, parents with young children have heavy demands on their time and have little left for leisure activities. Because of the scarcity of time, these families must find other resources to substitute in goal achievement. Money and material possessions are often also limited for young families. Sometimes scarity of several key resources causes a reevaluation of goals; or the family expands available resources through use of credit.

Families with limited resources are forced to make careful decisions about the amount of one resource to invest in a given goal. Understanding the characteristics of substitution and interchangeability of resources can help such families to attain their goals. Timing, determining how much of a resource is enough to achieve the desired goal without overexpenditure of resources, and deciding when to abandon goals and shift resources to a new goal are three of the most crucial factors relating to resource allocation. Juggling the quantity and quality of resources to be used at different times for different purposes can be learned with experience and deliberate practice.

Parkinson's Law—that a job expands to meet the time available to do the job—illustrates the elasticity of some resources, even one as rigid as time. When time is limited and people are busy, they tend to squeeze many activities into a short span of the clock and seem to accomplish more during peak pressure periods than when under less pressure.

The English economist backed up his theory of the elasticity of the demands of work on time, with a story of an elderly lady of leisure who spends the day writing a short note to her niece. She spends the first hour searching for a postcard, the next hunting for spectacles. It takes her half an hour to find the address, an hour and a quarter to compose the note, and another twenty minutes to decide whether or not to take an umbrella when going to the mailbox down the street. The total effort that would occupy a busy person for only a few minutes may leave another prostrate after a day of doubt, anxiety, and toil.[20]

Achieving balance among the resources used to reach goals increases chances of living what is referred to as a well-balanced life. Gross, Crandall, and Knoll concluded that the important factor in achieving balance among resources is not equal or even a specific distribution of resources among interests; it is, rather, insistence that all resources be represented.[21] Personal development, increased community service, companionship among family members, social interaction, civic involvment, and educational travel are qualities of life that are often slighted in the pursuit of life, liberty, and some degree of happiness. Conscious allocation of resources to these goals can improve the balance of life.

LIFE CYCLE AND FAMILY FACTORS

Family size, age, and sex of the component group greatly affects resource use. It simply takes more space and costs more to feed a family with five children than it does to feed only two adults.

The *Family Economics Review* publication of the U.S. Department of Agriculture reports, in each issue, the cost of food at home for families of different sizes for three levels of spending. The levels of spending represent different standards of eating. The cost differences within each level indicate the effect of size and composition of the family on food costs for an adequate diet. From Table 5.2, costs to provide an adequate diet for each size family can be studied. Costs vary by sex and age of the persons to be fed.[22]

Other costs vary with changes in family size and composition. The Bureau of Labor Statistics periodically develops and updates an equivalence scale for estimating budget costs by family type. Table 5.3 shows that the cost of an equivalent life style for a couple living alone is 60 percent of what it costs parents of a similar age with two children.[23] The third child increases the cost of living at the same standard by 16 percent.

The age of children in a family is a determining factor in resource use. With their estimated $30 billion per year discretionary incomes, today's teenagers have a particularly powerful influence on the family's use of economic resources, and they command control of many other forms of family resources.[24] Recent surveys indicate that teenagers between the ages of 16 and 19 have an average income of approximately $20 per week from earnings and parents. This represents more than a thousand dollars a year that these youths are spending during the last four years of their teens. Even for younger children (age 13 to 15)—the average annual income is reported to be more than $300—about $6 per week.[25]

In addition to money spent by teens, money spent on them by their families is also of great consequence. Urban families, in one area of the U.S., spend an estimated $1,380 per year on each child age 13 to 15 and $1,550 per year for a child aged 16 or 17. The cost of child rearing varies with the level of living and family size as well as the family's geographic location.[26]

The U.S. Department of Agriculture calculated the total cost of rearing a child to the age of 18 (in 1969 prices) to vary from $20,750 at a low-cost level to about $30,500 at a moderate-cost level. Those costs increase with spending for cars, television sets, private phones for the children, and a host of other purchases not calculated in the USDA estimates. The cost of supporting a child represents between 14 and 17 percent of the family's income, but the percentage decreases with each additional child.[27]

The life cycle of typical families with children and the economic life cycle of childless families was discussed in Chapter 1. Resources vary according to the stages of the life cycle. Time available for discretionary use tends to increase over the life cycle; available energy tends to decrease with age; wealth normally increases over the life cycle; and money income tends to reach a peak in the second stage of the family life cycle when the husband is between the ages of 44 to 55.[28] Reconciling the available supply of resources with resource demand is the control stage of management and requires skill in planning. The degree to which all available resources are recognized and the care taken in mixing and matching appropriate resources with goals determines the levels of living that families are able to achieve.

GOALS

The goals they set for themselves determine the quality and quantity of resources needed to achieve satifaction. Peer pressure is a highly influential fac-

Table 5.2 Cost Of Food At Home.[1] Estimated for Food Plans at Three Cost Levels, June 1975, U.S. Average.

Sex-age groups	Cost for 1 week			Cost for 1 month		
	Low-cost plan	Moderate-cost plan	Liberal plan	Low-cost plan	Moderate-cost plan	Liberal plan
	Dollars	Dollars	Dollars	Dollars	Dollars	Dollars
FAMILIES						
Family of 2:[2]						
20–54 years	28.70	36.10	43.40	124.40	156.50	188.20
55 years and over	25.40	31.70	37.90	110.20	137.30	164.30
Family of 4:						
Children, 1–2 and 3–5 years	40.40	50.40	60.70	174.90	218.80	262.80
Children, 6–8 and 9–11 years	48.90	61.40	73.80	211.90	266.30	320.00
INDIVIDUALS[3]						
Child:						
7 months to 1 year	5.40	6.60	7.80	23.40	28.70	34.00
1–2 years	6.50	8.00	9.60	28.10	34.70	41.40
3–5 years	7.80	9.60	11.60	33.70	41.80	50.30
6–8 years	10.10	12.70	15.20	43.90	55.00	66.10
9–11 years	12.70	15.90	19.10	54.90	69.00	82.80

Male:

12–14 years	13.50	16.90	20.30	58.40	73.20	87.90
15–19 years	14.90	18.70	22.50	64.70	81.10	97.60
20–54 years	14.50	18.30	22.10	62.80	79.40	95.80
55 years and over	12.70	15.90	19.10	55.10	68.80	82.70

Female:

12–19 years	12.00	14.90	17.80	52.10	64.70	77.30
20–54 years	11.60	14.50	17.40	50.30	62.90	75.30
55 years and over	10.40	12.90	15.40	45.10	56.00	66.70
Pregnant	14.30	17.70	21.10	62.00	76.70	91.60
Nursing	15.20	19.00	22.70	66.00	82.30	98.30

[1] These estimates were computed from quantities in food plans published in *Family Economics Review*, Winter 1975. The costs of the food plans were first estimated by using the average price per pound of each food group paid by urban survey families at three selected food cost levels in 1965–66. These prices were adjusted to current levels by use of *Retail Food Prices by Cities* released periodically by the Bureau of Labor Statistics.

[2] Ten percent added for family size adjustment. See footnote 3.

[3] The costs given are for individuals in 4-person families. For individuals in other size families, the following adjustments are suggested: 1-person—add 20 percent; 2-person—add 10 percent; 3-person—add 5 percent; 5-person—subtract 5 percent; 6-or-more-person—subtract 10 percent.

U.S. Department of Agriculture
Agricultural Research Service
Consumer and Food Economics Institute
Hyattsville, Maryland 20782

SOURCE: *Family Economics Review*, U.S. Department of Agriculture, Consumer and Family Economics Research Div., Washington, D.C., (Fall 1975), p. 38.

tor in goal establishment for young people and for "corporation families," such as those described in Vance Packard's *Pyramid Climbers*.[29] Even in a society that prizes free-thinking, the desire to do the "in thing" tends to lead free-thinkers down a narrow path in their use of resources. Regardless of the source of motivation behind goals, they do influence which resources will be used to reach the desired objectives.

Table 5.3 Equivalence Scale For Urban Families Of Different Size, Age, And Composition.

	Age of Head			
Size and type of family	Under 35	35-54	55-64	65 or over
One person	35	36	32	28
Two persons:				
Husband and wife	49	60	59	51
One parent and child	40	57	60	58
Three persons:				
Husband, wife, child under 6	62	69	—	—
Husband, wife, child 6–15	62	82	88	81
Husband, wife, child 16–17	—	83	88	—
Husband, wife, child 18 or over	—	82	85	77
One parent, 2 children	67	76	82	75
Four persons:				
Husband, wife, 2 children (older child under 6)	72	80	—	—
Husband, wife, 2 children (older child 6–15)	77	**100**	105	95
Husband, wife, 2 children (older child 16–17)	—	113	125	—
Husband, wife, 2 children (older child 18 or over)	—	96	110	89
One parent, 3 children	88	96	—	—
Five persons:				
Husband, wife, 3 children (older child under 6)	87	97	—	—
Husband, wife, 3 children (older child 6–15)	96	116	120	—
Husband, wife, 3 children (older child 16–17)	—	128	138	—
Husband, wife, 3 children (older child 18 or over)	—	119	124	—
One parent, 4 children	108	117	—	—

Table 5.3   (Continued)

Size and type of family	Age of Head			
	Under 35	35–54	55–64	65 or over
Six persons or more:				
Husband, wife, 4 children or more (oldest child under 6)	101	—	—	—
Husband, wife, 4 children or more (oldest child 6–15)	110	132	140	—
Husband, wife, 4 children or more (oldest child 16–17)	—	146	—	—
Husband, wife, 4 children or more (oldest child 18 or over)	—	149	—	—
One parent, 5 children or more	125	137	—	—

The scale values shown in this table are the percentages of the expendable income of the base family (4 persons—husband, age 35–54, wife, 2 children, older 6–15 years) that is required to provide the same level of living for urban families of different size, age, and composition.

SOURCE: Derived from BLS Survey of Consumer Expenditures in 1960–61. Derivation of the scale is described in *Revised Equivalence Scale: For Estimating Equivalent Incomes or Budget Costs by Family Type,* issued as BLS Bulletin 1570-2.

MEDIA

Communications media are influential in motivating goal orientation and in advertising products for consumption. Mass media contributes to the acculturation of a population and is capable of spreading biases, held by small segments of the population, to the nation and the world. Regardless of how realistic or unrealistic they may be, life styles depicted in television programs and magazine pictures affect the goals and expectations and, thus, the resource choices of many viewers. Television has had profound effects upon time usage in the average household and has even influenced housing designs and space utilization in the home.

THE FEMALE LABOR FORCE

Women's participation in the paid labor force is a factor that affects and is affected by resource allocation of all family members. Resource use of children is quite different depending on whether their mother works in the home or outside, part-time or full-time. Teenagers are reported to be doing more grocery shopping[30] and often assume responsibility for the laundry. Resource use of children is particularly important in homes headed by only a mother.

When the wife works, the children tend to do slightly more of the household tasks, and the wife spends less time and energy on home-related activities than her nonworking counterpart; but she is still responsible for the upkeep of the home and home management decisions.[31] Because the working wife has less time to devote to home-related tasks, perhaps she becomes more efficient at her home-keeping jobs. Do these research findings support Parkinson's Law, or are working women those who have less home-related work to do?

Not only does the total amount of time contributed by working wives differ from nonworking wives, but the hour of the day when work is accomplished also differs. Because the working wife usually carries out her home-related tasks in the morning before she goes to work and at the end of the day, her energy usage differs.

Families with working wives are inclined to use more purchased services, eat out more often, and spend more on transportation than those of nonworking wives. Job-related expenditures for such things as gifts, worker's compensation, professional dues, taxes, clothes, and lunches, demand a larger chunk of the family income. But the family has more money because of the wife's job—an average of one-third more.[32]

Many women work to support their families. Female heads of families were about 23 percent of all households in 1973 but were 57 percent of the fifth lowest in size of income and less than five percent of the highest.[33] Many women work to provide a college education for their children. Others work to raise the level of living, while still others work because they are educated to fill jobs and enjoy the challenge of working outside the home for pay. The satisfaction of family members and the sharing of home-related tasks appears to be connected to the attitudes and other human resources held by family members toward the wife's working. If all family members agree to the wife's working, there is a greater tendency to share in home responsibilities.[34]

INCOME AND OTHER ECONOMIC FACTORS

Factors of income and credit affect resource use by limiting potential purchases, by expanding purchasing power, or by making possible investments that bring greater family security. The supply, frequency, and certainty of income flow to a family affect the allocation of other resources to provide needs and satisfy wants. Although the group's goals influence how both economic and noneconomic resources will be used, the quality and quantity of material possessions to serve the family are also affected by the economic resources available.

Income may serve as a goal to one person and as as a resource to others. Income does not guarantee happiness, but it can oil the wheels of satisfaction. Its instrumental value should be recognized and utilized not only to bring personal satisfaction to its possessor, but to produce a better way of life for the community and the world.

Summary

In Chapter Five, resources were defined as the tools and talents with which people build their life styles and attain their goals. When used in goal attainment, tools and talents are assets. When left unused or underdeveloped, they become constraints on the potential accomplishments of the person and his family group.

Four universal characteristics of resources were identified: utility in goal satisfaction, accessibility to the user, interchangeability, and manageability.

Factors affecting the use of resources were explored. Among the most prominent factors discussed were the following: the quality, quantity, and combinations of available resources; family life cycle; family composition; education and goals of the group; media; and economic resources that expand or limit other resources.

References

1. Owen, R., "A New View of Society," reprinted in H. F. Merrill (ed.), *Classics in Management,* American Management Assoc., New York, (1960), pp. 21–25, Mayo, E., *The Human Problems of an Industrialized Civilization,* Harvard Business School, Division of Research, Boston, (1945), and Gilbreth, L., Thomas, O. M., and Clymer, E., *Management in the Home,* Dodd, Mead and Co., New York, (1964).

2. Otto, H. A., "New Light on Human Potential," in College of Home Economics, *Families of the Future,* The Iowa State University Press, Ames, Iowa, (1972), pp. 14–25.

3. *Ibid,* p. 14.

4. Mead, M., essay in Otto, H., *Explorations in Human Potentialities,* Charles C. Thomas, Springfield, Ill., (1964).

5. Gross, I. H., Crandall, E. W., and Knoll, M. M., *Management for Modern Families,* Appleton-Century-Crofts, New York, (1973), p. 152.

6. *Ibid,* p. 153.

7. Webster, N., *Webster's New Twentieth Century Dictionary of the English Language,* Unabridged, The World Pub. Co., New York, (1968), p. 1542.

8. Gilboy, E. W., *The Economics of Consumption,* Random House, New York, (1968); see also Kyrk, H., *A Theory of Consumption,* Houghton Mifflin, New York, (1923).

9. Gordon, L. J. and Lee, S. M., *Economics for Consumers,* Van Nostrand Reinhold, New York, (1972), p. 34.

10. Bratton, E. C., *Home Management Is . . . ,* Ginn and Co., Boston, (1971) pp. 107–108.

11. Mundel, M. E., *Systematic Motion and Time Study,* Prentice-Hall, Englewood Cliffs, N. J., (1950), pp. 23–26.

12. Landers, Ann, "Rape Story With O. Henry Ending," *Santa Barbara Newspress,* Calif., (May 13, 1974), p. B-5, Field Newspaper Syndicated column. Reprinted by permission of Ann Landers and Field Newspaper Syndicate.

13. Paolucci, B. and O'Brien, C., "Management of Resources," *Forecast for Home Economics,* 76 (1960), pp. 55–56.

14. Burk, M., "Problems in Studying Allocation of Family Resources," in *Issues in Family Economics,* Proceedings of National Conference, American Home Economics Assn., (1967), pp. 69–83. Also see, Burk, M., "On the Need for Investment in Human Capital for Consumption," *Journal of Consumer Affairs,* 1 (1967), 123–138.

15. Rice, A. S., "An Economic Framework for Viewing the Family," in Nye, F. I. and Berardo, F. M., (eds.), *Emerging Conceptual Frameworks in Family Analysis,* Macmillan, New York, (1966), pp. 223–268.

16. Coles, J. V., *Standards and Labels for Consumers' Goods,* Ronald Press, New York, (1949), p. 107.

17. Kyrk, H., *The Family in the American Economy,* The University of Chicago Press, Chicago, Ill., (1953).

18. Montgomery, J., "Housing Technology: How Does It Affect the Energy Crisis?"*Journal of Home Economics,* 65:9 (December 1973), 16–22.

19. *Ibid,* p. 17; and Stanford Research Institute, *Patterns of Energy Consumption in the U.S.,* U.S. Govt. Printing Ofc., Washington, D.C., (1972), pp. 33, 62.

20. Parkinson, C. N., *Parkinson's Law,* Houghton Mifflin, Boston, Mass., (1957).

21. Gross, I. H., Crandall, E. W., and Knoll, M. M., *op. cit.,* p. 179.

22. *Family Economics Review,* "Cost of Food at Home," (Fall 1975), p. 38.

23. Bureau of Labor Statistics, *Revised Equivalence Scale: For Estimating Equivalent Incomes or Budget Costs by Family Type,* U.S. Department of Labor, Washington, (1972).

24. "Young Adults," *U.S. News and World Report,* (January 17, 1972), pp. 16–18.

25. "An Important Group of Consumers," *MMI Memo* Money Management Institute, Household Finance Corp., Chicago, (Fall 1970), p. 3.

26. Pennock, J., *Cost of Raising A Child*, U.S. Dept. of Agriculture, Agricultural Research Service, (1970), pp. 22–23.

27. *Ibid*, p. 23.

28. U.S. Bureau of the Census, *Statistical Abstract of the U.S.:* 1974, Superintendent of Documents, Washington, D.C., (1974) p. 388, Table No. 628.

29. Packard, V., *The Pyramid Climbers*, Fawcett, Greenwich, Conn., (1962).

30. Belil, E. S., *Grocery Store Shopping Habits of the Young Consumer*, Co-Ed Survey Report, Scholastic Magazines, New York, (1974).

31. Walker, K., *Time-Use Patterns for Household Work Related to Homemakers' Employment*, Talk at National Agricultural Outlook Conference, Washington, U.S. Dept of Agriculture, Agricultural Research Service, Washington, D.C., (1970).

32. 1973 Statistical Abstract of the U.S., *op. cit.*, pp. 333, 335.

33. *Ibid.*

34. Hoffman, L. and L. Nye, I., *The Employed Mother in America*, Rand McNally, Chicago, Ill., (1963).

6

ASSESSING RESOURCES

It's one thing to recognize the resources of other people, but another to accurately evaluate present and potential personal resources. Most people are prejudiced when it comes to their own talents, and tend to over or under estimate them. Sometimes people believe they can "lick the world." Sometimes they are "all thumbs" and "left feet" and cannot do anything well. Self confidence is an important element in accurate resource assessment. The old adage, "The more you do, the more you can do," implies that self confidence is developed through action, through trying and discovering success along with effort. Assessment is partially based on experience in using resources and the degree of success associated with their use.

Resource assessment also depends on recognition of the utility of personal qualities, economic belongings, and the characteristics of the environment that permit or inhibit goal attainment. Seeing the use for talents to satisfy wants is the beginning of motivation. And motivation is the foundation of action.

One teacher with tremendous potential for creative thinking was content to work out her techniques for managing outdoor food preparation for her own use and that of her students. She shared her ideas with friends and professional associates but never considered writing for profit until her hobby of collecting art etchings created a need for additional income. The need for greater monetary resources motivated action in a new direction, and success added enthusiasm to her effort. If she had been asked to assess her resources before her need arose, this home economist would probably not have considered her writing talent as a valuable resource.

When faced with goals that cannot be reached with presently recognized resources, people seek to increase their supply of resources. Thus conscious awareness of the utility of undeveloped personal resources is often the beginning of a higher level of living for an individual and the family group to which he or she belongs.

Classification of Resources

In their efforts to increase awareness of individual and family resources, to explain the application of them to the process of management, and to assess their use in goal satisfaction, a number of management specialists have proposed various systems for classifying resources. These classification ideas have been ammended and refined by other researchers and theorists interested in clarification of resources and their function in the management process.

Although the resources generally included are similar, each system emphasizes a different characteristic of resources: the source of the resources, their function, characteristics of the environment, human versus nonhuman association, or economic elements of the resources. No single system of classification has yet received universal endorsement by management specialists. This diversity indicates that resource theory is still in a malleable stage of development.

Many systems have been used. The classical economists considered land, labor, and capital as the primary resources of the entrepreneur.[1] Time, energy, and money have been viewed, until quite recently, as the primary resources managed by families. Most family management texts still devote a proportionately larger number of pages to these resources than to other ones. However, the trend is currently moving toward greater emphasis on human, community, and environmental resource use. Interest in preserving environmental quality has spread beyond ecologists to the general public and to management professionals. Such issues and conditions are of vital concern in modern life and are bound to influence the consideration of many resources that may have been overlooked in earlier classifications.

Even the concept of economic resources is expanding. Stringent requirements of income tax reporting and inflationary trends of prices coupled with recessionary periods in the economy have made people more aware of the complexity of economic resources, the adequacy of incomes, and the necessity for accounting of stocks, wealth, and property. Scarcity of some resources often affects the usefulness of others and leads to investigation of alternate resources.

In their revised edition, Gross, Crandall, and Knoll describe three classifications of resources: human versus nonhuman, economic versus noneconomic, and a classification based on sources in the various environments surrounding the family.[2] These classifications represent the thinking of many people. Early management conferences were devoted to identifying and classifying resources used in the management of homes. Journal articles explored and questioned the classification of resources. The most generally accepted and widely used system has been the human versus nonhuman classification. But there are others that merit consideration. The framework proposal of Maloch and Deacon[3], the explanation of the management process by Schlater,[4] and the writings of Paolucci and O'Brien,[5] Steidl and Bratton,[6] and Manning[7] have expanded resource philosophy. This chapter presents several recognized systems of resource classification and develops two additional ways—one an interdisciplinary, eclectic approach to resource classification.

HUMAN VERSUS NONHUMAN RESOURCE CLASSIFICATION

Classification of household resources as either human or nonhuman stresses their nature and calls attention to the human aspects of resources that could be overlooked by the less skillful manager.

Human resources are abilities and characteristics of individuals and other resources that cannot be utilized independently of people. In earlier editions of *Management in Family Living,* Nickell and Dorsey identified human resources

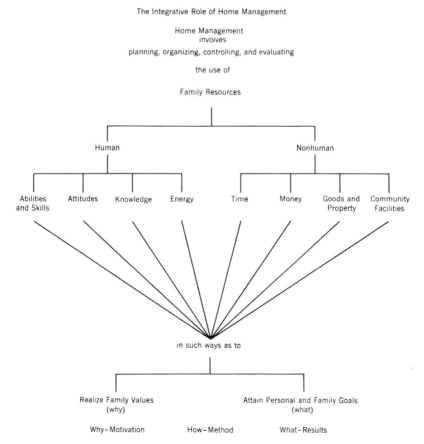

Figure 6.1   The Integrative Role of Home Management. Home Management involves planning, organizing, controlling, and evaluating the use of family resources.

as those existing within people—abilities and skills, attitudes, knowledge, and energy. They identified nonhuman resources as those existing outside people but controlled, utilized, or possessed by the family—time, money, goods and property, and community facilities.[8] Their diagram of the integrative role of resources and home management illustrated a consensus at that time of most management specialists regarding the classification of resources.

Gross, Crandall, and Knoll expanded the usual list of human resources to include intelligence, creativity, awareness, and standing plans. To the usual list of nonhuman resources they added space and power; as examples of space they cited large rooms for entertaining, storage space, and play yards for children. Electricity and fuels were noted as examples of power.[9]

For some time there has been controversy over whether time should be considered as a human or nonhuman resource. Time exists outside of individuals, but it cannot be utilized independently of individuals. The present trend is to classify it as a human resource.

Gross, Crandall, and Knoll further categorized human resources as personal—those belonging to single individuals, and interpersonal—resources that exist because of positive interaction of two or more people.[10] Knowledge, attitudes, abilities, awareness, and standing plans are examples of personal resources. Interpersonal resources are characteristics such as cooperation, love, loyalty, and communication which can contribute to group goals.

SPECIFIC VERSUS GENERAL RESOURCE CLASSIFICATION

At a Western Regional Conference of family economics and management teachers, Liston proposed the classification with two headings—*specific* or *general*—of eight basic types of resources involved in any managerial effort toward goal achievement.[11] According to this system of classifying resources, space, time, natural environment, and cultural environment would fall into the general, broadly available classification; and human resources, community opportunities, property, and income during a given period of time would be considered as specific resources.

Liston defines a resource as the properties of an object, person, or circumstance that can be used as a means to achieve a goal.[12] Time, a general resource in this classification, refers to clock time, biological time, perceived time, and the duration or sequence of time. Space, another general resource, implies social as well as physical space, perceived as well as measured space. Income during a given period of time and property (real estate, durable inventories, financial contracts) are considered as specific resources in this system. Human resources of group members and community opportunities, both human and nonhuman, are also specific resources.

This is a fresh approach to resource classification. Its unique features are its simplicity, emphasis on community opportunities and consideration of human resources of group members, and the natural and cultural environmental classes. At that point in time, Liston was still uncertain as to how she wished to classify energy, but recognized it as an essential resource intrinsic within so many of the others that she was hesitant to list it as a separate and singular dimension of the resource complex.[13]

HUMAN, PHYSICAL, AND PSYCHIC CAPITAL RESOURCE CLASSIFICATION

Using the land, labor, and capital philosophy of economic resources and building upon Burk's concepts of consumption economics, Rice classified the resources available to the family as: human, physical, and psychic capital.[14] The term capital, in its broader sense, meant any form of assets used or available for use in goal attainment.

According to this system, the components of human capital are: technology, capacity, motivation, and time. Capacity is the ability to adjust, to innovate and change. Technology is both production and consumption technology—skills, abilities and knowledge of each member of the group—as well as the education, training, and interpersonal environment through which these qualities operate. Motivation includes the power to act—energy.

Physical capital includes the frequency and amount of income as well as purchasing power, elastic income (credit), wealth (the pattern of family property and durables), and community facilities (protective agencies, educational systems, services, and recreational opportunities).

Psychic capital (the degree of satisfaction derived from expenditure of human and physical capital) is important because it regulates the amount and quality of other resources required in the pursuit of satisfaction by all family members.

ECOLOGICAL CLASSIFICATION OF RESOURCES

An ecological approach to management and resource classification is also appropriate because of recent experiences with scarcity of natural resources. Human ecology is the study of the spatial and temporal interrelationships between people and their economic, social, political, and physical environments. Cain explains the ecological system as the physical environment acting on living organisms, the living organisms reacting to the physical environment, and both co-acting with one another.[15] Bresler further explains that the basic interests of ecologists are the answers to three questions: How does the environment affect the organism? How does the organism affect its environment? How does one organism affect another organism in the context of the environment in which they both live?[16]

At a national conference on *The Family: Focus on Management* in 1969, Steidl proposed an ecological approach to the study of family managerial behavior.[17] She explained that the logic of an ecological framework originates in the fact that content and quality control of the environment in which managerial behavior takes place is a prerequisite to the ultimate realization of goals because the environment shapes behavior. According to this approach, the environment is composed of three elements: social, physical, and biological. Social components of the environment include social organizations (family, community, and other cultural institutions that embrace customs, mores, habits, and norms), economic institutions (business, industry, stock market, banks), and political institutions (different levels of government).

The physical components consist of man-made objects (clothing, furnishings, tools, appliances, and dwellings), less tangible surroundings (air, light, sound, temperature, humidity, and space), and natural tangible surroundings (soil, terrain, and rain). The biological components of the environment are human (physiological, anatomical, behavioral, and psychological) and nonhuman (animal, insects, microbes, and viruses).

According to Steidl, the *near environment* is intimate and has more potential for individual or family control of quality and content. Employment outside the family is the major reference point between a person and his *intermediate environment,* which is on a larger, less personal scale. The intermediate environment may require managerial adaptation because there is less opportunity for change by a family or individual. People seldom interact with the *far environment* except through televised space flights.[18] Although Steidl did not propose a classification of resources as part of this ecological framework, her organization of the components of the environment lends itself easily to a classification of the resources within the environment.

SOCIAL LINKAGE APPROACH TO RESOURCE CLASSIFICATION

A social linkage approach to resource classification, stressing the social orientation of the organization to which the resources belong, is still another possibility and could be more useful to the process-interaction approach to management than some of the previous approaches.

Since any cooperative system is an organization, even an individual can be considered an organization within a social-linkage framework based on classification according to who uses the resource. Figure 6.2 illustrates how social linkage might function as a resource classification system.

INTERDISCIPLINARY HUMAN-ECONOMIC-ENVIRONMENTAL APPROACH

Each resource classification system serves to increase awareness of specific resources as families seek goal attainment. However, the present authors

Figure 6.2   A Social Linkage Approach To Resource Classification.

Classification	Examples
Personal Resources	Abilities and skills, knowledge, attitudes, creativity, awareness, interests, energy, and time belonging to an individual.
Family Resources	Personal resources of all family members, family ritual, the extended family exchange, housing unit, cars, furnishings, equipment, and the family's pattern of wealth.
Compeer Resources	Social ties, friendships between individuals and families, and the pattern of cooperative human interaction systems influencing an individual's values, norms, and goals.
Community Resources	Career opportunities, the marketplace of goods and services for consumption, employment and investment opportunities, banks, savings institutions, and all social communal resources—police protection, fire department, local government, school systems, churches, and parks.
National Resources	Coal, oil, water, gas, trees, and all the natural resources of a nation, government parks and recreation facilities, national government and its network of protective laws, defense mechanisms, and world-trade agreements, the economic system, roadways and communication systems.
World-Society Resources	World-wide organizations such as the United Nations, international trade agreements, world airways, international social interaction, travel opportunities, and ambassadors.

believe each of these systems has limitations in practical use or places undue emphasis on limited properties of resources. Use of the prefix *non* (as in human-nonhuman, economic-noneconomic) tends to oversimplify the system and fails to completely identify what the non-category represents.

An efficient system would combine the best elements from each system of classification into a logical and usable eclectic approach to resources. Since each author or team of authors has predominately refined one area, it seems profitable for managerial resource theory to combine elements of each theory into one mutually exclusive, broadly based system of resource classification. This type of system should increase awareness of a larger variety of resources available for management. It may, thereby, expand the satisfaction most individuals and families can achieve in their pursuit of particular qualities of desired life styles.

The following classification system builds upon the human, economic, and environmental approaches, utilizes some of the social linkage groupings, and combines them into one eclectic classification of resources available for family management. This classification can accommodate a broader list of resources and, by so doing, should increase awareness of the breadth of resource possibilities. Figure 6.3 utilizes interdisciplinary terminology and is detailed in the definition and illustrations of each category.

Human Resources

According to this system, three large areas of resources are delineated: *human resources, economic resources,* and *environmental resources.* The classification of human resources is subdivided into four categories: cognitive, affective, psychomotor, and temporal resources. The first three terms are common in education relating to behavioral objectives and levels of learning.[19] The terms affective, cognitive, and temporal were utilized by Steidl and Bratton in their book, *Work in the Home.*[20]

Cognitive Resources

Defined for classification purposes as mental traits, these resources belong to an individual or individuals composing an organization. They are mental characteristics and are related to knowledge acquired through practice. They are intellectual abilities and include such human characteristics as aptitude, intelligence, judgment, goal orientation, and adaptability. The reader may wonder, is decision-making style a cognitive resource?

Affective Resources

Human traits pertaining to, or resulting from, emotions and feelings rather than from thought and reasoning, are affective resources. Examples of these traits are interest, appreciation, faith, taste, patience, tolerance, honesty, friendliness, and job satisfaction. Taste, as classified in this section, refers to characteristic preferences, such as taste in clothes, furnishings, art, or music.

Psychomotor Resources

Muscular activity and mental processes are combined through these resources in the development of traits and skills. They combine the ability to accomplish a job with proficiency in carrying out the activity; this usually requires some physical exertion. Some examples of psychomotor resources are energy, vitality, smell, sight, communication skills, and manners.

Psychomotor resources are particularly beneficial in the operation of the home and care of family members. Such skills as comparative shopping, record keeping, computing and filing income tax forms, driving a car, and administering first aid to bruises and cuts are all psychomotor resources. They are easier to analyze than cognitive and affective resources because they can be observed during action and evaluated following their use. Taste, as classified in the psychomotor section, refers to the ability to perceive differences such as sour, sweet, salty, or acid.

Figure 6.3 A Proposed Interdisciplinary Human-Environmental Approach To Resource Classification.

Resource Classification	Examples of Family Resources

HUMAN RESOURCES

Cognitive Resources
Mental traits or characteristics of an individual that are related to practical and perceptual knowledge.

Intelligence, knowledge, judgment, logic, articulation, aptitude, communication, ability, goal orientation, self control, curiosity, ambition, creativity, initiative, understanding, adaptability, resourcefulness, confidence, alertness, perception, and other traits either inherited or acquired and related to the thought/reasoning process of the human mind.

Affective Resources
Traits pertaining to or resulting from emotions and feelings.

Interests, attitudes, decision making style, tact, loyalty, sensitivity, consideration, trust, motivation, enthusiasm, intuition, perseverance, cooperation, appreciation, faith, tastes, leadership capacity, reputation, friendliness, patience, tolerance, integrity, honesty, sincerity, influence, poise, job satisfaction, and other emotional traits and attitudinal characteristics.

Psychomotor Resources
Resources that combine muscular activity with associated mental processes, both ability and proficiency in carrying out activities involving some physical exertion.

Energy, vitality, fatigue-tolerance level, smell, sight, hearing, taste, touch, appearance, metabolism, manners (systems of social conduct), communication skills, do-it-yourself skills, work habits, job skills, consumer skills, managerial skills, home-related work skills, motion-mindedness, posture, temperament, and other traits that combine muscular and mental activity.

Temporal Resources
The minutes, hours, days, weeks, and years of clock time, as well as an individual's characteristic methods of assimilating, using, and perceiving the passage of time.

Clock time—past, present, and future; physiological time, psychological time, sense of timing, pace of activity, industriousness and routine that an individual or organization assimilates.

ECONOMIC RESOURCES

Money Income
Monetary gains within a prescribed period of time, gross monetary receipts to all family members derived from capital or labor, frequency and pattern of such flow to the group.

Gross income, wages, commissions, bonus payments, rent on owned properties, interest, capital gains, dividends, transfer payments, retirement receipts, and royalties.

145

Figure 6.3 (Continued)

Resource Classification	Examples of Family Resources
Elastic Income Purchasing power expanded through deferred payment, ability to secure goods or present services through deferment of financial obligations.	Long-term real estate mortgage credit, short-term consumer credit, service credit, charge accounts, revolving charge accounts, cash loans, installment purchases, and all forms of credit and deferred payment plans that allow people to purchase and use goods and services before payment for the items.
Wealth The composite of holdings, real property, income-producing assets, durables, and personal possessions of all family members as well as the family's characteristic pattern of asset holdings.	One's home or apartment, personal possessions, household furnishings, cars, jewelry, sports equipment, stereos, clothing, tools, appliances, stocks, bonds, and all income-producing assets, as well as the pattern of family holdings.
Fringe Benefits Nonmoney income derived as a consequence of employment and for which the employer pays at least a portion of the cost.	Medical care programs, hospitalization, sick leave benefits, life insurance plans, paid vacations, retirement benefit programs, pension plans, worker's compensation for injury on the job, and low-cost or free housing, food, car, room and board, expense accounts, and club memberships.

ENVIRONMENTAL RESOURCES

Physical-Environmental Resources

  Natural tangible surroundings

Elements of the environment that can be perceived by the sense of touch.	Soil, terrain, rain, minerals, and other land resources.

  Nontangible surroundings

Elements of the environment and climate that are not tangible but are measureable.	Air, light, sound, temperature, humidity, space, and sunlight.

Social Environmental Resources

  Social Organizations

Cooperative human interaction systems which influence an individual's values, standards, norms, habits, mores, customs and goals.	Nuclear family, extended family, friends and associates, professional and business associates, community, nation, professional organizations, American Association of Retired Persons, consumer action groups, Boy Scouts, YWCA, and bridge clubs.

Figure 6.3   (Continued)

Resource Classification	Examples of Family Resources
Economic Institutions The business and industrial establishments that make goods and services available to the public for purchase or through private membership and that furnish employment and capital investment opportunities to individuals. Economic institutions have a profit base.	Business and industry, stores and shopping centers, service markets, supermarkets, department stores, drugstores, restaurants, variety stores, banks, savings institutions, stock markets, wholesale and retail outlets, and the national and international economic system in which business operates and families consume.
Political Institutions Governmental structures and systems that influence a person's behavior.	City, county, state, and national governments and their network of protective and enabling laws.
Community Facilities & Services Shared resources provided by nonprofit organizations or the government. Government facilities are usually financed through public taxation and support.	Police protection, water and sewage systems, garbage pick-up service, fire protection, churches, schools, roads and highways, recreation centers, parks, libraries, municipal golf courses, mass transit and other facilities commonly shared but for which no cost or only a part of the cost is paid upon use.

Psychomotor resources are also highly useful in employment situations. Typing, bookkeeping, filing, machine operation, waiting on customers, making change, supervising other people on the job, waiting on tables, cooking, planning menus, and many other employment activities are classified as psychomotor resources because they combine both muscular and mental activity.

Temporal Resources

In this classification system, time is considered a human resource and refers not only to Sideral "clock time", that everyone possesses in equal amounts, but also to a person's characteristic methods of assimilating and perceiving the passage of time. Perceived time is highly related to satisfaction with activity. Duration and time sequence are related to effectiveness of time planning for home-related work. People differ in their ability to gauge the passage of time or to estimate the amount of time that an activity will take. This is perceived time, or one's time sense, sometimes called psychological time. Biological time is related to the body's circadian rhythm—periods of alertness and periods of depression or fatigue—as well as to feelings of hunger at certain times of the day. These are all examples of temporal resources. They are considered resources because they can be managed. The industriousness or *pace of routine* which an individual assimilates is also a human, temporal resource.

Economic Resources

According to this classification scheme, these resources include money income, elastic income, and wealth.

Money Income

This resource is defined as a monetary benefit or gain derived from capital or labor. It includes not only the amount of gross monetary receipts to a person or family, but its characteristic pattern and frequency of flow to the family. Tips, bonus payments, royalty payments, wages, commissions, interest, dividends, and pensions are money income resources; but savings and investments are wealth.

Fringe Benefits

These resources are advantages in goods and services derived as a consequence of employment but exclude money income. A typical package of employee benefits includes medical care services, medical and surgical insurance, life insurance plans, paid vacations, and a retirement program toward which the employer pays at least a portion of the cost.

Credit

Because of increased use of credit and its potential to expand the purchasing power of such a large segment of the population, *elastic income* has a category of its own in the proposed eclectic classification of resources. Elastic income is current purchasing power expanded through deferred payments and includes not only long-term real estate mortgages, but also, deferred short-term methods of payment for soft goods and services. Availability and elasticity of this kind of income differs from person to person depending upon the character, capacity, capital, and collateral of the individual and money market conditions in the community. Examples are cash loans, service credit, charge accounts, installment buying, and all types of sales credit.

Wealth

The last subcategory of economic resources is *wealth*. As a resource, wealth is a composite of holdings, real property, and other income-producing assets, plus all the durables, household equipment, furnishings, and personal possessions of group members. Wealth also refers to the family's pattern of asset holdings, not just what is on hand at the present time.

Environmental Resources

Environmental resources are classified as either physical or social. The physical environmental resources include two types of surroundings—natural tangible surroundings and less tangible surroundings. The former are the elements of the environment and climate that can be perceived by the sense of touch, such as soil, terrain, rain, and minerals. Nontangible surroundings are the elements of the environment and climate that are less tangible but include those that can be measured, such as air, light, sound, temperature, and humidity. Some nontangible surroundings can be heard (such as sound), and some can be seen when the quality has been polluted but are relatively invisible when their quality is high (such as air).

The remaining resources utilized by families and individuals have been classified as different forms of social environmental resources: social organizations, economic institutions, political institutions, and community facilities and services. In this classification system, an organization is defined as persons or groups united for some purpose that contributes to the group welfare. *Social organizations* are the cooperative human interaction systems that influence an individual's values, standards, norms, habits, mores, customs, and goals. Examples include the nuclear and extended family circles, friends and associates, civic groups, and community, national, and world organizations. Thus the United Nations organization would be considered a social organization even though its purpose may be partially political. Schools and educational institutions would fit, more logically, in the category of community facilities and services.

An institution is a relationship—an established organization especially dedicated to public service, or a behavioral pattern of importance in the life of a community or society. *Economic institutions* are the business and industrial establishments that make goods and services available to the public for purchase, rent or use, furnish employment to individuals, and provide capital investment opportunities. Business and industry, stores and shopping centers, service markets, banks and other financial institutions, stock markets, and the national and international economic system in which business operates and families consume are classed as economic institutions.

Political institutions are the governmental structures and systems that influence a person's behavior, such as local, city, county, state, and national governments and the network of laws that each encompasses.

Community facilities are shared resources provided by organizations, by business, or by government, such as police and fire protection, churches, schools, roadways, recreation centers, parks, and libraries. Community facilities are usually operated on a low or nonprofit basis and their cost of up-keep is usually shared.

The list of examples given in the table is intended as suggestive only and is not all-inclusive in spite of the length of the list. However, the classifications should be mutually exclusive. Each resource should fit most appropriately into only one classification heading. For example, economic institutions and community facilities are similar in that they are both shared resources. There is, however, one primary difference between the two classifications into which these social environmental resources fall. Economic institutions are operated for profit and the costs of upkeep are financed through the earnings of the business organization and its owners. Community facilities and services are shared resources paid for through taxation or established specifically for public use without a profit motive. This continuation is a public responsibility. The cost of irresponsible use of community facilities deprives the population of additional community facilities. Responsible sharing of community facilities increases the satisfaction they bring to all.

While testing this system of classifying resources with college students, the authors encountered a number of questions that may also help the reader clarify uncertain points. The question of "Where do credit unions go?" arose. Credit unions are usually operated on a limited membership basis but are, like most mutual insurance companies, economic institutions. The question, "Where do educational programs go that aren't tied to a facility?" led to clarification of the term "facilities." *Facilities,* when used in the plural, are conveniences, provisions, or means used to facilitate an action or process. Facilities are more than buildings; they represent services as well, such as library facilities. However, in Figure 6.3, the word "services" was added to community facilities to avoid ambiguity. Both educational programs that are tied to facilities and those that are not are more appropriately classified as community facilities and services, unless they are operated for a profit, as are some business schools. In the latter case, they are economic institutions.

This interdisciplinary system of classifying resources is a comprehensive one; it includes not only economic and human resources, but the less-recognized areas of the environment as well. Examine the system critically. Are there resources that would not fit into one of the subcategories provided? Are there some that logically belong in more than one area of the classification system? Will the system work? Does it increase awareness of resources available for management within your scope of operation? As with all theory, the test of effectiveness is in its worth as an operational tool for raising the level of family managerial behavior.

Summary

In Chapter 6, several systems for classifying resources were discussed, including a human-nonhuman approach, an economic approach, and an environmental approach. A social-linkage classification was developed to show how the social orientation of the organization to which resources belong might be used as a classification system.

A comprehensive, eclectic, and interdisciplinary approach was presented as a means of increasing the reader's awareness of the breadth of potential resources and as a means of utilizing what is considered to be the strong points of each of the other classification systems described. Three large areas of resources were delineated in this eclectic system: human resources, economic resources, and the elusive environmental resources.

References

1. Heilbroner, R. L. and Thurow, L. C., *The Economic Problem,* Prentice-Hall, Englewood Cliffs, N.J., (1975), p. 17.

2. Gross, I. H., Crandall, E. W., and Knoll, M. M., *Management for Modern Families,* Appleton-Century-Crofts, New York, (1973), pp. 156–166.

3. Maloch, F. and Deacon, R., "Proposed Framework for Home Management," *Journal of Home Economics,* 58, 1 (January 1966), pp. 31–35; see also Maloch, F. and Deacon, R. E., *Components of Home Management in Relation to Selected Variables,* Research Bull. 1042, Ohio Agr. Research and Development Center, Wooster, Ohio, (November 1970).

4. Schlater J. D., "The Management Process," *Journal of Home Economics,* 59, 2 (February 1967), pp. 93–98.

5. Paolucci, B. and O'Brien, C., "Management of Resources," *Forecast for Home Economics,* 76 (1960), pp. 55–56.

6. Steidl, R., and Bratton, E. C., *Work In the Home,* John Wiley, New York, (1968); see also Bratton, E. C., "Management Process in Conceptual Framework—Strength or Weakness?" in *Conceptual Frameworks Process of Home Management,* Proceedings of a Home Management Conference, Michigan State University, East Lansing, (June 17–20, 1964), pp. 37–41.

7. Manning, S. L., *Time Use in Household Tasks By Indiana Families,* Purdue University Agr. Exp. Sta. Research Bull. 837, (1968).

8. Nickell, P. and Dorsey, J. M., *Management in Family Living,* (4th ed.), John Wiley, New York, (1967), pp. 82–85.

9. Gross, Crandall, and Knoll, *op. cit.,* pp. 156–159.

10. *Ibid.,* p. 160.

11. Liston, M. I., "Management As Interaction Process," in *Behavioral Aspects of Management,* Proceedings of a national conference, American Home Economics Assoc., Washington, D.C. (1972), pp. 37–48.

12. *Ibid,* p. 41.

13. *Ibid,* pp. 44–46.

14. Rice, A. S., "An Emerging Economic Framework for Analyzing Managerial Behavior," in *The Family; Focus on Management,* Proceedings of a national conference, American Home Economics, Washington, D.C., (1969), pp. 5–13.

15. Cain, S. A., "Can Ecology Provide the Basis for Synthesis Among the Social Sciences?" in Garnsey, M. E. and Hibbs, J. R., (eds.), *Social Sciences and the Environment,* University of Colorado Press, Boulder, Colo., (1967), p. 27.

16. Bresler, J. B., (ed.), *Environments of Man,* Addison-Wesley Pub. Co., Inc., Reading, Mass., (1968), p. 1.

17. Steidl, R. E., "An Ecological Approach to the Study of Family Managerial Behavior," in *The Family, Focus on Management,* Proceedings of a national conference, American Home Economics Association, Washington, D.C., (1969), pp. 22–34.

18. *Ibid,* p. 28.

19. Bloom, B. S. and others, *Taxonomy of Educational Objectives, Handbook I: Cognitive Domain,* David McKay Co., New York, (1956), and Krathwohl, D. R. and others, *Taxonomy of Educational Objectives, Handbook II: Affective Domain,* David McKay, New York, (1964).

20. Steidl, R. E. and Bratton, E. C., *Work in the Home, op. cit.*

Part II

MANAGING HUMAN RESOURCES

7

DEVELOPING HUMAN RESOURCES

If most people use between four and ten percent of their human potentialities, what happens to the unused capabilities?[1] Think of the change in Gross National Product that could result from a 90 percent improvement in national output! Think of the personal fulfillment and productivity that could result if each individual would develop unused capabilities and improve personal output by even 50 percent.

If twice as much could be accomplished in the same length of time, would it not be worth the extra effort to sharpen existing characteristics and to develop latent capabilities? The most challenging part of this dream is that its achievement is possible.

Most people have untapped potentialities simply because circumstances have never encouraged their use. Gardner describes society's failure to develop latent resources as a premature hardening of society's arteries. Failure to develop potential individual capabilities is a self-constructed prison formed of fixed relationships and set ways.[2]

People allow themselves to "go to seed." Each attitude or habit developed makes people less receptive to alternative ways of thinking and acting. People become more competent to function in a specific environment but less adaptive to change.[3] However, unlike the prisoner who seeks escape, people are often unaware that they imprison themselves until they have broken the bonds of habit and escaped to a new, higher plane of living. It often takes a major change in life—marriage, a new baby, a change of jobs, or a move to another city—to break the habitual pattern of living and to alter the circle of friends with which most people tend to smother themselves. Only through major changes do people often recognize the extent to which habit has limited self-development.[4]

Like the gold mines along the Trail of the Forty-Niners, the mind may be worked for a little while and then abandoned. By the time they are in their mid-thirties, many people have stopped acquiring new skills or new attitudes in any central aspect of their lives.[5] Preoccupation with comfort and complacency causes the mind to wither. As people mature, they are likely to progressively narrow the scope and variety of their lives. Deliberately developing resources to enrich and strengthen life, rather than to fragment and destroy, is an essential step in attaining and maintaining full use of personal potential.

Men and women need not mummify mind and spirit before they are old. Why should people relinquish the resiliency of youth and the capacity to learn and grow at any age? Within each individual is the capacity for lifelong learning and creativity. The process of self-discovery can be perpetuated through development of potentialities. When obstacles to individual fulfillment are removed, life becomes more interesting, more vibrant, and more rewarding to the society as well as the individual.

Apathy and lowered motivation are two constraints that present the highest hurdles to self-discovery and self-development. Discovery of personal resources depends on motivation, commitment, conviction, and the values people live by—those that give meaning to life. Apathetic people accomplish little for themselves and their society. People who believe in nothing, improve nothing.

This chapter explores ways to expand human resources. Through a motivation-oriented approach, techniques of discovery and development will be presented to motivate the reader to ask, "Who am I and where do I want to go in life?" "What resources will I need to get me there?" "How can I develop these resources?" "How soon can I start?"

Who Am I?

The phrase, "Know thyself," is such a simple one that people often overlook the difficulty that is inherent in self knowledge. There is a natural resistance to being objective about oneself. The Scottish poet Robert Burns expressed the difficulty clearly when he penned the words of "To a Louse" on the inside cover of his hymnal. He did this after watching a louse crawl out from under the elaborate hat of a splendidly dressed lady whose enormous hat completely obscured the poet's vision at church. While the louse made its way up the hat, over a ribbon, to the summit of the great plume that dominated the hat, Burns wrote his poem describing the lady's blindness to her real image. She was confident that all the women were watching and envying her and that all the men were desiring her, while the poet was thinking how dirty her hair had to be. The poem ends with the famous words:

> *Would some power the gift to give us,*
> *To see ourselves as others see us,*
> *It would from many a blunder free us.*

Some people would rather remain ignorant of their potential than risk even temporary rebuff or failure that could accompany a break from routine actions and relationships. Those who refuse to discover and develop *self* are at the mercy of outside forces. Like a straw blowing in the wind, they sway in one direction, then another; control of their destiny is impossible, and improvement of their station in life is unlikely. Realization and effective management of all resources at their disposal is improbable.

Lack of control over life situations causes uneasiness, creates fear and tension, and imposes a life that is far below potential. Lack of motivation, drive, or will power plays a dominant part in the combination of forces that prevent operating at capacity.[6] Restricted self-knowledge can lead to the progress-arresting qualities of complacency, fear, and confusion. Consequently, they lead to the neglect of abilities, talents, and capabilities that, as human resources, could be used to attain personal, family, and societal goals.

SELF CONCEPT

Have you ever been caught off-guard by the question, "Who are you?" A thoughtful answer to such a question usually reflects a person's self concept and value system. It may reflect roles that dominate current decisions. The answer to such a question sometimes reveals conflicts in roles or emphasizes resources being developed at the time. The person who answers, "I'm a student," is focusing life on developing knowledge and its symbol—a college education. The person who answers, "I'm a woman," may be questioning the traditional role of women as described by Betty Friedan in *The Feminine Mystique,* and may be reflecting concern over the employment equality rights of women. The person who answers, "I'm a plumber," describes the personal resources that have been mobilized into a salable skill.

People who are uncertain about their own worth may avoid major decisions, seek rigid patterns of activity, and limit their human potential. Yet, lack of self awareness and self understanding is a cultural norm.[7] Most people would rather avoid self knowledge than seek it. Knowing oneself can be painful because it involves unsettling feelings of uncertainty. To meet oneself face-to-face requires growth, and one objective of growth is the creation of an open self concept. However, self image is not a cure-all, for obviously, a turtle cannot jump a fence regardless of how positive his attitude becomes.[8] Self image is a reflection of what lies within. To enact change, the reflection and the actual form must be compatible.

Self image is the key to human behavior and personality.[9] It is, therefore, a powerful force in developing human resources. Maltz says that self image sets the boundaries of individual accomplishment and defines what a person can and cannot do.[10] By expanding the self concept in a positive direction, the "area of the possible" is expanded. Self-image psychology indicates that development of a positive but realistic self image tends to imbue people with new talents and capabilities and may literally turn failure into success.[11]

According to Gale, no one can make adequate personal or social adjustments to life if he dislikes himself.[12] Self acceptance is fundamental to human resource development. The longer self acceptance persists, the stronger it becomes.

Society may open or close doors to human development. Societies with hereditary privilege systems that determine "rights, privileges, prestige, power, and status in the society" can, and do, "keep a good man down."[13] Gardner points out that in extreme forms, the let-the-best-man-win philosophy can lead to something close to the *survival-of-the-fittest* law of the jungle.[14]

Although American society is not completely open, a wide range of opportunities do exist for upward mobility as a result of individual effort, and people do tend to "root for the underdog." Such a society allows, if not encourages, excellence and development of human potential.

For many years, development of women's potential has been limited by prescribed sex roles. The trend in philosophy and research away from a "child-centered" toward a "person-centered" family philosophy is compatible with human resource development and the building of a positive self image for women. There is growing recognition that well-being of all members of a family, including women, is important to the well-being of children in the family.[15] Women have a responsibility to select their route to self fulfillment. The directions chosen depend, in part, on the self concept that today's woman builds for herself, not only as a woman, but as a *person.*

Self image is changed, not by intellect alone, but through experiences.[16] The child who lives with love, learns to love. Poise and confidence are the result of cumulative experiences and the reaction of others to these experiences. Memories of past, and especially, of successful experiences provide a storage bank that enforces confidence and contributes to a positive image.

Both real and contrived experiences may contribute to a positive self image. The human nervous system cannot distinguish between a "real" experience and an imagined one,[17] any more than the digestive system can distinguish between natural and synthetically-produced vitamins. A focus on successful experiences is important to self-image clarification.

According to Hurlock, growth in self acceptance and the establishment of a positive self concept is aided by stabilizing self image, being realistic in self demands, narrowing the gap between real and ideal self concepts, and achieving compatibility between self concept and the concepts of others toward the person.[18] The better people understand themselves—recognize facts and perceive the significance of these facts about themselves—the more they can limit self demands to those that are realistic.

The process of self discovery may be enhanced by use of the following statement-reaction exercise. By reading each statement, considering it briefly, relating it to personal experiences, values and goals, reacting positively or negatively to the statements, and completing the written activity at the end of the exercise the reader may begin to build a composite picture of self concept. The written exercise can be especially useful in building a positive self concept.

SELF CONCEPT STATEMENT-REACTION EXERCISE

I am what I want to be. I am what I value, what I ardently believe in and can put my heart into. I can renew myself with things that can be seen, heard, and felt, by direct contact with nature, through face to face relations with other people, or by fashioning something with my own hands. I am what I really know to be of importance and worth in my life.

I am what I am prepared to be. I am all the education I have gained from schools and all the training and socialization I have learned from my family and community—the traditions and character our culture has developed in me. I am the personality my early years gave me, the independence my adolescent years released in me. I am all the skills, abilities, knowledge, and intelligence I have mustered in my years of living. I am what I am presently prepared to be.

I am part of my people's past. Coming to terms with my past revolt and rebellion in youth, I realize that revolt is the tool of the creative seeking independence. As I felt the emotional intensity with which the children in *Fiddler on the Roof* watched the ritual of the Sabbath and the wedding, I began to feel a part of my own people's past. I am a part of the folklore of my past—phrases in everyday speech, proverbs, childhood rhymes and games, and making willow whistles and quilts. I am a part of all that I can remember, and all that my parents and their parents can remember.

I am what I am expected to be. I am what my parents have taught me to be and required of me. I am what society expects of me. I am what my peers lead me to be and what I mediate in them. I am what my religion teaches me to be.

I am what I eat and wear. I know that fine feathers do not make fine birds, but I am also realistic enough to know that I am judged by the wrapping on my package. I want to express wholeness of myself in my appearance. My costumes are expressions of my state of mind, my freedom to express creativity without distinction of wealth, status, elitism, or sex-identified roles.

I am the masks I wear, and I do sometimes wear masks. I am the roles I play today and tomorrow. I am the games I use to manipulate other people, the masks I seek to hide my real feelings from others. My masks are like the colors of a chameleon that allow me to play one role today and another tomorrow, not insincerely, but not unconsciously either.

I am what I do for other people. I am a part of all the experiences I have engaged in with a helping hand. I am a part of the Peace Corps, the migrant workers I tried to help, the Heart Fund, United Way, Headstart, and the summer recreation program where I waited on tables. I am a part of the 4-H club I taught, the Boy Scouts I led, and the handicapped I helped. I know that across the world there is a universal desire for improved and decent standards of living, and for improved welfare and opportunities for children and adults.

I am a part of all that I see, all that I hear, and all that I read. I am wondering what astrology has going for it and why the anti-intellectual movements of the times are formed. I am influenced by the crime and violence, the bigotry and fighting that I see. I am affected by affluence and by the hunger and anguish of poverty. I am distressed by pollution and waste of resources, by rising costs, and unemployment. I am troubled by dishonesty in governments, by shoplifting in local stores, and by inferior and unsafe products in the market place. I am grateful that the majority of this world is not represented by these troublesome problems and that there are capable hands and minds to find solutions to these social issues. I am excited by all that is good about my country and my world.

I am becoming "me." My self image is becoming clearer. I can face my weaknesses without apology and accept my strengths for what they are. I know what I am and what I can be; and I want to be more than I am today!

What are my reactions to these statements? I'd like to write my own profile of self concepts including statements to which I can positively relate. I'd like to add original statements that encompass my own value system and have more personal meaning than those in the reaction-statement exercise.[19]

SELF-ACTUALIZATION

No serious attempt at self discovery would be complete without reexamining Maslow's hierarchy of needs (see Chapter Three). It may be helpful to review these needs and to determine how far up that ladder each of us has climbed. Few people actually take the time and trouble to discover their own resources and abilities in depth; yet, it is Maslow's basic concept that emotionally healthy people seek to improve themselves.[20] Most people remain only partially aware of their strengths and personality resources. It was a perceptive person who said, "If you want a helping hand, look for it at the end of your arm." Another apostle of success described big shots as "little shots . . . that kept on shooting."[21]

Examine the first rung of Maslow's ladder of needs. To what extent have basic physiological needs—food, air, and shelter—been satisfied? They obviously command first priority. Shelter in today's society is more than protection from the elements. It is a primary goal of many people and has earned an undisputed place in the list of commodities indirectly referred to as "the American way of life." Shelter means not only a house or apartment, mobile home or condominium; it means adequate space for each member of the group to develop, privately and collectively, the personality characteristics needed to interact with society throughout life. Housing adequacy may be judged more effectively when a person has been away for a period of time and, upon returning, examines the shelter with an unbiased view for ways of making more adequate personal and group use of space.

Safety needs

Freedom from fear, threat, danger, and deprivation are also basic to living. Genuine development of the self requires honest evaluation of the *status quo* and a philosophy that the *status quo* is not enough. Otto suggests listing evidences of attitudes.[22] For example, in a notebook small enough to keep near at all times, label one page, "What do I fear most?" Give some serious thought to this question. Be honest, for honesty and dissatisfaction are the seeds of progress and challenge in life.[23]

A productive exercise would be to write down, without evaluating *why*, all the "fears" a person feels—fear of a job loss, fear of failure, fear of not keeping a time commitment, and fear of being left out of a group. Continue the list for a number of days, perhaps a week, and then analyze the list for patterns. Consider them in light of all safety needs. Do the fears indicate social or financial insecurity? Do the fears indicate areas of weakness or do they indicate strengths that may be further developed? Fulmer tells the story of a man who said, when analyzing his own potentialities, that Mother Nature had handed him a lemon . . . and so he decided to make lemonade.[24]

Attitude

Attitude is often the primary difference between a strength and a weakness in human potential. It is easy to misinterpret a strength for a weakness and vice versa. Fulmer's laboratory mouse illustrates this view. It seems the mouse, on returning to his cage after an experiment, said to his wife, "I have the professor conditioned perfectly now. Every time I run through the maze, he gives me a piece of cheese."[25]

Make a list of personal strengths and weaknesses and then turn the list around and call the weaknesses strengths: think how each weakness might function as a strength. It is reasonable for a person—man or woman—with small children, to fear premature death. It is not reasonable to worry about and dwell upon death. The rational person protects dependents against financial losses occurring as a consequence of premature death, provides for distribution of wealth to loved ones, practices safety precautions when driving, and may even discuss and investigate burial alternatives. Fear of premature death may be called a weakness, but it is a strength when it causes positive action to eliminate stress and hardship upon loved ones if the fear becomes an actuality.

Affection

The person who truly knows himself will have experienced love, the third step in Maslow's ladder of self actualization. Love and belonging are essential components of effective individual and family living. Affection and companionship between mates and personality development of children are primary functions of the modern family.[26]

Social needs form the foundation of personal interaction and are instrumental in determining its quality. Often, a primary focus of the family with teenagers is a search for ways of satisfying social needs. A family that overlooks this level of need, within and outside the home, is failing to launch its young with the capacity to function as self-reliant, satisfied, and acceptable persons in society. Yet many people reach adulthood without having fulfilled their need for love, affection, acceptance, and a feeling of belonging. There are some who spend their entire lives searching for love and desiring to belong. Deprivation of love can be as disasterous to a person's development as deprivation of the more basic needs for safety and shelter.

People need to relate emotionally to other people. McClelland, et al., classified man's need for affiliation as one of three basic motivational drives that affect the nature of thoughts and accomplishments.[27] People have a natural craving for close interpersonal relationships with others. In addition to family life, many lifelong friendships satisfy this need. Lasting friendships are usually built through reciprocal trust, confidence, and interaction about shared interests.

Belonging involves outside managerial relationships. The division of labor within a family is, as it was with primitive people, a way of establishing working relationships, roles, and a hierarchy of interaction patterns among group members. Some conflict and disagreement is normal, and people must learn to deal with normal conflict. One well-adjusted woman, recognizing her need for releasing pent-up emotions, had a habit of wearing her apron backwards as a signal to her family that she was in a provocative mood. When her husband and children came home to find her with an apron on backwards, they were more careful of what they said and how they approached her. This family gradually developed a particularly high regard for the rights of others, an important requisite for achieving belongingness within a group.

Social movements aimed at separating division of labor from sex-identified roles are making some headway in freeing people to seek their desired or earned status of belonging within groups. Such movements strengthen the need for self discovery and self evaluation, and they impose individual responsibility to develop an accurate self image.

To have friends, a person must *be* a friend. Friends communicate, support, sympathize, display trust, show loyalty, appreciate companionship, generate warmth, and join the struggle for common causes to be counted truly as friends. Lasting friendships are usually closely associated with self esteem and self actualization.

Qualities of Self-Actualized People

Maslow places self esteem and self actualization at the top of his ladder, where needs get harder to satisfy. Unlike many psychologists who dwell on the abnormalities of personalities, Maslow described the psychologically healthy individual. He outlined the following characteristics of mentally healthy, self-actualized persons:[28]

1. They are *realistic.* They can accept the way things really are. Instead of dwelling on "what should be," self-actualized people accept themselves as they really are—flat feet, overweight, bunions, bifocals, and all. They see the natural world for what it really is. They are basically acceptors. They are neither self-satisfied nor content with the *status quo,* but because they accept themselves, they can accept other people as they are.

2. They are *not afraid* to get close to others. Although they are autonomous and independent, have an air of detachment, and a need for privacy, their appreciation of people and things is fresh rather than stereotyped. Because they feel secure and happy with themselves, they are not threatened by others and can afford to have deep interpersonal relationships with others, although these deep relationships are reserved for a special few.

3. They are efficient *judges of situations* and can accomplish more because they waste less time. They are problem-centered rather than

self-centered. They are able to solve problems more efficiently because of their ability to make decisions in realistic terms.

4. They are *appreciative* and *creative*. Unlike others who respond the way they have always responded, Maslow's self-actualizing people respond to problems with natural, logical solutions. They have the capacity to repeatedly appreciate the basic goods of life and to find excitement in everyday living. They have a philosophical rather than hostile sense of humor.

5. They *resist conformity* to the culture. These self-actualized people "march to a different drummer." They are self-reliant, make their own judgments, and are autonomous in thought and judgment because they feel good about themselves and generate confidence in others. They emanate the feeling of "I'm O.K., You're O.K."[29] They rely on their own behavioral standards and values and are more likely to set the pace for a group than to follow everyone else.

6. They are *willing to learn* from anyone. Their values and attitudes are democratic. Because self-actualized persons are confident and aware of their worth, they are not fearful of appearing uninformed. They are more interested in getting information and gaining understanding than in building a reputation for knowledgeability. In the words of Fulmer, Maslow's self-actualizing people realize "that it is better to blunder into learning than to learn nothing gracefully."[30]

Rogers was also interested in rational people, and consistently found the following four characteristics in emotionally mature people: confidence in their own ability and judgment, willingness to accept experiences for what they are, greater reliance on self than on society or friends, and willingness to continue to grow as persons.[31]

It is not surprising to learn that only a few people achieve this level of complete self-actualization. To know thyself is a difficult task. It requires, above all, honesty; and it is probably harder to be completely honest with oneself than it is with anyone else. Self inquiry is a painful process in which life must be viewed with new perceptions of awareness.[32]

Honesty is a relative term. It implies a willingness to assert what is perceived to be true. How accurate is self reflection? If perception is the root of honesty, those who are most in need of self discovery are least capable of achieving it because a reasonably objective view of self is closely aligned with mental health.

Achievement of self actualization may be promoted through practice of the following concepts: good physical health, a healthy self concept, knowing and accepting personal strengths and weaknesses, a creative and stimulating environment for existence, a positive attitude toward decision making, habitual exercise of desired personality traits, conscious effort to eliminate personal weaknesses that constrain growth, constructive compatible outlets for interests and energies, attacking the causes rather than symptoms of misbehavior in personality improvement, and seeking assistance from trained specialists in human development.[33] Some steps toward self realization may need the assistance of a psychiatrist.

Two final concepts are critical: (1) to achieve self actualization, a person must have a strong desire to become his or her own best self; and (2) self realization involves the ability to relate constructively to others and to achieve a balance between maintaining independence and yielding to authority.[34]

Where Am I Going?

Setting goals for self development is an essential part of developing usable personal resources. There is something quite remarkable about people who know where they want to go: they usually get there. It would be difficult to reach San Francisco from Los Angeles, California, if a person headed south instead of north. Yet many people approach life with few long-range goals and even fewer plans for self growth and development. There are families who never consciously determine the direction they expect family life to take.

Butler placed people in three classes: the few who make things happen, the many who watch things happen, and the overwhelming majority who have no idea what has happened.[35] Of these three groups, the first is obviously the only group to know where its members want to go. It takes much effort and direction to make things happen—a determined path to follow.

Odiorne says management means action, not reaction, and a manager must be more than a problem solver.[36] Managers are goal setters. Odiorne's ideal manager sets a course, envisions things that should happen, and thinks through the possible paths through which the goal can be reached. This manager is active in thought as well as deed. Personal talents are utilized to accomplish established goals.

The person who sets development of human resources as a goal and works actively for growth should eventually reap a greater capacity for living and achieving. It is the nature of human resources to expand, rather than diminish, with use. The more a person does, the more he is able to do, given adequate energy and health. There are, however, inevitable risks in the early stages of self development, and temporary setbacks can be anticipated. When setbacks are anticipated, failure does not bring about the utter emptiness and destruction of self esteem. Willingness to accept risk is the first step toward growth.

Fear of failure demands a heavy price. It is a powerful obstacle to development of personal resources. Any deviation from the customary patterns of living can create uneasiness and disruption and will almost invariably affect others. Growth of even one member of a family group can affect the patterns of interaction with other family members. In fact, one of the more effective methods of self-actualization is the use of a second person as a sounding board for ideas and for the strenthening of a healthy self esteem.[37]

Failure to search out and utilize the attitudes which are latent within a person or those talents of which he is clearly aware often leads to a sense of guilt. This guilt, in turn, serves as a barrier to creative living. Waste of potential has both psychological and physiological ramifications. Otto reports that unused energy available for developing human resources is often channeled into self-destructive processes.[38] Conversely, he reports that the more a person develops potential, the more energy and capacity for creative living become available. Exploration of potentialities is not something that the self-renewing person can leave to chance. It must be set as a goal and pursued systematically and vigorously.[39]

WHICH RESOURCES TO DEVELOP?

It would be ideal for every member of each family group to develop all potential human resources to the fullest at the earliest possible date. It is impractical to suggest such an undertaking within a short period of time. Therefore, the logical approach is to start with a plan for developing the personal resources that are most crucial to successful management—those that seem to be causing the greatest amount of difficulty will give the greatest satisfaction. The following guidelines may prove useful in setting priorities for developing personal resources.

Develop the personal resources that are most crucial to successful management

Although there are many human resources used in the processes of management, studies of accomplished managers indicate that intelligence to discriminate between alternative activities and to focus upon those that will produce the greatest gains is essential.[40]

Intelligence, according to Woodworth, is closely related to intellect, but there must be some application of the intellect before a resource can be called intelligence.[41] The latter includes, not only ways of observing, understanding, thinking, remembering, and gaining knowledge, but also includes the use of these qualities for problem solving or reaching a goal.

Woodworth cites the ability to count as an example of intellectual activity that yields knowledge; but whether or not this knowledge is useful depends on its adaptability to the solution of problems at hand. When entertaining, the problem may be how to provide enough chairs for a roomful of guests. Counting the available chairs is intelligence, since it utilizes knowledge of how to count in the solution of a personal problem. It is intellect put to use, application of intellectual abilities to accomplish tasks.[42] Counting the appropriate number of plates and flatware before taking them to the dining room is an intelligent aid to setting the table; but counting the cookbooks on a shelf is scarcely an intelligent way to prepare a main dish.

To identify the essentials of a problem, to see the situation as a whole, to see relations between past, present, and future, and to apply previously acquired knowledge to new issues or to new goals requires the use of intelligence. The latter is one resource nearly everyone can further develop because possibilities for knowing more about almost everything are practically unlimited, and the problems to which this knowledge can be applied are also unlimited in most people's lives.

Judgment is one of the most valuable of human resources used in management. Judgment is an ability to distinguish between relationships or alternatives, a capacity to make reasonable appraisals that enables fairness in weighing facts in a situation, and to see the issue in relation to the conflicts. The ability to weigh critically, to analyze, to evaluate, and to interpret experiences is of vital importance in making decisions. Judgment can eliminate costly mistakes, expand relationships, and reduce embarassing predicaments. Judgment is acquired through experience and grows slowly but can be purposefully developed at any age.

Adaptability is that human quality which contributes to flexibility in living. Success in meeting daily problems depends largely on the ability to adapt to changing circumstances. The human environment is not static; conditions and demands change from day to day. Plans must frequently be shifted or given up. People move and change jobs. They marry, but some divorce and remarry. People lose their jobs. Loved ones die. Conflicts must be resolved, and difficulties must be overcome. Failure to meet changing conditions reflects an inflexibility that stifles growth and progress and causes a lack of harmony within the person and with his surroundings.

Enthusiasm is another characteristic of successful managers. This quality is partially a byproduct of well-balanced mental and physical health, of temperament, of a conviction of the worth of the undertaking.

Enthusiasm is contagious. It stirs others to become interested in an activity and stimulates people to higher levels of proficiency and productivity. A sustained, lively, and healthy enthusiasm is preferable to erratic enthusiasm that may be bubbling or excessive at one time but nonexistant at another time. The latter may be exploitive and suggests emotional immaturity. The manager who is enthusiastic about work imbues others with this spirit. Through encouragement, an enthusiastic manager develops positive excitement in others and is, thereby, able to accomplish more in life than the unenthused manager.

Initiative is not a magical power bestowed upon a few. It is an ability coupled with a trained instinct to introduce needed action and to follow through to produce some desired result.

One evening, following a class reunion, a group of successful senior citizens were visiting. After a series of success stories, somebody posed a challenging question to the group. "What's the biggest financial mistake you ever made?" There were a variety of answers. One had invested in the stock market at the wrong time. Another had failed to change jobs when he was offered the chance to go with a larger company. Finally, someone said, "The biggest mistake I ever made was all the opportunities I missed because I decided too late to try them." Although successful managers do not dwell on hindsight, they evaluate past experiences, store these lessons, and apply conclusions to new opportunities. From past experiences, good managers learn decisive action.

Initiative is willingness to take the lead, interest in finding new methods, and contribution of ideas. Initiative is prompt action. Odiorne described five characteristics that are basic qualities of people with initiative and pointed out that most of these traits are acquired and can be taught to others. These five characteristics follow.[43]

- *Inner drive,* a vigorous and positive approach with a desire for improvement.
- *Goal Orientation,* the ability to identify important rather than trivial goals. This is a "first-things-first" way of dealing with priorities for action, a way of eliminating bottlenecks that delay other activities.
- *Tough-mindedness* to encourage a person working at less than his best, to persevere with ideas, and to impose ideas if there is no other way to assure progress.
- *Inspiration,* skill in instilling a desire to excel in others by building a climate in which ideas can be applied. Inspiration also includes listening patiently, probing to help the initiator develop his ideas fully, and making it worthwhile for a person to excel at tasks.
- *Intelligent action* requires a goal that is realistic and attainable and a plan to arrive at the goal in an orderly fashion.

Perseverance is another valuable quality of managers. This characteristic combines courage and patience. The person who possesses it believes in the inherent value of the idea or task at hand and is willing to work for its achievement. Perseverance requires courage to face facts, to act in full knowledge instead of blindly, and to see the relationship of short-term goals and less-challenging routine jobs to the accomplishment of the more important and the more distant goals.

Perseverance is steadfastness, the quality of holding to a course of action, belief, or purpose without giving up. It depends on conviction and determination and is often the main difference between success and failure in management. Dreams are ideas that have not yet been put to use. Those who have the ability to set goals, but lack perseverance, seldom reach their goals.

Communicativeness involves the conveying of accurate meaning to others. It is essential in working with people and putting plans into action. The ability to successfully communicate within the family leads to the sharing of knowledge, feelings, desires, and experiences. Lack of or misinterpretation of communication among family members often leads to delay in attainment of goals.

One busy young couple began to furnish an apartment. The overall goal of a tastefully decorated apartment furnished with durable, well-designed furniture, within a limited budget was agreed upon. After the couple had purchased a sofa and chairs for the living room, the wife began looking for a coffee table. She narrowed her selection down to two Danish modern teakwood tables before taking her husband to see them and to help in the final decision. "Neither of these will do," he said. "All my life I've stumbled over the legs of coffee tables because my feet are size 12. In my own home, I want a coffee table with recessed legs so I don't have to bang my feet on the legs when I sit down." The woman thought, "Well, why didn't you *say* so and save me all this time?" Then she remembered she hadn't said much about the style of the table either. Their only communication had been about the cost and the wood. Why is it that people often fail to communicate with those they are nearest to and with whom they spend most of their time?

Communication, like good clean air, is often taken for granted until its absence makes life uncomfortable. Fulmer calls communication an idea transplant.[44] Almost every aspect of everyday living revolves around the efforts of people to transmit ideas to others. Communication is essential for job success, for purchase decisions, and for education. Although today's information explosion causes some communication overload, lack of effective communication between those who live or work closely together is often of great personal negative consequence. How the family communicates with the community, the society, and the government, however, is equally important.

As described in the next chapter, all modes of communication should be improved if the quality of management is to be strengthened. Such modes include not only verbal behavior such as speaking, writing, listening, and reading; but nonverbal behavior that is equally crucial to effective communication:

facial expression, posture, tone of voice, visible signs of emotion, touch, and body motion.[45] Communication is such an important human resource for management that the next chapter is devoted to understanding and strengthening communication.

Improve the personal resources that seem to be causing the greatest amount of difficulty

In addition to developing resources crucial to successful management, priority should be given to those resources that cause bottlenecks in goal attainment. Self control, commitment, empathy, and work habits are human resources that often impede progress. A plan for developing personal resources may well begin with these four characteristics. Ways of developing two of these resources are explored as follows.

Work habits may either impede or implement management and are often the cause of job stagnation. Habit is a predisposition to use resources in a certain way, a constant, often unconscious inclination to perform tasks in a particular way. Habit is an established routine and is acquired through frequent repetition.

There is evidence to indicate that the average healthy person is deeply habit-bound; daily personal activities are dominated by routines; vocational functioning is also heavily routinized.[46] Habit appears to have four distinguishable dimensions: daily routines, habitual modes of perceiving, habitual modes of thinking, and habitual modes of feeling—emotional responses to recurrent situations.[47] Although some habits are purposeful and appropriate, many habits impede development of human resources. The person who watches the same television programs day after day, rationalizing that they are favorites, seldom uses television as an educational tool and seldom explores new or better programs for entertainment. The eating patterns of many people are so limited that they eat the same cereal for breakfast every morning and consider only five or six favorite dishes in the same two or three restaurants when eating away from home. The nutritional value of the habitually-chosen foods is seldom questioned. These are examples of the daily routine dimension of habit.

People who are only marginally aware of the landscape through which they travel to work illustrate how easily habitual perception dims awareness of surroundings. People who use habitual modes of thinking deepen some intellectual powers, but fail to develop others. There is a tranquility trap in becoming too comfortable with established ways of thinking.

When a person reacts in a similar manner each time he or she is confronted with a certain situation, "habit emotion" may develop—a habitual mode of feeling or a routine emotional response to recurrent situations.[48] Habit emotions can inhibit personal development if the emotion elicits an inappropriate response. For example, many people habitually react with suppressed anger and confusion to criticism, whether constructive or damaging.

Firmly entrenched clusters of habits, including habit emotions, may function subconsciously. A habit-ridden person may restrict his choices and deprive himself of new experiences, spontaniety, and flexibility. Creativity and adaptability are thereby stifled. People who participate in many experiences but open themselves only to a narrow band of feelings or emotions tend to become increasingly controlled by their habits. A husband and wife who habitually go out for dinner every Friday may fall into a pattern of going to the same small circle of restaurants and ordering approximately the same foods at each one. The experience can become what Otto calls a pseudo-pleasure.[49] Cumulative exposure to pseudo-pleasurable experiences continued by habit long after the vitalizing, enjoyable feelings have diminished seems to destroy the capacity for real pleasure.

Vocational routines are often even more rigid and firmly entrenched than habitual patterns of everyday living. Entering by the same door, using the same greetings to the same people day in and day out, and following the same habitual modes of thinking can easily lead to bland, unimaginative, sterile feelings about one's job and to stagnation in work.

Not all habits are deterrents to personal development or to promotions on the job. Some habits are desirable precisely because they save time for use in more profitable and more enjoyable ways. Programming the human body to accomplish specific tasks routinely without conscious thought releases thinking for fresh decisions. Thus habit may have a marked influence on management. The more tasks a person can refine and relegate to the point of routine habit, the more mental resources are released for other activities. The danger lies in becoming a slave to ineffective habit, in allowing the mind and emotions to be mesmerized. Effective work habits can be a tremendous aid in personal life as well as employment.

Work habits seem to be developed from four main sources:[50]

- Early training—schools and family,

- Experience on the job—especially earliest experiences,

- Habits of peers—friends and neighbors, work associates.

- Expectations of family—particularly those of parents.

Some principles of changing work habits include: observing and analyzing the current work pattern, replacing ineffective habits with more useful ones, establishing reasons for change, observing effective work patterns of others, changing the time or location of the task, or eliciting participation from others.

Utilizing these principles of changing work habits, a parent, wishing to improve the study habits of a child, might combine the following strategies:

- Observe the child's study habits for a few days.

- Try studying, himself, in the same location and under similar conditions of lighting, time, posture, and noise interference.

- Show the child the possible areas of change, for example, no centralized place for pencils, paper, books, inadequate lighting, poor posture which decreases mental attitude, or studying in bed which unconsciously is associated with relaxation.

- Set a good example by organizing family reading material near a well lighted, comfortable reading chair.

- Help the child substitute workable habits of study for less useful methods. Set the time for study so the child is not sleepy or hungry. Change the location. Provide a desk where books, pencils, reference materials, and proper lighting are centralized.

- Establish motivation to change study habits—higher school grades, increased knowledge, or other rewards.

Honesty and commitment to a task begin the improvement of work habits. Chart 7.1 contains clues to personal work habits that impede management and personal advancement. An honest self appraisal on the questionnaire may help the reader to identify problem areas associated with work habits.

Commitment is an emotional and intellectual pledge to some course of action and, as such, is a highly motivating human resource. When the Green Bay Packers hired Bart Starr as head coach and general manager, he was being compared to his former coach, Vince Lombardi, and those who had preceeded him as head coach. Starr, quiet and religious, and a student of the game, seemed poles apart from Lombardi, a fierce, inspirational leader. But Starr, the football hero turned businessman and television commentator, cautioned that there was more to him than met the eye. "On the football field I'll cut your heart out," he said with a smile. He added, the greatest lesson he had learned from

Chart 7.1 What Kind Of Worker Are You?[51]

Are you:	Always	Some- times	Never
A BustleBeaver? Lacks time for leisure, community activity, or family recreation.			
A ProcrastoOffer? Puts things off then rushes at the last minute to get things done.			
A PrissyPerfectionist? Wears everyone out with unnecessary work.			
A PapyroManiac? Accumulates papers compulsively.			
A Filophiliac? Arranges and classifies papers and references continuously.			
A Phonophiliac? Possesses a passion for talking on the telephone and has several phones.			
A Paper Putterer? Picks up and shuffles papers forever.			
A PlayItByEarofiliac? Lets things happen rather than plans.			
A WortWorrier? Spends so much time thinking about what has to be done that there is no time to do it.			
A Merry Martyr? Glories in being exhausted at the end of the day.			
A Master Manager? Makes things happen the desired way.			

Lombardi was that the quality of a man's life is in direct proportion to his commitment to excellence no matter what his chosen field of endeavor.[52]

Commitment is often the missing link in the lives of many people. Less than ten percent of the participants of the University of Utah's human potentiality research indicated that they had ever written their life goals, listed their values, or actively committed themselves to a persistent cause.[53] A person with no binding commitments to any cause is like a boat adrift without a rudder. Lack of commitment or fear of becoming personally involved—even with one's own life—causes operation at only a fraction of its true capacity. Commitment to excellence is rare. Those who have definite commitments usually have a limited number of goals, and these are often self-centered. Some are family-centered goals, but few people have commitments to a purpose larger than self. Yet it is possible that man must give himself to something greater if he is to fulfill his destiny.[54] Commitment to even limited life goals is helpful in mobilizing personal resources. Vast energies become available to those who serve a cause, whatever that cause may be. Commitment is the first step in motivation, but it is more than a fleeting interest; it is binding and lasting interest coupled with directive action.

Commitment and motivation may be undercut by childhood experiences that constrict self image, by interpersonal family relationships that mold personalities into habitual patterns, or by social, cultural, and vocational pressures that create excessive demands. Sleep is also a constrictor of personal development and is one of life's great thieves. When sleep is an escape, there is usually little commitment to vitalize living and to temper the emotions. It appears that as dedication and creative commitment to life increase, the need for sleep decreases. Thomas A. Edison, Einstein, and many other intensely creative people are said to have required little sleep.

A simple and logical way to begin developing human resources is to commit oneself to the task; but commitment cannot be dictated: it must be felt! When it is felt, it is directive. It consumes a person's thoughts, motivates action, and demands perseverence. It is vitalizing; it gives meaning to action and purpose to living. Commitment is a necessary ingredient in management.

Develop the personal resources that produce the greatest amount of satisfaction

Creativity, skills, talents, appearance, and friendliness are human resources that can bring a high degree of personal satisfaction and are, thus, logical candidates for purposeful development. *Creativity* is not a psychic wonder drug, a powerful, painless prescription for all ills. It is a revolt against conformity. It is part of a growing resistance to the everyday, everybody pattern that society tends to impose as the price of success.

Creativity is not intelligence alone, nor just mastery of a craft, and it is not always predictable. A scientist may schedule lab hours, but cannot schedule the time of innovations or best ideas.[55] Nor is it desirable to be creative in all endeavors, for creativity in spelling would scarcely bring accolades from a spelling teacher. There is not much difference between a creative accountant and an embezzler. Judgment is an important factor in channeling creativity.

How would you describe a creative person? One who is original, imaginative, expressive? When Gregory drew up his list of characteristics of creative persons, he included a number of unexpected ones: believes nothing is impossible; has written and spoken language fluency; has sensitivity in isolating problems; believes that truth, as man understands it, is relative; thinks in abstract figures, design, and constructs; is flexible and adaptive in making changes to achieve goals; is open-minded; vacillates from periods of creativity to periods of judgment; is enthusiastic, self-actualized, strong-willed, broadly experienced, goal oriented; and is often a poor speller.[56]

Popular beliefs tie creativity to eccentricity. However, Gardner, Jay, Fulmer, and others seem to agree that there are certain responsibilities associated with creativity and that efficiency is as much a characteristic of creative people as creativeness is of the best managers.[57] According to Jay, people who flaunt their creativeness to conceal their laziness might well have their poetic licenses revoked.[58] Unlike the exhibitionist who rejects convention in matters that will give him the most attention, the truly creative person, as a rule, chooses to conform in routine, everyday matters of life such as speech, dress, and manners, reserving his independence for what really concerns him—his area of creative activity. Some people hide behind the word "creative" to disguise bad habits, using creativity as an excuse for overspending, slovenly appearance, tardiness, evasiveness, or lethargy.

Creativity requires openness, independence and flexibility of character, zeal and drive, order in chaos, confidence, self assertiveness, and determination—an intense and sustained absorption in changing something. Creativity is almost always focused on change. Most creative people change in spite of, not because of, popular opinion and because they are willing to investigate the obvious. The truly creative person is willing to endure popular opposition because of personal faith in his capability to do the things that he wants and needs to do in the chosen creative endeavor.

Creativity does not occur in a vacuum. According to Fulmer, "We need not decide which parent is more important (in producing the offspring)—but we are selling ourselves short if we fail to recognize the teamwork of creativity."[59] Creative people accept and build upon the inventions of others. Sometimes they put existing parts together backwards in an effort to see new relationships, and they use the productive teamwork of others.

There is some degree of creativity in all persons, and as with intelligence, only a small percentage of creative potential is used. Research indicates that creativity, like the qualities of character, temperament, and intellect that contribute to it, is formed in childhood and depends to a degree on family relationships. Certain environments smother creative impulses and other kinds promote them. A family climate that can nurture creativity will usually contain many of the following characteristics and may serve as a check list for establishing a climate for creativity in work groups.

CHARACTERISTICS OF A CREATIVE ENVIRONMENT

_____ Allows open communication between members and with the outside

_____ Provides space and materials for experimenting with new ideas

_____ Encourages self direction and definition of personal goals

_____ Accommodates change but does not encourage change for the sake of change alone

_____ Allows members to be themselves

_____ Utilizes flexible scheduling

_____ Allows objective task assignment without stereotyped sex-role connotations

_____ Encourages freedom of thought and inquiry.[60]

A creative environment is an interesting place to live or visit.

Specific research techniques used to promote creative abilities were grouped by Fulmer into three headings: analytical (logical attack), free association (the blue-sky technique), and forced relationships (the systems approach). A fourth approach combined the first three.[61] Most of these techniques involve some form of brainstorming or collective listing over a period of time, prediction of effectiveness of each course of action, and model building.

Fulmer's list of eleven "creative blockbusters" can be used to develop creativity as a resource. He says the creative block may be cracked by: isolating the problem, avoiding excessive narrowing of the problem, defining terms, observing the problem from every possible angle, putting the parts together backwards, investigating the obvious, not worrying about conforming to the adopted pattern, forgetting practicality and economy until what ought to be done is established, not trying to reinvent current ideas, not being nice or polite if it means sacrificing creativity, and asking a nonexpert.[62]

Build your own success pyramid

John Wooden, for many years a basketball coach at U.C.L.A., built a highly successful reputation among his players through the use of a pyramid of success. His pyramid was originated and developed in the late 1930's for his own self improvement as a high school teacher and coach. He believes adherence to the blocks of the pyramid can stimulate people to be the best they are capable of becoming, regardless of how others may judge them. He defined success, the object of this pyramid, as "peace of mind which is a direct result of self–satisfaction in knowing you did your best to become the best that you are capable of becoming."[63] Wooden utilized, as the cornerstones of his success pyramid, the characteristics of industriousness and enthusiasm and added friendship, loyalty, and cooperation to form the foundation. Self control, alertness, initiative, and intentness were near the foundation. The sides of his pyramid were formed by ambition, adaptability, resourcefulness, integrity, honesty, and sincerity. His explanation of competitive greatness as "When the going gets tough, the tough get going," and his admonition to "be at your best when your best is needed," is challenging.[64]

To build your own success pyramid is even more challenging! The following Management Pyramid illustrates one approach to building a success model that exemplifies human resources needed in effective management. In the model, the foundation consists of five value-oriented qualities important to successful management. The next two levels of the pyramid are built from work habit characteristics needed in management. The fourth level consists of people-oriented traits affecting the quality of management. The uppermost building block utilizes a self-actualizing quality of management. Success may be defined as satisfaction derived from use of resources in achieving goals. The value of developing one's own success model lies in the commitment of the designer to a hierarchy of human resources that he believes is important to a particular goal—in this case, successful management.

Many human traits and characteristics are important to successful management. Each resource can be developed and improved through conscious effort. Each has tremendous potential to raise the quality of life of individuals, families, and societies. Each exists within people to varying degrees. Each lies waiting to be harnessed for activity of achieving goals.

How to Increase Satisfaction from Human Resources

To some, achieving greater potential means the attainment of wealth and riches. To others, it is love and affection, a heightening of personal awareness for living, and the intellectual resources to cope with heightened awareness. Whatever its meaning, an understanding of the nature of human resources,

Chart 7.2 A Management Success Model.

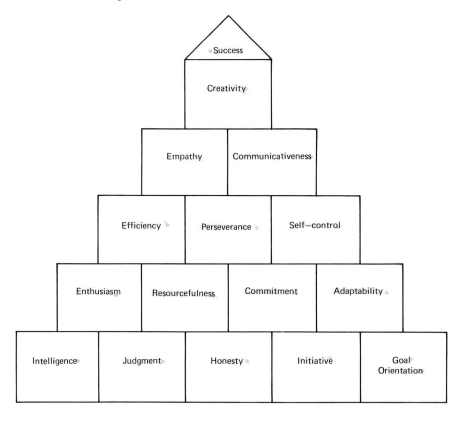

principles of human resource development, and techniques for managing human resources should help individuals develop them.

NATURE OF HUMAN RESOURCES

Human resources expand as they are used, like a muscle that becomes stronger with use. The more opportunity a person has to make decisions and use personal resources, the more able he becomes to assume managerial responsibilities, and the more enjoyment he can derive from life. Human resources can be expanded through a variety of experiences. Through deliberate exercise and refinement of a human resource, such as honesty, its quality and potential quantity are increased. Every time a person tells the truth, it becomes easier to use the truth as an explanation for subsequent situations.

Personalities change slowly, and a person may be unaware of the new heights to which resources have been developed until some situation activates them. The capacity for self development is immense. Undeveloped human potential may be the greatest inhumanity man brings upon himself. Development of human resources can bring a new quality of freshness into all experience, including everyday existence. To deny this potential ignores the realities of life. In describing man's potentialities and the future, Otto said:[65]

A man is not his past record; he is his potential—what he wishes to be, what he wills to be, and what he is actively striving for. A man's past need not determine his future; what matters is what he is now and what he chooses to become . . .
Your potentialities represent your undiscovered self—the search for and the discovery of this self can leaven the journey through life with joy and transcendent purpose. By becoming truly committed to the search for the undiscovered self, man grows into something larger than himself, which touches, at least by implication, all of mankind.

With the exception of time, human resources can be expanded or improved in their application to management. The utility of even time is expanded through the refinement of other human resources. Many management problems involve personal adjustments and relationships. A parent who can be calm when personal conflicts arise is more capable of guiding a situation intelligently than one who has little self control. Self management is required to work amicably and harmoniously with other members of the family and to handle emotional entanglements without excessive display of anger. The effective manager is one who can stand up under strain.

Nonhuman resources may decrease, increase, or retain the same value if saved. What happens if human resources are saved? As an arm bound too long in a cast loses its agility, human resources decrease in value if they are not used. The only way to save and expand human resources is to use them.

Human resources interact with nonhuman resources in the system of management. Empathetic understanding of differences among family members and their probable reactions to situations is a great aid in solving many money-management problems and to reducing friction and disappointment that frequently occur when economic resources are limited. Skills can be substituted for paid services. Managers who know what they and their families want from life can improve their uses of human resources to attain goals, maintain standards, realize values, and meet human needs.

Human resources are, however, not completely interchangeable with nonhuman resources. It is not always possible to substitute a human for a nonhuman resource. Although a person has developed skill and speed in walking, it may not be practical to substitute this skill for a daily 20 mile drive to work.

Human resources are usually abundant; they are plentiful in the potential rather than developed stage. The adequacy of supply depends upon development.

PRINCIPLES OF HUMAN RESOURCE DEVELOPMENT

Although knowledge of the development of the human potential is still exploratory, the evidence of experience and observation leads to the following tentative conclusions regarding human resource development:

- Human resources can be improved. Seldom, if ever, does a person utilize all the potential human resources at his or her disposal. Developing and using this enormous reserve of potential is the great challenge of the age.

- Personal development requires personal commitment. It is possible to stimulate growth from outside the individual, but conscious development of resources comes when the outside stimulus motivates internal commitment to expand potential. Commitment opens the door to personal development and provides dedication to achieve human potentialities.

- Habit is both a deterrent and an aid to the development of human resources. Habit limits perception and prevents change. Growth is change. When habit is used to simplify daily routine so creative resources may be devoted to personal development, it then becomes an aid to development of latent resources.

- Change involves risk of personal security. Fear of failure and risk of personal security leave many human capabilities untapped. The person who wishes to develop human resources must be willing to accept risk and temporary setbacks for greater, longer-lasting satisfaction of fulfilling goals.

- Effort required for change and personal development increases with age. Children expect change. Young people thrive on and openly court change. During middle age, the greatest threat to lifelong learning occurs. Complacency can become too comfortable. Mesmerized by the idea of comfort and security, personalities begin to slowly die from disuse.

- Personal development is slow and costly in time. Like values, personalities change gradually and require repeated experiences to develop desired characteristics.

- Development of human resources involves broadening relationships. Creation of purposeful, multiple relationships helps to develop human potential. No one in today's society can exist in a vacuum for very long. Fixed relationships demand little beyond habit and routine ways of reacting. Meeting and interacting with new personalities requires greater use of human resources and, thus, challenges growth.

- Change resulting from outside stimuli is frequently more forceful and compelling than that prompted from internal motivation. Travel tends to shake people out of apathy. Crises produce unimagined personal resources. A move, a marriage, or a change of job are all forms of outside stimuli that force changes in routine and open the door to personal resource development. Few people are sufficiently motivated, without some prompting from outside sources, to overhaul personal traits or characteristics. The person who seeks growth will, however, use outside stimuli to remove the callousness that naturally protects the self and will develop sensitivity to change.

- Human resources are influenced by the environment in which people live. If man is to be thought of as a whole, other than as the sum of his characteristics and traits, all aspects, including the environment, must be analyzed to direct the needed changes.

- The more human resources a person develops, the greater is his or her capacity for continual development. The belief here is that other human resources, like muscles, may be developed through the exercise of chosen resources which will produce growth.

INVESTING IN HUMAN CAPITAL

Is all this work and risk worth the reward? For those who are satisfied with the *status quo,* perhaps not. For those who would not allow their capabilities to diminish and their personalities to die of "habititis," investment in human capital is a most profitable investment. No relationship is as permanent as the one a person has with his own personality. Operation "talent salvage," to assist young people in achieving the promise within them, is worthwhile. But youth are not unique in their need for education, vocational training, and guidance toward self actualization. People of all ages can profit from capital investment. But what kind of investment? What is the investment to produce?

Consider potential *for what*—capabilities, capacities and characteristics for what? For greater monetary return through increased abilities, talents, and skills? For more effective and satisfying relationships with other people—within the family, with friends and neighbors, or associates on the job? For a higher level of living for the nation? For a society in which resources are treated as precious possessions to be developed for the greatest good for all? Is investment in self awareness, self knowledge, self realization, self renewal, or self actualization investment in human capital?

Investment in human capital includes all activities that increase human resources. Using this definition, the concept of investment in human capital may be expanded beyond the customary reference to education as an income-producing investment to include investment in any resource that can increase satisfaction. Investment in education, health, and career-related knowledge and skills are, without a doubt, investments in human capital because they relate to the future monetary income potential of a person or family.[66]

There are examples in research and professional literature of investment in human capital that influences psychic income—satisfaction. Schultz opened the door to this broader view of investment in human capital when he called the satisfaction that people get from education, the consumption component of capital investment.[67] Burk further refined this theory when she identified the forms of consumption-oriented investment in human capital as: (1) basic education that indirectly affects capacity for satisfaction from consumption, (2) managerial knowledge and skills required to allocate family financial resources, (3) consumer technology or knowledge of attributes of products and services and how to use them in meeting the needs and wants of family members, (4) knowledge and skills in home production of goods and services for family consumption, including such services as maintenance of household durables, clothing, and standards in meal preparation, (5) capacity to learn and innovate, and (6) human value development related to consumption.[68]

Although the concept of investment in human capital has not previously been applied to activities that contribute to success in home-related work or personal living, there is no reason why it should not. It is reasonable to consider investment in any human resource that will increase managerial ability and, thereby, increase satisfaction, as an investment in human capital. Establishing a satisfying life style is more challenging and rewarding than simply making a living.

Managing Human Resources

Use of resources determines the degree of satisfaction derived from possessing them. Understanding basic concepts for managing resources can yield greater satisfaction from their use. However, in this chapter the concepts are discussed primarily in terms of human resources.

RESOURCE CHOICE AND GOAL ATTAINMENT

This concept specifies "most appropriate" not "most efficient." The most appropriate resource is not always the most efficient if the goal is to further develop human resources. It can be more efficient for one person to do all household tasks and, thereby, become most proficient at housekeeping. But other members of the family would not learn to care for the home if this practice was continued, and the energy of the one person could be overtaxed.

Learning to make decisions is a vital step in management and can be taught to children by repeatedly guiding them through decision situations, even by creating the situation. Note that the word resources is plural in the concept. This is because one human resource is seldom used alone. Human resources are used in clusters. Decision making, for example, requires this sort of cluster—time, energy, intelligence, skills, perseverance, and others depending on the complexity of the decision.

If the goal is new clothing for a party and time is limited, the tendency is to buy the clothing. But not just any garment will do. There are times when "the goal" is really several goals—to secure an item that will fit well, be especially becoming, and enhance the wearer's esteem among peers—at reasonable cost in resources. If the person sews, he or she could probably make a dress or suit for less money but it would take more time and would utilize more home space and equipment. If another family member also has a goal of helping the person learn to make clothes, the most appropriate resources would probably be a cooperative effort to make the item, although this may not be the most efficient way of providing the clothing.

REASONABLE RESOURCE INVESTMENT

What is reasonable—enough but not too much. Consider how much of any resource is reasonable to invest for the return. With savings, it is often impractical to invest in high-risk ventures that offer low returns. Likewise, human resources should be considered in terms of the potential return. There is a tendency for people with large blocks of time and particularly high standards to overinvest human resources. Of course, overinvesting or underinvesting is often a matter of judgment, but the quality and quantity other people invest is one measure for comparison.

Drucker's point that timing of resource input is important has particular meaning with human resources. Larger amounts of human resources are usually needed to "get going" and to learn, after which smaller amounts will produce similar results.[69] To increase output, Malone and Malone caution against stopping short of the most efficient effort. They also caution against wasting resources by exceeding the optimum.[70] With practice, the utility of human resources can be increased to affect the amount of human resource input needed to produce the same or better output. A person learning to cook will have to invest more time, energy, intelligence, and decision-making skill in food preparation than would an experienced cook.

How many words per minute of accurate copy should a secretary be expected to produce? How long should it take a teenage boy to make his bed? With human resources, the matter of standards must be considered with clusters of resources such as equipment, working conditions, and human resources including knowledge, skill, and motivation. Guidelines can be set and standards established, and many have been, to help the novice estimate "How well am I doing?" But the final determination of quantity of a resource to invest depends upon the individual and his life goals.

CONSIDER ALTERNATIVE USES OF RESOURCES

Time, as a human resource, imposes limitations on people's use of other resources in that it forces choices between how other resources will be used. Time spent swimming cannot be used for horseback riding. Time spent building friendships with others cannot be spent studying. Or can it? Studying together for a common cause might accomplish both goals better than some social activities.

It is possible to conserve environmental resources through appropriate use of human resources. Management of environmental resources is discussed in Chapter 13. Some mention of possible human resources that may be substituted for environmental ones is in order here. Walking or riding a bicycle will conserve natural resources and retain air quality in highly populated areas. Preserving homegrown or surplus food commodities reduces the need for commercially canned foods. Substituting talent for purchased items and making home repairs that will reduce heat loss are but a few possibilities to conserve environmental resources through substitution of human resources. How many others could be added to the list? As human resources are increased, their possibilities for substitution are also increased.

Because many resources have more than one use and because human resources are not consumed with use (except for time), alternative uses of human resources are almost unlimited. It has been said that the most binding decision a person makes is probably choice of occupation. To a large extent, occupation determines income and often prescribes social standing. It surely affects level of living because it limits the economic resources available for buying goods and services. Think of possible alternatives available in career choice. Developing skills to succeed in more than one occupation can increase likelihood of achieving satisfaction.

There are three ways of considering alternative uses of resources: consider the total supply, consider their utility, or consider the satisfaction derived from their use. Increasing any one of these can increase the satisfaction from goal attainment.

BALANCE RESOURCE CHOICES

A balance of interests stimulates and refreshes other resources to bring a sense of balance to life and to promote greater satisfaction from resource use. Balance is achieved by choosing enough of some resources to counter others. "Too much work makes Johnny a dull boy," is an age-old parable, but it should also be remembered that too much play would also make Johnny uninteresting.

While balance can best be determined by the person whose human resources are being used, most experts agree that community needs as well as basic cultural interests provide ballast to life. Balance occurs when human resources are allocated in satisfying proportions to a variety of personal values, needs, and interests, such as those defined as basic cultural values by Hoyt: comfort, aesthetics, empathy, environmental control, intellect, gregariousness, and satisfaction of physical demands.[71]

COMBINE GROUP RESOURCES

Human resources are applicable to organizations as well as to individuals. Sharing resources means sharing responsibilities for goal attainment; it could mean both specialization and group action. There is strength in joining with others for the good of the group. What one person may lack, another may have. By sharing responsibility in group action, it is possible to observe ways of developing latent personal resources. Self confidence is usually bolstered by the group, and competition is lessened.

Many nonhuman resources are shared by the family—money, houses, cars, and appliances. Aren't human resources shared? If the income derived from work is considered a family resource, why not consider also the earning power of all family members as a family resource? Many community resources are primarily human resources—police and fire protection and government at various levels. These resources are created by cooperative human concern to serve community needs. Work associated with maintaining house and family is a shared resource. Differing needs may require more than an equal share of an individual's resources. Differing interests and capabilities may allow more of a resource to be contributed by one member of a group. This is specialization partially required by technological development. Group needs, whether they be family or society, can be served more effectively by combining group resources.

Summary

This chapter is based on a philosophy of personal fulfillment through self improvement. Effective development and utilization of all available human resources, without limiting qualities available to society, was its focus. The importance of a healthy self concept and methods of achieving self actualization were explored. A three-step personal development plan was outlined. It included personal resources that:

- are crucial to successful management

- cause greatest difficulty

- can give the possessor the greatest satisfaction

The unique nature of human resources to expand, rather than diminish with use, was examined, along with five basic concepts for managing resources and some principles of human resource development.

If, after studying this chapter, each reader would commit him- or herself to life-long development of just one human resource, think what a change this would make in each person's life, and what a change it could produce in the world around us!

References

1. Otto, H. A., "New Light on Human Potential," in *Families of the Future,* Iowa State University Press, Ames, Iowa, (1972), pp. 14–25.

2. Gardner, J. W., *Self-Renewal,* Harper and Row, New York, (1963), pp. 9–10.

3. *Ibid.,* p. 4

4. Fiske, D. W., Maddi, S. R., *Functions of Varied Experience,* Dorsey Press, Homewood, Ill., (1961).

5. Gardner, J. W., *op. cit.,* p. 10.

6. Otto, H. A., *Guide to Developing Your Potential,* Charles Scribner's Sons, New York, (1967).

7. Otto, H. A., (ed.), *Human Potentialities: The Challenge and Promise,* Warren H. Green, St. Louis, Mo., (1968).

8. Fulmer, R. M., *The New Management,* Macmillan, New York, (1974).

9. Maltz, M., *Psycho-Cybernetics: A New Way to Get More Living Out of Life,* Pocket Books, New York, (1969).

10. *Ibid,* pp. vii, 4, 10.

11. *Ibid,* p. ix.

12. Gale, R. F., *Developmental Behavior,* Macmillan, New York, (1969).

13. Gardner, J. W., *op. cit.,* p. 3.

14. *Ibid,* p. 20.

15. Harbeson, G. E., *Choice and Challenge for the American Woman,* Schenkman, Cambridge, Mass., (1967).

16. Maltz, M., *op. cit.,* p. x.

17. *Ibid,* p. 32.

18. Hurlock, E., *Child Development* (4th ed.), McGraw-Hill, New York, (1964), pp. 743–744.

19. Developed from notes taken during an "idea swap meet" at Utah State University, Logan, Utah, Spring, 1972, to consider proposal of a new interdivisional personal management course. Persons involved included Drs. Alison Thorne, Jay Skidmore, and Ann Rice.

20. Maslow, H. H., *Toward a Psychology of Being,* D. Van Nostrand, Princeton, N.J., (1962).

21. Fulmer, R. M., *op. cit.,* p. 106.

22. Otto, H. A., *op. cit.,* pp. 236–239.

23. Moustakas, C. E., *Creativity and Conformity,* D. Van Nostrand, New York, (1967).

24. Fulmer, R. M., *op. cit.,* pp. 107–109.

25. *Ibid.,* p. 95.

26. Lippeatt, S. F., and Brown, H. I., *Focus and Promise of Home Economics: A Family Oriented Perspective,* Macmillan, New York, (1965).

27. McClelland, David, et al., *The Achievement Motive,* Appleton-Century-Crofts, New York, (1953).

28. Maslow, H. H., *op. cit.*; R. M. Fulmer, *op. cit.,* pp. 99–101.

29. Harris, T. A., *I'm O.K., You're O.K.,* Harris-Avon, New York, (1969).

30. Fulmer, R. M., *op. cit.,* p. 101.

31. Rogers, C. C., *Client-Centered Therapy,* Houghton Mifflin, Boston, Mass., (1951).

32. Moustakas, C. E., *op. cit.,* p. 121.

33. Bernard, H. W., *Human Development in Western Culture* (2nd ed.), Allyn

and Bacon, Boston, Mass., (1966), pp. 476–477; and Rogers, D., *The Psychology of Adolescents,* Appleton-Century-Crofts, New York, (1962), pp. 49–51.

34.   Bernard, H. W., *op. cit.,* p. 477.

35.   Butler, H. M., in Odiorne, G. S., *How Managers Make Things Happen,* Prentice-Hall, Englewood Cliffs, N.J., (1961), p. 3.

36.   Odiorne, G. S., *How Managers Make Things Happen,* Prentice-Hall, Englewood Cliffs, N.J., (1961), p. 5.

37.   Otto, H. A., *op. cit.,* p. 170.

38.   *Ibid,* p. 122–123.

39.   Gardner, J. W., *op. cit.,* p. 13.

40.   Odiorne, G. S., *op. cit.,* p. 28.

41.   Woodworth, R. S., *Psychology,* Henry Holt and Co., (1940), pp. 97–98.

42.   *Ibid.,* p. 98.

43.   Odiorne, G. S., *op. cit.,* pp. 49–57.

44.   Fulmer, R. M., *op. cit.,* p. 297.

45.   Berlow, D. K., *The Process of Communication,* W. W. Norton, New York, (1951).

46.   Odiorne, G. S., *op. cit.,* pp. 78, 86–87.

47.   Otto, H. A., "Human Potentialities Research at the University of Utah," in Otto, (ed.), *Explorations in Human Potentialities,* Charles C. Thomas, Springfield, Ill., (1964), pp. 403–437.

48.   Otto, H. A., *Guide to Developing Your Potential, op. cit.,* pp. 112–113.

49.   *Ibid,* p. 114.

50.   Odiorne, G. S., *op. cit.,* pp. 78–83.

51. Three of the terms in the questionnaire (PapyroManiac, Filophiliac, and Phonophiliac) have been adapted from Peter, L. J., Hull, R., *The Peter Principle,* William Morrow and Co., (1969); and *The Peter Principle Game,* Skor-Mor Corporation, Carpinteria, Calif., (1973).

52. Santa Barbara News-Press, Santa Barbara, Calif., (December 24, 1974). p. C-4.

53. Otto, H. S., *Guide to Developing Your Potential, op. cit.,* p. 116.

54. *Ibid,* p. 115.

55. Gardner, J. W., *op. cit.,* p. 41.

56. Gregory, C. E., *The Management of Intelligence,* McGraw-Hill, New York, (1967), pp. 188–190.

57. Jay, A., *Management and Machiavelli,* Holt, Rinehart and Winston, New York, (1967), pp. 85–88; also see Gardner, J. W., *op. cit.;* and Fulmer, R. M., *op. cit.*

58. *Ibid,* p. 85.

59. Fulmer, R. M., *op. cit.,* p. 366.

60. These nine characteristics for establishing a climate for creativity in family groups were selected from a list of 78 personality traits attributed to creative people, in Gregory, C. E., *op. cit.,* pp. 188–190.

61. Fulmer, R. M., *op. cit.,* pp. 373–377.

62. *Ibid.,* pp. 377–379.

63. Wooden, J., *Practical Modern Basketball,* Ronald Press, New York, (1966), p. 12.

64. *Ibid,* p. 13.

65. Otto, H. A., *op. cit.,* pp. 218–219.

66. Becker, G. S., *Human Capital,* National Bureau of Economic Research, New York, (1964), p. 1.

67. Schultz, T. W., *The Economic Value of Education,* Columbia University Press, New York, (1963), pp. x, xi, 8.

68. Burk, M. C., "On the Need for Investment in Human Capital for Consumption," *Journal of Consumer Affairs,* 1 (Winter 1967), pp. 123–138.

69. Drucker, P. F., "How to Manage Your Time," *Harper's Magazine,* 233 (December, 1966), pp. 56–60.

70. Malone, C. C., and Malone, L. H., *Decision Making and Management for Farm and Home,* State College Press, Ames, Iowa, (1958), p. 47.

71. Hoyt, E., *Consumption in Our Society,* McGraw-Hill, New York, (1938), pp. 16–30.

8

STRENGTHENING COMMUNICATION

Although some aspects of the environment cannot be controlled as yet, people can and do influence their personal and social environments through communication. Radio, television, neighborhood gossip, classroom discussion, a pat on the back, or a frown all influence behavior. Because people constantly communicate, the ways in which families interact often become habits. Because of its habitual and frequent nature, communication is sometimes assumed to be a simple process that anyone can master. People who find their ideas misinterpreted or ignored, or who try to listen to someone who is mumbling or rambling, recognize that communication is not always easy or effective. Becoming aware of the impact of communication is a step toward improving its effectiveness.

Communication is the process of human interaction that involves generating, organizing, and sending ideas to one or more receivers. Although alarm clocks and barking dogs communicate, the emphasis, here, is on interpersonal interaction. Ideally, the meaning sent in a message should be comparable, if not identical, to the meaning received if the process is to be effective. The purpose of this chapter is to help the reader understand the components of human interaction, to appreciate personal differences in communications, and to consider some suggestions for improving communication.

The importance of communication to quality of life is evidenced throughout this text. Imagine a personal or family life style with no communication. How would people demonstrate values, achieve goals, or meet their needs without some form of interpersonal contact? The development of human resources, decision making, and the managerial processes all involve communication.

The purpose of communication is to change or to maintain behavior. When a patient talks to a physician about symptoms the patient has observed in himself, he is attempting to influence the doctor to discover and to remove the cause of the problem. In a family mealtime discussion, a child may send hints about his or her desire for a 10-speed bicycle; while another family member may be discussing an upcoming party to learn if the family will approve his or her attendance.

A problem in communication is that the messages people send either clarify or confuse issues. The patient in the doctor's office may complain of a backache while the problem may originate in his or her hip or knee. The child who wanted the bicycle might send the following message: "Johnny has a new 10-speed. Boy, is it something!" The response might be mere recognition that a neighbor's child has a new bicycle, without an understanding of the child's real meaning. The message about the party might be ignored by others in the group who are busy discussing bicycles. Confusion or lack of understanding of communication can frustrate goal attainment.

Components of Communication

Effective communication—assigning comparable meanings to messages—can clarify individual perceptions and can produce the cooperation needed to reach group goals. An understanding of the components of interpersonal communication may help the reader to develop criteria for assessing his or her effectiveness as a communicator. The components include perceiving meanings, sending messages, receiving messages, and providing feedback.

PERCEIVING MEANINGS

People react to their environment in individual ways. The same stimulus can generate varying reactions in the same person over a period of time and, in different people, at any given point in time. Two individuals walking into a living unit that is for rent are, for example, experiencing the same stimulus. Because of differences in their backgrounds and expectations, the two people will notice differing features of the housing situation. One might notice the color scheme and furniture styles, while the other could pay special attention to the quality of construction, the spatial arrangement, the view from the kitchen window, location of convenience outlets, or its cleanliness. Even if the two people notice exactly the same aspects of the living unit, their reactions to these features could differ.

Perceptions involve interactions between a person's brain and a stimulus—a situation, object, or experience.[1] Differing reactions to color, furnishings, or ideas result from these perceptual differences. Biological, psychological, and social factors affect perception. Bartley, for example, described some perceptual differences between blind people and those with normal sight. He concluded that the world is different for people with an absent or with an abnormally functioning sense.[2]

These sensory inputs are combined, and meaning is attached to what is seen, felt, heard, smelled, or tasted. Combinations of such sensory inputs, over time, lead people to conclusions about what is "real" or "true" in life and form a perceptual basis for future behavior.

Hayakawa compared a person's frame of reference to a map. For example, a community may design a map to locate points of historical interest, major streets, and the specific buildings or locations rather than including all streets and buildings. Maps, as many a driver or hiker have learned, may or may not conform to reality. Like maps, perceptions may or may not conform to what is happening, may ignore some details and emphasize others, and may vary with intentions and experiences of the perceiver.[3] The degree of influence in a message depends in part on how accurately the message conforms to the reciever's perception or map of reality.

SENDING MESSAGES

The sending of messages is the second component of communication. Ideas, feelings, or experiences are coded into words or other expressions to be shared with others. Although little is known about how people code ideas or feelings, the codes or symbols must be understood by others if communication is to occur. Sending can be either verbal or nonverbal. Touch—as in a handshake or a hug, body movements—as in a nod of a head or leaving a room, and sensory symbols—like some road signs, sirens, works of art, or graphs—are examples of *nonverbal communication.* Additionally, people give meaning to words in the *tone* and *rhythm of voice* they use. One researcher estimated that in face-to-face communication, at most 35 percent of the meaning is in the form of verbal or word messages.[4] Nonverbal cues are most frequently used, followed by tone of voice or vocal inflection, and finally, the words themselves. People who emphasize word choice in speaking or in listening, without considering other forms of communication, may encounter problems of accuracy in interaction.

The *channel* used for most face-to-face communication is sound waves through the air. This channel includes much extraneous noise, such as other people's conversations, the sound of a television, or a fan operating in the background. It is slow in comparison to other communication channels such as wires or cables;[5] however, people talk at an average rate of 125 words per minute,[6] and sound waves are sufficiently fast to handle interpersonal, face-to-face communication.

Radio, telephone, letters, and television are other vehicles for interpersonal communication. The selection of a channel influences the speed and accuracy of a message as well as the forms of communication that can be used. As an example, there are now more telephone calls placed per person than there are letters mailed per person.[7] The speed of communication via telephone is more immediate, both words and tone of voice are combined, and feedback of some variety is assured. Although receivers can infer tone of voice through letters, the sender's meaning may or may not be accurately conveyed. Use of letters does, however, allow senders time to carefully choose words and receivers time to think before responding.

RECEIVING MESSAGES

People are able to listen to more words per minute than most individuals can speak per minute. While the average speaking rate previously has been mentioned as 125 words per minute, the listening rate is approximately 400 words per minute.[8] Listeners can use this difference in rates to concentrate on the meaning of a message, to prepare an argument, to daydream, or for a number of other purposes depending on their interest in the sender and his or her message.

In *decoding,* receivers translate the sender's codes in terms of personal experience. If the communication is unrelated to the receiver's experience or if the receiver is not paying attention to the message, the communication process can end.

Because words can be used in varied ways and because other forms of communication are combined with words, sensitive receivers consider both the meaning and context of communication in addition to the works.[9] A child, for example, may say something—like hating a neighbor's child or never wanting to go to school again. Receivers, in such a situation, can more accurately determine the meaning of the message from an analysis of the reasons for the sender's statements. Interpreting interpersonal communication too literally without concern for intent or context can minimize effectiveness. Empathy can help listeners sort even confusing messages to determine meaning.

Receivers are influenced not only by what is said, but also by confidence in the sender. People tend to prefer relationships with those holding similar beliefs to their own.[10] A person might, therefore, be more receptive to messages that are based on religious, political, philosophical, or other notions similar to his or her own beliefs. Distrust, fear, or lack of confidence in a sender's abilities can also influence the meaning attached to messages. If a neighbor's suggested household hints have failed in the past, a receiver might discount future messages from the neighbor on that topic. Some people, with or without reason, instantly distrust an entire class of people such as youth, salespeople, minority group members, or women executives. If effective communication is to occur, trust in the other participants and in their messages should develop.

While intended receivers may accurately decode messages, it is sometimes possible for others not directly involved in the relationship to become receivers. People may pick up a party-line telephone and overhear parts of a conversation without understanding the context. Neighbors may observe a backyard family argument. Family members may overhear comments, about the family situation or about themselves, that were not meant to be over-heard. If senders in these examples recognized that people other than the intended receivers were involved, it is possible that the content and forms of communication would be changed.

Field estimates that people spend from 45 to 75 percent of each day mentally or physically interpreting messages. Although much time is spent in listening, retention is short-lived. Within two weeks, most people forget 75 percent of what they have heard or read.[11] Reinforcement through seeing, hearing, and touching, for example, can help people to remember messages that have been received.

Because of the vast variety of daily input, people screen what they receive—accepting some, ignoring others, altering some meanings, and reject-ing still other messages. Because of screening, the original intent of a one-to-one message can be altered by the receiver to the extent that the sender no longer can recognize the message. If the idea or experience is shared several times by a number of people, as with gossip, meaning may be seriously dis-torted.

Some communication stops after decoding, as illustrated:

$$\textbf{SENDER} \xrightarrow{\textit{message}} \textbf{RECEIVER}$$

This one-way communication, as in textbooks or news reports, is organized in its presentation, eliminates much noise, is fast, and offers little or no challenge to the sender's power or expertise. The limitations of one-way communication are that the sender does not know if the receiver is understanding the mean-ing of the message, and the reader or listener cannot ask questions of a text or television set for clarification or for additional information.

FEEDBACK

Two-way communication helps both senders and receivers to correct miscon-ceptions or to expand knowledge. *Feedback,* the process of returning informa-tion, usually with the intent of influencing behavior, turns one-way communi-cation into a cycle or loop, as is illustrated:

$$\textbf{SENDER} \xrightarrow[\textit{response}]{\textit{message}} \textbf{RECEIVER}$$

People attending a church service or a community meeting may not speak out in the meeting, but their behavior is a form of feedback. Members of the audience who fall asleep, smile and nod in agreement, wiggle in their chairs, or leave are intentionally or unintentionally sending messages to the speaker. These nonverbal messages may or may not be correctly interpreted, or may even be ignored by the speaker. For example, wiggling can be caused by a short attention span or physical discomfort as well as by a boring conversation. Misinterpreting nonverbal communication can needlessly reduce a speaker's confidence or can create a false sense of confidence.

Oral exchange between people involves the receiver taking the role of sender in asking questions, in reacting to messages, in developing additional ideas, or in clarifying ideas provided by the sender. This interaction may be rapid, and the roles of sender and receiver may change quickly enough for the roles to be blurred. In discussing financial plans, family members may exchange comments in rapid succession without later being able to identify specific sender and receiver roles. Other communication can involve a number of sequences of sending and receiving called *chains* or *loops*, as illustrated by the following example.

Noting that the lawn has not been cut lately, an adult family member assigns the task to a teenage member of the group through face-to-face communication. The teenager, in turn, questions why he has to cut the grass at home while the neighbors pay him to do the same work. The adult responds with examples of tasks performed by other members of the household for no pay and asks if the teenager would want to pay these other people for meals, laundry, household repairs, and other tasks performed for him and for the family group.

After some additional interaction, the parent suggests that a younger family member help with trimming the lawn. The teenager then reports this information to the younger family member. If the child does not believe the teenager, he may check with the parent to determine the truth of the communication and to see if the work can be avoided. This example involves a number of sender-receiver cycles but also includes the teenager acting as an intermediate between the parent and a younger family member. It is easier to determine the original sources of communication in a family than in a larger group, and the intent of messages sent through others is more easily verified because of the proximity of family members.

Readers might assume that the above discussion implies that communication is effective only if behavioral change occurs. If a family with money problems changes their buying practices, a financial counselor might assume, for example, that messages he or she sent to the family are understood. If a family member who has been withdrawn begins to reenter family conversations, the family knows that their messages of concern have been received.

At times, however, receivers will understand messages but will not change behavior. If the message is threatening to the receiver's view of

himself or of the world, he may be unwilling to change. If the messages conflict with personal motivations, can the receiver be expected to change behavior? If the proposed behavioral change appears too difficult or too complex,
the message, although understood, may be rejected as unrealistic. While some
people believe that these are examples of ineffective communication, others
will point out that the message was indeed understood, so the interaction was
effective.

Although knowledge of communication is increasing, many questions are
not yet completely answered. Is communication effective if the receiver does
not behave as directed? Do senders recognize that they, too, can be affected
in two-way communication? Is there a set of characteristics that should be
used in separating "effective" from "not so effective" communication in
families or in other groups? Although there may not be enough research to
formulate a theory of communication in families, the following section explores some research and opinions about family communication.

Communication in Families

The components of communication apply to interpersonal communication in
family and in community settings. Communication occurs between people
who have something—a goal, a role, or a problem, for example—in common.
Pierce states that this sharing of experience, interest, or understanding is more
important to effective communication than is a common language.[13] If a relationship is to be developed, one psychologist recommends that this area of
common experience be enlarged.[14]

Self disclosure is the term Jourard uses to describe people's sharing of
information about themselves. Jourard reports a lack of self disclosure among
family members,[15] although Americans are generally more open about
themselves than are people of a number of other cultures.[16] People may find it
easier to discuss very personal matters with total strangers than with family
members, partially because the stranger will probably never be seen again.
Women are also more inclined to self disclosure than men.[17]

Why is self disclosure important, and how do people develop this ability
to be open with others? People who share knowledge about themselves promote openness in others. Family members, for example, who share their
experiences and feelings with others in the household promote self disclosure
in the entire group.[18] Because people gradually change, establishing a pattern
of sharing personal feelings and experiences helps to adjust perceptions and
to expand family relationships even in times of stress. According to Jourard,
love and trust also promote self disclosure. The risk in self disclosure is that
others might use this knowledge to hurt the sender or tell others.

In families and other groups, the significance of the relationship will influence the degree of openness. If two people are indifferent toward each other or do not want to develop a relationship, there is little need for self disclosure. People may be frank with fellow employees about some aspects of their life, but they may prefer privacy regarding other aspects of their lives.

COMMUNICATION BETWEEN ADULTS

Through communication, people learn how to live together. Husbands and wives learn about themselves and about each other by talking about roles and goals. Communication can also be an expression of love and respect. Interaction between a couple is related to marital satisfaction[17] and can lead to accurate and mutually appreciated role perceptions in family life. Luckey also observed a direct relationship between marital satisfaction and agreement in a couple's perceptions of their roles.[20]

Openness, however, does not guarantee marital satisfaction. Komarovsky observed that some self-disclosing women were not satisfied with their marriage.[21] If a marriage partner does not reciprocate—does not return information about himself—others in the family may feel a decreasing desire to be open.

Komarovsky also observed a trend toward decreasing communication with increasing years of marriage. An exception was the younger, less educated males whose communication increased with the length of the marriage.[22] At least three reasons for decline or lack of communication were given—differentiation in interests, socialization not to share, and psychological barriers.[23]

If a man's and woman's roles are clearly separated, there is little basis in common experience for self disclosure. In a London study, Bott observed that couples who had close, extended family and friendship ties were likely to segregate their individual, marital roles. If extended family ties were not as close, husbands and wives were more inclined to share—to communicate.[24] If companionship is not a goal in marriage, Komarovsky concluded that sharing may be limited—at least on the verbal level—but the relationship can be satisfying.[25]

In such situations, companionship may be achieved in a peer-group relationship. Of the blue-collar families Komarovsky studied, three-fifths of the females and one-fifth of the males had close, primarily same-sex, extra-marital friendships.[26] Berado concluded that in geographically mobile families, women play dominant roles in maintaining kinship ties, although these ties weaken across time.[27] If sharing is absent both within and outside marriage, loneliness can result.

In at least some parts of society, men have been taught to disclose little or nothing about themselves.[28] Strength, in some people's minds, is related to a lack of complaints and to nonexpression of hurt feelings. There is, however, an increasing trend toward openness in family life of the younger, educated males.

Psychological barriers to open communication in husband-wife interaction include the fear of hostile feelings and the danger that shared information can be used against the self-disclosing person.[29] These fears can motivate defensiveness in marital communication.

PARENT-CHILD COMMUNICATION

Children learn to communicate and are socialized through participation in family interaction. In a study of Kibbutz families, Kaffman concluded that parent-child interaction is essential for the full development of a child's potential. Children in this study lived in separate housing from their parents and were provided stimuli for learning by teachers and by others in the community. Those children who also received stimulus toward learning from their parents appeared more healthy and better adjusted in contrast to those who received little parental attention.[30] If parent-child interaction has such an impact on children who are not living with their parents, how great is the impact for those residing with their families?

The frequency and quality of family communication can influence children's mental health. According to Westley and Epstein, families who communicate often have healthier children than those who seldom communicate.[31] The quality of family communication may also affect children's potential. Satir recommended that family communication should be honest, clear, specific, and direct. Behavioral limits, rules, or policies should be known to all family members, but Satir believes that these limits should be applied in a flexible, human spirit. In applying these guidelines with openness to experience, Satir believes that individuals' feelings of self worth can be promoted.[32]

The Changing Nature of Communication

Initial parent-child communication is nonverbal. The frequency and ways in which a baby is held, cuddled, or ignored is the child's introduction to the world. The child makes its needs known through fussing or crying. Because newborn children are so completely dependent on others, some husbands and wives find their parental roles conflicting with their concern for each other's companionship.[33]

Children's growth toward autonomy and adult status can be facilitated by parent-child interaction. By example more than by discussion, parents provide initial models of adult behavior. Adults who can satisfactorily resolve difficulties, who can manage their aggressive feelings, and who are interested in life tend to promote their own growth as well as that of their children. Adults who physically or verbally attack children not only can damage a child's self concept but can teach the child that violence is an acceptable part of adult behavior.

Children can be guided in their development of human resources through communication. Mothers, for example, who emphasize how to solve problems rather than offering specific solutions promote the development of problem-solving abilities in their children.[34] Parents who recognize the developing, unique capabilities of their children can promote positive self concepts in children through verbal reinforcement.

Parent-child communication, either consciously or unconsciously, also teaches children about sex roles. Male babies are often treated more roughly than are female babies.[35] Men may communicate more with male children in a learning activity and women more with female children.[36]

Children in other cultures and those in lower-class Western civilization may experience more verbal communication with peers than with parents.[37] Children's recognition that parents are fallible human beings is a step toward emotional independence. In transition, young adults in this society may rely on peers or on other significant adults or on important reference groups while moving toward autonomy.[38] While these changing relationships can be frustrating and confusing for an entire family, parents may find new freedom as their children move toward independence and may renew or expand husband-wife communication.[39]

Does family size have an impact on communication? Small group research indicates that communication in a laboratory setting varies with the size of a group and with the nature of the activities being shared.[40] Family activities can be varied through an increase in the number of family members, which, in turn, can increase interest in and satisfaction received from family interaction. Age differences of more than five years between children or where there are more than four children, can produce too much diversity in individual interests, according to Blood and Wolfe.[41] The reader may want to consider what actions people can take to promote family interaction in larger families or in those with a great age span between children.

Impact of Television

Television sets are available in 96 percent of the American households,[42] and the uses of television affect family communication. Coffin observed that increased hours of television viewing decreases time spent in interpersonal communication.[43] Preschool children watch an average of two to three hours of television daily, and the number of hours per day increases with the age of the child through early teenage years.[44] Adults view an average of six to seven hours of television daily.[45] While some of this viewing may occur as a family, how much time remains for developing interpersonal competence?

Television can either help or hinder personal development, depending on selectivity in viewing and on evaluations following television programs that conflict with or reinforce family motivations. Cases of children and young adults physically hurting other people after having watched similar behavior on television have been documented. Children and young adults also can grow cognitively from television viewing and can be less fearful of new experiences.[46] Television is not inherently good or evil—it is a resource that can be used to enhance or to interfere with goal attainment. Its worth varies with the quality of programs and with the uses people make of it.

A group of 158 preschoolers, in a study by Lyle and Hoffman, made the majority of their decisions about television viewing without parental guidance.[47] Although adults may be able to evaluate the appeals used in advertising and to separate reality from fantasy, are young children able to evaluate the meaning and reality of programming without adult guidance? Are adults able to manage their own viewing time to promote personal and family goals, or does television manage individuals and families? These questions are deliberately left unanswered to generate thought.

CONFLICT RESOLUTION

Conflict is a struggle with values, with power, or with resource allocation. The emphasis here is placed on interpersonal conflict in the means or ends of family life. People who interact across time are bound to have differing opinions or perceptions about some aspects of family life. People can walk away from disagreements in insignificant relationships, but if the relationship is an important one, people attempt to make their opinions known and to continue the relationship. If disagreements cannot be successfully resolved, tensions may be expressed in alternate ways such as sulking, nagging, or belittling others in the family.

Successful conflict resolution is based, in part, on established and effective patterns of open communication. When faced with new decisions, couples who have developed effective communication patterns are more inclined toward spontaneous agreement than are unrelated couples or disturbed families. Married couples also reach new decisions faster and with less concern for politeness than do dating couples.[48]

The presence of conflict, according to Scanzoni, need not threaten a relationship.[49] Some conflicts, such as those that include redefinition of a relationship, require more serious adjustments than do those involving peripheral issues, such as the amount of money to be spent for a needed item or the time to leave a party.

Is fighting or quarreling an effective way to resolve conflicts? The answer to the question depends on the results of the quarrel and on the strategies used in resolving conflict. If problems are clarified and if participants are satisfied with the outcomes of conflict resolution, tension is reduced and the relationship is maintained or possibly enhanced. If a quarrel is destructive, however, the issues may grow rather than diminish across time; frustrations may increase and the relationship may become strained.[50]

This section of the chapter has described only a small portion of communications research and theory. The intent has been to illustrate some of the observed differences in communication among families and within families. The following section explores suggestions for improving interpersonal communication.

Improving Communication

Communication is learned behavior, and communication skills, like other human resources, can be improved with practice. Resolving conflict is the most difficult aspect of interpersonal communication because people are faced with heightened sensitivity and sometimes do not consider the long-term consequences of what they say and do when angry or upset. For this reason, this section begins with suggestions for effective conflict resolution. Also included are ideas for developing skills for receiving and sending messages.

TECHNIQUES FOR RESOLVING CONFLICT

"Constructive fighting" is the term that is sometimes employed when discussing effective resolution of conflict. The principles involve empathy—putting one's self in the other person's roles, judgment, and a human-centered outlook on life. Readers who believe that arguments or fights are harmful will observe that some of the guidelines for fighting can be applied in a number of other situations.

Some people enjoy family arguments; others seek to avoid them regardless of the costs in self esteem or feelings of equity. In either case, the suggestions for constructive fighting or quarreling, developed by the University of Maine Cooperative Extension Service, may be helpful:

1. Seek to understand, not to win.

2. Let the conversation clarify the issues and differences.

3. Make your position clear through a careful explanation of exactly what you think and how you feel.

4. Try to completely understand your mate's point of view and feelings by careful listening, questioning, and by a sympathetic attitude.

5. Stick to the point and avoid side issues.

6. Listen not only to the words said but try to understand and accept the feelings expressed.

7. Get it out, don't let it fester.

8. Pick the right times to quarrel, if possible, when fatigue, hunger, illness, a rushed schedule, or the lateness of the hour do not prevent a happy outcome.

9. Attack the problem, not each other. Avoid words that shame, belittle, or damage the other's ego.

10. Quarrel privately.

11. Let the quarrel end when it is over. This does not necessarily mean that a solution is found, but it does mean that tensions are relieved for now.[51]

These suggestions or guidelines parallel those presented by Back and Wyden in *The Intimate Enemy.*[52]

Because quarreling is a type of bargaining directed toward resolving conflict, emphasis should be on changeable behavior and the participants should request specific changes. Telling someone that he is too tall, too old, or that her feet are too big cannot bring about a change, because emphasis is placed on a physical trait that is difficult if not impossible to change. Telling someone that he talks too much might cause confusion in the receiver—does it mean, "Do not talk at all," "Don't talk while I'm reading the paper," or just that "I need a few minutes of privacy right now?" If receivers in such settings wanted to resolve conflict, they would not have enough specific information to do so.

Some readers might assume that constructive fighting involves complete openness, but letting out all hostile feelings may not be appropriate or constructive. Although verbalizing anger has been suggested to prevent physical violence, Straus observed verbal and physical aggression occurring together in a study of college students' families.[53] While this small study based on responses to questionnaires is not conclusive, it could give people a reason to be cautious in excessive venting of angry feelings. Even if verbal expression of anger does not lead to physical harm, hurting and angry communication can inhibit trust. Communication based on anger can also inhibit perception and limit alternatives for resolving conflict.[54] Handling conflict before it becomes a crisis can minimize problems of excessive anger.

The list of suggestions for constructive resolution of conflict includes the possibility that resolution may take some time. If disagreements have developed across time, determining their causes and implementing change may also require some time and patience. Because of serious, thoughtful interaction, people may evolve totally new and acceptable solutions to their differences. Compromise is possible only if a range of alternatives exists. In such situations, participants in a conflict each yield to some of the demands or requests of the others. Dominance, temporary withdrawal, or dissolution of the relationship are other possible alternatives for resolving conflict.

The worth of each of the forms of conflict resolution depends on people's satisfaction with the results. It may be upsetting, for example, to dissolve a dating relationship that has been enjoyable; but if the couple believes that conflict can only be resolved by going their separate ways, this may be an effective form of conflict resolution. However, to give up a relationship without understanding the causes of the conflict and without considering other alternatives is management by, rather than of conflict.

Although these guidelines are developed for handling complaints or differences of opinion, these principles are broad and can be used in many situations. Timing of communication, for example, applies to a variety of day-to-day interactions. Tired, hungry, or preoccupied people have difficulties in paying attention to and in understanding messages. If a family member is distracted, or if others notice preoccupation within a family member, postponing communication for a short time can be an asset to interpersonal communication. The above suggestions and those that follow can help to develop more effective communication.

SEEKING COMMON MEANING

If both sender and receiver hold similar perceptions of the meaning of a message, then communication has been effective. Receivers do not necessarily need to agree with the perceptions, but perceptions must be mutually understood. To clarify meanings from both senders' and receivers' perspectives, the meanings of words, nonverbal cues, and combined forms of messages should be explored.

Words and Multiple Meanings

Using words appropriately and being sensitive to the impact of words on other people is part of effective communication. Most commonly used words have more than one meaning, so the interpetation of verbal communication should include consideration of the context in which the terms are used. Additionally, words have emotional as well as cognitive meanings that should be considered in developing effective communication. Misunderstanding can be avoided through careful attention to selection and combination of words and to listening or reading for the intended meaning of the message.

Take a moment to consider the many meanings people give to word symbols like *table, free, cut, play, or right.* Each of these words has accumulated varied meanings across time. Webster's *New Seventh Collegiate Dictionary* includes seven different meanings for the word "table," alone. Not all of these meanings are presently in widespread use, but people are continuing to add new meanings to existing words. Is it any wonder that people sometimes confuse or misinterpret the intended meaning of words?

Carefully choosing words requires an understanding of the receiver, as well as of the words. Professions sometimes develop specialized, fancy-sounding words or develop specialized meanings for common words. Using these terms with family members or with those who are not in the profession, without clarification of meaning, can be frustrating to the receiver. Terms like "mole," for example, mean one thing to the chemist and another to the gardener. Additionally, consider how the receiver will react to the emotional meaning of terms like "disturbed," "aggressive," or "slow learner." Labeling may cause people to be defensive and may weaken their willingness to listen. If thoughtfully selected, however, words can facilitate interpersonal understanding.

Combining Forms

Have you ever observed yourself or someone else saying one thing with words, but saying something else in voice tone or in nonverbal cues? If you were the receiver, would you pay more attention to the words or to the other forms of communication? In such circumstances, tone of voice or the nonverbal cues often, but not always, convey more accurate meaning. People are taught to be polite, to say appropriate things; but it is more difficult to control nonverbal forms of communication. Senders can facilitate interpersonal understanding by combining all three forms of communication to clarify and emphasize intended meanings.

Interpreting Nonverbal Cues

People demonstrate their emotions and disclose much about themselves through the use of nonverbal messages. For example, the distance that people keep between themselves communicates the nature of a relationship.[55] People who have a positive relationship with others in a group tend to adopt each other's posture.[56] It is important to remember that patterned or repetitive nonverbal cues rather than one-time gestures or body movements convey people's personality and reactions to others.

The ways in which people use their bodies and space to communicate deserves serious attention by those who want to strengthen communication. The way a person walks into a room—if his shoulders are hunched over or straight, if his eyes are focused on the floor or directly at someone, if he moves hurriedly or slowly—is interpreted by others in the room. These combinations of nonverbal messages are often more accurate reflections of people's feelings than are their words.

Before assigning meaning, the reader should be cautioned that there are cultural and age differences in nonverbal communication. Hall, for example, notes that generally Americans' sense of smell is poorly developed because people in this society mask odors rather than communicating by smell. In other cultures, people use this sense to send and receive many kinds of messages.[57] Older people and those in Arab society seek body warmth in personal interaction. In contrast, younger people in the United States prefer more distance when communicating.[58]

How can receivers know if their interpretation of nonverbal cues is accurate? Because misinterpretation of nonverbal cues is such a common problem, people do need feedback to clarify the meaning of messages: asking questions to clarify issues and ideas, or restating others' messages to avoid assumptions can help senders and receivers to understand individual perceptions.

The Role of Evaluation

Premature evaluation of messages leads to misunderstanding ideas. If a person quickly decides that he or she likes or dislikes an idea or a person before fully understanding the message, communication can become polarized into those who are "for" and those who are "against." Rogers, among others, suggested that people first need to understand ideas before evaluating them.[59] Understanding others' ideas and feelings demands a certain amount of courage because empathetic listeners can be changed by what they hear. Without empathy, can there be effective communication?

Judgment—the evaluation of meanings and consequences of alternatives—is an important human resource.[60] For example, if a person tells another that for 69 cents a week, he or she can receive six magazines for the next four years, judgment may be necessary. The receiver, in determining the meaning of the message, may consider whether the 69 cents is available on a weekly basis or may figure the total cost of the offer. In evaluating the consequences, he or she could ask—"Are these magazines that I want to read?" "Do I want to receive the same publications for four years?" "What other uses can I make of that money?" Advertising messages, such as the above example, and other persuasive interpersonal communication need to be evaluated for their personal meaning and consequences—after each message is understood.

Meta-Communication

If families or other groups are seriously concerned about strengthening their communication, it can be advantageous to discuss how they communicate—*meta-communication*.[61] If a family member is displeased with the tone of a discussion, verbalizing the cause of the communication problem can lead to a further understanding of group members and of their individual styles of communication. If someone believes, for example, that his privacy has been invaded, that someone is rehashing old complaints, or that other family members are expecting too much of him, the problem cannot be handled unless others in the group are aware of it. If families do evaluate how they communicate and apply what they have learned, they will have incorporated a flexibility that allows for and respects growth in individuals and in the group.

Summary

Effective communication is needed for interpersonal understanding in family decision making and management. Communication is a complex process that appears simple because people interact often. Effective communication involves similar perceptions of both senders and receivers. Because of long-term, day-to-day interactions, families develop unique styles of communication that gradually change. Because it is learned behavior, communication can be improved through concern for others and appreciation of intended meanings of messages.

References

1. Fabun, D., *Communications: The Transfer of Meaning,* Glencoe, Beverly Hills, Calif., (1968), pp. 2–12.

2. Bartley, S. H., *Perception in Everyday Life,* Harper and Row, New York, (1972), pp. 204–218.

3. Hayakawa, S. I., *Language in Thought and Action,* Harcourt, Brace, Jovanovich, New York, (1972).

4. Campbell, J. H., and Helper, H. W., (eds.), *Dimensions in Communication: Readings,* Wadsworth, Belmont, Calif., (1970), p. 258.

5. Busignies, H., "Communication Channels," *Scientific American, 227:3* (September 1972), pp. 98–113.

6. Field, P. A., "The Receiving End of Communication, Listening," *Proceedings of the 1962 Institute of Technical and Industrial Communication,* Colorado State University, Fort Collins, Colo., (1962), p. 34.

7. Pierce, J. R., "Communication," *Scientific American, 227:3* (September 1972), p. 39.

8. Field, *op. cit.,* p. 34.

9. Hayakawa, *op. cit.,* pp. 55, 82–83.

10. Rokeah, M., *The Open and Closed Mind—Investigations into the Nature of Belief Systems and Personality Systems,* Basic Books, New York, (1960), p. 391.

11. Field, *op. cit.,* p. 34.

12. *Ibid.,* p. 35.

13. Pierce, *op. cit.,* p. 36.

14. Jourard, S. M., *The Transparent Self,* Van Nostrand Reinhold, New York, (1971).

15. *Ibid.,* p. 6.

16. *Ibid.,* p. 12.

17. *Ibid.*

18. *Ibid.,* p. 13.

19. Karlsson, G., *Adaptibility and Communication in Marriage,* Bedminster, Totowa, N. J., (1963), pp. 80–81.

20. Luckey, E. B., "Perceptional Congruence of Self and Family Concepts as Related to Marital Interaction," *Sociometry, 24* (1961), pp. 234–250.

21. Komarovsky, M., *Blue-Collar Marriage,* Random House, New York, (1962), p. 137.

22. *Ibid.,* p. 145.

23. *Ibid.,* pp. 149–169.

24. Bott, E., *Family and Social Network—Roles, Norms and External Relationships in Ordinary Urban Families,* Tavistock, London, (1971).

25. Komarovsky, *op. cit.,* p. 177.

26. *Ibid.,* p. 215.

27. Berado, F. M., "Kinship Interaction and Communication among Space Age Migrants," *Journal of Marriage and the Family, 29* (August 1967), 549.

28. Komarovsky, *op. cit.,* p. 156.

29. *Ibid.,* p. 169.

30. Kaffman, M., "Family Conflict in the Psychopathology of the Kibbutz Child," *Family Process, 11:2* (June 1972), pp. 171–198.

31. Westley, W. A., and Epstein, N. B., *The Silent Majority,* Jossey-Bass, San Francisco, Calif., (1969).

32. Satir, V., *Peoplemaking,* Science and Behavior Books, Palo Alto, Calif., (1972), p. 4.

33. Blood, R. O., and Wolfe, D. M., *Husbands and Wives, The Dynamics of Married Living,* Free Press, New York, (1960), p. 157.

34. Bee, H. L., "Socialization for Problem Solving," in J. Aldous, T. Condon, R. Hill, M. Straus, and I. Tallman, *Family Problem Solving,* Dryden, Hinsdale, Ill., (1971), p. 200.

35. Davis, F., *Intuition—What We Know about Nonverbal Communication,* McGraw-Hill, New York, (1973), p. 7.

36. Hubbell, R. D., Byrne, M. C., and Stachowark, J., "Aspects of Communication in Families with Young Children," *Family Process, 13:*2 (June 1974), pp. 221–222.

37. Gumperez, J. J., "Sociolinguistics and Problem Solving in Small Groups," in J. Aldous, T. Condon, R. Hill, M. Straus, and I. Tallman, *Family Problem Solving,* Dryden, Hinsdale, Ill., (1971), p. 165.

38. Chickering, A. W., *Education and Identity,* Jossey-Bass, San Francisco, Calif., (1969), p. 12.

39. Blood and Wolfe, *op. cit.,* p. 160.

40. Hackman, J. R., and Vidmar, N., "Effects of Size and Task Type on Group Performance and Member Reactions," *Sociometry, 33* (1970), pp. 37–54.

41. Blood and Wolfe, *op. cit.,* pp. 156–157.

42. U.S. Bureau of the Census, *Statistical Abstract of the United States, 1973,* U.S. Government Printing Office, Washington, D.C., (1973), p. 499.

43. Coffin, T., "Television's Effects on Leisure Time Activities," *Journal of Applied Psychology, 32* (1948), 550–558.

44. Liembert, R. M., Neale, J. M., and Davidson, E. S., *The Early Window— Effects of Television on Children and Youth,* Pergamon, New York, (1973), pp. 8–9.

45. Rue, V. M., "Television and the Family: The Question of Control," *The Family Coordinator, 23:*1 (January 1974), p. 73.

46. Liembert, et. al., *op. cit.,* pp. 38–89.

47. Lyle, J., and Hoffman, H., "Explorations in Patterns of Television Viewing by Preschool–Age Children," in *Television and Social Behavior, 4,* U.S. Government Printing Office, Washington, D.C., (1972).

48. Ferreira, A. J., and Winter, W. D., "Stability of Interactional Variables in Family Decision-Making," *Archives of General Psychiatry, 14* (April 1966), pp. 352–355; Winter, W. D., Ferreira, A. J., and Bowers, N., "Decision-Making in Married and Unrelated Couples," *Family Process, 12:*1 (March 1973), pp. 83–94.

49. Scanzoni, J., *Sexual Bargaining,* Prentice-Hall, Englewood Cliffs, N.J., (1972), p. 72.

50. Deutsch, M., "Conflicts: Productive and Destructive," *Journal of Social Issues, 25:*1 (1969), pp. 10–11.

51. "Compatibility and Conflict," Cooperative Extension Service, University of Maine, (November 1969), p. 4. Reprinted by permission.

52. Back, G. R., and Wyden, P., *The Intimate Enemy, How to Fight Fair in Love and Marriage,* Avon, N.Y., (1968).

53. Straus, M. A., "Leveling, Civility and Violence in the Family," *Journal of Marriage and the Family, 36:*1 (February 1974), 13–29.

54. Deutsch, *op. cit.,* p. 13.

55. Hall, E. T., *The Hidden Dimension,* Doubleday, Garden City, N.Y., (1966), pp. 112–117.

56. Davis, *op. cit.,* p. 106.

57. Hall, *op. cit.,* p. 43.

58. DeLong, A. J., "The Micro-Spatial Structure of the Older Person: Some Implications of Planning and the Social and Spatial Environment;" in Pastalan, L. A., and Carson, D. H., (eds.), *Spatial Behavior of Older People,* University of Michigan, Ann Arbor, Mich. (1970), p. 72.

59. Rogers, C. R., and Roethlisberger, F. J., "Barriers and Gateways to Communication," *Harvard Business Review, 30:*4 (July–August 1952), pp. 46–52.

60. Foote, N. N., and Cottrell, Leonard S., "Interpersonal Competence," in *Kinship and Family Organization,* John Wiley, New York, (1966), pp. 444–445.

61. Scoresby, L., "Applying the Managerial Process," in *Behavioral Aspects of Management,* Proceedings of the Western Regional College Teachers of Home-Management-Family Economics, Salt Lake City, Utah, (1971), p. 52.

9

MANAGING TIME

Each day, people throughout the world have an equal amount of one resource—time. How it is used affects each person's goal attainment and the development or use of other resources. If a person wants to learn something, to travel somewhere, or to build or create something, he or she must use time with other resources to reach the goal. Although skills and materials may be available, goal attainment is also dependent upon time allocation.

Contributions to a family, a community, a nation, or the world are not always proportionate to the number of years someone has lived. People's use of time influences the quality of their lives to a greater degree than does the number of years, months, hours, or seconds they have lived.

The Concept of Time

In American society, people generally perceive time as a material resource,[1] in that it is spent, saved, wasted, measured, and scheduled. Among some subcultures within this society and in other societies, time is viewed differently. Some languages have no words to express the concepts of time or future, and some cultures have alternate views of promptness and timing. Others emphasize the "here and now," rather than the future.

An older Eskimo, for example, might wonder at some young Eskimos' and white persons' use of clock time. According to Pryde, Eskimos traditionally eat when they are hungry and sleep when they are tired, regardless of clock time.[2] People in more technically-oriented cultures may wake to an alarm, eat at specific times whether or not they are hungry, and return to bed according to clock time. In applying time—referred to here as a human resource—to reach goals, there are individual as well as cultural concepts.

TIME SENSE

Individuals differ in their orientations to time. While some people can accurately estimate the length of time they have been reading, working, or visiting, other people consistently overestimate or underestimate time.[3] Individual sense of time can be affected by extremes in temperature, by the presence or absence of light, by loneliness, enthusiasm or boredom, and by a number of other factors.[4] Meerloo theorized that an individual's subjective *sense of time* has four dimensions: biological time, estimates of time spans, historical time, and continuity.[5]

Biological Time

Natural rhythms provide people with their initial exposure to time. The *circadian rhythm* is the term used to describe cycles of approximately 24 hours—day and night, sleeping and waking time.[6] Natural phenomena, such as changes in the phases of the moon or in seasons, are examples of other rhythmic cycles that signify the passage of time. The regularity of breathing, heart rate, and other physiological functions are parts of biological time.

People are exposed to these rhythms before birth; in technological societies, however, people free themselves from some of the impact of biological time. Without some form of artificial lighting, people are completely dependent on the sun; they would be waking and sleeping according to solar rhythm. Interior lighting allows people to alter the impact of natural day-night rhythms. However, people who have drastically changed hours of employment or who have flown long distances report problems in making time adjustments. Orme[7] and Strughold[8] report that a number of days are needed to adjust to a new time zone or work schedule because of the change in circadian or 24 hour rhythm. If these rhythms are completely ignored, a person's concept of reality can become distorted or confused.[9]

Time Span

The passage of time is indicated by clocks, but people differ in how accurately their subjective estimates approach objective *clock time*. For example, a young child may ask how long it will be before lunch time, and his mother may respond with an estimate of one-half hour. Because children are present-oriented, view life as a large number of changing events, and feel the immediacy of hunger, time seems to pass more slowly for the child than for the parent.[10] Moods, such as boredom, and the specific nature of an activity, such as its urgency, also affect people's estimates of duration or time span.[11]

Historical Time

Orienting past events in time is another dimension of a subjective sense of time. Meerloo explained that this ordering results in memories, aids in understanding a cause and effect relationship, and is influenced by cultural heritage and language.[12] Historical time gives order to previous events. If, for example, a family can recall the sequence of an argument, the cause of the problem can be identified. Without memory, however, such learning would be impossible.

Like perception, interpretation of past events is influenced by culture and language. History or personal experience as viewed by an Arab citizen might be interpreted differently than by a Chinese or a South American because of language and cultural background.

Continuity

The dimension of continuity somewhat parallels the concept of historical time. Rather than sequencing and linking past events, continuity is the linkage of past, present, and future activities. In continuity, people become attuned to the flow of time and to their personal identities. As mentioned in Chapter 4, people may orient themselves more to one time element—past, present, or future. These orientations can shift as a person ages and can also change within a culture. Gross, Crandall, and Knoll, for example, observed that while Americans have demonstrated a future time orientation, a recent trend has been more present-oriented.[13]

A person's subjective sense of time, then, forms a part of a perception of reality, influences the arranging of activities in time, and affects goal setting and goal attainment. It is this subjective sense of time that causes the authors of this book to classify it as a human resource. If only objective, clock time would be considered, time could be classifed as a standard against which progress is measured.

TIME MEASUREMENT

Formal time measurement helps people socialize and synchronize their activities with those of others. A person who wants to talk to a physician, teacher, city official, or employer often has to make an appointment for a specific time in the future. In such a situation, a secretary or receptionist may schedule the meeting for the following Tuesday at 3 p.m. The appointment is based on the understanding that those involved know when Tuesday is, and understand the meaning of the term "3 p.m."

While a person's sense of time helps to orient himself to the world, formal time is useful in coordinating events with other people and other places or things. Formal time somewhat parallels the biological concept of time. Because people differ in awareness of these biological cycles and because of the need to coordinate activities, the passage of time has been formalized. The divisions of centuries, decades, years, seasons, months, days, hours, minutes, seconds, and even smaller time divisions are based on natural cycles. Clocks and calendars orient people to this formal system of time measurement.

Learning about time is a gradual process, and the formal measurement of time is the last in a series of time-related learnings. Piaget reported that children initially need to become sensitive to the order of events in their lives and to the duration or lengths of events. He observed a relationship between time and rate in young children's concept of time. In other words, a faster moving person or object seemed to use less time than a slower moving one. An understanding of the objective measurement of time may not be completely developed until a child is between 8 and 12 years of age.[14]

Meerloo reported that in at least some psychological illnesses, people may be faced with a blocked or distorted view of time.[15] Consistent tardiness or guarding personal time too carefully is sometimes termed mismanagement of time because of psychological factors.

Time is a concept that is understood gradually and, as a resource, is measured and both subjectively and objectively understood. A perception of time as a manageable resource can give order and direction to life.

Patterns of Time Use

Time use has been categorized according to its specific application for purposes of personal analysis and for scientific research. Some of the classifications that have been applied in research include: work and leisure;[16] employment for pay, personal and family care, sleep and leisure;[17] and work time, personal work, consumption, cultivation of the mind and spirit, and idleness.[18] Patterns of time use are further explained as follows.

WORK TIME

Is work only those activities for which people are paid? Is work production only made real through tangible results? Is work the activities needed for survival? These are among the questions that researchers and theorists have struggled with to develop classifications of time use. *Work* is defined here as activities producing measurable results for one's self or others. The varieties of work time include time used for work for pay, household or home-related work, and volunteer work.

Employment

Time devoted to employment for pay is one category of work time. If people are paid by the number of hours, weeks, or months they work, time seems more economically valuable than if work is purely related to meeting survival needs without monetary return.[19]

Employment time differs with the specific job. Work days are not always the standard 8 a.m. to 5 p.m., and work weeks do not always extend from Monday through Friday. The specific nature of work hours influences the duration of nonwork activities and also affects synchronization of personal activities with those of others. A person who concentrates work time into 10 to 12 hour days in a four-day work week has three consecutive days for other activities but has more limited time for such activities during the work week. People in executive or professional positions generally have more choice in their work hours but work longer days or weeks than do those with more regular work hours.[20] Such people may, for example, bring work home from the office or may work beyond closing time, leaving less time for other activities.

Some people, faced with shortened work hours, may seek second jobs to increase income or to pass time. Approximately five percent of all employed persons work at two or more jobs.[21] A second or third job provides a person or family with a more adequate income but may leave the wage earner with less time for enjoying the benefits of such income.

Time spent traveling to and from a place of employment is also a form of work time. Consider two people employed the same number of hours each day: if one worker commutes two hours each day, that worker has less discretionary time. than does the worker who can walk to work in five or ten minutes. If the commuting worker drives to work, his or her travel time is completely occupied by driving. If the person can join a car pool or use a form of mass transportation, however, the travel time can also be used for some alternate activities. Employed people may read while commuting, and, for some people, commuting time may be most creative.

Home-related Work

Household care, personal care, and care of other family members is another form of productive or work time. Although the time requirements of specific household work have changed in the last 40 years, the average total time for this work is about the same. For example, food preparation time and after-meal cleanup took 30 minutes less in 1967 than it did in a similar study done in 1927. During the same time, average marketing, record keeping, and household-management time increased by 30 minutes.[22] Women spent a minimum of four hours a day in household work, and this time increased with the presence of children—especially young children. Men averaged one and one-half hours in household work, and their contributions increased only as their hours of employment decreased. Children's time for home-related work was similar to that of adult males.[23]

Readers might be surprised at the amount of time used for household work, but as people purchase more goods and larger houses, the time needed to purchase, prepare for use, clean, and maintain these items also tends to increase. As household work is made easier through technology, people may also do the cleaning and laundry more frequently. New tasks, such as chauffering children to and from school or to leisure activities, have also been added to household work during these 40 years.

Volunteer Work

Time contributed to a church, a community, or a nation for no monetary pay is termed *volunteer time*. It could be classified as leisure, but its productive nature causes these authors to classify it as a variety of work time. In the mid 1960's, volunteers were estimated at 16 percent of the population over 14 years of age.[24] Time spent in volunteer activities may vary from a once-a-year fund drive to weekly community meetings or service time at a local library or hospital. Although people using time for community or household work are not often paid a wage, this time use does affect personal, household, community, and national quality of life.

NONWORK TIME

Sleep is one of the most time-consuming of all human activities. It accounts for about one-third of an adult's day and an even larger share of a child's day.[25] Although sleep is needed for survival, the specific amount needed varies with each person. While one person may be refreshed after six hours of sleep, others may need nine or more hours of sleep each day. In addition to sleep, free time and leisure are classified as nonwork time.

Free Time

Time not devoted to work or to sleep is called *free time*.[26] Free time may be imposed or may occur by choice. A person who seeks full-time work but can find only a part-time job or cannot find work is faced with *imposed free time*. If the man or woman has insufficient nonhuman, economic resources—money, transportation, or tools—or lacks interest in free-time activities, this time can be a constraint rather than as a resource. Young adults, people over 65 years of age, minority group members, and female heads of households are more likely than members of other groups to be faced with imposed free time.[27]

Leisure

Time spent in activities chosen by the individual and rewarding for its own sake is *leisure*. In other words, leisure is unimposed free time. If a person sits because he or she wants to, this time is classified as pure leisure. Family pic-

nics, water-skiing, horseback riding, tennis, reading, or other activities not related to work roles are also considered leisure-time activities.

Some leisure time may overlap with employment, and some leisure
activities involve more freedom of choice than others. An employee who enjoys golf, bowling, or basketball may feel pressured to join a company-
sponsored team. Is this pure leisure? A family who purchases and remodels an
older home in their spare time also overlaps elements of work and leisure. A
Sunday school teacher who prepares lessons for the coming week's class
mixes volunteer work and leisure time. An exhausted child, who turns on the
television set for diversion from homework, uses time for escape, but is this
pure leisure? If the reader were to study use of pure leisure time, he or she
would need to ask about the discretionary nature of the activities and about the
relationship of these activities to work roles.

Studies of leisure time have utilized individual definitions of leisure.[28] One
study of nonrural households excluded employment, sleep, and personal and
household care time, but considered volunteer time and class time as leisure
activities. In this study, full-time housewives had slightly more leisure time than
did employed males, while employed females had the least leisure time of the
three groups. During a week, the average for all respondents was five hours of
daily leisure time.[29] These researchers recognized the problem in studying
leisure time and asked, "Should, for example, eating be considered a leisure-
time activity or a personal- and family-care activity?"[30]

Informal social activities and television viewing were the most frequently
reported leisure activities in an international study of time use.[31] Citizens in
less-developed countries generally reported a wider variety of free-time
activities than did those in economically-developed countries. Ferge attributed
part of this relationship to the presence of television in more affluent
societies.[32] These researchers observed leisure patterns within countries, supporting the conclusion that society influences people's definitions of acceptable uses of free time.[33]

The characteristics of available time may also influence the choices of
leisure activities. If free time is available in small bits, people may select different activities than if larger blocks of free time are available. A few minutes a
day can be used for visiting, reading, television watching, walking for recreation,
or bike riding; but a longer *duration* is needed for a camping trip. Likewise the
regularity of free time can affect choices of leisure activities. A person who
knows that he or she has two specific days a week free from employment may
select different leisure activities than others whose jobs or home-related roles
require that they be always available. People who consider leisure activities
extremely important may select or reject specific employment roles because of
the impact these commitments have on free time.

From the above discussion, it can be concluded that the use of time for specific roles and activities limits choices available for other time uses. Although the data presented here illustrates general trends in time use, individual and family priorities also need to be considered in managing time.

Applying the Management Processes to Time Use

Time is an influential resource because it is used with other resources to reach goals. Through the application of management, individuals and families can utilize time to achieve desired qualities of life. In the processes of managing time, people may develop other resources or recognize priorities in life that had not been previously considered.

EVALUATING TIME USE

A person or family, dissatisfied with current time use, may feel pressured by time demands and may want to improve the effectiveness of its use. Evaluating current uses of time is a logical beginning for improvement. This evaluation provides a benchmark against which change can be evaluated. This analysis alerts people to possible improvement in the uses of time or other resources.

A simple technique for evaluation is recalling time use during the previous 24 hours. Listing activities and the amount of time used for each, as well as totaling the overall amount of time, is involved in this technique. People who overlap activities, such as listening to the radio while doing something else, will total more than 24 hours of activity in a day. An analysis of activities by major groups such as work, sleep, or free time can lead to an understanding of the balance between activities. Because people differ in their recall abilities,[1] some activities may be forgotten, and time estimates may not be completely accurate. Thus, additional forms of evaluation may lead to a more complete understanding of time use patterns.

A time log of weekly activities may sound tedious; however, the knowledge gained from such an experience can lead to more realistic management of time. In evaluating the listed activities, a number of questions can be asked. The person may, for example, want to consider time devoted to sleep; too much or too little sleep in relation to personal needs can inhibit goal attainment. If some listed activities are evaluated as unimportant or excessively time-consuming, it may be necessary to consider omitting or altering the frequency of such activities or to learn short cuts to task completion. Considering the reasons for delays or avoidance can help to later accomplish these activities or to revise priorities. An awareness of time-use routines, frequent interruptions, or unanticipated activities, as well as questions related to goal attainment during the week, can lead to more realistic planning.

PLANNING TIME USE

Formal or informal time schedules are used by most people, but not all manage time equally well. Some people act as if they are in a race with time—trying to do everything before the day ends. Others, who can anticipate demands on their time and sort priorities, may be faced with some frustrations but are able to manage, rather than be managed by, a time plan.

The value of time plans is that before action the person or family setting them can consciously consider long-range goals, needed and desired short-range activities, as well as possible problems in time use. Situations change and time plans are revised, but without some plan, would people be able to anticipate the meaning of these changes and the need for revision? Carefully considered time plans can increase satisfaction and reduce indecision or worry in the application of time and other resources to reach goals.

Bases of Time Plans

A general goal of time management is the conservation of time to match needs and wants. Time plans should, therefore, reflect personal and household goals. Based on these goals, people decide on activities to be included in the day, week, month, or year for which they are planning.

Freedom in planning time use is restricted by prior decisions and by other members of the environment. Work or school hours of family members affect the times at which meals can be prepared and served. Music lessons, participation in social or professional clubs, or membership in community organizations are examples of other activities that have definite time demands. These activities must be considered in planning time use because they affect its use in the household. Previously set standards in home-related work or time for family interaction are also examples of factors that affect time planning.

Two general restrictions in time planning are individual preference and the inflexible nature of some activities.[34] *Inflexible activities* are those that occur at a fixed time. For example, a church service scheduled for 10:30 a.m. cannot be attended at noon, or a train departing at 10:43 cannot be boarded later that day. Other activities are available during a limited time, while still others, like 24-hour shopping or banking, are available at any time. People may also choose to consider some events as completely inflexible by deciding, for example, that lunch will be served at 11:30 each day or that bedtime is at 11 each night. Because there is a range of rigidity in activities, this restriction is illustrated as a continuum in Chart 9.1.

Evaluations of the need for activities reflect personal and family preferences as well as the situation. Such evaluations are illustrated as a continuum in the chart. Although people will place activities in different positions on such a chart, the essential, inflexible events must be planned for in available time if people are to be satisfied with their use of time.

Chart 9.1   Two Restrictions in Planning the Use of Time. This model illustrates one person's view of the flexibility and importance of a specific group of activities. While the placement of activities may vary with the person and the situation, this chart illustrates that the roles and activities selected by a person or group do influence time management.

In Chapter 2, a variety of plans were discussed, and the usefulness of each mental and written plan was explored. To apply these concepts to time management, the reader should be aware that the processes of planning and organizing often overlap.

ORGANIZING ACTIVITIES IN TIME

Organizing activities in time involves an orderly arrangement of planned events, the assignment of responsibilities, and the delegation of authority when others are involved. To realistically organize activities in time, managers must consider three factors—the rate or pace, sequence, and synchronization of activities in managing time.

Rate or Pace

Some people are slow and methodical, while others seem to rush through life; personality and physical attributes affect the tempo or speed of action. In addition to personality, resources affect the organization of time as illustrated in the following examples and in Chart 9.2 (see page 231). If a family member is learning a new skill, like changing a tire or doing the laundry, a longer period of time will be needed than if an experienced person is carrying out the activity. Additionally, there may be a need for another family member to supervise the learning. The supervisor needs to recognize this pace adjustment to avoid shared feelings of frustration with the experience.

In addition to knowledge, other human resources affect the rate of activity. A person who is tired or has a cold may not think clearly, and this change can affect pace. People who lack interest in a planned activity may either rush through an activity or may work at a very slow pace, while hoping that others will complete the disliked activity.

Economic resources also affect the speed at which an activity is carried out. Household appliances can be more quickly readied for use if there is convenient and adequate storage for each appliance in the work area. A family member who enjoys woodworking will be able to work at a more comfortable pace if he or she has an adequately sized and arranged work space as well as the appropriate tools.

Knowledge of the effects of resources on pace can help a manager to adjust the tempo of activities and make plans more workable. A student who feels sluggish while studying may observe that a slightly lower room temperature or improved lighting can improve reading speed and comprehension.

Sequence of Activities

The sequence or order in which activities follow one another in a schedule is influenced by the number and duration of inflexible events, by the relationship among tasks, and by personal or group preferences. Some sequences are fixed by the nature of the activity. The sequence in starting a car or baking bread needs to be carefully followed in order to achieve satisfactory results. Useful, frequently repeated sequences can become *procedural routines* that reduce time and other resource demands, to allow people to employ other improvements in time management.

Some general suggestions for sequencing activities in time follow, but each person will need to decide how to apply the ideas of his or her situation. Time and motions are saved by *clustering* or grouping activities that fall into sequence and that fit into an available block of time. Combining a number of errands into one trip on the way home from work is an example of clustering. A national study reported that people overlapped activities on an average of

4.9 hours each day.[35] This *overlap* involves at least two activities occuring simultaneously—one that is active and the other that requires only occasional attention or does not fully occupy the person's mind. In preparing an oven dinner, a cook does not have to focus constant attention on the oven while the dinner is cooking but may need to occasionally check on the meal. During the cooking process, then, the cook's time is somewhat free for other, nearby activities. Overlapping driving and reading—two primary activities—is an ineffective use of overlap because of the great degree of attention needed for each of the activities. Combining tasks that use the same tools or equipment is another effective sequence because time and effort needed to assemble, clean, and replace tools and equipment is minimized through this technique.

To achieve practical daily, weekly, or longer sequences of activities, people may also want to consider their biological clocks as well as peak-time loads. If early morning or late evening is a productive time for a person, demanding activities might be scheduled during that time. If a person finds that he or she does not accomplish much during the early afternoon, it may be possible to schedule less demanding, less tiring activities for that time. Alternating physical with mental activities is another way to conserve effort in a given time period and to avoid fatigue.

Synchronization

Meshing events, people, and nonhuman resources in time is *synchronization*. To bring order to varied activities, estimates are made of the length of time needed for each activity or group of activities, and these estimates are integrated into the plan. Previous evaluation of time use supplemented by time-use norms (see the section on patterns of time use and Chapter 10) can serve as a basis for these estimates. The levels of organization, referred to in Chapter 2 and in Chart 9-2, illustrate the varying degrees of complexity in synchronizing activities.

While people may unconsciously consider their preferences in pace in synchronizing group management, there is a danager of assuming that others also prefer this pace. For example, completing a group of household repairs may require that, or may be more enjoyable if, several group members participate. If one family member tends to work constantly and to relax only when the project is done, his or her pace differs from another who takes short, frequent rest breaks during the activity; this difference affects the synchronization of action. A manager faced with such a situation can delegate separate areas of responsibility to each person or can help family members to coordinate their pace in synchronized work. Coordinating the varied pace of such a group requires an appreciation of individual differences if all family members are to be involved in the activity.

Chart 9.2 Organizing Activities in Time. The rate, sequence, and synchronization of activities influence the organization of these activities in time.

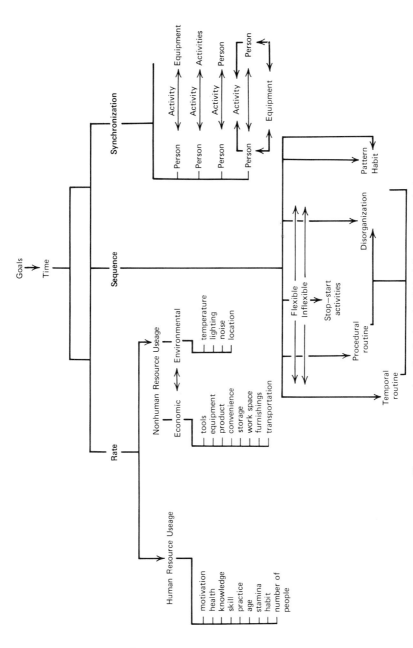

The rate, sequence, and synchronization of activities influence the organization of these activities in time.

This integration of individual and group activities into a synchronized unit is a very complex level of organization, and the complexity may not be apparent unless part of the organizing effort is out of phase. In the temporary absence of a family member who has done most of the home-related work, other family members may assume these responsibilities. Because of little experience, these family members might find that getting all the dishes for a meal ready at the same time and at appropriate temperatures is more difficult than anticipated. Although each individual's work load is lightened by a number of people's involvment, the synchronization in this case is made more complex because a number of people with individual pace and differing availability of time are working in a limited space with a limited number of tools and equipment.

In living units, as opposed to factories, space may be used for a number of purposes, and this multiple use of space makes synchronizing activities in time essential. The use of a living room or family room, for example, as a television room, a study, a game room, a party room, and a spare bedroom must be sequenced and synchronized if it is to be effectively used. Communication among family members is an essential resource to synchronize such individual and family activities in time.

Planning and organizing processes are integrated into what is commonly called a time plan. As described above, the process can seem too difficult to attempt; however, people develop these plans gradually, and much of the activity may be mental. If a person or family is developing a new plan for time use, however, plans should include all important and necessary activities, should be relatively simple, and should be workable for the person or group who will implement the plan.

IMPLEMENTING TIME PLANS

Unless time plans are used, they are not resources but are constraints for management. The resources invested in making the plans could have been put to other uses. The utility of a plan is partially determined by the ease with which it can be implemented. A workable plan will facilitate action in a normal household situation and, with adjustment, can provide stability in times of crisis.

Resources in Implementation

If a homemaker plans to finish weeding the garden before lunch and is interrupted by a neighbor who wants to visit, the homemaker is faced with a decision—should she combine the visiting with the weeding, postpone the garden work until later, or alert the neighbor to her plans and schedule the visit for some later time. Minor control decisions like this one occur throughout the process and are guided by a person's or family's awareness of priorities in goals, values, and standards. Self discipline, supervisory skills, and flexibility are among the human resources that are also important to the effective implementation of time plans.

Self discipline is the will power needed to complete an activity. People who are enthusiastic and confident in their planned use of time will be more motivated toward completion than will those who are bored, overwhelmed by, or lack confidence in the plans. To increase self discipline, people may find it practical to divide large activities into smaller, more measurable ones. A person who wants to refinish a room full of furniture, for example, may be able to complete the project if the labor involved is performed one step at a time and if goals are kept in mind. As each piece of furniture is completed, pride in the accomplishment will motivate further progress. Contrast this attitude with that of a person who just looks at the room full of furniture and wonders if he or she will ever find the time to do all that work.

Self discipline may also be enhanced by the use of a reward system, a written plan, or outside reinforcement. The student who studies every evening during the week so he or she can go canoeing that weekend is using a system of rewards in managing his or her time. Being able to check off completed activities on a written plan may also enhance motivation because progress can then be identified. If someone else comments favorably about the progress in implementation, the manager's confidence in his or her ability to implement time plans may also be enhanced.

If a number of people are involved in an activity, *supervisory skills* may enter into the implementation of time plans. The case of a household move can illustrate the importance of supervisory skills to implementation. If a location change is within the same community, it may be logical to clean the new living unit before the furniture is moved, to pack dishes and other small household possessions before the moving process is begun, and to deliver full truck or car loads to the new location. If family members help with the activity, they will need to be alerted to the sequence of activities and to the planned location of items with the living unit if resources are to be effectively used. The communication needs to be clear and direct if the moving process is to be effectively implemented. Those carrying out the activity may also enjoy knowing that their help is appreciated.

During implementation, a manager's skill in adjusting plans will also come into play. If a need or opportunity arises for an activity that is more important than the planned one, should the need go unmet or the opportunity overlooked because it was not included in the original plan?

Problems in Implementing Time Plans

Procrastination, delays, interruptions, discouragement, or guilt are among the problems in implementation that can be avoided through conscious management of time. *Procrastination*—delaying activities—can cause havoc with time but can be solved by a more complete understanding of personal motivation. Some people manage and function quite effectively only when faced with imposed deadlines. If such people can substitute self-set deadlines for those that are imposed, they, rather than other people or other situations, will be managing their time. If the reasons for procrastination are sought and if adjustments are made, a more workable management of time can be developed, and work will no longer accumulate.

Some delays or interruptions may require adjustments from managers, while it is possible to creatively manage others. The case of a couple on vacation who were told that their connecting flight would be two and one-half hours late is an interesting example. Rather than adjusting to the change in schedule, the couple chose to fly stand-by and arrived at their destination only one-half hour later than originally planned. A manager must recognize the number of available alternatives if such a change in implementation is to be attempted. If the one mechanic in town, for example, says it will take one week before he or she will be able to fix a car, adjustments may have to be made in the family's mode of travel.

As previously mentioned, knowledge of personal and family priorities can guide a manager faced not only with interruptions, but also with discouragement or guilt. In one homemaker's case, discouragement with time management resulted from a plan that was inappropriate for her family. To conserve time and money she developed a detailed written menu and a time schedule for the week. The menu was posted on the refrigerator, and during the second evening's meal, her husband became extremely angry at the plan. After his anger subsided, he was able to recognize that constantly seeing the week's menu seemed to take the spontaneity and enjoyment from meal time. He also said he missed the involvement in meal planning. This knowledge aided the couple in developing a more workable time plan.

Guilt is frequently associated with the implementation of leisure-time activities, but this guilt appears to be less of a problem for younger people.[36] If people schedule leisure activities into a time plan and recognize that the plan is adequately developed to allow for this variety, guilt should be reduced.

CONTROLLING TIME PLANS

As illustrated above, evaluation and adjustment enter into making and carrying out plans and in reviewing the final results of time management. In planning to reach goals through the use of time, individuals and families evaluate alternative or combined activities to develop a workable plan.

As time and activity plans are carried out, there is continual evaluation of performance and checking of accomplishments to be certain that activities conform to plans. If time requirements have been over or underestimated or if adjustments must be made in a day's activities, the evaluation of a number of factors enters into these controlling decisions. This evaluation aids in the development of future time plans.

In analyzing a plan at its completion, it may be worthwhile to ask these questions:

- Was the plan workable?

- Did it help to accomplish what had to be done as well as the less essential but enjoyable activities?

- Were the needs of others met? If not, what changes could be made in future plans?

- If there were difficulties, were these in planning? Were these in organizing? Was the difficulty in controlling the plan in action or in implementation?

Successful time management makes the attainment of individual and family goals possible without misusing resources or causing unnecessary tension. Because clock time serves, to some degree, as a standard against which progress toward goals is measured, understanding of time use can also lead to a more integrated perspective of the use of other resources.

Summary

This chapter has included an analysis of the concept of time including its cultural, psychological, and objective components. Typical time use patterns for work—including employment, home-related work, and volunteer time—and groups of nonwork activity were then described. Lastly, the processes of management were specifically applied to the resource of time. In applying these general suggestions, readers were reminded to adapt the guidelines to their needs, values, goals, standards, and resources.

References

1. Hall, E. T., *The Silent Language,* Doubleday, New York, (1959), p. 29.

2. Pryde, D., *Nunaga: Ten Years of Eskimo Life,* Walker, New York, (1971), pp. 277–278.

3. Orme, J. E., *Time, Experience and Behavior,* Elsevier, London, (1969), pp. 9–12.

4. Cohen, J., "Psychological Time," *Scientific American, 211:*5 (November 1964), p. 117.

5. Meerloo, J. A. M., *Along the Fourth Dimension: Man's Sense of Time and History,* John Day, New York, (1970).

6. Hamner, K. C., "Experimental Evidence for the Biological Clock," in J. T. Fraser (ed.), *The Voice of Time: A Comparative Survey of Man's Views of Time as Expressed by the Sciences and the Humanities,* G. Braziller, New York, (1966), p. 288.

7. Orme, J. E., *op. cit.,* p. 111.

8. Strughold, H., *Your Body Clock: Its Significance for the Jet Traveler,* Charles Scribner's Sons, New York, (1971).

9. Meerloo, J. A. M., "The Time Sense in Psychiatry," in J. T. Fraser (ed.), *op. cit.,* pp. 235–252.

10. Piaget, J., "Time Perception in Children," in J. T. Fraser, *op. cit.* p. 212.

11. Orme, J. E., op. cit., p. 9.

12. Meerloo, J. A. M., *op. cit.,* p. 118.

13. Gross, I. H., Crandall, E. W., and Knoll, M. M., *Management for Modern Families,* Appleton-Century-Crofts, (1973), p. 375.

14. Piaget, J., *op. cit.*

15. Meerloo, J. A. M., *op. cit.*

16. Kelly, J. R., "Work and Leisure: A Simplified Paradigm," *Journal of Leisure Research, 4:*1 (Winter 1972), pp. 50–62.

17. Executive Office of the President, Office of Management and Budget, *Social Indicators, 1973,* United States Government Printing Office, Washington, D.C., (1973), p. 223.

18. Linder, S. B., *The Harried Leisure Class,* Columbia University, New York, (1970), pp. 13–14.

19. Moore, W. E., *Man, Time and Society,* Wiley, New York, (1963), p. 25.

20. Executive Office of the President, *op. cit.,* p. 214; Wilensky, H. L., "The Uneven Distribution of Leisure: the Impact of Economic Growth on 'Free time'," *Social Problems, 9* (Summer 1961), pp. 32–56.

21. United States Department of Labor, *Manpower Report of the President,* United States Government Printing Office, Washington, D.C., (1972), p. 209.

22. Steidl, R. E., and Bratton, E. C., *Work in the Home,* Wiley, New York, (1968), pp. 84–85.

23. Walker, K. E., "Effect of Family Characteristics on Time Contributed for Household Work by Various Members," speech to American Home Economics Association meeting, Atlantic City, New Jersey, (1973).

24. *Americans Volunteer,* Manpower/Automation Research Monograph #10, United States Government Printing Office, Washington, D.C., (April 1969).

25. Strughold, H., *op. cit.,* p. 36.

26. deGrazia, S., *Of Time, Work and Leisure,* Free Press, New York, (1967).

27. Young, A. M., and Michelotti, K., "Work Experience of the Population in 1970," *Monthly Labor Review, 94:*12 (December 1971), pp. 12–71.

28. Kelly, J. R., *op. cit.*

29. Executive Office of the President, *op. cit.,* p. 214.

30. *Ibid.*

31. Converse, P. E., "Country Differences in Time Use," in A. Szalai (ed.), *The Use of Time: Daily Activities of Urban and Suburban Populations in Twelve Countries,* Mouton, The Hague, (1972) pp. 156–157.

32. Ferge, S., "Social Differentiation in Leisure Activity Choices," in A. Szalai (ed.), *op. cit.,* pp. 219–220.

33. *Ibid.,* p. 226.

34. Bratton, E. C., *Home Management Is. . .*, Ginn and Company, New York, (1971), p. 280.

35. Executive Office of the President, *op. cit.*

36. Neulinger, J., and Breit, M., "Attitude Dimensions of Leisure: A Replication Study," *Journal of Leisure Research, 3:*2 (Spring 1971), pp. 108–115.

10

MANAGING HOME-RELATED WORK

People will consider personal and home-related work to be a frustrating or a rewarding experience depending, to some degree, on their managerial skills and on their attitudes toward the work. Even those who choose to, and can afford to, pay someone else to perform home-related work must know about the work to adequately supervise its completion.

Home-related work is the group of activities that keeps a household functioning while meeting a certain standard of cleanliness and safety in daily living. The general task groups include meal preparation and after-meal clean up, physical care of family members, care of a living unit, laundry and other care of clothing, and shopping and record keeping. Each of these groups includes a variety of tasks utilizing varied resource mixtures. The monetary value of these services provided to individuals and families through home-related work has been estimated at approximately one-third to one-fourth of the total Gross National Product.[1]

The goods and services produced within households for members are most often provided by females who have limited training for this career.[2] In assuming the role of wife, these persons also become "homemakers". A small amount of technical knowledge may have been gained in school, or limited observation and practice may have occurred as children at home; however, rapid technological change applied in the home can rapidly outdate homemakers' knowledge. However, the recent trend toward co-educational home management, family living, or consumer education courses at a variety of educational levels illustrates an increasing recognition of the importance of developing human resources in home-related roles.

What do people need to know in order to successfully manage home-related work? The concepts of time management from the previous chapter, as well as the concepts of financial mangement in the following chapters, are interwoven in home-related work. This chapter will specifically explore home-related tasks—general concepts related to work, findings from home-management research, specific techniques borrowed from industrial management but applied to home-related work, and the performance of these tasks by those in nontraditional settings.

Work-Related Concepts

Fatigue, in its general context, signifies a reduced performance of work—it is caused by either physical exhaustion, aversion to work, preoccupation with some other aspect of life, or any combination of these and other factors.

A study of the fatigue of homemakers with young children illustrates some of the problems in managing home-related work. The number of tasks within a given period of time and shifting from task to task were factors closely related to the fatigue these homemakers experienced.[3] Attitudes toward household tasks and the energy demands of specific tasks, combined with personal feelings of adequacy in carrying out the activities, and the characteristics of the work place all have been related to feelings of fatigue. Factors that have implications for reducing fatigue in home-related work depend on the person performing the work, the nature of the work, and the design of the work place.[4]

THE WORKER

Human resources—cognitive, affective, and psychomotor—affect performance of household work. Examples of some important *cognitive resources* include knowledge of materials used in household equipment and furnishings, understanding of the developmental tasks of children and adults, and the ability to plan meals that are economical, attractive, varied, and nutritious. Examples of *affective resources* applied to home-related work include judgments of the desired quality and quantity of goods to be purchased, appreciation of the contributions of other household members, or tolerance of the repetitive nature of some work. *Psychomotor resources* have been emphasized in writing and research on home-related work but interact with cognitive and affective resources to help families reach goals. A more detailed discussion of physical energy, posture, and rest follows.

Physical Energy

Human energy required for the performance of any task is a combination of normal body functions—respiration, circulation, secretion, and excretion—and the energy used to move about and to complete the task. The pace of work, the tools used, and the position of the worker are among the factors affecting energy use in household work.

Measuring the energy costs of household tasks, though useful in planning

Chart 10.1   Energy-Demanding Tasks

Light: 1.4–2 Calories per Minute	Moderate: 2–3.5 Calories per Minute	Heavy: 3.5–4.5 Calories per Minute
Hemming	Using carpet sweeper	Scrubbing floor
Knitting	Using vacuum sweeper	Mopping floor
Crocheting	Polishing furniture	Waxing floor
Hand sewing	Kneading dough	Taking out and hanging
Machine sewing	Hanging clothes from	laundry
Preparing meals	utility table	Bedmaking
Washing dishes	Ironing	Lifting heavy baskets of
Dusting furniture and		wet clothes
floors		Lifting young children
Sweeping kitchen floor		

work and in designing living units, provides only a partial understanding of the fatigue the worker experiences. Some light tasks, listed in Chart 10-1, may be tiring because of personal attitudes, postural strain, muscle tension, or the concentration and skill required. Other energy-demanding tasks may be less tiring than light work because of the cognitive or affective resources of the worker.

Posture in Home-Related Work

To avoid strain and to reduce the likelihood of fatigue, attention can be given to posture and effective use of body mechanics. Homemakers, male and female alike, can avoid visits to their doctor for painful back problems or other muscle strain through the application of these principles.[5]

Posture involves keeping the natural balance of the body aligned, whether sitting, standing, or moving. If the three major weight centers—head, chest, and pelvis—are balanced, less strain or fatigue results.[6] If an imbalance occurs, muscles work to keep the body in equilibrium, and that is wasted energy. For example, when bending or pushing a heavy object, as illustrated in Chart 10-2, spreading the feet apart widens the base of support and keeps the body properly aligned. Static positions are tiring because of muscle tension; thus, it is also wise to alternate activities involving standing and sitting.

A second principle that applies to home-related work is the use of *efficiency in effort*. Hazelton and Russell describe efficient use as "the one that (1) uses only those muscles or parts of the body that are necessary to the operation, and (2) uses those muscles or parts of the body that are best able to do the work."[7] In lifting a heavy baby or a bag of groceries from the floor, stronger leg muscles can be utilized if a person bends the knees and hips. If the worker bends only at the hips, he or she is using weaker back muscles and is ignoring this principle of efficiency in body mechanics.

There are related principles that apply to weight and body movement. Lifted objects carried close to the middle of the body require less effort than if they are carried away from the body. Smooth, continuous, and rhythmic motions are less tiring than sudden, sharp changes in movement.[8] Pushing, rather than pulling, large objects such as furniture and aligning the worker's and the object's center of gravity so they are close together, are also energy-and stress-reducing guidelines, as illustrated in Chart 10-2.

Rest

Rest periods during a day's work help prevent fatigue and inefficiency. The length of needed rest depends on the nature of the work and on the individual's human resources. Industrial researchers have concluded that rest periods are most effective if taken when productivity begins to decline—when fatigue is starting. After all but very strenuous work, complete relaxation may not be helpful.[9] The length of rest periods in home-related work depends on the fatigue level of the worker. The time should be long enough to achieve a relaxed feeling and to return to work with enthusiasm.

Chart 10.2   Applying Principles of Body Mechanics.

Ok	Ok	Avoid this
Bending	Lifting	Lifting

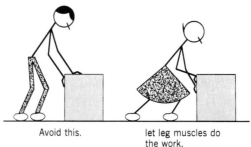

Avoid this.	let leg muscles do the work.

Managing home-related work, therefore, includes consideration of the person doing the work and an appreciation of individual capacities and limitations. The work and workplace can, through this knowledge, be made suitable to the person or group doing the job.

THE WORK

A number of authors have compared and contrasted the work of a full-time homemaker to paid employment.[10] Those authors agree that home-related work is varied, demanding, and requires specific, current knowledge, but also agree that it is accorded low status by others, including some homemakers in society. This section of the chapter will explore the role of a homemaker, some methods for evaluating specific household tasks, and guidelines for dividing responsibilities in home-related work.

Homemaker's Role

A *homemaker* is a person responsible for most or all of the home-related work performed by or for a family. In this role, people provide a variety of services, all of which require knowledge and skill. Teacher, chef, counselor, chauffeur, gardener, interior decorator, and purchasing agent are some of the more specific occupational roles combined in the role of homemaker.[11] Also, full-time homemakers manage other roles, such as that of husband, wife, mother, father, or neighbor, along with the specific corresponding demands.[12]

The time commitment for full-time homemakers varies with the number and ages of children. This work load is comparable to or greater than full-time employment in other occupations.[13] While other careers may have specific work hours, home-related work is more flexible yet more demanding in its time requirements. A homemaker can sequence a number of tasks in the morning so afternoon hours are free for other activities. In contrast to many occupational roles, homemakers do not advance to more prestigious roles within the household; their work-week extends over a seven- rather than over a four–to six-day work-week, and there is usually no paid vacation. These characteristics compare with the work of a farmer, a self-employed professional, or a small-business owner. Like persons in these occupations, homemakers do most of their work alone but may be able to occasionally hire someone to help.

Uniform performance standards exist for a variety of occupational roles, but overall performance standards are lacking for the role of homemaker. Standards regarding the quality of overall results are left to the discretion of the homemaker or of the household group. This lack of specification provides freedom to carry out the work but entails frustration if the homemaker and significant others do not agree on specific procedural or performance standards, as illustrated in the following example.

Chart 10.3 Composition of The Work-Day Of Full-Time Homemakers. Adapted from Walker, K. E., "Homemaking still takes time," *Journal of Home Economics, 61:8* (October 1969), p. 622. Full-time homemakers used an average of eight hours per day for home-related work. This 56-hour work-week compares to and, in some cases, exceeds the weekly hours of employment and home-related work for husbands in the study.

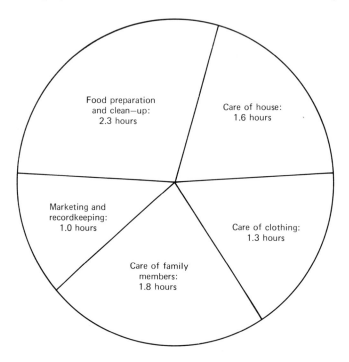

A homemaker with small children may discover that the late-evening hours are a good time for ironing, mending, or after-dinner clean up. If, however, her husband wants her sole attention devoted to her role as a wife and companion at this time, or, if he believes that a homemaker should go to sleep early enough to use early morning hours to fix a large breakfast for the family, a role conflict may exist. Family members who can discuss these role expectations will usually be able to resolve their differences; a lack of communication about role expectations can lead to prolonged conflict and dissatisfaction with individual and family qualities of life.

The advantages of individual and family determination of standards for home-related work can outweigh the disadvantages. Cooperatively determined and understood standards enhance motivation to complete the work. There is also a potential for experimentation with new products and methods, with the frequency of repetition of tasks, and with combinations of activities in the absence of externally-set standards. These standards can reflect the life style of the person or group.

An interesting assumption explored by Lopata is that home-related work is ignored by those not performing the work until it is incorrectly done or unfinished.[14] If this is the case for a number of families, how will this attitude affect the worker's motivation or another person's willingness to take on additional home-related work?

Homemakers' Preferences

Generally, cooking is a preferred household task, while ironing or cleaning are among the least liked tasks.[15] Researchers have examined some reasons for homemakers' preferences. Results of two such studies were in complete agreement on the primary reasons homemakers disliked specific tasks. In priority order, these reasons were monotony, fatigue, the short-term results, or dislike of work time. General agreement was found in the primary reasons for liking a task; although the ranking of the characteristics differed for the two groups of homemakers. These primary reasons included results being appreciated by other family members, self-satisfaction, and pride in results.[16] The reader may want to consider how homemakers and families can design work days and activities to emphasize the *positive* features of household tasks and to minimize the less desirable features.

Work Methods

Guidelines for procedures used to complete home-related work are numerous. Homemakers in Lopata's study listed printed or other secondary sources more frequently than interpersonal, primary sources for evaluating their performance of home-related work.[17] Magazines, newspapers, Cooperative Extension Service publications, books, as well as television and radio programs feature "how to do it" hints. If they are to be useful, these ideas need to be adapted to the life style of the person or group.

Additionally, homemakers can study bothersome or time-consuming tasks to improve work methods. Some industrial engineering methods for studying time and motions in work can be adapted to household tasks for use by homemakers or by professionals working with families to evaluate work methods. These techniques include the pathway chart, the process chart, and the operation chart.

The *pathway chart* is a simple device for time and motion study. A scale-sized floor plan of the work area, pins, and thread are all that are needed to make such a study. Pins are placed on the floor plan to indicate where a worker turns; the line of travel or pathway is measured from thread wound around each pin. In this way, the distance traveled in an initial work method and in an experimental method can be compared by the length of threads.

Chart 10.4   Process Chart

An Explanation of the Chart and Its Symbols. The Chart shows graphically the flow of activities from their start through their completion. Each symbol represents a particular function, as illustrated below. Operation changes the characteristics of an object, such as cutting fabric, opening a door, or turning on an oven. Moving or Transportation changes the location of an object, such as carrying a pan to a sink, pushing a chair to a dining table,

Activity   Making a Pot of Coffee

Distance in Feet	Steps	Move	Operation	Inspection	Delay, Storage	Description of Method
	3		○	☐	▽	To sink
		○	○	☐	▽	Get coffee pot; turn on water
		○	☐	☐	▽	Add water to measuring line
	2		○	☐	▽	Get coffee
		○	○	☐	▽	Open can
		○	○	☐	▽	Insert basket in pot
		○	☐	☐	▽	Pour coffee into basket to measuring line
		○	○	☐	▽	Put lid on pot
		○	○	☐	▽	Attach cord; plug cord into outlet
		○	○	☐	▽	Put lid on coffee can
	2	▽	○	☐	▽	Put coffee away
		○	○	☐	▽	Wait for coffee to perk
	4	○	○	☐	▽	Take coffee pot to table
		○	○	☐	▽	

Summary

4 Moves	1 Storage
8 Operations	1 Delay
2 Inspections	11 Steps

or wheeling a vacuum cleaner from storage to the room where it will be used. Inspection examines an object for identification or for comparison with performance standards, such as reading a thermometer, measuring ingredients, or checking the water level in a humidifier. Delay or storage occurs if the next step cannot be completed immediately, such as waiting for water to boil, putting food in a refrigerator, or hanging clothes in a closet. Note that the processes overlap if performed at the same location or at the same time. The number of processes, steps, or the distance traveled in a typical and altered work method can be compared through the use of process charts if the beginning and end points are the same for each work method. Adapted from R. M. Barnes, *Motion and Time Study: Design and Measurement of Work,* Wiley, New York, (1968), pp. 63-67.

An Explanation of the Chart and Its Symbols

The chart graphically shows the flow of activity from the start of activities through their completion. Each symbol represents a particular type of function, as illustrated below.

○   *Operation* changes the characteristics of an object, such as cutting fabric, opening a door, or turning an oven on.

○   *Movement or Transportation* changes the location of an object, such as carrying a pan to a sink, pushing a chair to a dining table, or wheeling a vacuum cleaner from storage to the room where it will be used.

□   *Inspection* examines an object for identification or for comparison with performance standards, such as reading a thermometer, measuring ingredients, or checking the water level in a humidifier.

▽   *Delay or Storage* occurs if the next step cannot be completed immediately, such as waiting for water to boil, putting food in a refrigerator, or hanging clothes in a closet.

Note that the processes overlap if performed at the same location or at the same time.

The number of processes, steps, or the distance traveled in a typical and altered work method, can be compared through the use of process charts if the beginning and end points are the same for each work method.

Adapted from R. M. Barnes, *Motion and Time Study: Design and Measurement of Work,* Wiley, New York, (1968), pp. 63-67.

The *process chart* is a step-by-step description of the method used in completing a task. It shows the flow of movement in the task and helps to reveal unnecessary steps and motions. The *operation chart* is used to make a more detailed study of a part of the process. In this chart, the movements are broken down into the activities of both the right and left hand.

Researchers used these techniques to develop task sequences in washing dishes,[18] ironing,[19] or making a bed.[20] Additionally, these techniques can be used to compare time or effort reduction through the use of products, tools, or equipment purported to make household tasks easier. One study compared the time used in washing dishes by hand and machine. The daily time, when washing dishes by hand, averaged 73.2 minutes or about one hour and 15 minutes a day. During 30 days of machine washing, the average was 35.6 minutes. Across a year, this use of a dishwasher represents a reduction of 28.5 eight-hour days.[21]

These techniques can help workers to understand the components of a specific task and to evaluate the time and effort used to complete it. Improving work methods requires practice and may, at first, seem uncomfortable. As illustrated in the dishwashing example, it is possible to free hours or days in a year's time through study and improvement of work methods. This freed time can be applied to other goals.

Dividing Responsibilities

Home-related work can also be shared by other family members. The tasks can be delegated to individual workers, or a number of people can cooperate to complete a specific task or a group of tasks. Resources and goals of the household need to be considered to decide whether to divide responsibilities, to cooperate, or to do the work alone.

Resources affecting pace listed in Chart 9.2, Chapter 9, also enter into the division of household tasks. For example, if only one person is available and able to do grocery shopping, he or she will have to perform the task. If a number of people are available, alternative resources and consideration of family goals and individual preferences may be involved.

Tradition may be a factor in dividing responsibilities in household work as well as in decision making. Males traditionally perform work outside the living unit—lawn work or car maintenance—while females traditionally perform tasks inside the living unit.[22] Parents who want to train their children for independent adult life, however, might choose to provide their children with experience in a variety of tasks.

Tradition also affects the sharing of tasks. Daughters in one study worked with mothers more than sons or fathers did. This study of low-income, urban families also reported ethnic differences in cooperation on general household tasks, with black fathers, daughters, and sons cooperating more than those of white or Puerto Rican origin.[23]

The methods of home-related work, homemakers' role satisfaction, and divisions of responsibility are also affected by the nature of the workplace. The next section includes a discussion of situational factors affecting the performance of home-related work.

THE WORKPLACE

Concepts of work heights, work centers, and arrangement within centers are also involved in effective management of home-related work. Families who are considering a change of residence can apply these concepts to evaluate the usefulness of specific work areas such as the kitchen, laundry, sewing, or child-care areas for individual or family activities. The concepts can also help to adapt the work areas in current housing to users' needs; some of these changes can be made with small expense and the creativity of household members.

Work Heights

The height of a work surface affects posture and fatigue. A tall homemaker, for example, will find most kitchen sinks too low. This homemaker will need to bend at the waist and stoop at the shoulders to wash dishes, and this is a tiring position. Too high a work surface requires the worker to raise arms and shoulders—another tiring position. Stretching and bending are among the adjustments made because of an inappropriate work surface. Comfortable work heights permit good working posture.

The suitability of work heights is relative to the worker's physique. A number of studies have revealed that work surfaces slightly lower than elbow height are preferred by most workers.[24] The specific distance below elbow height varies with the nature of the task. For example, the recommended height of work surface for using a rotary beater is 6 to 7 inches below elbow height, while that for serving food is 3 inches below elbow height.[25] In Chart 10.5, notice that comfortable standing or sitting work heights are those that allow the worker to keep his or her arms at right angles to the body. Workers can experiment with varied heights to determine those most comfortable for specific tasks.

The height and depth of seating surfaces also affect human performance. A comfortable chair or stool induces good posture without physical strain. To evaluate a seating surface, the following questions can be asked:

Can both feet rest comfortably on the floor?

Is there enough support in the areas behind and under the knee?

Chart 10.5   Equipment suited to worker permits good working postures.

Comfortable working height for handling supplies and equipment.

Comfortable working height for beating, stirring, kneading.

Comfortable working height for lap table and work chair for sitting-down tasks.

Comfortable working height for sink.

Poor sitting position. Stool too high for table.

Good sitting posture. Stool comfortable height. Footrest provided.

Equipment suited to worker permits good working postures.

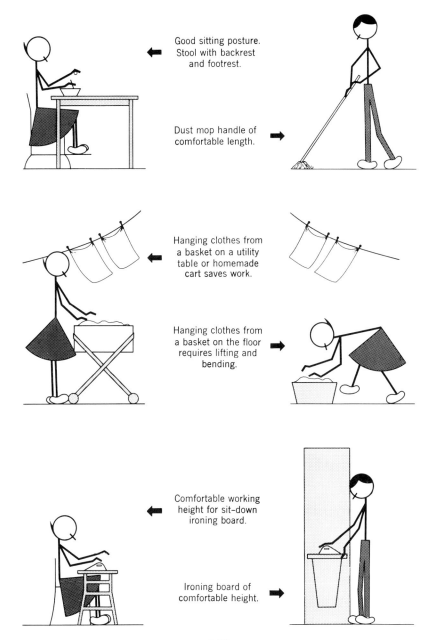

Good sitting posture. Stool with backrest and footrest.

Dust mop handle of comfortable length.

Hanging clothes from a basket on a utility table or homemade cart saves work.

Hanging clothes from a basket on the floor requires lifting and bending.

Comfortable working height for sit-down ironing board.

Ironing board of comfortable height.

Is the seat depth shallow enough to permit comfortable movement?

Is the seat sloped slightly backward to prevent a forward slide?

Is there adequate support for the small of the back?[26]

A "yes" answer to the above questions denotes a comfortable chair or stool for work.

People faced with inappropriate work heights can adapt their work place to their needs. A cutting board can be placed on a work surface that is too low for a worker's comfort. A small footstool can be placed under a worker's feet if the seating surface is too high. Perching or sitting on a stool can help a person adjust to a work surface too low for standing. Slide-out cutting boards, storage or equipment with adjustable heights, a sink base, or a kitchen table also provide flexibility in heights. Creative thinking combined with a knowledge of needed work heights helps to adapt existing work areas to human needs.

Work Centers

A *center* is an area designed for the performance of a specific activity. According to Steidl, each center has three components: (1) equipment, supplies, and utensils needed for the work, (2) storage space for needed items, and (3) work surface.[27] A woodworking center would, for example, contain the wood, nails, glue, sandpaper, and other tools and equipment, as well as storage for these items and space for work. Centers can be organized for gardening, for children's play, for musical entertainment, or for many other activities. Research has applied the concept of centers to kitchen design because food activities are an important part of home-related work, because homemakers spend over one-fourth of their home-related work time in kitchens, and because of the expense in building or remodeling kitchens.

The placement of major appliances influences the flow of work and the distance traveled in food preparation, serving, and after-meal clean-up. Kitchen centers are based on three or four major appliances—a sink with or without dishwasher, a range, and a refrigerator. Although researchers have used differing names and numbers of kitchen centers,[28] more work time is spent at the sink than at any other center.[29]

Research on the number of trips between centers has also influenced kitchen design. Researchers concluded that the range and sink should be placed relatively close together, dish storage should be near the sink, and the distance from the range to refrigerator is more important than that from refrigerator to sink.[30] As new appliances are introduced, new products become available, or trends in home building change, so may the standards in kitchen design.

Not only major appliances, but tools, supplies, and small equipment can also be organized by centers. Food and utensils first used with water should be stored at the sink center. Foods using boiling water and cooking utensils used without water should be stored near the range. Foods that are ready to eat and dishes, serving utensils, or equipment to be used at the dining table—a fondue pot or toaster—are easiest to use if stored where they are first needed. Storage containers for leftovers should be kept near the refrigerator. Also, the duplication of small items like salt and pepper, can openers, or spoons in more than one center can reduce travel time within a kitchen.[31]

Each center should include a *work surface*. Recommendations for the widths of work surfaces in kitchens include the following:

Sink—	36 inches to one side for dirty dishes and foods
	18 inches to the other side for clean items
Range—	21 inches of work surface
Mix—	36 inches of work surface
Refrigerator—	18 inches adjacent to the latch side
Serve—	24 inches of work surface.[32]

These are minimum space standards. If food is prepared for more than four people, if complex food preparation or food preservation is done, additional work space will be needed. Using one work surface for more than one center can reduce the total work surface needed.

Kitchen centers are usually organized in one of the following shapes: "L," "U," corridor, one-wall, or island. *Arrangements* that include centers at right angles to each other, as in the "L" or "U" shapes, shorten the distance between centers but require creativity in arranging corner storage.[33]

To evaluate kitchen arrangements, consideration should also be given to the number of people involved in food preparation and clean-up, to other nearby activities, and to the work methods used. If several workers are to use the kitchen at the same time, they will need separate work surfaces and space to move about comfortably and efficiently. This space need is further complicated by the need to open doors or drawers. If visiting is normally carried on in a kitchen, seating space is required outside the work area. Family members who want to see a specific outdoor area, such as a child's play yard, from the kitchen will also need to check the location and visibility from kitchen windows or doors. If a number of other rooms connect with the kitchen, the chance of interruptions and the danger of burns when moving hot food are increased. If a worker prefers sitting to standing for some kitchen activities, work space and under-counter knee space should also be included at this lowered height. Evaluating a kitchen's work-space arrangement involves consideration of the space needs for the work and the patterns of personal or family life.

Storage

Arranging supplies and equipment within easy reach reduces unnecessary walking, reaching, and stretching. To store items within kitchen centers and throughout a living unit, the following guidelines can be applied:

1. Sort items to be stored.
2. Place items at the point of first use.
3. Arrange items so they are easy to see, reach, grasp, and replace.[34]
4. Consider maximum reach.[35]
5. Plan storage to fit the items.

These guidelines apply to storage of any items used by household members—toys, sports or cleaning equipment, personal-care items, or household linen. Rather than revising all household storage at one time, it is less overwhelming to apply these principles to one center or room and to evaluate results before reorganizing the next center.

The initial step in arranging functional storage is to *sort items* according to the frequency and location of use and to who will be using them. Frequently used items such as toothbrushes, shoes, or everyday glassware, should be more accessible than items that are used monthly or seasonally. If some items are not used, decisions must be made regarding storage or disposal. Thinking about where an item is used and the characteristics of needed storage—hung, stacked, or separated in drawers—is a further step in defining storage needs.

Knowledge of household activity centers aids in placing items where they are first used. Tools, equipment, and supplies frequently used within a center should be stored nearby. Seasonal items such as holiday decorations or canning equipment, although first used at a specific location, can be placed in more remote storage because of infrequent use. If items are used together, such as parts of a coffee pot, walking can be reduced when they are stored together.

For safety and convenience, stored items should be easily *seen, reached, grasped,* and *replaced.* For example, clothes crammed into a closet are not easy to see, reach, grasp, or replace and usually become wrinkled. Transferring infrequently worn clothing to other storage or hanging shorter items like blouses, shirts, or slacks at two levels can make the items more accessible. Turntables, slide-out shelves, or step shelves are examples of adaptations that can make needed items more accessible in deep cabinets or refrigerators. Bratton also suggested, "Store items one row deep and unstacked, except for things such as cups, plates, or bowls of one size. No item in frequent use should be stored behind or inside another unless it is a duplicate."[36]

Consideration of *maximum reach* is another factor in devising accessible storage. Heiner and McCullough concluded that a height of 72 inches could be reached without difficulty by homemakers of average height—about 5 feet 4 inches.[37] Frequently used items should be stored within the limits of maximum reach, the outer circle formed by extended arms with fingers curved, as illustrated in Chart 10.6.

The *normal work area*—the inner circle in Chart 10.6, formed by bending the elbows—illustrates the least fatiguing height for storage. Research on energy use supports the need to consider limits of reach. For example, it takes four times the energy to reach 72 inches as to reach 46 inches; bending to 3 inches from the floor takes eleven times the energy to reach 46 inches.[38] For these reasons, storage of frequently used, heavy, and large items near counter level or within comfortable reach is suggested.

Chart 10.6 **A guide for planning kitchen cabinets that fit both the worker and equipment. (Adapted from a chart prepared by Naomi Shank in** *Make Your Kitchen Modern,* **Iowa State, Agriculture Extension Service, Bulletin P92 (1948), p. 51.**

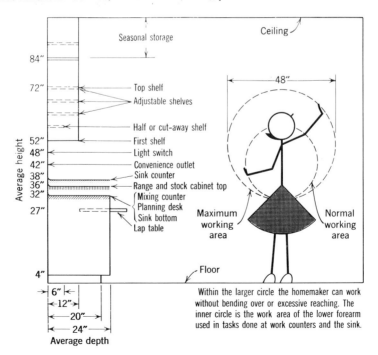

Within the larger circle the homemaker can work without bending over or excessive reaching. The inner circle is the work area of the lower forearm used in tasks done at work counters and the sink.

Selecting Products, Tools, and Equipment

Items used in home-related work should be appropriate to the task and the worker. Household items that are easy to assemble, to use, to maintain, and to store can enhance motivation for the work.

Fatigue and frustration can be reduced by selecting products, tools, and equipment suitable to the worker, to the nature of the task, and to the work–place, as illustrated in the following examples. Volume purchases may be less costly than smaller purchases, but the economic advantages are nullified if inadquate storage exists. A small appliance may be attractive and convenient, but if the worker cannot read the dial, its usability is limited. The metallic trim on an oven may be attractive, but will it collect fingerprints and retain heat? Currently used household items such as knives that fail to hold an edge, mixing bowls that tip or are difficult to clean, a washer that is excessivly noisy, or a spoon that is poorly designed waste time and energy and can cause dissatisfaction with the task.

Concepts of home-related work have been discussed in relation to the person or group doing the work, to the nature of the work, and to the design of work areas. Although the concepts have been explored separately, they are interrelated; a change in products or equipment may change work methods and the worker's attitude. The concepts are further integrated in the next section on simplifying home-related work.

Simplifying Home-Related Work

Busy people who want to conserve time and energy for certain activities, disabled people who need to conserve energy, or people who want to improve results or to reduce frustration with work can apply the concepts of home-related work to their household situation. Likewise, people who want to incorporate physical exercise into household work can also use these concepts to reach their goals. For example, storing items higher or lower than normal involves bending and stretching exercise.

Improvements in household work involve a number of steps: selecting the task, gathering facts, challenging details, revising procedures, and using the new plan. Some activities may be eliminated; others may be combined. The location of work, its sequence, the division of labor, or procedures may also change. These changes should reflect the goals and standards of the person or group.

A homemaker, for example, may be frustrated with the task of dressing a three-year-old child because of the number of other simultaneous household activities needing her attention. Motivation to improve work methods is enhanced through the selection of tasks that are frequently performed but are dissatisfying in some respect.

Next, the homemaker would need to review procedural and performance standards for the dressing activity. Use of a process chart, with the help of a neighbor or family member, may alert the homemaker to other facts about the activity.

After this objective recall of current procedures, every detail can be challenged—what is being done, why it is done, where it is done, how it is done, and when it is done. Although it may not be possible to eliminate the entire activity, perhaps some parts of the process may be shortened or eliminated. One item of clothing can be substituted for a number of garments, such as slippers that combine the features of shoes and socks or a one-piece play-suit.

The location or time at which the task is done might also be changed to reduce frustration. With some adaptations in storage and clothing, the preschooler may be able to dress himself. Lowering the closet rod height or storing folded garments in lower drawers or shelves permits the child access to the clothing. Additionally, clothing with elastic waistlines, large buttons, front openings, and simple styles will enable the child to dress himself if he is ready for and encouraged to assume this independence.

Change and improvement are possible in work methods. Because of household differences, a number of "best ways" can be found to perform household tasks.

Home-Related Work in Nontraditional Settings

Because of resource limitations, family heads, whose roles or resources differ from the full-time female homemaker and full-time male employee, have as great or a greater need to apply the concepts of home-related work. Adaptations of the concepts to situations of physical disabilities, employed homemakers, one-parent or low-income households will be discussed in this section of the chapter. Although the management of home-related work has consequences for the quality of life in all households, individuals and families faced with reduced psychomotor resources, scarcity of time, or limited economic resources may find that improvement of managerial skills permits more effective use of scarce resources to reach household goals.

DISABILITIES AND HOME-RELATED WORK

People—disabled or not—desire an independent life.[39] In addition to the 12 percent of all homemakers who manage home-related work with some form of disability, many men and children with disabilities can learn to care for themselves and their surroundings through an understanding of their capabilities and limitations, the tasks, and the workplaces.[40] These individuals are faced with the normal challenge of daily activities and with the special challenge of the disability. Professionals in home economics, occupational therapy, social work, or nursing are examples of people who can be useful resources to facilitate this independent living.[41]

Some disabilities, such as those associated with the heart or circulatory system, require that energy expenditures be limited. Partial paralasis or amputation may cause work to be performed with one hand or from a wheel chair. Visual limitations may call for compensation through the use of other senses. For people with a physical limitation, *acceptance of the disability* is the beginning of rehabilitation.[42]

Evaluation of household needs, standards, goals, and the physical capabilities of the worker is a continual process in managing home-related work; but it is necessary for those with some form of disability. Developing effective *work methods* is important because the performance of some tasks requires more time with a disability.[43] Deciding what activities to eliminate, what other members of the household or paid workers can do, and which purchased services to use is a part of this managing process. The worker's self concept interacts with other people's attitudes to affect the kinds and successfulness of adjustments made to even temporary disabilities. Overprotective family members or fear of failure can hinder adapting to a disability.[44]

After evaluation of current housing, family life style, and personal abilities, alternatives for completing home-related work can be explored. In a number of states, advice can be obtained from work-simplification programs for homemakers with limited work capacity. Publications, including lists of sources for adaptive equipment, clothing, and tools, ideas for using existing equipment and products, and adaptations in work space are also available.[45]

Architectural barriers are a special problem for people using wheelchairs; these barriers also restrict movement of others with limited mobility—such as the aged. Ground-level entrances to a living unit or public building permit access by those with physical limitations. Additionally, doorways at least 32 inches wide, gently sloping ramps or elevators in multi-story buildings, and hallways that are at least four feet wide permit mobility once the person is inside the building.[46] These and other standards of accessibility are inexpensive to include in the initial design of a building but are of maximal cost in remodeling.

People with limited mobility may find it less expensive to move from, rather than to remodel, a living unit that is architecturally unsuitable. If moving is too costly or if the family wants to remain in current housing, adaptations like selecting a narrow wheel chair, removing doors under the sink to permit sitting to work, or adding grab bars in the bath area can facilitate mobility. As in any managerial situation, creativity and self confidence aid the disabled in discovering other resources to reach goals.

EMPLOYED HOMEMAKERS

An increasing proportion of married females combine home-related work and gainful employment.[47] Most of these women retain primary responsibility for home-related work. In one study, professional women tended to avoid conflict between these roles by placing family and homemaker roles in higher priority than employment roles. These researchers said that women doctors, lawyers, or professors generally accepted this situation without resentment.[48] Similar findings were reported in another study of dual-career families. Household help was hired by most of these families, and other family members helped with a variety of tasks.[49]

Fewer mothers of preschool children than those with schoolage children are employed, but an increasing proportion of mothers of young children are joining the labor force.[50] For these families, adequate child-care facilities are an important concern. The child-care center should not only be a safe environment but one that also promotes personal growth of the children. Of the mothers who left a job during one year, over one-fourth of the whites and one-fifth of the blacks gave child care as their reason.[51]

Decisions to seek or continue employment depend on income needs, interests, and household time demands. Mothers with a college education are more likely to enter the labor force than those with less education. Some concern has been expressed about the effects of employment on children; but one study determined that children of mothers who are happy in their roles— whether as full-time employees, as full-time homemaker, or as some combination of the two—seem to do well in school.[52]

Flexible employment hours are an asset for working women who occasionally need to be home for emergencies: however, few jobs allow this flexibility.[53] In two-parent families, a husband's attitude toward these role combinations influences whether or not married women work. Husbands who were secure in their roles had a more favorable attitude toward their wives' employment.[54] Readers who plan to combine careers and family life may want to consider characteristics of careers and select potential marriage partners receptive to such a combination.

Employed married women generally have fewer home-related responsibilities than those whose primary career is homemaking. Combining home-related work and employment, however, leaves these women with fewer hours of free time than employed males or full-time homemakers.[55] With this reduction in discretionary time, employed females can ease the time pressures by application of the management concepts. As in the case of disabled homemakers, these families must choose standards and priorities in home-related work. Although research does not indicate that a large number of families do so, a more equitable division of household tasks is one possibility.

INCOME LIMITATIONS

Among these employed women are heads of households. This group comprises 10 percent of women workers and has been increasing as a proportion of the work force.[56] An additional 10 percent of female workers had husbands who were unemployed. The income supplied by these women often supports their families. For these two groups, combining employment and home-related work is a necessity, but these women earned an average of slightly more than one-half the amount earned by males who were the only source of income for their families.[57]

Risk-taking is a part of trying to manage with too little money and too little time.[58] Family members faced with decisions of buying food or paying rent will probably buy the food because of its immediate need. Households needing two incomes to make ends meet may decide to have one person work days and the other work evenings to lessen the costs of child care. Older children may stay home from school to take care of younger ones when they are ill. The goods and services that make home-related work easier and sometimes less time-consuming are not easily afforded by low-income families. To overcome feelings of deprivation, low-income families may purchase convenience items on credit or sometimes splurge on more expensive food items. These risks are not free but they illustrate individual or family priorities.

Jeffers also observed that the quality of home-related work varies with the worker's moods.[59] If life is going well, household tasks are effectively performed; in contrast, depression or poverty inhibits motivation for this work. Homemakers who can uncover the causes of these mood changes and deal with them will probably find home-related work to be less of a problem.

Disabled, employed, and low-income homemakers are people with individual needs and situations—not stereotypes. A technique judged workable by one family for the improvement of home-related work may be inappropriate for another family. This discussion has focused on families with scarce resources and on examples of adaptations that can be made. It is important to remember that people have a vast number of potential resources that can be applied to home-related work. These resources and the refinement of current skills and abilities help people to sort priorities, to develop appropriate work methods, and to adjust work spaces so they are suitable to the person or group.

Summary

Evaluation is both the beginning and the end of home-related work management. To evaluate progress, people can ask questions, such as the following:

Are important tasks accomplished?

Are performance standards met?

Are people in the situation satisfied with the results?

Because management is not magic, progress will be gradual. Further clarification of reasons for dissatisfaction and satisfaction can help to improve the performance of home-related work and to re-use workable solutions to problems.

For some readers, home-related work may seem trivial, but trivial matters are the fabric of daily life. If this work is integrated and performed with personal and family goals in mind, people are free to concentrate on the interpersonal aspects of life. If conflicts develop, knowledge of the worker, the nature of the tasks, and the workplace can help to isolate the cause of the conflict and to resolve problems.

REFERENCES

1. Gauger, W. H., "The Potential Contribution to the GNP of Valuing Household Work," speech to American Home Economics Association Annual Meeting, Atlantic City, N.J., (June 26, 1973).

2. Lopata, H. Z., *Occupation: Housewife,* Oxford University, London, (1971), p. 141.

3. Wiegand, E., and Gross, I. H., *Fatigue of Homemakers with Young Children,* Michigan Agricultural Experiment Station, Technical Bulletin 265, (1958), pp. 3–4.

4. Steidl, R. E., and Bratton, E. C., *Work in the Home,* Wiley, New York, (1968), pp. 1–2.

5. Galton, L., "How You Can Cure Your Backache," *Parade,* (September 30, 1973), pp. 12–14.

6. Steidl, R. E., and Bratton, E. C., *op. cit.,* p. 107.

7. Hazelton, H. W., and Russell, M., *Keeping Fit for Farm Work,* Purdue University, Bulletin 299, (1943), p. 3.

8. Burtt, H. E., *Psychology and Industrial Efficiency,* Appleton, New York, (1929), pp. 122–123.

9. Burtt, H. E., *Applied Psychology,* Prentice–Hall, Englewood Cliffs, N.J., (1957), p. 438.

10. Lopata, H. Z., *ibid.;* Steidl, R. E., and Bratton, E. C., *op. cit.,* pp. 169–179.

11. Bell, H. E., "How Many Persons Is a Homemaker?" Pennsylvania Extension Service Leaflet 223, nd.

12. Lopata, H. Z., *ibid.*

13. Walker, K. E., "Homemaking Still Takes Time," *Journal of Home Economics, 61:*8 (October 1969), p. 622: Vanek, J., "Time Spent in Housework" *Scientific American 231:*5 (November 1974), pp. 116–120;

References to historical studies: Nickell, P., and Dorsey, J. M., *Management in Family Living*, Wiley, New York, (1967), pp. 149–151.

14. Lopata, H. Z., *op. cit.*, pp. 137–181.

15. Maloch, F., *Properties, Qualities, and Characteristics Of Most and Least Liked Household Tasks*, Cornell Agricultural Experiment Station, Memoir 284, (July 1963), p. 7.

16. *Ibid.*, p. 11; Ronald, P. Y., Singer, M. E., and Firebaugh, F. M., "Rating Scale for Household Tasks," *Journal of Home Economics, 63:*3 (March 1971), p. 178.

17. Lopata, H. Z., *op. cit.*, pp. 149–165.

18. Goble, E., "Work Simplication in Dishwasing," *Journal of Home Economics, 40:*4 (April 1948), pp. 195–196.

19. Muse, M., *Seating Housewives at Their Ironing*, Vermont Agricultural Experiment Station, Bulletin 559, (1951).

20. *Easier Homemaking*, Purdue University Agricultural Extension Service, Bulletin 529, (1948), pp. 21–24.

21. Weaver, E. K., Bloom, C. E., and Feldmiller, I., *A Study of Hand versus Mechanical Dishwashing Methods*, Ohio Agricultural Experiment Station, Research Bulletin 772, (1956), pp. 15, 18.

22. Blood, R. O. and Wolfe, D. M., *Husbands and Wives: The Dynamics of Married Living*, Free Press, New York (1960), p. 50.

23. Wheeler, N., *As They See It: A Study of Urban Home Management*, Time and News, Gettysburg, Penn., (1973), pp. 39–40.

24. McCullough H. E., Philson, K., Smith, R. H., Wood, A. L., and Woolrich, A., *Space Standards for Household Activities*, Illinois Agricultural Experiment Station, Bulletin 686, (May 1962), pp. 4–5; Wilson, M., Roberts, E. H., and Thayer, R. *Standards for Working–Surface Heights and Other Space Units of the Dwelling*, Oregon Agricultural Experiment Station, Bulletin 348, (1937), p. 37.

25. Steidl, R. E., *Functional Kitchens*, Cornell Extension, Bulletin 1166, (July 1969), p. 12.

26.   Bennett, H. E., *School Posture and Seating,* Ginn, Boston, Mass., (1928), pp. 49, 51–61.

27.   Steidl, R. E., *op. cit.,* p. 4.

28.   Mundel, M. E. and Armstrong, J., "Easier Housekeeping," *Life, 21,* (September 9, 1946), pp. 97–107; Steidl, R. E., *op. cit.,* p. 12.

29.   *Ibid.*

30.   *Ibid.*; Mundel, M. E., "Factors Affecting Ease of Kitchen Work," *The Kitchen Reporter,* Kelvinator Kitchens, (March 1947).

31.   Steidl, R. E., *op. cit.,* pp. 7–8.

32.   *Ibid.,* pp. 10–11.

33.   *Ibid.,* p. 20.

34.   Bratton, E. C., "Making the Most of Household Storage," Cornell University, Home Economics Extension Leaflet 27, (1968).

35.   Heiner, M. K. and McCullough, H., *Functional Kitchen Storage,* Cornell University Agricultural Experiment Station, Bulletin 846, (1948).

36.   Bratton, E. C., *op. cit.*

37.   Heiner, M. K. and McCullough, H., "A New Look at the Kitchen," *Architectural Forum, 84* (1946), pp. 155–158, 187–190.

38.   Bratton, E. C., *Oxygen Consumed in Household Tasks,* Cornell University Agricultural Experiment Station, Bulletin 873, (August 1951), p. 12.

39.   May, E. K., Waggoner, N. R., and Boettke, E. M., *Homemaking for the Handicapped,* Dodd, Mead, New York, (1966), p. 5.

40.   *Ibid.,* p. xiii.

41.   Rusk, H. A., Kristeller, E. L., Judson, J. S., Hunt, G. M., and Zimmerman, M. E., *A Manual for Training the Disabled Homemaker,* Institute of Rehabilitation Medicine, Rehabilitation Monograph VIII, New York, (1970), pp. 149–150.

42. *Ibid.*, p. 21.

43. Manning, S. L., *Time in Household Tasks by Indiana Families,* Purdue University Agricultural Experiment Station, Research Bulletin 837, (1968), pp. 5–6.

44. Hawkins, M., "Rehabilitation for Homemaking Activities," *Journal of Home Economics, 55:* 5 (May 1963), p. 340.

45. Klinger, J. L., Frieden, F. H., and Sullivan, R. A., *Meal-time Manual for the Aged and Handicapped,* Essanders, New York, (1970); Wheeler, V. H., *Planning Kitchens for Handicapped Homemakers,* Institute of Physical Medicine & Rehabilitation, Rehabilitation Mongraph XXVI, New York, nd; McCullough, H. E. and Farnham, M. B., *Kitchens for Women in Wheelchairs,* Illinois Extension Service, Circular 841, (November 1961).

46. Boaz, J. N., *Architectural Graphic Standards,* Wiley, New York, (1970), pp. 4–6; Department of Transportation, *Travel Barriers,* U.S. Government Printing Office, Washington, D.C., (1970), p. 27.

47. Hayghe, H., "Labor Force Activity of Married Women," *Monthly Labor Review,* (April 1973), p. 31.

48. Poloma, M. M. and Garland, T. N., "The Dual Profession Family: Summary of Research," Business and Professional Women's Foundation, Washington, D.C., (1971).

49. Holmstrom, L. L., *The Two Career Family,* Schenkman, Cambridge, Mass., (1972), p. 67.

50. Hayghe, H., *op. cit.*, p. 33.

51. Hedges, J. N., and Barnett, J. K., "Working Women and the Division of Household Tasks," *Monthly Labor Review,* (April 1972), p. 11.

52. Williamson, S. Z., "The Effects of Maternal Employment on the Scholastic Performance of Children," *Journal of Home Economics, 62:*8 (October 1970), pp. 609–613.

53. Poloma, M. M. and Garland, T. N., *op. cit.*; Hedges, J. N. and Barnett, J. K., *op. cit.*

54. Arnott, C., "Husbands' Attitude and Wives' Commitment to Employment," *Journal of Marriage and the Family, 34:*4 (November 1972), pp. 673–684.

55. Executive Office of the President, Office of Management and Budget, *Social Indicators, 1973,* U.S. Government Printing Office, Washington, D.C., (1973), pp. 214.

56. Hedges, J. N. and Barnett, J. K., *op. cit.*, p. 9.

57. Hayghe, H., *op. cit.*, p. 31.

58. Jeffers, C., "Hunger, Hustlin' and Homemaking," *Journal of Home Economics, 61:*10 (December 1969), pp. 755–761.

59. *Ibid.*, 760.

Part III

MANAGING ECONOMIC RESOURCES

11

MANAGING INCOME AND CREDIT

Despite being "installment-plan millionnaires," most families will juggle income and expenses in a challenging, sometimes discouraging race to make ends meet. Some years the family will "win;" some years it won't. Across time, a family financial institution will part with about $15,000 of its income on interest payments for cars and other goods and another $25,000 to $40,000 on home mortgage interest.[1] Thus, credit detracts from as well as contributes to the family's accomplishment of a satisfying life style.

This chapter is about people and their incomes. Its goals are simple. The chapter seeks to help people to assess their lifetime income pattern, find ways to keep more of what they earn, and to increase satisfaction from the income they use. Based on management, these principles are designed to work for both individuals and groups. The chapter stresses goal setting and systematic management, not abstractions. It stresses a decision framework for the use of economic resources. It analyzes financial management problems of people at different income levels and with irregular incomes. It stresses the interrelatedness of human, economic, and environmental resources and the importance of goals in guiding the financial management process.

This chapter is dedicated to helping the reader plan and build a satisfying financial future. But it will do nothing unless its principles are applied—the sooner the better; for many financial goals depend on early identification and early establishment of a plan so that resources can work effectively. There is no more appropriate time than NOW to start a financial plan and no more opportune resource to develop than earning capacity. Income—and the expansion of income through credit and investments—conditions the content of living through the standard of goods and services it allows, the cultural opportunities it provides, and the experiences, possessions and comforts it furnishes.

Financial Management by Objectives

Financial management is an organized, goal-oriented system of allocating and controlling human, economic, and environmental resources to achieve specified goals that are usually purchased with economic resources. Management by objectives, whether for industry, for individuals, or for families begins with the fundamental step of defining objectives or goals before operating with assets. It also requires systematic control of the assets in line with identified objectives.

GOALS AND MANAGEMENT

Some people manage their money; with others, the money manages them. Some people have "too much month left at the end of the money" and spend most of their management effort defensively reacting to money problems. These people are *not* managing effectively.

People who are slaves to their bills and have little choice about who they are and would like to become are *not* managing by objectives. Whyte described this kind of living as "budgetism," where people do not budget what they will spend their money on; they just turn over all their income to a bank to be applied toward mounting bills for things that have been bought on credit.[2] Obviously, this system works only if no one demands full payment of bills or garnishees the wages of workers if cash is not needed for current expenses.

Credit counselors call this kind of management, "brinksmanship" because these people are habitually living on the brink of financial disaster. They may cringe every time they go to the mailbox, every time the phone rings. Creditors may haunt them at home and at work. One minor, unexpected expense can collapse the whole system for "brinksmanship" families. They are the people who are most likely to seek bankruptcy as a way out of harassment.

Personal bankruptcies are increasing rapidly. When people want their tomorrow today, and credit makes it possible, they may become confused over what their goals and standards for living really are. People who become enamored with "the good life" and unrealistic but immediate possessions often have their financial future end in heartache, embarassment, tragedy, bankruptcy, or even dissolution of partnership—divorce.

Bankruptcy is not new. What is new is the dramatic increase in personal bankruptcies and the diminishing stigma associated with them. In recent years, at least 180,000 of roughly 200,000 bankruptcies declared each year have been personal bankruptcies.[3] During the prosperous sixties and early seventies, the number of personal bankruptcies doubled, causing a higher ratio of bankruptcies per 1000 households than during the depression years.[4]

Reasons for families becoming hopelessly in debt are numerous. For some, it is unexpected illness or accident, irresponsible acts of a family member, untimely death, or a freak of nature—hurricane or earthquake. For other families, financial troubles are caused by a combination of lack of long-range goals, unrealistic estimates of income or costs of living, lack of patience for what may be afforded more easily at some future time, unexpected changes in the economy, or loss of job. Materialism, inflation, the tendency of some newly married couples to expect their life cycle to begin at the same level of living that their parents have achieved over a lifetime, and excessively generous credit that makes possible a debt level higher than can be handled have all been blamed for financial difficulties of families.

It is important to recognize that families with serious money problems may suffer emotionally and experience family disharmony. Those in financial trouble have little control over their lives.

FINANCIAL SUCCESS AND MANAGEMENT

Odiorne is considered the originator of the management by objectives philosoply and has written books describing its application to situations in business, industry, and education.[5] Management by objectives is based on the principal of cybernetics, which has to do with goal-striving, and goal-orientated behavior of mechanical systems. When applied to human behavior, Maltz calls this system of goal-striving, "psycho-cybernetics."[6]

By adapting these philosophies to personal financial management, it is possible to construct an organized system—Management for Financial Success (MFS)—consisting of orderly steps leading to specified goals. Such a system would utilize seven financial operations: earning, saving, borrowing, lending, investing, insuring, and spending. Each of these monetary operations requires both internal and external decisions. If the Browns, who are currently facing hard times, decide to spend their money for groceries, they do not have it for the car payment. If they borrow to make the car payment or buy groceries, they will have less money to spend next month. If the Osburns invest their money in human capital—their son's education—they have less to spend for housing or transportation for the remaining family members. If the Matins invest their money, they do not have it to spend now. If they insure their income and possessions, they have less money to spend for additional current possessions but more security in return for the insurance premiums. These are *opportunity costs*—the weighing of one alternative against another—rather than merely considering the cash price of a specific good or service.[7]

The following diagram provides a decision framework for the financial management process. In a simplified manner, it explains what can be done with money—the operations that make up the Management for Financial Success system.

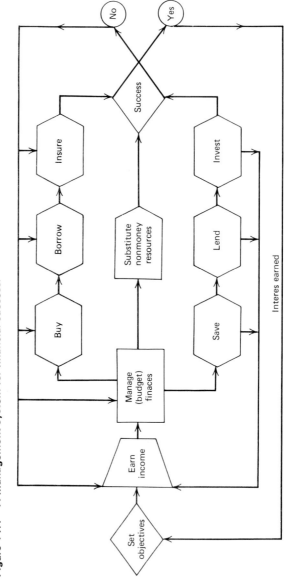

Figure 11.1   A management system for financial success.

276

TEN STEPS TO MORE SUCCESSFUL FINANCIAL MANAGEMENT

The following outline of steps in the Management for Financial Success system is designed to aid families or individuals in improving the quality of living that can be "bought" with their resources.

1. *Define success in terms of overall goals for living*—in terms of the life style, income, or other economic and environmental resources, and the people necessary to make life satisfying.

2. *Identity objectives and subgoals*—such as reducing debt, eating steak once a week, providing a college education for children, taking a trip to Mexico, owning a home, or buying a camper.

3. *Establish priorities and timing for objectives*—determine which objectives are most important, need to be started early in order to take advantage of interest accumulations, and can be attained with the least effort.

4. *Estimate the cost of objectives*—use realistic guides. Consult newspaper advertisements, use previous records of spending, visit open houses, and examine catalogs of possible colleges. Record the cost estimates and the date.

5. *Analyze financial resources*—money income, potential credit, fringe benefits, net worth, quantity and inflow pattern of money income, and annual as well as lifetime expectations.

6. *Formulate a plan of action*—a current consumption plan for fixed and flexible expenditures, protection, and growth.

7. *Organize all efforts*—establish goal-oriented behavior; set up measurable subgoals; determine who pays the bills, makes the purchasing decisions, does the shopping, reconciles the checkbook, and keeps records. Decide when and if credit is to be used.

8. *Control activities*—eliminate waste, motivate goal-striving, spend for planned objectives, compare before buying, read before signing, and pay yourself first.

9. *Keep adequate records*—establish a financial management center, read and file warranties, record installment payments, keep tax

records together, and establish a system suitable to family needs and interests. Know your money's purchasing value.

10. *Evaluate regularly*—review insurance coverage before premiums are due, compare net worth statements periodically, and adjust spending to changes in income and changes in objectives. Abandon or revise unworkable plans. Consciously develop a credit reputation. Evaluate decision making and assignment of financial management tasks. Determine satisfaction derived from the system.

To be workable and satisfying, each plan for using income and other economic resources must be worked out *by,* or at least *for,* the person or group concerned. No one else can tell a person what to do with money in order to bring personal satisfaction. Any family that expects to accomplish its goals by having someone else direct the plan or by following some ready-made plan may have less motivation than a group who plans its own future.

Rapid social and economic changes in the present-day environment require flexible patterns or models of expenditures. However, the *system* for managing money to achieve individually–determined goals will work for one family as well as for another and for one individual as well as another. As with the management process on which it is based, these ten steps to successful financial management depend on the quality of decision making and control for the satisfaction to be achieved. Therefore, it is important to examine each process in the system carefully and to understand the underlying concepts within each step.

DEFINING SUCCESS IN TERMS OF LIFE STYLE

The first step in the MFS system requires a clear definition of what financial success means to persons in the group—what overall, long-term life style is desired by the group and for its members. Life style is more than a single economic goal. It is a clear and concise view of the kind of living that will bring satisfaction to all members of the group and to other people necessary to make that life style satisfying.

It is a composite of consumer practices, goods and services, income and financial security, occupation and employment patterns, and roles and role combinations.

Agreement About Success

The desired life style is more likely to be achieved if there is an agreement about goals and harmony in the attitudes of persons in the group. Values are strongly reflected in views of what is satisfying. Choice of life style is a central decision that produces many satellite decisions related to specific goals that contribute to the desired style of living, such as the choice of an occupation to support the chosen way of life, or selection of a living unit to provide an appropriate environment for family interaction.

Several life style profiles are presented in Chapter 15. Each case study is developed from market research, consumer behavior studies, national surveys of consumer finances and expenditures, census reports, or sociological studies. The studies describe styles of living typical of families in the United States in the early 1970's. A study of these profiles illustrates what is meant by life styles and why it is important to establish goals early in a financial management program. People can set the course in a financial management by objectives system rather than allowing resources or chance to determine goals.

CHARTING GOALS

Financial plans should be discussed with all family members. Specific personal and group goals should be listed—vacation plans for next summer, the kind of house wanted, educational objectives for each family member, or retirement plans. Less expensive items should also be included for they may be high on the priority list and can be attained more easily than expensive things.

Small purchases can become big budget-wreckers. People may discover that they are "nickel and diming" themselves right out of the large items they really want in life. If a person took coffee to work in a thermos it could be better coffee than from the vending machine, and the person would have $100 or more to spend on vacation next summer. But if coffee in a nearby restaurant is high on the priority list, something else is compromised. That's what management for financial success is all about. Important activities are not omitted if spending is directed toward important goals and quality of life is improved in the process. The first guideline in income management requires an objective, unemotional, and mature outlook on finance problems and desires.

TIMING GOALS AND ESTABLISHING PRIORITIES

The more limited the funds, the more urgent it is to set priorities on specific goals. Those identified goals discussed and listed in step two should be ranked in terms of their importance to each family member and the length of time it will realistically take to achieve them. Classify them as:

- *immediate goals*—those that can be accomplished in one year or less such as buying a winter coat or eating steak once a week, or

- *intermediate goals*—those that can be accomplished in two to five years, such as getting out of debt, building a savings account for the down payment on a house, or a second car, or

- *long-range goals*—those that take more than five years to accomplish and are illustrated in examples such as an education for children, an adequate retirement program, or a recreation home.

People in all income levels and at all stages of the family life cycle have financial goals. Theirs may be different from the typically middle-status goals given as examples above. Objectives may be accomplished in less or more time than the examples. For low-income families, it is most important to set goals.

ESTIMATING THE COST OF GOALS

Price of Goals

To keep planning realistic and balanced, actually price or at least estimate the items listed as goals. Consult a mail order catalog as a reference for costs of appliances and furnishings. Learn the price of large purchases from the source likely to be used at the time of purchase. For smaller items, estimate their prices from a newspaper or catalog. Visit open houses or new and used car lots. Check out school costs in college catalogs.

Figure 11.2 lists goals and ranks them, giving an overview of the cost of personal objectives. The cost column should be dated and each sample goal priced or estimated for best results. It is important to complete each column of such a chart now, although the goals may not be reached for several years. This action gives direction to current spending and saving. If a person's goal is to buy a house, requiring $8,000 for down payment and closing costs at the end of five years, he must begin now to save $114 every month for the next five years if he is to achieve that goal in the planned time period. Furthermore, a rate of 7 percent interest on the savings will have to be earned to assure $8,000 in this length of time. To determine current savings needed to reach specific amounts of money at specified dates, see Table 12.3 "Reaching Savings Goals" (Chapter 12).

ANALYZING FINANCIAL RESOURCES

Reaching financial goals requires knowledge of available resources—inventorying the financial resources of those whose goals are being sought. Financial resources are the economic assets that come within the managerial scope of an individual or group. They are specifically money income, elastic income, fringe

Figure 11.2   Estimating The Cost of Goals.

Priority Ranking	Immediate goals	Cost estimate Today's date _____	Target date
3	10 speed bicycle	$150	October 1976
2	pay loan at credit union	$230 ($23 per month for the next 10 months)	July 1977
1	winter coat for _____	$75 during winter clearance sale in November	November 1976
	Intermediate goals		
2	trip to Mexico	$900 for three people traveling by camper	Summer 1978
1	new house	$8,000 for down payment and closing costs	Spring 1980
	Long-range goals		
1	college educations— bachelor's degrees for both children	$4,500 per year for eight years	Beginning in 1984
2	˙ retirement	$1,200 per month income	June 1995

benefits, and wealth. Fringe benefits—group insurance, health services, private pensions, employer contributions to social security and other retirement plans, vacation pay, sick leave, expense accounts, and stock options—play an important role in financial planning and should not be overlooked as financial resources.

Analyzing financial resources involves three steps: (1) clarifying current financial status through a net-worth statement, (2) evaluating the current quantity, certainty, source, and pattern of income flow and predicting its continuation over the short term (one year), and (3) estimating the pattern of financial resources over the lifetime of the family.

Clarifying financial status

Statements of net worth should be computed annually to measure financial progress. *Net worth* is a comparison of financial assets to liabilities. A net-worth statement is a balance sheet as outlined in Figure. 11.3.

Assets are usually computed first. The value of nonliquid assets is difficult to determine but should be estimated yearly. The current market value of such assets as owned cars, home and other real estate, furnishings and equipment,

Figure 11.3 A Sample Net-Worth Statement.

Assets	Now	Goal year from now	Liabilities	Now	Goal year from now
Cash on hand			Long term		
Cash in banks			Mortgage on home		
Savings accounts			Mortgage on real estate		
Value of bonds			Personal loan balance		
Value of stocks			Notes payable		
Value of house			Installment accounts		
Value of real estate			Car		
Value of cars			Others		
Value of personal property			Short term debts		
Value of household goods			Charge accounts		
Cash value of life insurance			Medical and dental		
Notes receivable			Personal loans		
Value of pension or profit-sharing plan			Others		
Value of tax-sheltered annuities			Stock margin accounts		
Value of business interests			Loans on life insurance		
Other assets			Other debts		
TOTAL ASSETS			TOTAL LIABILITIES		

NET WORTH (Total Assets — Total Liabilities = Net Worth)

DATE:

Net Worth serves as a barometer of financial wellbeing. If net worth declines annually without justifiable reasons such as education, trouble is indicated and a need for revision in annual budget is probable.

clothing, and other forms of wealth can be estimated. Use newspaper advertisements for indications of value, but remember advertised prices are "offer prices", and buyers usually negotiate the prices they pay for used items. For cars, average the wholesale and retail values quoted in a standard reference on market values of used cars such as Kelly's "Blue Book."[8] A representative of a credit union, bank, or savings institution will usually quote the blue book value of a client's car. To estimate the value of a living unit, compare it with another of similar size and construction in the same neighborhood that sold recently. What price did the house bring? How long was it on the market? When calculating the value of assets, consider the total market value. Do not deduct, at this point, what is owed on the items.

Liabilities are the negative side of a net-worth statement. The major liability of most families is the mortgage on a living unit. Charge account and installment purchase balances are also liabilities. Insurance premiums due, medical and dental bills, bank loans, life insurance loans, and all bills payable should be included in the total of liabilities. Taxes—federal, state income taxes, real property taxes due, and other special assessments—must also be considered.

Net worth is the difference between total assets and total liabilities. The statement should be dated for future comparisons. Such a financial analysis tells a family what its financial health is, much as a physical examination tells a person's state of health. Its real value is in repeated analysis at regular intervals over many years. Financially healthy families, at any income level, usually show growth toward goals and an increased annual net worth. An effective net-worth statement is one that is *used* as the basis for revising financial plans and for encouraging a policy of goal-mindedness.

It is interesting that the tangible possessions of a family are traditionally listed on a net-worth statement, but the most important assets of the family are not, namely the human resources. Should the lifetime earning potential of workers and the value of the services rendered within the home be included in the net-worth statement of a family?

Analyzing Income

The second step in analyzing financial resources is to consider the current quantity, certainty, source, and pattern of income flow and to predict its continuation over the short term. Money income, value of fringe benefits, and increased purchasing power through use of credit are central foci in this step toward management for financial success.

Money income includes all monetary gains, gross receipts of money to all family members, and the frequency and pattern of this flow. Gross salary, wages, commissions, bonus payments, rent on owned properties, interest on savings, capital gains from mutual funds, dividends from stocks, social security retirement income, royalties, and all other forms of monetary receipts to any member of the family should be considered as money income when analyzing the financial resources available to reach goals. Money income is dollars and cents purchasing power that goes into the family treasury in a given period of time—week, month, year, or a lifetime.

Occupational choices affect the regularity and characteristic flow of income and, consequently, the financial planning that is possible. The quality of living that can be exchanged for financial resources is dependent not only on how much income is available but even more importantly, on the regularity and stability of income. For salaried workers with regular employment, money income is usually predictable not only by the year but also over a lifetime. Both time periods must be considered to realistically manage. For those who have irregular incomes and those with uncertain employment, planning is both more difficult and more necessary.

Annual Income Profiles

Few people are fortunate enough to have monthly expenditure demands that exactly parallel monthly income. Examining the characteristics of annual income through the use of a *profile* makes it possible to visualize the essential process of reconciling periodic monetary inflow and expenditure. Income profiles are more *effective* if they can be made for the year ahead.

To construct a personal annual income profile, list income from all sources on a form similar to Figure 11.4 and chart the monthly totals on graph paper. Let the horizontal axis line represent months and the vertical axis represent dollars.

Figure 11.4 represents a personal income profile of a Georgia family with one child. The husband is employed as a teacher and has no income in July

Figure 11.4   A Personal Annual Income Profile.

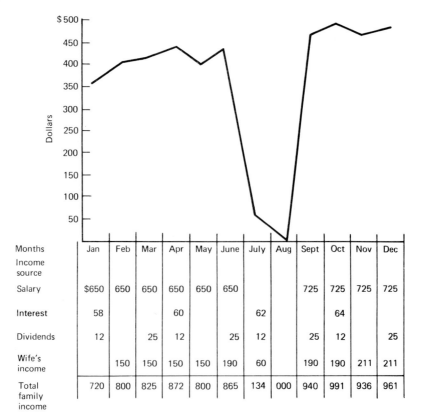

Months / Income source	Jan	Feb	Mar	Apr	May	June	July	Aug	Sept	Oct	Nov	Dec
Salary	$650	650	650	650	650	650			725	725	725	725
Interest	58			60			62			64		
Dividends	12		25	12		25	12		25	12		25
Wife's income		150	150	150	150	190	60		190	190	211	211
Total family income	720	800	825	872	800	865	134	000	940	991	936	961

Average Monthly Income = $737

and August. The profile shows a small increase in salary the following September. The wife works part-time as a secretary but takes off during the summer to travel with the family. Additional income is earned from quarterly dividends from stocks in two companies and from a savings account. Although income exceeds $800 during nine months of the year, the average monthly income is $737.

The money income profiles, typical of several occupational groups, are presented in Figures 11.5 through 11.9. These examples help to explain the flow of income that is typical of different occupations during a year's time, show when points of high or low supply can be anticipated, and provide a graphic guideline for spacing and spreading large expenditures, such as life insurance premiums.

Profile 1 (Figure 11.5) is typical of income derived from wages or salary that is constant throughout a year. People with retirement pensions or social security often have this type of annual income profile. This income pattern is the easiest to budget and to focus on goals because it is highly predictable. It is typical of office and clerical workers, laboratory technicians, sales clerks not on commission, and public officials such as firemen, policemen, or mayors during years when they do not receive a pay increase.

Figure 11.6 represents an increase in pay that continues throughout the remainder of the year. Teachers and others whose income depends on the number of years of experience or longevity on the job typically have this kind of annual profile. The profile is typical of any steady salaried worker who receives a raise in pay at some time during the year. Income the next year may follow the same pattern of one raise per year at a predictable time, as represented in Profile 2; or income may remain steady at the higher rate and follow Profile 1.

A salary decrease would be represented by a drop in the profile line, requiring downward adjustments in expenditure patterns. However, the flow of income would still remain predictable, and planning and controlling its use would still be relatively certain.

Profile 3 (Figure 11.7) represents a constant wage or salary for part of the year and none for the rest of the year. Part-year workers have this profile. Periods of no income occur on a regular, predictable basis. Teachers on a nine- or ten-month pay plan also follow this pattern. Income is assured except

Figure 11.5 (left) Annual Income Profile 1: Money income is constant throughout the year.

Months

Figure 11.6 (right) Annual Income Profile 2: Money income increases during the year.

for brief interruptions during certain months. This knowledge is useful in eliminating large, single payment expenditures from the months of no income. Savings can be accumulated during the remaining months to accommodate ordinary living expenses.

Profile 4 also depicts periods when there is no income but differs from Profile 3 in that the times of unemployment do not usually occur regularly. Seasonal workers, such as fruit pickers or wheat harvesters who have seasonal employment, or those who may be laid off at unpredictable periods when business is slow have annual incomes that flow in this manner. Some workers are helped through the periods of unemployment by insurance that provides a subsistence income during periods of no income.

Periods of no income are usually a cause for concern because they add difficulties in financial management. Long-range goals are pushed aside in favor of immediate needs for food and housing, transportation, and medical care. If income is low during months of employment, there is nothing to save for the no-income months. Grave problems can arise, and perspective can become present-oriented. For such families, it is easier to use the money as it comes and hope that somehow the future will be provided for than it is to attempt planning in the face of so much uncertainty. Can a person plan if income is scarcely sufficient for immediate essentials—if there are literally no choices? Why plan if there is nothing left to save anyway? Yet, these are the people who have greatest need for financial management and a goal orientation.

Income irregularity may not, in itself, be a disadvantage. If income during periods of employment is higher than expenditure needs, there is usually less difficulty in managing. This might be the case with an older couple who have

Figure 11.7 Annual Income Profiles 3 and 4. Annual Income Profile 3: There is no money income during part of the year. Annual Income Profile 4: There is no money income at several intervals during the year.

Months   Months

accumulated furnishings and clothing, whose housing is provided by children or whose mortgage is paid off, and whose current needs are easily met by the irregular income. Adequacy of income is determined not only by quantity and regularity of inflow but by level of needs and wants.

Families whose income is provided solely from investment dividends could have an annual profile similar to Profile 4. They may or may not have adequate income to accomplish the goals they have set for themselves without dipping into the investment principal.

Profile 5 illustrates the income of a professional or businessperson whose income fluctuates with productivity or number of clients. Some persons receive a salary plus commissions; with others, the irregular income is augmented by earnings from investments. When income flows in this manner, a definite "spendable income" is often declared for budget planning, and the fluctuating amounts above this level are put into investments or used to augment the "spendable income" during months when it is lower than usual. Minimum monthly earnings are usually relatively predictable, and the "spendable income" may be the same if high-month returns are used to equalize low-month earnings. In families with incomes that match Profile 5, there is often a tendency, especially among young families, to live beyond the average monthly expenditure and to accumulate debt slowly from year to year to an often insurmountable level. Individuals with a plan find it easier to spread the use of their income than do those who attempt to change their way of living after having become accustomed to using all their income as it arrives.

Profile 6 (Figure 11.9) represents an income with two major peaks and a lower, more steady income throughout the year. Income of farm families derived mainly from sale of livestock in spring and grain in fall, is an example of this pattern. The income base throughout the year includes monetary value of real income obtained from the farm and used by the family as well as added cash income from the weekly sale of produce.

Real income is the flow of goods and services used or available for any given period of time. Real income is derived from the use made of human as well as economic resources and includes the service derived from owned property and possessions. Specifically real income includes such contributions as food furnished by a garden or the use of an automobile or equipment. Real income varies with resource use, kind, quality, and amount. Only monetary return from the use of monetary investments is charted in income profiles; but, in the case of farm income and perhaps the fringe benefits usually provided ministers (including house and automobile), an accurate annual profile would also consider these forms of real income.

A creative person—artist or writer—who has a position and an occasional or frequent sale of creative production, has an annual income that follows Profile 6. A salaried person who earns a commission may also follow this pattern.

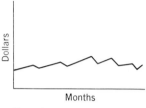

Months

Money income is irregular.   **Figure 11.8**

Profile 7 (Figure 11.9) shows the probable income pattern of groups such as artists, writers, inventors, promoters, or freelancers who may have one or a few sales a year but no regular base income, as in Profile 6. There is one single point of productivity when a large sum is received, although the profile of such a person might include one or more lesser peaks as well.

Fringe benefits

Although people rarely consider the importance of fringe benefits in financial management, the U.S. Chamber of Commerce and Changing Times magazine report that fringe benefits have become so important that they are currently being taken for granted.[9] In fact, they are considered employee rather than fringe benefits and are eagerly bargained for in labor-management negotiations.

Included in a typical package of employee benefits costing the average American company 30.8 percent of payroll (about $2,500 per employee) are various medical care programs and sick leave benefits, life insurance plans, paid vacations, and some retirement-benefit coverage.[10] In the early 1970's, the most frequent fringe benefit of working was hopitalization insurance. At that time, 60 million employees (80 percent of all the civilian wage and salary workers) and 93 million of their dependents were covered by hospitalization in

Figure 11.9

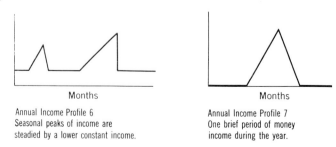

Months   Months

Annual Income Profile 6   Annual Income Profile 7
Seasonal peaks of income are   One brief period of money
steadied by a lower constant income.   income during the year.

addition to required worker's compensation.[11] Employees receive 89 percent of their fringe benefits in the form of wages or salary, overtime, vacation, or holiday pay.

Some fringe benefits are required of employers such as Social Security and workers' compensation. Other benefits are optional. Company-paid services such as parking space; free or low-cost meals; club, trade, and professional association memberships; company-owned recreation facilities; tuition for further training; medical care at work; and discounts on company products are examples of some optional benefits.

Investment and savings programs offered as employee benefits may directly affect financial management. Such plans are early retirement, vesting (equity in a pension plan that allows full or partial benefits if the employee leaves the company after a specified number of years), profit sharing, stock options, bonuses, and saving and thrift plans in which a company will typically match one-half of the employee's contributions up to a maximum of 5 or 6 percent of salary.[12]

Figure 11.10 may be used to estimate the worth of employee benefits and should be included in estimates of net worth and other analyses of financial assets. It may also be useful to compare job opportunities.

Lifetime Income Profiles

While annual income profiles are useful in reconciling expenditures with income within a year, many expenditures must be planned over a longer period of time. A lifetime income profile is more useful in reconciling expenditures and income over the family life cycle and for predicting potential earnings in future years.

Average lifetime income for men 18 years of age in 1972 is estimated by the Census Bureau at $470,795,[13] but this figure varies according to the amount of education a person achieves. Completion of elementary school brings a lifetime income of $343,730; high school brings a lifetime income to $478,873; four years of college points to a lifetime income of $710,569; and graduate study of one or more years should add another $113,190 for a lifetime income of $823,759.[14]

Average lifetime earnings for women is considerably less; yet, one-third of all wives worked full time in 1972, and another 15 percent worked part time.

Lifetime earnings differ from one family to another depending on the number of earners pooling their incomes, education, occupation, sex, and race of the earners and even the age at which work begins. Similar characteristics such as occupation and education do not insure equal earnings among all groups in the population. Talents, hard work, property ownership, location, luck, and discrimination are listed by Unger and Wolf as reasons why people in the

Figure 11.10 Computing the Annual Dollar Value of Fringe Benefits.

Health Programs

_____ Hospitalization
_____ Surgical Insurance
_____ Dental Insurance
_____ Optical Plans
_____ Sick Leave Allowance
_____ At-work Clinics
_____ Major Medical Insurance
_____ Other

Insurance Programs

_____ Life Insurance
_____ Worker's Compensation
_____ Disability Insurance
_____ Income Protection Insurance
_____ Other

Retirement Programs

_____ Social Security
_____ Pension Plan

Vacation Time

_____ Paid Holidays
_____ Vacation Pay
_____ Overtime Pay
_____ Accrued Sick Leave
_____ Travel Time Between Jobs

Company-Paid Services

_____ Free Parking Space
_____ Free or Low-cost Meals
_____ Club Memberships
_____ Professional Dues
_____ Company-owned Recreational
          Facilities
_____ Discounts for Company Pro-
          ducts and Services
_____ Room

Investment and Savings

_____ Savings Programs
_____ Vesting
_____ Profit Sharing
_____ Stock Options
_____ Bonuses and Awards
_____ Thrift Plans
_____ Credit Unions
_____ Low-cost Loans

Education Benefits

_____ Reimbursed Tuition
_____ Trade-school Training
_____ Paid On-the-job Training
_____ Apprenticeship Programs
_____ Executive Training Programs

Expense Allowances

_____ Company Car
_____ Mileage
_____ Meals
_____ Lodging
_____ Entertaining
_____ Expense Account Allowance
_____ Moving
_____ Housing
_____ Settling-In Allowance

Compute the cost of comparable services if purchased
outright by the employee in the
open market and list to the left
of all services offered by the
company. Total the value of all
company benefits below.

_____ Total Annual Value of
All Benefits

same age group with the same education and ability cannot expect to earn the same amount of money over a lifetime.[15]

Lifetime income profiles help people visualize the probable changes in money income that is typical over a lifetime within certain occupations. Five typical lifetime profiles are presented in Figure 11.11.

Lifetime Profile 1 pictures the typcial lifetime income stream of an average regularly employed wage earner. Income begins in childhood, gradually increases though youth to a plateau in middle age (40 to 60), finally tapers off in retirement, and ends with pension or social security payments. This profile is based on annual median incomes for various aged persons. Although a large part of the population will have an income pattern that somewhat follows this trend, there are a number of important variations that are typical of occupational subgroups.[16]

Lifetime Profile 2 represents the money income stream of individuals who inherit wealth, position, or both, and receive an early money income from this accumulated fund. Such people are likely to have a high income immediately. The direction income takes after inheritance depends on the managerial ability of the person to protect what has been inherited, as well as the occupation and productivity of the person. Dotted lines represent failure to

Figure 11.11   Profiles of Lifetime Family Incomes

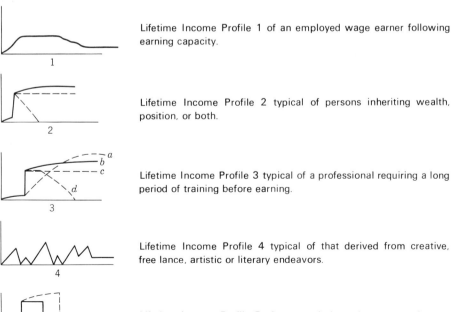

Lifetime Income Profile 1 of an employed wage earner following earning capacity.

Lifetime Income Profile 2 typical of persons inheriting wealth, position, or both.

Lifetime Income Profile 3 typical of a professional requiring a long period of training before earning.

Lifetime Income Profile 4 typical of that derived from creative, free lance, artistic or literary endeavors.

Lifetime Income Profile 5 of persons in hazardous occupations or those with short duration such as professional athletes.

increase or a decrease in the principal inheritance. The amount of the inheritance is unimportant in this analysis; the direction the income takes is the issue.

Profile 3 represents the income trend for a professional or vocationally trained person who undergoes a longer period of preparation before earning. During training, the individual may be subsidized by a fellowship, relatives, friends, or governmental aid. A portion of expenses may be earned during training or borrowed against expected income. The period of lower income may be short or long, depending on the demands made by society for the training of specialization in the chosen field.

The direction income takes depends on the circumstances at the end of the training period. Line *b* shows the income of people who receive a definite salary immediately after completing the training period, such as teachers, scientists, or businessmen, and who have corresponding income increases with professional maturity.

Line *c* represents the income of those who receive a salary at the end of the training period but go through life with little income change over the years. Some are not successful and are lost to the profession, while others choose to serve some other occupation; their income follows the direction of line *d*.

Persons in fields requiring time to build a practice, clientele, or business are represented in line *a*. Eventually income of persons in this group may go higher than that of the salaried group. Incomes, for example, in Lifetime Profile 3 tend to increase and stay higher longer than in the case of the average wage earner shown in Profile 1.

Lifetime Profile 4 is typical of people who freelance and depend on creativity or luck for income. They are not regularly employed and, thus, do not have a regular wage or salary. They may have investments or savings for maintenance between sales or commissions. This profile is typical of some architects, actors, authors, speculators, and promoters. Any one of these may be found in another group with a regular income. The distinguishing characteristic here is that they *depend* on the infrequent acceptance of their work for monetary resources. This is the only group that has a lifetime pattern similar to annual income because any single income peak in the lifetime may be the peak for a given year.

Lifetime Profile 5 is typical of persons in occupations in which earning power is high but short in duration. Professional sports participants and others whose earning power depends on physical skill that may be lost with age are examples of such occupations. The income profiles of some airline pilots may follow the general pattern of Profile 5. Line *a* represents those who fail to find additional work to sustain earnings. Line *b* is typical of those who are able to maintain high income from capital accumulated during their high-earning periods or who are able to exchange their fame for related work, such as that of a sports announcer following a career as a professional football player.

West and Wood identify three stages through which lifetime incomes typically move: Stage 1, the income source is from parents and lasts until a person is about 20 years of age; Stage 2, the increased income is from productive work and reaches a peak at about age 50; and Stage 3, productivity and income decline somewhat prior to retirement, gradually at first and then drastically at retirement. The last stage continues until death.[17]

Figure 11.12 provides a form and a pattern for charting a personal or family lifetime income profile. The form itself may be drawn on graph paper and the actual income plotted on an annual basis from old tax records. This would produce a "current" income profile with buying power fluctuating with the cost of living. Instead of the earner's age as the horizontal axis, number of years of employment may be easily substituted. Either will allow the person or family to compare progress or lack of it on the profile. To use the form, combine annual income from all sources and start at any point on the chart. Past income records will produce complete and accurate profiles.

In Figure 11.12, the dotted line represents the actual median 1971 income of all familes in the U.S. by age of the husband in constant 1971 dollars.[18] The solid line represents the median income of white families with both husband and wife in the labor force.[19] Personal lifetime income profiles may differ from both of these median profiles because of factors such as race, occupation, luck, number of persons employed, motivation, education, and location of residence during the family's life cycle.

A personal lifetime income profile is a tool for analyzing long-term financial assets and can be highly useful to chart growth toward financial security and specific goals. Knowledge of typical income profiles of people in similar situations can help a family predict and plan for changes in income.

Credit: Elastic Income

Credit is a method of obtaining money, goods, or services in the present and paying for them in the future. The use of credit expands purchasing power at any given time and, thus, makes possible the provision of more goods or services than the cash on hand would allow; but repayment of the amount borrowed, together with interest for its use, must eventually be made.

This system of expanding current purchasing power should not be overlooked when analyzing financial resources because it is a financial resource. As with income and wealth, the quality of living credit will buy is dependent on the effectiveness of management. Although some people consider credit a method of securing goods and services that cannot be afforded, it is true that practically everyone in modern society uses credit in one form or another.

Figure 11.12 Personal Lifetime Income Profile Form

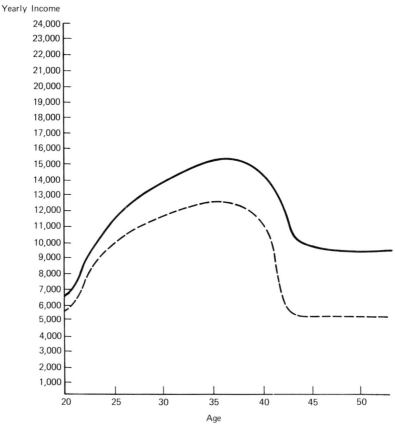

Service credit—utility, telephone, and doctor or dentist bills—is so common that people forget it is credit. This is noninstallment credit, and if paid promptly, this form of credit usually costs no more than paying cash and is more convenient. Monthly charge accounts also fall into this category.

Many people routinely purchase their cars through *installment credit*, another form of credit resources. About 50 percent of used cars and 57 percent of all new cars purchased in a year are typically bought through installment credit and other forms of borrowing.[20]

Few people can afford to pay cash for a home. If they delay home ownership until they can pay cash, the need or desire for a home may pass. *Mortgage credit* provides a way of owning a living unit while paying for it. However, mortgage credit is costly. A mortgage of $30,000 at 8 percent interest would require a minimum monthly payment of $231 excluding taxes and insurance, for 25 years. Of the total $69,300 repaid (25 years × 12 months = 300 months at $231 = $69,300), $39,300 is interest. The remaining $30,000 repays the original loan. If the same amount of money ($231) is deposited monthly in a savings account paying 8 percent, it would take 7 years and 9 months to save $30,000. This way the interest earned helps pay for the house, instead of adding cost.[21]

By setting goals early and starting a rigid savings program, a young couple could own their own home *without a mortgage* in less than eight years after marriage—about the time the average family buys its first home. The $39,000 that would have been spent on mortgage interest will buy many advantages that the average family is missing. The problem is that many young couples would find it difficult to pay rent *and* save $231 per month, even for 8 years. With home ownership via mortgage, people can live in the house while paying for it, but the period of paying is prolonged—to 25 years in the case described.

Another variable is the increase in the cost of housing even in an eight-year period. There is also an income tax deduction offered home owners with mortgages that helps offset the cost of the mortgage. Other reasons why more families do not follow the save-first, buy-later plan are willpower and a sense of direction—goal orientation. There are often multiple, conflicting goals at this time. Cars, television sets, and other goods compete for current dollars and for credit. People are enticed to use installment and other credit for smaller items with cost equal to rent plus a rigid savings plan. Credit is a costly example of the price of interchange in resources—money for time.

Who Uses Credit?

The ratio of consumer debt to disposable personal income in 1973 was 18.7.[22] This ratio varies with the income level of the spending unit and is lowest among those with incomes under $3,000 and highest among families with incomes of $10,000 to $15,000. Those who use installment credit most frequently are young, middle-income families, especially those with children. Almost half of all families have some installment debt, and 60 percent of those in the $10,000 to $15,000 bracket have installment debt. More white families own bank and retail credit cards than black families, and black families use installment credit more often than white families, but the amount owed is usually less.[23]

According to a study of excessive indebtedness by Ryan and Maynes, 19 percent of all debtors were in some degree of trouble because of too high a debt load, and 11 percent were in deep trouble. People under the age of 25 and over the age of 65 were more likely to have debt troubles as were poor and unmarried persons. Laborers, service workers, unemployed, and retired persons had above average chances of debt troubles. At least half the households headed by a woman who used credit had some trouble, and about the same proportion of black credit users had problems.[24]

A U.S. Department of Agriculture study reported current expenditures for young married couples, with the family head under 35 years, averaged slightly more than current income; debts averaged about 81 percent of current income, and liquid assets and investments were only 39 percent of the debt owed.[25]

Building a credit reputation

While some families have severe debt troubles, others consciously seek to establish credit and to locate channels of credit that may be used in case of emergencies. Families who have not used credit find it hardest to get it when they need it most. Building a credit rating is as important in financial planning as developing other resources.

Today's credit is based on what are sometimes called the four "C's" of credit: character, capacity, collateral, and capital.[26] Confidence and conditions have also been identified as "C's" of credit.[27] Confidence of the lender is faith built on the borrower's character—desire to repay—and his or her capacity, collateral, and capital—ability to pay. Conditions are the current national and local economic conditions that limit or expand available money and confidence in job security. Figure 11.13, "Building Credibility", shows how lending institutions and credit-extending merchants evaluate a person's credibility—ability to get credit.

Single and recently divorced women may find it difficult to get credit. Laws are being passed to eliminate sexual discrimination, but it may take some time for the practice to be actuated. Many people are denied credit, not because of a poor credit rating, but because they have simply no rating. Credit information is provided by a bureau that collects information about those who use credit from a variety of sources—merchants, landlords, personal references, employers, banks, savings institutions, court and police records, press stories, and even from neighbors, schools, or medical records. Legal records, federal tax liens, and collection agency records are also consulted. In fact, it is said that credit bureaus know more about people than people do about themselves.[28] It is also believed that a person may move away from a shady moral reputation, but a credit reputation follows wherever one goes because of the well-developed network of communication and data storage techniques used by credit bureaus.

Anyone interested in building a credit file may do so by visiting the local credit bureau, filing an application form, paying a small fee to establish the file, and listing references useful to determine character, capacity, capital, or collateral. The cost to establish a credit file is usually paid for by a merchant who requests information on a customer applying for credit in the store. Either

Figure 11.13   Building Credibility.

The four C's of credit	Meaning	What lending institutions look for
Character	Intent or desire to repay	Application behavior, accurate information on application, personal characteristics as age, length of residence at one address, neighborhood of residence, number of credit cards or accounts, prior credit experience with repayment, credit history with absence of collection, past-due notices, or law suits.
Capacity	Ability to repay	Education, few dependents, steady income sufficient to meet normal needs, employed with good firm, steady job prospects, job involving skill, amount of pay, length of time on the job (two years or more desirable).
Capital	Money and securities owned, financial standing in the community, amount of down payment	Checking account in one or more local banks, savings accounts, owning a living unit and automobile, and lender's ability to exercise command over borrower's assets.
Collateral	Assets pledged as security for a loan or credit sale	Resale value of goods pledged as security, accessibility of person (even a telephone adds points on a credit point scale), police power to tap existing equities in home and cars, cosigner.

SOURCE: Based on interviews with managers of lending institutions and merchants using sales contracts for installment purchases.

system will establish a file, and careful management of debts will maintain a positive record in the credit bureau's files. Developing characteristics listed in the column labeled "What Lending Institutions Look For", in Figure 11.13, can also help build credibility.

The Fair Credit Reporting Act of 1970 requires the credit reporting agency, when requested, to tell the consumer the information that is in the file, the source of information, and recipients of reports. The law also provides recourse on disputed information.

Managing credit includes determining when to use credit and when its use has become excessive. Credit is a useful resource when handled with understanding of its potential and its cost. It allows people to take advantage of sales that save more than the cost of the credit. It can provide a home during the years when family members are there to enjoy and use the home. Credit can finance investments in human capital—education—that might not be possible otherwise. And credit can pay for emergencies, such as illness or accidents. It may encourage more prompt service on cars or durables purchased on installment. It may also provide better family living, better health, more satisfaction, or it may buy equipment that saves human resources.[29]

Credit may also bring disastrous results. Many a family has lost property used as security; wages have been assigned by creditors to collect overdue indebtedness, or available goods have been sold to make payments on a loan. Avoiding unnecessary use of credit or finding it at lowest available cost when it is used is the first target for most families.[30]

Learning to compare the dollar and percentage costs of sources of credit is a vital skill in installment credit management. Because consumer credit is expensive and the risk involved in its use may be quite real, the importance of investigating various sources of credit before it is needed cannot be overemphasized. When the pressure of urgent need is on a family, the choice of the source of credit is sometimes hasty and unwise. Prior investigation provides practice in credit source comparison in addition to indicating the probable source of lowest-cost credit.

Figure 11.14 presents a comparison of six sources of cash credit for buying an automobile in one community.[31] There is a *difference* of $525.60 in interest between the highest-cost source of borrowing $3,000 (Small Loan Compay #1) and the lowest-cost source (Credit Union #2). This difference is more than the *total* interest cost of borrowing the money from Credit Union #2. Of course, not everyone is eligible to borrow from credit unions, but there is still $307.80 difference between Bank #1 and Small Loan Company #1's cost of financing. Extra money spent on interest due to lack of credibility or failure to compare costs of borrowing reduces choices in financial management and wastes resources. Although some credit sources may provide money faster, the

Figure 11.14   Credit Cost Comparison.

Source of loan	Annual percentage rate (APR)	Monthly payment	Total interest in dollars
Bank #1	13.26%	$101.45	$652.20
Bank #2	13.69	102.08	674.88
Credit Union #1	10.8	98.04	529.44
Credit Union #2	9.0	95.40	434.40
Small Loan Company #1	18.25	110.00	960.00
Small Loan Company #2	18.25	109.66	947.87

quality of the needed service—money—is no better from one source than another. A comparison of credit costs may require no more than a few phone calls. Most lending agencies will provide the dollar cost and true annual interest rate by telephone.

The Consumer Credit Protection Act, called the Truth-in-Lending Act, requires full advance disclosure of finance charges in dollars-and-cents cost as well as a clear statement of the annual percentage rate that is charged on all credit contracts and monthly charge bills. Under the law, each contract involving credit offered by merchants, banks, and other creditors must disclose, in advance, the cash price, down payment, total amount financed, late charges, total number of payments, amounts of payments, and certain other information, in addition to the annual percentage rate and dollar cost of interest. In some states, a contract must be in the same language in which the sales presentation is made. This law and its amendments have increased the information available to consumers to compare sources and costs of using credit.

Another consideration in managing credit is to determine how much credit is excessive. More people are in debt today than at any other time in the nation's history. The average American family owes between $800 and $1,000 in installment debts, not counting home mortgages, and the average debt ratio to disposable income approaches 19 percent. Most experts say that debt should not exceed 20 percent of the husband's take-home pay if the family is to consider itself in a safe economic position; and this would be safe only when the head of the household's job is secure.[32]

Margolius recommends the following credit management procedures: using credit for only "genuine" uses, such as large purchases that will last beyond the final payment, using credit moderately, borrowing the least a person needs, not borrowing until the cash is actually needed, and shopping for the lowest cost of credit.[33]

Protecting credit vulnerability is equally important in financial management. Possession of credit cards includes responsibility for use and control. Although a 1971 amendment to the Truth-in-Lending Act limits liability to $50 worth of unauthorized purchases, many people carry several credit cards. Their loss can mean responsibility for an uncomfortable sum of money, especially if notification of loss is delayed. It may take court action to prove which purchases are unauthorized. The rightful owner is responsible for items charged until the company is notified that the card is missing. Knowledge of method of notification and the number of cards a person carries can both be crucial to limiting total liability. Just as with other resources, credit can be a constraint on goal attainment; with effective management, it can help people reach their goals earlier and more conveniently.

Wealth

Many families overlook wealth as a financial resource. Inventorying and analyzing the pattern of wealth as a financial resource is a useful step in achieving goals. Rather than considering wealth as a goal, it may be managed as a means to other, more satisfying ends. It is the *use* of the goods and services that compose wealth that determines satisfaction.

FORMULATING A PLAN OF ACTION

Once the desired life style and goals of a family are established and the current financial resources have been evaluated, the approach will need to be formulated. This is one of the most exciting and challenging steps of successful management. It is also one of the most difficult.

Controlling and successfully using financial resources takes planning. Families use two types of plans—an *annual plan* or budget that identifies classifications of expenditures and estimates the proportion of income to be devoted to each category, and a general *overall financial plan* that describes a spending pattern for lifetime goals.

Annual Plans

Essentially, an annual budget is a plan for allocating income to current committments and to supply funds for identified short-term goals. It also includes provision for reaching long-term goals. It usually covers roughly a year and is broken down into monthly time periods. If the plan proves unsuccessful at any time, it should be revised immediately. Otherwise, it is usually revised at the end of the year or when changes occur in income, goals, or family circumstances.

The budget year may begin at any time, and there is no better time than the present to establish the plan. Once it is developed and refined, the budget year may be reestablished to coincide with an occupational fiscal year (September through August for teachers), or with income tax records (usually January through December).

If the budget is to serve as a master plan to gain satisfaction from financial resources and not just a bookkeeping system, it will need to be personal, goal oriented, realistic, flexible, and workable.

Goal-Oriented Plans.

A financial plan can do many things. It helps to choose a suitable standard of living within the limits of present earnings; it helps people mature in their attitude toward financial facts of life; it encourages rational consumer action in the marketplace; it can eliminate family arguments about finances, help solve financial problems, and encourage people to study their values and gain satisfaction from the use of their financial resources.

If a plan is not directed toward the identified short-term goals and does not provide avenues for achieving long-range goals, it is not achieving its purpose. If completion of college has been set as a primary goal during the year and money is not planned for college expenses, the budget cannot accomplish its function. Even when financial security is established as a long-range goal, a budget cannot guarantee financial security, but it can identify steps necessary to reach what the group has defined as financial security, and it can identify problems before they reach the crisis stage.[34]

Realistic Budgets

Financial plans are usually related to a particular standard of living—that of the people who are to use the budget—but must also be related to the expected income of that group. Realism in financial management is learning to live on less than one earns and allocating remaining funds toward long-range goals.

In a realistic budget, some methods of reducing expenditures to a manageable list are essential. Bymers and Rollins[35] use one method of classifying expenditures for budgets and the bulletin *Helping Families Manage Their Finances*[36] uses another, but both classifications of budgets include categories for:

- long-range goals and possible emergencies

- repayment of due bills, debts, and notes

- commitments—both regular (as mortgage payments) and irregular (such as taxes and insurance)

- current living expenses such as food, clothing, allowances, and transportation

- miscellaneous, overlooked items, unexpected expenses, and extra spending

- satisfaction of near-future goals.

Since financial plans are personal, there is no one "right" system to classify expenditures. The system that reduces probability of oversight of potential expenses, reconciles expenditures with plans for spending, and compares the proportion of expenditures with priorities in goal attainment is a realistic system.

In Figure 11.15, several of the expenditure classifications are grouped as either *flexible expenses*—those that fluctuate from month to month and may be manipulated to balance the budget—or as *fixed expenses*—those previous obligations with known amounts or due dates, some of which occur each month in the same amounts or once or twice a year in roughly predictable amounts. On such a form, the dollar amount owed by any member of the family should be written in the appropriate month for all fixed-cost obligations. Note that repayment of due bills and debts are included in the fixed expense category.

For large, fixed obligations that are due once a year and cannot realistically be paid out of a single paycheck, a reserve savings fund into which a suggested $\frac{1}{12}$ of the total payment is deposited each month will smooth out the payment of such bills. If an annual insurance premium is divided by 12 and that amount deposited into a reserve fund each month, the appropriate balance will be on hand to pay the premium when due. Similarly, other fixed expenses may be so divided and the reserve fund used for their payment. The interest earned on such a fund is a reward for planning.

Flexibility

If a budget is inflexible, it will not be functional. If the cost of living increases and the budget does not include a "buffer" for this increase, the family will be that much in debt unless the income increases by a similar proportion.

A flexible plan lists the family's usual fluctuating expenditures by headings such as utilities, clothing, gifts, or home repairs and assigns an estimated percentage of income for each category. All other unaccounted-for items should be given a category in the budget as "other flexible expenses." The budget for flexible items may be assigned by averaging the previous year's receipts and adding a cost of living adjustment. Dividing this adjusted total of like expenditures from the previous year by 12, will allow an equal estimate for each month. Or, if more clothing is purchased in September and April, the clothing budget for these months may be set higher than other months and other categories reduced by a similar amount. This latter system is more realistic but may not be practical for people whose incomes barely stretch to cover monthly essentials.

A flexible budget will also allow for impulse buying within a prescribed limit. Most people enjoy emotional spending, and when these self-satisfying splurges are planned in the budget, they do not impinge on goal attainment. Even families with low incomes are inclined to pacify emotional wants through spending. If these are planned in the budget and held to controllable limits,

Figure 11.15 A Sample Budget Form.

	% Budgeted	FIXED EXPENSES												
		Jan.	Feb.	Mar.	April	May	June	July	Aug.	Sept.	Oct.	Nov.	Dec.	Total
		$	$	$	$	$	$	$	$	$	$	$	$	
SAVINGS														
Emergencies														
Goals														
HOUSING														
Mortgage or rent														
INVESTMENTS														
Education														
Professional advancement														
Retirement														
Securities														
Social Security														
Other														
MONTHLY PAYMENTS														
Auto Loan														
Appliances														
Furniture														
Revolving charges														
Other														
TAXES AND LICENSES														
Auto licenses														
Federal income taxes														
Property taxes														
State income taxes														
Other														
TOTALS														
		FIXED OR FLEXIBLE												
TRANSPORTATION														
Car upkeep and repairs														
Gasoline and oil														
Servicing														
Public transportation														
UTILITIES														
Electricity														
Fuel														
Gas														
Telephone														
Water														
OTHER														
$ TOTALS														

303

Figure 11.15 (Continued)

	% Budgeted	Jan.	Feb.	Mar.	April	May	June	July	Aug.	Sept.	Oct.	Nov.	Dec.	Total
		\$	\$	\$	\$	\$	\$	\$	\$	\$	\$	\$	\$	
CLOTHING														
New purchases														
Care & upkeep														
Laundry														
Dry cleaning														
CONTRIBUTIONS & GIFTS														
Anniversaries														
Birthdays														
Christmas														
Church														
Charities														
Civic groups														
Professional groups														
Social clubs														
Schools														
Weddings														
Other														
ENTERTAINMENT														
Hobbies														
Movies														
Equipment														
Sports														
Special events														
Travel														
Vacations														
Other														
FOOD														
Meals at home														
Meals out														
FAMILY PERSONALS														
Cosmetics														
Incidentals														
Family allowances														
Soaps & sundries														
Other														
HOME FURNISHINGS														
Household equipment														
Furniture														
Repairs														
HOME IMPROVEMENT														
Repairs														
Upkeep														

FLEXIBLE EXPENSES

% Budgeted	FLEXIBLE EXPENSES												
	Jan.	Feb.	Mar.	April	May	June	July	Aug.	Sept.	Oct.	Nov.	Dec.	Total
	$	$	$	$	$	$	$	$	$	$	$	$	
HOUSEHOLD OPERATION													
Cleaning supplies													
Household help													
Inside													
Outside													
Baby Sitters													
INCIDENTALS													
Stationery													
Postage													
PERSONAL IMPROVEMENT													
Papers													
Magazine subscriptions													
$ TOTALS													

they contribute to satisfaction that money can bring without jeopardizing other, higher priority goals.

Flexibility in a budget is increased when a *range* of expenditures is estimated for certain items that normally have a fluctuating pattern. Problems arise when too wide a spread is established for an item and the added expense must be taken from some other category, such as "other flexible expenses."

Workable

For a budget to be workable, it must include some practical method to achieve the goals that have been identified for its time period. A workable budget is complete. It does not omit items that are normal for the spending pattern of the group. Incidentals such as stationery, postage, cosmetics, meals eaten out, car repair, auto licenses, or Christmas gifts are sometimes forgotten. If such items are considered as miscellaneous expenditures in the budget, the category must be adequate enough to include them.

Deciding on an appropriate category of expense is a part of planning. Do reading materials—books, magazines, newspapers—best fit into the recreation or the education category? Are lunches at work job-related expenses or food away from home? Where would unexpected car repairs fit in the plan—transportation or savings? There are no binding rules that govern these questions because financial plans are personal. Plan for the unexpected and for the incidentals, and inform the person who reconciles expenditures with budget, about the decisions.

Gaining maximum satisfaction from the financial plan requires accurate estimates of the costs of living. Flexible expenditures are more difficult to determine in advance than are fixed expenses. If the income pattern is irregular and income is lower than anticipated one month, the flexible side of a budget must be trimmed, savings used, or credit substituted for money that month.

Records of past expenditures are helpful to establish accurate estimates of flexible expenditures. If analyzed in light of new and more pressing goals or changes in situations, such records can contribute valuable information. Newly-established families with no previous records, single people who have had little experience with money plans, and debt-ridden families whose financial circumstances have reached a problem state may find suggestions in records of what other people spend. Also, information in standard budgets such as the three-level budgets prepared periodically by the Bureau of Labor Statistics for different geographic areas may prove helpful to determine a realistic estimate of expenditures for items in the proposed budget.[37]

Families with similar incomes and ages tend to follow similar patterns of spending. More important than dollar amounts are percentages used for different items characteristic of the life styles of people at different income levels. For example, Dorries, Smith, and Young report the following ranges of expenditures by families:[38]

Food	from 19 to 31 percent
Clothing	from 8 to 11 percent
Shelter	from 11 to 21 percent
Household Operation	from 12 to 14 percent
Transportation	from 14 to 10 percent
Personal Advancement	from 15 to 12 percent
Savings	from 21 to 1 percent

The first number for each item is the proportion spent by highest-income families, and the second figure is for the lowest-income families. High-income families tend to spend lower percentages for such necessities as food, clothing, shelter, and household operation. They spend higher percentages for transportation and personal advancement, and they save at a considerably higher rate than low-income families whose spending is devoted primarily to food, shelter, and household operation.[39]

Caplovitz[40] and Harrington[41] discussed problems the poor face in managing money and credit. For those with regular incomes, stretching weekly income through the week is the main problem. Because income is inadequate, often grossly inadequate, to meet the food, shelter, clothing, and household operational expenses, there is no money left to save. The goals that can be realistically established are those that relate to "getting by." Resisting the notion of planning for the future is the norm because scope of living is only "today."[42] Banking facilities may seem unnecessary because "Why put money in a bank if you have to draw it out before the end of the week?"

Campbell outlines the shopping habits of the economically disadvantaged as present-time oriented and characterized by feelings of insecurity. Disadvantaged people often buy the first item presented and are conscious of brand names but are often uninformed about features of the products they desire. They generally spend a large portion of the income in the store where they cash their pay check and stay close to the residential neighborhood for shopping because of insecurity and distrust as well as transportation problems.[43]

Because there is not enough money to save for larger annual payments, life insurance is purchased weekly or monthly with a high service charge for more frequent payments. The insurance salesman may come to the house to collect his payments. Often door-to-door merchants know the day welfare payments or paychecks arrive and time their calls to coincide with these payment dates.

The poor do pay more for many of the items they buy because of these characteristics, problems, and conditions. Disadvantaged people tend to spend, with abandon when they have money and make more impulse purchases partly because of the satisfaction gained from spending the cash that jangles in their pockets on payday and partly because they need almost everything.[44]

Lack of education and poor storage facilities often lead to improper care of clothes, appliances, and household goods. Warranties are not read and are soon lost; care instructions are disregarded. Lack of equipment for adequate care of clothes and fear of the unknown surroundings that may be necessary to use commercial laundry facilities leads to shortened life span of clothes.

Financial planning is difficult for the economically disadvantaged, but it is one of the most crucial procedures to improve quality of life. Saving even small amounts of money can lead to a "future oriented" attitude of money management and provide needed hope to stimulate goal-striving which, in turn, may provide motivation to increase income efforts. Saving may also reduce the cost of current expenses by helping to decrease borrowing. Although the ratio of debt to income is relatively low for the poor, their sources of credit are apt to be pawnbrokers and high-cost merchants. Eliminating these costs can improve economic wellbeing. Planning and consumer technology may help to increase return from expenditures and also contribute to the wellbeing of economically deprived families.

A final process in financial planning for families in any income level is to make sure the percentages assigned to individual categories of expenditures do not add up to more than 100 percent of spendable income.

Workable budgets are seldom achieved with one attempt. Reviewing the plan to assure that it is directed toward achievement of indentified goals, meets the needs of all members to use it, assures solvency, and allows funds for emergencies is a necessary process in developing workable financial plans. Using a budget for a period of several months will further test its effectiveness. Complete revision or minor adjustments can be made during this trial period. Records of income and spending during the trial period and comparison with the budget can help to identify specific budgetary changes.

Some budgets that are solely based on previous spending records perpetuate old problems without focusing spending on goals. Analyzing a budget with goals clearly in mind and questioning each item's relationship to the goals may help eliminate the least productive expenditures.

A budget is not meant to frustrate wants; its purpose is to provide a plan for gaining wants that are important. If the budget does not balance—income is insufficient to include fixed obligations, normal flexible living expenses, savings, and high-priority goals—a study of the plan may indicate the areas that provide least satisfaction.

Long-Range Financial Planning

A workable, short-term, goal-oriented budget is the foundation for longer-term planning. Any worthwhile budget includes plans for growth toward financial success—not just gratification of short-term goals. Each family needs an overall financial plan to reconcile income with wants throughout the life cycle of the family to build long-term financial security.

People—individuals and families—have different wants and different needs at various life cycle stages. Consumer behavior grows out of situations that occur in a familiar cycle—couples marry, establish households of their own, some bear children and raise them to maturity, others concentrate on work, education, or building a satisfying life for themselves and society during their middle years; they retire from active employment and eventually die. The economic life cycle of childless families was discussed in Chapter 1, along with the life cycle of families with children. Families of varying compositions have both a life pattern of income and expenditures. Reconciling the two to achieve life goals of all members of the group is the function of a long-range financial management plan.

Stages in family life cycle and use of money

An analysis of money income use is incomplete unless the long-time family life is paralleled with the probable long-time income. The family life cycle with children passes through three stages, each with a number of substages. Each phase makes specialized demands on the family income. The accompanying chart (Figure 11.16) shows the impact of the family's demands on income at the various stages of the life cycle.

Figure 11.16   Stages in Family Cycle. Patterns of income and expenses during the three stages of the average wage earner's life cycle.

Family stage		Substage	Demand on income
I. Beginning	1.	Period of establishment	Light to heavy
II. Expanding	2.	Childbearing and preschool	Heavy
	3.	Elementary school	Light to heavy
	4.	High school	Moderately heavy
	5.	College	Heaviest
III. Contracting	6.	Vocational adjustment of children	Heavy
	7.	Financial recovery	Light or heavy
	8.	Retirement	Lightest

Recognizing the influence of various stages in the family life cycle on income use is necessary to forecast goals during the stages. To show how such forecasting for each stage aids the family to analyze its income use, the family stages have been superimposed on two of the lifetime income profiles and the typical expenditure pattern of families. In this way, the force of the demand within the various stages may be more easily identified. If a family can forecast on a curve its probable lifetime income and locate the particular stage through which it is passing at a given time, the long-time view of needs and the resources to meet them can be visualized.

Figure 11.17 shows the three family life stages and the phases of each superimposed on the lifetime income profile of a wage earner. Figure 11.18 shows the same stages and phases superimposed on the lifetime income profile of the professional man. In both cases, the force of greatest demand is during college and recovery phases; the second force of demand is in vocational adjustment. The professional group has another period of heavy demand during the time children are being professionally trained. The elementary school phase is a period of light demand. The lightest demand for both groups is during retirement.

Observe the differences between the two groups in the intensity of demand related to the change in the earner's age during the various stages. For the professional, the periods of establishment and childbearing may be longer than for the average wage earner because training may delay marriage in this group; marriage during training usually is associated with a limited income. The period of accumulation in the professional group is shorter because of fewer children. With smaller families, the succeeding stages are shortened and do not overlap as much as in the wage-earner group. Substage 5, college, will in all probability be longer for the professional because the likelihood that the children in this group will receive advanced training and family subsidy is greater than for the average family. In the average family, advanced training for

Figure 11.17   Stages in Family Cycle. Professional man's lifetime income profile and the three stages of the family cycle.

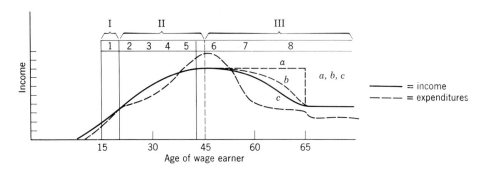

Figure 11.18

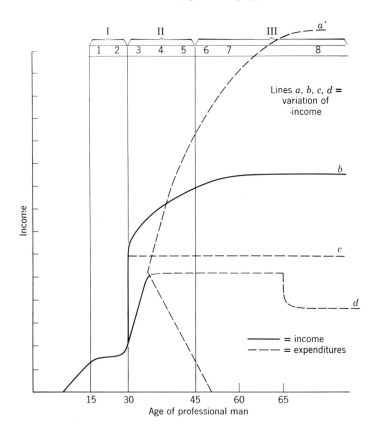

children is frequently financed, in part, from some source outside family funds—scholarships or other grants and subsidies plus work during training.

The recovery phase will be longer for the average wage earner than for the professional man because of the likelihood that the wage earner will need to liquidate indebtedness incurred during the period of sending children to college or providing vocational help. Moreover, the recovery stage is shortened for the professional because the income stream still tends to be high during this period. Both groups have about the same period of retirement, the difference being that the professional man's income tends to stay higher longer than the wage earner's because of the character of his employment plus the possibility of greater accumulation of funds supplemental to the earned income. The average wage earner's income levels off during retirement because of a pension and Social Security.

It is evident that many family financial ills arise from lack of strong motivation to plan for and control the long-term use of income. No matter how large or how small the income, an effective job of using income is possible if patterns of income and expenses are recognized and if annual budgets reflect long-term financial plans.

Organize all efforts

The organization stage of financial management is the same as the organization stage in the management of other resources. Establishing goal-oriented behavior, determining who will pay the bills, making purchasing decisions, doing the shopping, reconciling the checkbook, keeping records, or deciding when to use credit instead of cash are all parts of organizing efforts.

Different families use different systems to handle money matters. The choice of a method of handling money that gives all family members a feeling of satisfaction is a matter of major importance in the life of any family. Not all families use a budget or follow a management system for handling money. Some use a dole system; some use an allowance method; others use an equal-salary method with varying degress of satisfaction. One system may work more effectively for authoritarian families, while another may be better when both husband and wife are employed. Several methods, that have proven satisfactory for some families, are described and diagrammed as follows.

The family finance plan

The family finance plan, utilizing a budget, is a method of using income as a planned and shared family project. Husband and wife direct the system cooperatively, sharing jointly in planning and distributing income into the expenditure pattern that represents their desired living. As children become old enough to understand financial matters and have wants and desires of their

own, they may share in the planning along with the adults. Such a plan becomes part of the way of life of the family using it and is based on an understanding by both partners of the importance of shared experiences in human
development and financial management.

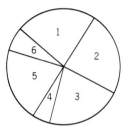

Diagram 1

Briefly stated, the method is one of analyzing goals, needs, and resources
to meet demands, of making decisions on what is important, and of working out
a plan for the use of money in accordance with the analysis. If husband, wife,
and children operate as colleagues, this method of handling money is a logical
development.

The allowance or apportionment method

In this method, a certain portion of the money is allocated for all or a part
of family living expenses. The husband generally gives the wife a stipulated
amount to cover specified expense items in family living. The remainder of the
income is used to cover other living costs such as payments on a house, investments, insurance, taxes, or any other items for which the husband wishes to
carry the responsibility. This system is likely to be used by business or

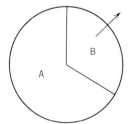

Diagram 2

professional people with irregular incomes. The apportionment system is sometimes used as a means to establish a family living salary from an irregular income stream. When such an equalizing process is used with careful planning, it
becomes a form of family financial planning described previously.

The equal salary method

This method is one in which all family expenses are paid from total income,
and the remaining amount is divided equally between husband and wife as a

"salary" for the contribution of each to the enterprise. The system assumes not only that the income is large enough to have a surplus but also that each division of the surplus represents an appreciable sum. The plan makes no visible provisions for managing the major portion allocated to family living. Thus, that part of the income can be operated as a handout or as a highly planned system of spending. Nor does the plan indicate whether area A includes funds for savings and investments for long-term goals.

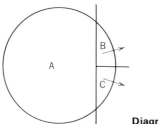

Diagram 3

This method is most often used in families where the wife has had an independent income or is currently working and desires the independence that a "salary" provides her. When area A is administered through a budget plan, the equal-salary method of handling financial resources can be a satisfying and productive method of handling money.

The fifty-fifty system

This system is a method in which total income and expenditures are divided into two equal parts. The system operates by the husband's assuming half of the specified expenditures and paying them from his half of the income; the wife assumes responsibility for the other half and pays for expenditures from her half of the income. The system assumes a known and regular income and known expenditures; otherwise an equal division could not be made.

This system is often used when the wife had an independent income before marriage and wishes to maintain a degree of independence, when the wife earns, or when there are no children.

The handout method

The handout or dole system is explained by its name. One person, usually the husband, although sometimes the wife, maintains complete control of the income and hands out small or large sums of money as needs arise or as wants are insistent enough to interest him in making the dole. The system is a carry-over from patriarchal family life when the father was controller of his domain and dealt out money, justice, and judgments in all areas of family life.

The handout method is likely to be used in a family that has little knowledge of its exact income, or one that still operates under the patriarchal system. It is based on a "first come, first served" philosophy and is often used in families where income is simply insufficient to meet obligations and living needs. The bill that is presented first, or with greatest persistence, is paid first. If the paycheck is cashed at the grocery store, it is there that the largest amount of money is spent that week.

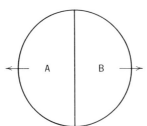

Diagram 4

Organizing efforts in financial management is largely a matter of human relations and cooperative action of the family to secure common goals as well as individually held goals. Organizing requires decisions about who is to keep the records, what kind of checking account to use when banking, timing of purchases, and what kind of records to keep. In most families, these jobs are

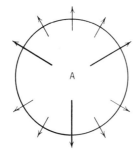

Diagram 5

already being accomplished. The questions are, "How well are the tasks performed; could someone else with more time, knowledge, or skill perform them in less time, and how satisfied are all members of the household with their usual tasks?"

Organizing financial resources to accomplish goals can be more effective if there is an established center for keeping records with easy access to necessary information. Computing income taxes for example, can be efficiently accomplished if adequate records are kept in one centralized place in the home. Possible equipment that could aid in the recordkeeping process includes:

adding machine or calculator   adequate lighting
file cabinet   storage cabinet or desk
large drawers   drawers for supplies
shelves for record books   typewriter
telephone

The home recordkeeping center, should contain such items as:

a copy of the household inventory

a list of credit cards and appropriate procedure for reporting loss or theft

savings account numbers and the maturity dates if they are of the fixed-rate, fixed-time variety

records of installment notes and payments

a list of items in the safe deposit box

automobile, boat, motorcycle, trailer and boat licenses, and registrations and serial numbers

records of insurance policy numbers, companies, and location of the policies

safe deposit box numbers and locations

securities and investments and their location

bank checking account numbers and addresses

brand, serial number, and location and expiration date of warranty for major appliances, such as stove, refrigerator, and dishwasher

These records can be gathered over a period of weeks and added to as new purchases are made or as the situation changes—sale of a car, purchase of additional insurance, or expiration of savings certificate. Once established, updating financial records presents little challenge to a busy manager, except to make sure they are safely stored, away from the hands of intruders, but readily available for need.

CONTROLLING ACTIVITIES

Ben Franklin said, "The use of money is all the advantage there is in having it." There is just one catch in his theory. It is *how* money is used that determines the advantages it brings to people. Money can buy an abundance of products that become mightier junkyards and auto graveyards lining the byways of communities; or money can be used to buy a quality of living that is founded on economic security and serviced by limited quantities of useful products, so carefully chosen that each actively contributes to an improved quality of living.

In an overabundant economy, where rational decisions are difficult, controlling financial activities is not an easy job. Communication is essential in motivating goal-striving. Self discipline is a real asset; and harmony of attitude of all family members will expand achievement of group and individual goals.

Many strategies have been offered for achieving success in financial management—eliminating waste from the budget, stretching the dollar by comparing before buying, reading before signing, and paying oneself first are only a few. Several of these strategies are examined as follows.

Eliminate Waste

Margolius identifies ten common "money leaks" that prevent families from reaching their goals. Included are: large finance charges resulting from habitual installment purchases, heavy outlays for car and household operating costs, larger-than-necessary expenditures for insurance, and failure to shop at appropriate times. He also suggests that many people pay more income taxes than necessary, often because of lack of records to substantiate deductions.[45] Since waste adds nothing, its elimination can only improve quality of life.

Plan Purchases

Emotional spending is a great detriment to reaching goals, and it has kept many a family from having things desired most in life. People who make shopping lists and buy only from the list are more likely to achieve their goals. About half of all supermarket customers shop without lists, and 70 percent of bakery goods are bought on impulse. Shopping from a list cuts extras to the minimum, but lists should be flexible enough to substitute frozen peas for fresh asparagus if there is a special on peas and the asparagus is too dry. If a need is for a nourishing green vegetable that is liked by the family, flexibility within limits should be a part of the process. However, with large items, impulse buying can wreck a budget. Closets are choked and charge accounts turn into monsters from emotional bargains that just couldn't wait. A bargain is a bargain only if it is something that would have been purchased anyway. Real bargains can always be added to another shopping list if, after consideration at home, they are determined important for one's way of life.

Time Purchases

Shopping for groceries once a week or less often with a list based on the weekly advertisements saves time and money. Knowing the arrangement of grocery stores and making the lists follow an orderly progression through store, from one special to another, makes management sense.

Timing large purchases to coincide with annual "white sales," end-of-month department store sales, or seasonal sales may save many dollars or allow purchase of a higher quality than could have been afforded at regular prices.

The time of day for grocery shopping may affect food prices. People tend to buy more foods and do less comparative shopping when they are hungry. Shopping after instead of before meals can save food dollars. Purchases may also be timed to coincide with higher income and avoid low-income periods during a year or over the life cycle of the family. Thus, timing may help eliminate need for using credit and save the cost of interest in large purchases.

Compare Alternatives

Comparing alternatives is an essential part of decision making in management. Comparative shopping is a vital part of financial management, and its techniques should be mastered, not only when choosing products within one store but in determining where it is most economical to shop. In times of inflation, even those with adequate funds enjoy getting their money's worth through comparative shopping. For low-income families, it is a constant need.

Studies have indicated that a variance of from 15 to 20 percent in a standard week's grocery list is customary between food markets in the same general locality. For those who are cost conscious, choosing a regular shopping place may be more realistic if a typical week's grocery list is priced in several convenient food stores and the market offering highest quality for lowest cost is determined on a personal basis. However, prices and policies change rapidly in stores, and specials at each store may make it worth using several markets if they are close together or if they are on a usual travel route.

The process of choosing consumer goods and services that meet the needs and wants of family members yet stay within the prescribed budget is a demanding task. Some families never buy a product that costs more than $10 without first comparing at least two brands in at least two sources. A waste of time? Not necessarily, if comparative shopping is done while a person is marketing or in between errands in a neighborhood.

Even the cost of services may vary widely. In a recent comparison of auto insurance premiums, a driver with no major citations or accidents for the last three years found a range in premium charges of from $149 to $189 for the same coverage on her car from four AAA-rated insurance companies.[46] The charges of hospitals, doctors, and other professionals may differ widely and merit investigation before they are needed. Comparison of quality of services, as well as product and service costs, can release funds for higher levels of savings or spending for other priority goals without decreasing the value of the services.

Use Information

Reading warranties and instruction manuals is another control mechanism that pays in financial management. The time to read warranties is before purchase. The length of warranty or quality of its services may tip the scales in favor of one product over another. After purchase, there is little that can be done about warranties except read, register, record, and file them so they can be located easily. Recording warranty dates and making a thorough check of the product several months before expiration of the warranty may save costly service bills after a warranty has expired. The Major Appliance Consumer Action Panel's pamphlet on "Warranties and the Consumer" may serve as a guide to comparing warranties.[47]

KEEPING ADEQUATE RECORDS

Each family will need to establish its own system of financial record keeping according to the family needs and interests, yet adequate for tax purposes and for evaluating growth toward financial goals.

The records most people dislike are a continual recording of expenditures. After a budget has been established, refined, and compared with long-term as well as short-term objectives, it may not be necessary to keep monthly records of expenditures beyond cancelled checks, check stubs, and records of paid bills. For families beginning their financial management system, for troubled families whose income simply does not stretch to cover necessities, or for those facing debt crises, it is important to know what the money is buying. These families may profit from expenditure records.

Some financial records are required by law—those that support income tax returns. Record keeping for tax purposes is an all-year job but if carefully executed can save many dollars of unnecessary tax payments that may be used for better living. Margolius estimated that about one-third of the families he interviewed paid more taxes than they needed to pay.[48] Even when an accountant figures the taxes, he must be provided accurate and complete records.

The law requires people to keep records that will enable them to prepare a complete and accurate income tax return, but the law does not require any special form of records. All receipts, cancelled checks, and other records that support an item of income or a deduction claimed on a return must be kept for three years after the date when the return was due or filed. When property or a home is purchased, checks, receipts, and records relating to purchase, and improvements made on the property through the years should be kept until the property is sold, and the transaction should be reported on an income tax return as either a loss or gain. Including a copy of each year's income tax returns— both state and federal—in the permanent financial record center is helpful for preparing future returns and serves as a record of income changes and financial worth over the years.

Tax records must be kept for all items claimed as deductions. The following items are deductible *under certain conditions* if records are available to support them: business auto expenses, bad debts, casualty losses, child care costs, contributions to charitable and educational organizations, employee business trips and other expenses, interest, and medical expenses including medical insurance.

Regular record keeping can save money at tax time. Other forms of records can do the same throughout the year. Overall financial records and a central financial management center is a step toward order in a financial estate, no matter how large or how small that estate may be.

EVALUATING PROGRESS TOWARD FINANCIAL SUCCESS

One of the most exciting results of evaluation is trust in choices made. As people learn to manage income, instead of letting it manage them, they learn self-reliance and self-control—two valuable human resources.

Reconciling checks with bank statements is one form of evaluation. Checks provide a record of spending; and when reconciled, not only with check stubs and bank statements, but with the management plan, they are clues to problem areas in the budget.

At least once a year, each family will benefit from a review of its overall long-range financial plan as well as its money-handling system. Few money-management systems work perfectly at first. They may be checked to see that needs of all family members are being met, that solvency is assured, emergencies are covered, leaks in spending are plugged, progress is being made toward long-range goals, credit ratio is manageable in light of present and future job realities, and family members are growing in their ability to practice self-control.

As records are being kept during trial periods and revised budgets are being established, people practice other management skills—communication skills, shopping abilities, organizational powers, investment judgment, and interaction with community specialists who can provide financial services. Time estimates in relation to goal realization are improved; and cooperation with others in achieving individual group goals is fostered. These are the experiences that expand abilities to manage—not just financial resources but all resources—toward a better way of life for all people.

Summary

Management was presented as an achievement-oriented system in this chapter, emphasizing results to be attained rather than effort expended. In the process, goal-oriented financial management exacts self-control and self-direction.

Ten steps to more successful financial management were outlined in the chapter with practical suggestions for carrying out each step. Progress was related to goal attainment. The clearer the idea of what financial success means, the better the chances each family and individual has of achieving it.

References

1. Ambassador College Editorial Staff, *Managing Personal Finances,* Ambassador College Press, Pasadena, Calif., p. 8.

2. Whyte, W. H., Jr., "Budgetism: Opiate of the Middle Class," *Fortune,* (May 1956), p. 172.

3. *Finance Facts Yearbook, 1973,* National Consumer Finance Assn., Washington, D.C., (1974); see also *Finance Facts Yearbook, 1974,* National Consumer Finance Assn., Washington, D.C., (1975) and Troelstrup, A. W. *The Consumer in American Society,* McGraw-Hill, (1974), p. 174.

4. Troelstrup, A. W., *The Consumer in American Society,* McGraw-Hill, New York, (1974), p. 174.

5. Odiorne, G. S., *Management by Objectives—A System of Managerial Leadership,* Pitman, N.Y., (1965); see also Odiorne, G. S., *Training by Objectives—An Economic Approach to Management Training,* Macmillan, New York, (1970).

6. Maltz, M., *Psycho–Cybernetics,* Pocket Books, New York, (1969).

7. Campbell, S., *Consumer Education in An Age of Adaptation,* Consumer Information Services, Sears, Roebuck, Chicago, (1971), p. 99.

8. *Kelley Blue Book Auto Market Report,* Official Guide, (Bi–monthly Periodical), Kelley Blue Book, Long Beach, Calif., (September–October, 1974).

9. "How Much Do 'Fringes' Boost Your Pay?", *Changing Times,* 27: 1 (January 1973), pp. 15–18.

10. *Ibid,* U.S. Chamber of Commerce survey reported on p. 15; see also "Fringe Benefits of Urban Workers," *Monthly Labor Review,* (November 1971), p. 4, (Table 2).

11. *The American Almanac, Statistical Abstract of the U.S. 1974,* Grosset and Dunlap, New York, (1974), p. 246, (Tables 388 and 389).

12. "How Much Do 'Fringes' Boost Your Pay?", *op. cit.,* pp. 17–18.

13.   "Lifetime Income," *op. cit.,* p. 1.

14.   *Ibid,* p. 1.

15.   Unger, M. A. and Wolf, H. A., *Personal Finance,* (3rd ed.), Allyn and Bacon, Boston, Mass., (1972), pp. 18–19.

16.   Data for lifetime income profiles are based on U.S. Department of Commerce, Bureau of the Census, P–23, P–30, and P–60 series; Survey of Consumer Finances monographs from Survey Research Center, Institute for Social Research, University of Michigan, Ann Arbor; and Rice, A. S., *An Economic Life Cycle of Childless Families,* unpublished doctoral dissertation, Florida State University, Tallahassee, (1964).

17.   West, D. A. and Wood, G. L., *Personal Financial Management,* Houghton Mifflin, Boston, Mass., (1972), pp. 39–40.

18.   The 1971 median family incomes charted are as follows: $6,861 for husbands under 25, $10,265 for those 25–34, $11,862 for those 35–44, $12,763 for families with husbands 45–54, $10,993 for those 55–64, and $5,511 for those 65 and over. Source: U. S. Bureau of the Census, *Current Population Reports,* Special Studies Series P–23, No. 47, "Illustrative Projections of Money Income Size Distribution for Families and Unrelated Individuals," (February 1974), Supt. of Documents, Washington, D. C.

19.   The charted median incomes of white families with husband and wife both earners in 1971, by age of the husband are as follows: $8,291 for husbands 14–24, $11,991 for those 25–34, $14,073 for those 35–44, $15,551 for those 45–54, $14,254 for those 55–64, and $9,821 for those 65 years and over; derived from American Almanac, *op. cit.,* p. 333.

20.   American Almanac, *op. cit.,* p. 549, (Table 905).

21.   Data derived from computer computations for savings; see also *Equal Monthly Loan Amortization Payments $4\frac{1}{2}$ to 10 Percent,* Financial Publishing Co., Boston, Mass., (1960).

22.   American Almanac, *op. cit.,* p. 455.

23.   Finance Fact Yearbook, (1973), *op. cit.*

24. Ryan, M. E. and Maynes, E. S., "The Excessively Indebted: Who and Why," *The Journal of Consumer Affairs, 3:* 2 (Winter 1969), 107–126.

25. *Finance Fact Yearbook, 1971,* National Consumer Finance Assn., Washington, D. C., (1972); U.S. Dept. of Agriculture study cited on p. 38.

26. Bigelow H. F., *Family Finance,* Lippincott, Philadelphia, (1953), p. 370.

27. Burda, E. T., *Consumer Finance,* Harcourt Brace Jovanovich, New York, (1975), p. 89; see also Nickell P., and Dorsey, J. M., *Management in Family Living* (4th ed.), Wiley, New York, (1967), pp. 309–310.

28. Troelstrup, A. W., *op. cit.,* pp. 180–181.

29. *Ibid,* pp. 166–197.

30. Margolius, S., *How to Make the Most of Your Money,* Appleton-Century-Crofts, New York, (1966), p. 55.

31. Survey of lending institutions in Santa Barbara, Calif., (Spring 1975).

32. "Do You Owe Too Much," *Changing Times,* 28, 6 (June 1974), pp. 6–9.

33. Margolius, S., *op. cit.,* p. 57.

34. West, D. A. and Wood, G. L., *op. cit.,* p. 91.

35. Bymers, G. J. and Rollins, M. A., *Classification Systems: Household Expenditures Data and Household Accounts,* Cornell University Agricultural Experiment Station Bulletin No. 1014, (July 1967).

36. U.S. Department of Agriculture, *Helping Families Manage Their Finances,* Agricultrual Research Service, Report 21, (1968), pp. 11–20.

37. U.S. Department of Labor, Bureau of Labor Statistics, *Autumn 1973 Urban Family Budgets and Comparative Indexes for Selected Urban Areas,* (June 14, 1974).

38. Dorries, W. L., Smith, A. A., and Young, J. R., *Personal Finance: Consuming, Saving and Investing,* Charles Merrill, Columbus, Ohio, (1974), p. 158.

39. Phillips, E. B. and Lane, S., *Personal Finance: Text and Case Problems,* (3rd ed.), Wiley, New York, (1974); see also Dorries, Smith, and Young, *op. cit.,* p. 158.

40. Caplovitz, D., *The Poor Pay More,* Free Press, New York, (1963).

41. Harrington, M., *The Other America: Poverty in the United States,* Penguin Books, Baltimore, Md., (1962).

42. Phillips, E. B. and Lane, S., *op. cit.,* pp. 40–41.

43. Campbell, S. R., *op. cit.,* p. 43.

44. Phillips, E. B. and Lane, S., *op. cit.,* p. 40.

45. Margolius, S., *op. cit.,* p. 35.

46. The financial standing and insurance rating of insurance companies is issued annually by Alfred M. Best Co., Morristown, N. J. in *Best's Insurance Guide to Key Ratings.*

47. Major Appliance Consumer Action Panel, *Warranties and the Consumer,* MACAP, 20 North Wacker Drive, Chicago, Ill.,

48. Margolius, S., *op. cit.,* pp. 35, 163–170.

12

WEALTH AS A RESOURCE

Wealth is a result, as well as a resource, of management. Galbraith called America "The Affluent Society" as early as 1958. "Wealth," he said, "is not without its advantages,"[1] But he also observed that until a person learns to live with wealth, "he will have a well observed tendency to put it to the wrong purposes or otherwise to make himself foolish."[2] Galbraith was writing about the transition from an era of poverty to the relatively recent "access to amenities—foods, entertainment, personal transportation, and plumbing—in which not even the rich rejoiced a century ago."[3]

It has been said that income is earned; wealth is accumulated. Wealth is seldom accumulated at one time. Its flow and timing are determined by many qualities—wants, aspirations, effort, motivation, frugality and thrift, perseverance, inheritance, education, gifts, and many other factors. Wealth is usually a product of previous income management. Wealth often reflects a family's level of living and its pattern of income, for it is through the use of income that wealth is acquired, especially discretionary income. Wealth is built and preserved through management.

Components of Wealth

Wealth consists of all resources having economic value. Personal wealth usually includes:

- fixed dollar assets—savings and checking account balances, cash on hand, value of life insurance policies, annuities, pension plans, and various other forms of insurance

- variable income investments—stocks, investment companies, trusts, mutual funds

- real estate—land and income properties, home

- durables—household appliances, furnishings, equipment

- automobiles

- personal possessions of worth—jewelry, furs, clothing, sports equipment

- collectibles and antiques—stamp or coin collections, silver and gold, limited edition plates, antique glassware

- art treasures—paintings, etchings, carvings, sculpture.

Wealth also refers to the characteristic pattern of asset holdings and investments in human capital—earning capacity. Wealth is sometimes referred to as a person's estate which means all property, real and personal, tangible and intangible, in which a person has investments.

America is a society of consumers who have been criticized for obsession with acquiring material possessions. Yet, this country is also the wealthiest nation in the world in terms of technology, Gross National Product, per capita income, and the level of living achieved by its population. Many of the nonconsumable, longer-lasting possessions that people strive to attain are classed as wealth.

ASSET HOLDINGS

An estimate of the total net worth of the average American family in the early 1970's is about two and a half times the median family's annual income.[4] The largest portion of net worth, for most families, is achieved through "forced savings" from regular earnings: through the purchase of a home with monthly mortgage payments, through purchase of furnishings and appliances on credit which adds assets faster than liabilities, or through accumulated cash value of life insurance policies and retirement plans. Most of the latter are deducted from salaries, and, in many cases, employers contribute to the retirement or pension plan, thereby building equity more rapidly.

The median amount of equity owners had in their homes was $11,500 in 1970.[5] That year, 62.9 percent of all occupied housing units in the country were owner-occupied. The median value of these owner-occupied housing units was $17,000.[6]

Liquid assets are an important part of personal wealth. In the United States in 1971, 84 percent of all family units had some liquid assets. The median amount of liquid asset holdings that year was $700, a decrease of $100 over the year before. Liquid assets include savings, certificates of deposit, checking accounts, and government savings bonds according to a Bureau of Census definition. In 1971, liquid asset holdings were distributed as follows:[7]

Amount of Liquid Assets	Percent of Families
Less than $500	42
$500 to $2,000	24
$2,000 to $10,000	22
$10,000 and over	12

Liquid assets are related to income. Families with incomes ranging from $7,500 to $10,000 in 1970 had a median amount of liquid assets worth $500; families with $15,000 and over incomes had liquid assets of $3,700. The trend, especially among older people seeking higher returns and the more sophisticated younger persons who are also yield conscious, is toward certificates of deposit with fixed-time limits and fixed-interest rates. Eight percent of the population had certificates of deposit with a median amount of $5,000 in 1970.

In 1970 only one in five families had total liquid assets of more than $5,000. About two-thirds of American families had a savings account with a median balance of $1,300 in 1970. More people of middle than other income groups reported dissatisfaction with their savings and reserve funds.[8]

Three-fourths of American families had a checking account with a median balance of $250. More than one-third of the check-writing families wrote more than 20 checks per month.[9]

About 21 percent of middle-income families owned real estate other than their homes. Undeveloped real estate was the most popular type of holding, and about 6 percent of families with $15,000 and over income in 1970 owned summer or vacation homes. That year, the median value of real estate owned by families with incomes of $7,500 to 10,000, was $7,500. For families with incomes of $15,000 or more, the median value of all real estate was nearly $20,000.[10] One in seven Americans owned securities; the median income of individual shareowners was $13,500, and the median value of shares held at that time was between $5,000 and $10,000.[11]

The median family believes in life insurance but not to the extent that many feel is safe. Average face value coverage per family in 1970 was $19,500. That year, 41 percent of families with $5,000 to 7,500; 22 percent of families with $10,000 to 15,000, and 11 percent of families with $15,000 or more had *no* life insurance other than that carried through their employer.[12]

By 1973, the average life insurance coverage per family had risen to $24,400.[13]

American families spend a large portion of consumption expenditures for transportation. The asset value of an automobile is low because a car often depreciates as fast as the equity in the car accumulates. Although small on a household level, asset value in cars is important on a national scale because of the large percentage of households who own one or more cars—nearly 80 percent in 1971. The percentage of automobile ownership increased with income. Of families in the $10,000 to 15,000 income bracket, nearly 95 percent had one or more cars and 45.6 percent had two or more.[14]

Since the median family has an income in the $10,000 to 15,000 bracket, it fairly represents ownership of other possessions counted as wealth. Seventy-eight percent have black and white and 58 percent have color televisions; 83 percent own washing machines; 65 percent have clothes dryers; 88 percent have refrigerators, 39 percent have freezers; 29 percent have dishwashers and 44 percent have air conditioner systems, either room or central.[15]

Montgomery reported that in 1973 more than 93 percent of all wired housing units had electric coffee makers, 95 percent had toasters, nearly 97 percent had vacuum cleaners, and 99.9 percent had radios.[16] All these small appliances contributed to wealth.

These are stationary data—median characteristics from the early 1970s. At that time, half the population exceeded these measures of wealth; however, to those with less than adequate income, these medians sounded like wealth beyond measure. These data illustrate what has happened in the past.

TRENDS IN WEALTH ACCUMULATION

What will the future bring with inflation that erodes the buying power of savings at a rate that is equal to, or greater than, the interest gained on savings? Will the homes purchased at high costs today continue to appreciate or will they, like cars, produce little asset value because of high-interest rate mortgages? Will individual home ownership become a luxury few can afford? Will some other commodity replace the home as the major asset for American families? What effect does inflation coupled with recession have on the wealth components of people? What trends in wealth accumulation are predicted?

U.S. News and World Report, Changing Times, Money, and other magazines indicate that investors are growing more sophisticated and more alert to emerging forms of investments and their high yields but are still tempering their accumulation of wealth with caution and are stressing savings.[17] Federal Reserve Board data indicates eras of tight money and rising interest rates tend to bring savings from conservative, lower-yielding invest-ments and shift them into riskier, higher-return assets. Recession generally causes more cautious investing, but following each recession, consumers retain more of their savings in higher-yielding assets.[18]

Between World War II and the mid-seventies, cash assets (currency and checking accounts—money that earns no return) decreased from more than 19 percent of individual financial holdings in 1946 to about 8 percent in 1975. Credit use and overdraft privileges with checking accounts have reduced the need for large cash reserves.

Less wealth is now devoted to life insurance, another conservative in-vestment. Between 1950 and 1975, the percent of financial assets devoted to life insurance was cut in half.

Forced savings in pension reserves (including both private plans and Social Security) increased from 3.7 percent of individual financial holdings to 3.5 percent in early 1975. Money in savings institutions also expanded from about 14 percent of financial holdings of all individuals in 1950 to more than 30 percent. As savings institutions raise their interest rates, the number of savers increase.

When people are free to choose their investments, the long-run trend has turned toward assets of high-yielding types, such as notes, bills, and debt se-curities, especially Federal government securities other than savings bonds. There is also an increase of investment in tax-free bonds of states and munici-palities. In 1974 40 percent of new consumer investments in financial assets were for market securities of these types, up from about nine percent in early 1973.

However, the newest trend in wealth composition began in 1973.[19] Called a "Money Market Fund," it is a mutual fund invested in short-term market securities—primarily Treasury and other federal agency bills and notes—and bank and savings and loan certificates of deposit. These new funds make it possible for individual investors to realize a yield of 11 to 12 percent on investments in 1974.

Federal Reserve Board data indicate the following distribution of assets held by individuals on October 1, 1974:

Savings accounts	30%
Stocks	26%
Pension reserves	14%
Checking accounts and cash	8%
Life insurance reserves	7%
U.S. Government securities	5%
Corporate and tax-exempt bonds	5%
Other assets	5%[20]

THE VALUE OF HUMAN CAPITAL

The definition of wealth presented earlier in this chapter included not only the financial assets and pattern of such holdings but also the value of a person's economic contribution to a family. Thus, earning potential—human capital investment—is a factor of wealth, as is the controversial economic value of services of each family member. The earning power of people—both women and men—has been an accepted index of wealth for some time. Law suits have been awarded widows and widowers for the expected lifetime employment earnings of a spouse killed as a result of negligence of another.[21]

The value of an unemployed wife's services to the family becomes news when this amount is awarded to her widower in similar court negligence suits. When discussing the monetary value of household work to families and to the nation, Walker and Gauger predicted, "The dollar value may come to be seen as a new 'family-life' index, a way of telling us a 'cost of living' that doesn't show up on the grocery bill."[22] These authors concluded that an unemployed homemaker with two children contributes $5,600 worth of household work and the family as a whole annually contributes $8,300 toward the well-being of the family. Working wives contribute an average of $3,600, and the total family time-service value is $6,700. If the value of human contributions to family welfare are included as wealth, most families are wealthier than they think.

HOW WEALTH IS MEASURED

Wealth is often measured by inventories and by net-worth computations. Net worth is the difference between assets and liabilities and is a more accurate indicator of economic position than inventories because net worth deducts the liabilities from the value of the inventoried items.[23] However, net-worth statements, such as the sample form presented in Chapter 11, summarize wealth by categories and show only totals for each category. Stocks are not listed individually, clothing and furnishings usually appear on the net-worth statement as "other assets," and even real estate that may be worth thousands of dollars is treated on the net-worth statement in one simple total.

If the components of a family's wealth had to be replaced, no insurance company would pay the value without specific lists, serial numbers, and purchase records for appliances and furnishings. Even the owner would find it taxing to recall the exact possessions accumulated over the years without records. Inventories and net-worth calculations are an important part of managing wealth.

National wealth is measured in terms of Gross National Product—the market-price dollar value of goods and services attributable to production—labor and property supplied by people of the nation. Why not devise a measure for Gross Family Product that would include the calculation of market value of goods and services attributable to the productive factors—including labor and wealth—of the members of a family? Such a measure would include the economic contribution of all family members' services to the wellbeing of the group as well as the earnings from outside employment and the return from wealth.

Building Wealth

Wealth is accumulated in a number of ways: through inheritance, consumption, lack of consumption and application of the surplus to savings and investments, forced-savings plans, and for some families in a combination of motivation, perseverance, advice of professional financial advisors, luck, and goal-oriented management.

PATTERNS OF ACCUMULATION

Generally, wealth accumulation is an unconscious by-product of consumption during the first half of most families' life cycle. The typcial family satisfies the need for an automobile first, purchases household equipment, then buys a housing unit and adds luxuries next, and finally expands assets rapidly in the prime earning years of the life cycle. Small savings are accumulated during most of these years, but most savings are earmarked for later purchases or down payments, including the down payment on a home.[24]

Williams and Manning report that increases in net worth of the 60 Indiana families they studied were not merely a result of past income, initial net worth, or anticipated progress. The significant factors in net-worth increases were increased cash income, high current income, increased real estate, business or farm assets, and a decrease in use of credit for purchasing durable goods.[25] These family assets consisted primarily of household equipment, automobile, life insurance cash value, and interest accounts. Some 80 percent included such items in their net-worth statements, and these assets appeared to be the earliest components of net worth. As net worth increased, the percentages of assets contributed by these items decreased, and greater risk items and monetary gain increased. The findings of this study indicate that "after durable goods, some life insurance, and an emergency cash reserve are obtained, use of current income for asset accumulation in real estate, business or farm, and stocks would contribute to a larger net-worth increase than in reducing debts or increasing other assets."[26]

Only a small proportion of households inherit wealth and the amount inherited is usually less than $10,000.[27] For most people, its value is negligible. Even though some families are fortunate enough to receive inheritances, generations overlap and the inheritance may not come when security is most needed or in time to take advantage of long-term inheritance growth. Furthermore, an inheritance is seldom in the form of cash but is in securities, business, or real estate on which debts must be paid before the estate may be transferred to a beneficiary.

In this section, four methods of building wealth—saving, investing, acquiring, and pension planning—will be discussed with emphasis on saving strategies.

SAVINGS—THE SEEDS OF WEALTH

Savings do not grow automatically; in fact, they may not accumulate at all. Savings are the result of careful management of current income and expenditures so that there is something saved. Saving usually requires the delay of present desires.

Most people who build sizable savings accounts do so in one of three ways: incomes are larger than needs and the surplus is saved by curbing the desire for spending; incomes are barely sufficient to meet current needs and desires, but present desires are renounced in favor of some future purchase; or motivation to save is strong enough to consider savings as a regular budgetary item, and they "pay themselves first." The pay-yourself-first philosophy is one that has worked successfully for many people. In this approach, a predetermined amount of money is set aside regularly. The regularity of the savings causes growth. People who save regularly often accumulate more than those who save larger amounts on an irregular basis. A savings program should fit the family's needs and be accomplished without undue hardship. An overly ambitious or poorly planned savings goal may cause so much tension, discouragement, and frustration that the entire program will be abandoned.

Why People Save

People usually save for: (1) future emergencies that cannot be met with current income, (2) income needed after earnings decline or cease, (3) needs and wants too costly to be paid for with regular income; and (4) investments to build an estate or increase wealth.[28] How much each family should save for each purpose is a matter of family goals and needs. Some say an adequate emergency fund should equal six months' take-home pay; others say three. The type of occupation, size of regular income, and likelihood of being without a job because of strikes or lay-offs will partially determine the amount of needed savings. The number of persons contributing to the family's financial resources, the number of people to be supported, debts, age and condition of household goods, and many other factors—not the least of which is the normal living expenses of the family—will also influence the amount of savings to be earmarked for emergencies.

Where People Save

Selecting forms of savings and determining institutions that offer maximum satisfaction of savings goals are important financial decisions that require investigation and planning. Savings for emergencies and contingencies in the financial budget need to be relatively liquid—readily accessible and easily converted to cash—and they should be convenient and safe. Savings for investments may be selected on the basis of yield with some sacrifice of liquidity. The purpose of the savings, immediacy of goals, age and composition of family, and current level of expenditures need to be considered when choosing institutions in which to invest savings and the type of account that can best satisfy individual needs.

There are at least four major savings institutions from which families choose when investing savings:

Commercial banks offer checking and savings accounts, extend loans, rent safe deposit boxes, provide investment advice, perform trust services, sell traveler's and cashier's checks, and may handle utility bills, bond coupons, and food stamps.

Credit unions offer savings accounts and extend loans to members of associated groups. Some credit unions offer financial counseling.

Savings and loan associations offer savings accounts, extend loans, and provide safe deposit boxes and most of the services offered by commercial banks. Two major services of savings and loan associations are to provide savings depository and to provide sources for home mortgages.

Savings banks and *mutual savings banks* are primarily savings institutions that do not provide checking accounts or most other services commercial ·banks offer. Mutual savings banks are owned essentially by depositors.

The U.S. Government may also be considered a savings institution for U.S. savings bonds are still among the most popular and the safest methods of saving. The two most popular U.S. savings bonds are: Series E Bonds that are bought at a 25 percent discount and gradually grow to full face value in seven years; and Series H Bonds that are current-income bonds for which the buyer pays the full face value and receives interest checks semiannually. The guarantee of redemption by the government, the ease of "bond-a-month" deductions from pay checks or checking accounts, together with the fact that, if necessary, the bonds can be cashed before maturity with no loss of interest after the second month of issue adds to the attractiveness of these bonds.

When comparing financial institutions for savings, Garman and Eckert suggest that the following criteria be considered: size of institution, location and convenience, number of years in business, rate of interest and frequency of compounding interest, type of plan used for computing interest, penalty for withdrawal, assurance that money deposited is insured and by whom, availability of money for emergency withdrawals, and additional services that the institution offers such as safe deposit boxes, traveler's checks or conference or reference room.[29] The three most crucial factors in choosing a savings institution are:

1. *Safety*—freedom from danger or risk and assurance of getting back the number of dollars deposited.

2. *Liquidity*—ease and speed of converting savings deposits into cash.

3. *Yield*—return or profit, usually expressed as interest or dividends and customarily calculated as a percentage of the amount deposited.

Table 12.1 is a rating of these three factors in choosing a place to save and two additional ones: services and convenience. The rating of 1 is assigned to those factors that are highest in satisfying the usual needs of typical families. The ratings may vary in different localities and with specific needs of

Table 12.1   Comparing Savings Institutions.

Institution	Safety	Liquidity	Yield	Services	Convenience
Commercial banks	1	1	2	1	1
Credit unions	2	2	2	1	2
Savings banks	2	1	2	2	2
Savings and loan associations	1	1	1	1	1
U.S. savings bonds	1	2	2	2	1

a family or individual, but they may serve as a guide for comparing savings institutions.

How People Save

The concept of earning money through saving is exciting. Table 12.2 shows how quickly money will double at various rates of compound interest. Depending on the frequency of compounding and the rate of interest paid, money placed in savings will double itself in a few years at high rates and frequent compounding. At 7-$\frac{3}{4}$ percent compounded daily, money will double in nine years. It is on this concept that investment in land is based. If land purchased for an investment does not double in value in a period of ten years or less, the investment is not keeping up with inflation and the cost of ownership, according to most investor's standards.

Ben Franklin's gift of $5,000, in 1781, to the residents of Boston is one of the most dramatic illustrations of the way money multiples when allowed to compound. Franklin stipulated that the money must be allowed to accumulate compound interest for 200 years. By 1891, the original $5,000 had grown to $322,000 and part was used to build a school building. The remainder continued to accumulate interest until, in 1961, 30 years before the 200 year goal, Franklin's fund exceeded $17 million.[30]

The importance of regular saving is illustrated in Table 12.3, which shows the growth of $100 in worth if deposited in savings compounded annually at various rates of interest. If a person began depositing $100 per month in savings paying 8 percent interest at age 20 and continued the practice for 26 years, that savings of $100 a month would be worth $104,936 when the person was 46. Currently, savings and loan associations in this country are returning more than 8 percent on fixed-rate, fixed-time certificates of deposit; and as money increases beyond certain minimums, it is possible to earn higher rates of interest.

If the person continued depositing $100 per month until age 64 and one-half, that continual deposit of $100 would be worth over half a million dollars.

This example hinges on one assumption—that the taxes on earned interest would be paid from current income. There is no high-risk element in this accumulation of wealth, only regular deposits and a willingness to forego $100 worth of current spending for a lifetime accumulation.

For a person who is strongly motivated, a decision to place a certain amount into savings until the sum is large enough to invest or spend is all that is needed. A student wanted to buy a bicycle that cost $280 and wanted to know how long it would take to reach the goal if $4 per month could be saved from current income. A computer analysis developed for the purpose indicated the goal would be reached in five years if deposited at an institution paying 6 percent compounded annually.

Table 12.2 How Long Does It Take To Double Your Money?

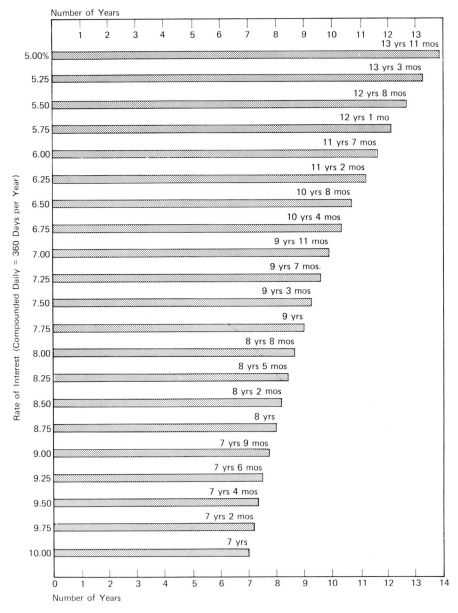

SOURCE: Calculated from *Savings Deposit Growth Tables* for money at interest compounded daily (360-day year).[28]

Table 12.3   Growth of $100 per month deposits compounded annually.[31]

Years	Rate Of Interest Paid On Deposit			
	6%	8%	10%	15%
2	$2,556	$2,611	$2,667	$2,814
4	5,437	5,673	5,921	6,604
6	8,684	9,264	9,893	11,712
8	12,344	13,476	14,740	18,593
10	16,470	18,417	20,655	27,866
12	21,120	24,211	27,874	40,358
14	26,362	31,008	36,684	57,190
16	32,270	38,980	47,436	79,869
18	38,929	48,329	60,557	110,425
20	46,435	59,295	76,569	151,595
22	54,896	72,156	96,111	207,065
24	64,432	87,242	119,960	281,803
26	75,181	104,936	149,065	382,501
28	87,297	125,688	184,584	518,176
30	100,953	150,029	227,931	700,979
32	116,347	178,577	280,832	947,278
34	133,697	212,062	345,391	1,279,128
36	153,253	251,335	424,179	1,726,246
38	175,297	297,398	520,331	2,328,672
40	200,143	351,425	637,674	3,140,351
42	228,149	414,793	780,878	4,233,968
44	259,717	489,116	955,643	5,707,453
46	295,298	576,289	1,168,924	7,692,755
	6%	8%	10%	15%

SOURCE: Computer program developed for the book by Ralph Schiferl, Director, Computer Programming, Santa Barbara Community College, California.

Table 12.4 shows the amount of money needed to be saved at various rates of interest to reach specific goals. This table allows a person to pick a savings goal and determine the amount of money to be saved at local interest rates for specified times to reach the goal.

Another interesting characteristic of savings and compounded interest is that if a set amount of money is deposited monthly in a savings account until the money has doubled, then the same amount of money may be *withdrawn* monthly for the rest of your lifetime, your dependent's lifetime, and forever, as long as the rate of interest paid on the balance continues the same or better than during the savings period. In this case, the balance in the account will

Table 12.4 Reaching Savings Goals. Monthly savings needed to reach specific goals at various rates of interest compounded daily.[32]

Savings goal	Months to save	Interest rates			
		5.25%	5.75%	6.50%	7.50%
$500	12	$40.49	$40.38	$40.22	$40.00
	24	19.72	19.60	19.46	19 25
	36	12.80	12.70	12.54	12.35
	48	9.34	9.24	9.10	8.90
	56	7.86	7.77	7.62	7.43
$1000	12	80.99	80.77	80.44	80.00
	24	39.43	39.22	38.91	38.49
	36	25.59	25.39	25.09	24.69
	48	18.68	18.49	18.19	17.81
	56	16.02	15.53	15.24	14.97
$3000	12	242.96	242.30	241.31	239.99
	24	118.29	117.67	116.74	115.50
	36	76.78	76.17	75.25	74.08
	56	47.17	46.59	45.73	44.60
	84	29.49	28.94	28.13	27.07
	120	18.97	18.45	17.70	16.73
	180	10.93	10.48	9.82	8.99
	240	7.05	6.65	6.07	5.37
$5000	12	404.94	403.84	402.18	399.99
	24	197.16	196.11	194.56	192.50
	36	127.96	126.95	125.45	123.46
	56	78.62	77.66	76.22	74.34
	84	49.15	48.23	46.88	45.12
	120	31.61	30.76	29.50	27.89
	180	18.22	17.46	16.36	14.98
	240	11.75	11.08	10.12	8.95

grow at the same rate as withdrawals so the balance, therefore, remains constant. For example, if a person can save $50 a month for 12 years 1 month at 5-¾ percent interest, deposits will have doubled by this time and withdrawals of $50 a month can be made for the rest of one's life without ever touching the balance. At higher rates of interest, withdrawal may begin sooner.

Using smoking again as an example of savings, if a person has been smoking a pack of cigarettes a day (60¢) and was willing to stop smoking for 12 years and put that 60 cents a day ($18.25 per month) into savings, he could then start smoking again at no further cost for life, assuming they still cost 60 cents. Or, if preferred, he would have $18.25 per month to spend as he chose and still have more than $2,997 deposited money plus approximately the same amount accumulated from compounded interest—a balance of nearly $6,000—all derived from the price of a pack of cigarettes per day.

But there are flaws in this direction of reasoning. Even though the student diligently saves $4 per month for five years, by the time the $280 has accumulated for a ten-speed bicycle, inflation will probably have increased the price of the bicycle to the point where $4 per month may *never* increase fast enough to pay for the bicycle. The pack of cigarettes may also have doubled in price by the end of the 12 years.

If the student saves for a reasonable down payment, then buys the bicycle on credit, at least the price of the bicycle will be controlled. The questions are: When does the rate of interest received from savings equal the rise in price due to inflation? When is the rate less; when is it more? On the other hand, when does the cost of credit equal the rise in price due to inflation? When is it more; when is it less? These are serious questions that affect the savings goals of people in a time of inflation, especially those saving *for* things. In 1974, the consumer price index rose 11.7 percent. The highest savings and loan association certificate of deposit paid 7.75 percent compounded daily or an equivalent annual yield of 8.06 percent. During that year, inflation eroded the value of the dollar faster than savings interest added to it.

INVESTING—THE ROAD TO WEALTH

Although investing is called the "road to wealth," thousands of people lose millions of dollars each year through "get-rich-quick" schemes for increasing their assets. There is no *quick* method of gaining wealth that is also *safe*. There are ways of getting rich slowly, but each method requires an element of risk. Most investing centers around four markets: stocks, bonds, mutual funds, and real estate. Each is associated with varying degrees of risk. It is generally felt that people are not ready to invest until they have an adequate emergency savings fund, have sufficient insurance to protect dependents and themselves against undue losses, and have accumulated a fund for investing that can be absorbed without unnecessary hardship if the investment should fail and the entire amount be lost. Whether to shift money from savings into investments depends on the amount of money a person has, the immediacy of need for goals that are inflexible in time or amount—such as college tuition when a child is ready for college—and on the capacity to absorb risk.[33]

Where People Invest

Not all investments carry the same amount of risk, and one investment vehicle may not be suitable for all requirements. Some characteristics of the common opportunities for investing and their limitations follow:

Government Securities, Treasury Bill, Notes, and Bonds

The bills have shortest maturity—from three months to a year. They are sold at weekly auctions at Federal Reserve Banks, may be bought by individuals by a noncompetitive mail bid or through a bank or broker, and come in denominations of $10,000 and in $5,000 multiples above that. Interest is paid immediately in the form of a discount from the face value, and at maturity the full value is paid when the bills are cashed in. Treasury notes mature in one to seven years, come in denominations of $1,000 or more, and pay a fixed rate of interest semi-annually. They are announced in financial pages of newspapers. The price of Treasury notes varies with the amount of premium a small investor pays for the notes—if the cost of buying a $1,000 note is $10, the average yield is 8.59 percent on a 9 percent note. Treasury bonds are similar to treasury notes in size, method of announcement, and purchase but have a longer maturity date—seven or more years.

Government securities are probably the safest of the five discussed forms of investing, and when interest rates are high, their yield may be higher than that of savings institutions. Bills have the advantage of short maturity time. The inconvenience and cost of purchase and the high investment denominations of Treasury bills is a disadvantage to most families.

Corporate and Municipal Bonds

These range in safety from secure to highly speculative. A bond is a promissory note for a loan which the investor makes to a corporation, municipality, or government and is usually issued in multiples of $1,000. Bonds are purchased through stock brokers or banks and may be issued for as many as 25 or 30 years. The bondholder can depend on a consistent rate over a number of years because the interest rate is fixed. If interest rates are high at the time of issue, the maturity date is far away, and the company or municipality issuing the bond is financially secure, bonds can be a profitable form of investing.

The quality of bonds is rated by *Moody's Investors Service* and by *Standard and Poor's Corporation*.[34] High-grade corporate and municipal bonds are relatively safe, but the risk is that a bondholder could lose part of the $1,000 principal if it becomes necessary or desirable to sell the bond before maturity date. Bonds are traded on the stock exchanges, and prices are quoted in the financial pages of newspapers. If interest rates rise generally, the bond price will fall and if the money invested is needed, the bond can be sold, but the price will be less than paid. The original investment can be safely assured only if the company remains solvent and the bondholder retains the bond until maturity.

Interest paid on municipal bonds—those issued by towns, cities, or other government subdivisions to raise money for local improvements and costs—is usually lower than that of corporate bonds, but they have a tax-free advantage that makes them particularly attractive to people in high-income tax brackets. The safety of these bonds depends on the financial soundness of the municipality backing the bonds.

Common and Preferred Stocks

These stocks represent part ownership in a company. They are purchased by investors who expect the price of the stock to increase equally or above that of the buying power of the dollar, as "a hedge against inflation." Their effectiveness as an investment is dependent on many factors—changes in the economy, stock market performance, growth of the industry and the companies whose stocks are purchased, profits of the company, and many unanticipated situations, such as law suits, news, product popularity, and availability of the resources necessary to produce or operate the products. Some stocks pay dividends that may equal or exceed interest rates of savings institutions, but the safety of the money invested is reduced with stocks.

Money is not made by buying stocks; it is made when stocks are sold for a profit. Investment strategy for building and maintaining wealth in the stock market includes many cautions about the selectivity of quality stocks, timing of purchases and sales, choosing companies in growth industries with good management and high profits for a number of consecutive years, setting performance goals and selling when goals have been met, and regularly weeding out nonperformers.[35]

Most investors depend on a broker to determine which securities to buy, when to buy them, and when to sell them. *Money* magazine's controversial article, "What Your Broker Doesn't Know Can Hurt You," called attention to the inadequate training and selection process for most securities salespersons.[36] Investment advisors must pass an examination before they can be licensed to sell securities, but that examination is not sufficiently demanding to assure quality of financial advice. Brokers are salespersons who make their income from commissions or from salary plus commissions. They vary in their ability to advise people regarding the market and should be chosen as carefully as selecting any other important service. Quality of investment advice is a crucial factor in building wealth through investing in stocks.

Mutual Funds

These funds provide management of investments in stocks and bonds by a type of holding company whose business is investing in specified markets. Mutual funds are managed by professionals, have the capital to make large buys and sells at strategic times, and are able to spread their investments to many companies so the chances of loss should be minimized. But mutual funds, like many corporations, do not always perform as expected; there is no guarantee of increase in value in a "poor market." Mutual funds transfer decisions from individuals to professional management of the fund but do not eliminate responsibility to determine which mutual fund or funds meet individual investment objectives or when to purchase and to sell shares of the fund.[37]

Choosing appropriate investments is no easy task.[38] Even when the decision to invest in a mutual fund is made, there are about 575 mutual funds from which to choose. Some specialize in growth companies, some in yield; others are balanced to serve a variety of purposes. Some are sold by salespersons and by stock brokers and charge a purchase fee of from 6 to 10 percent. Others, called "no load funds," are sold directly by the mutual fund or its trustee bank and are advertised in financial pages of newspapers and the *Wall Street Journal*. These no-loads charge no fee for purchase or sale of shares. Both types of funds charge about the same amount for management that is a part of the overhead and is not paid directly by the investor at time of purchase or sale.

Mutual funds are often used in an investment plan to provide funds for retirement. When purchased over a long period of time on a monthly or quarterly basis with a regular fixed number of dollars, the cost is averaged. When the price of the fund is down, the fixed investment dollars buy more shares; when the price is up, fewer shares are purchased.

Real Estate Investments

Purchase and management of real estate is a fifth avenue to wealth. In fact, it is said that nine out of every ten people who achieve the status of millionaire do so partially through real estate investments.

In real estate investments, location is the one most important consideration. Land cannot be moved; therefore, it is critical to monetary growth that the land be located in a desirable area.

Nelson identifies three reasons real estate investments are potentially attractive: rapid growth in population forces people to compete for available homes, apartments, and land; real property values tend to keep pace with inflationary trends; and real estate investments do not fluctuate rapidly like stock prices do.[39] But there are also limitations that can ensnare the unsophisticated investor. Land investments usually require down payments of one-third the total value and are traditionally repaid with large annual payments unless the land has been subdivided, and this reduces potential profit. The investment is usually a long-term one making it less liquid. It is seldom possible to make small additions to the investment as can be done with stocks, savings, or Treasury bills, and there are often heavy costs related to real estate holdings.[40]

When considering land as an investment, environmental factors and housing or business potential need to be evaluated. Is its potential for recreational use? Are the oil, gas, water, and mineral rights intact, and is the land located in an area with potential for mineral exploration? What is the potential for timber sales, oil leases, or grazing leases? Another consideration is the length of time before the real estate investment results in profit and the amount of net profit that can be realistically expected from the investment. What improvements are necessary to make the venture profitable? How much are the taxes? Are water and sewer connections established? Many people have bought property lacking in a water supply and found that the property is worthless because of this one limitation. Using the length of time it takes money to double in value in a savings institution (illustrated in Table 12.2) as a base for comparison, if a real estate investment cannot reasonably be expected to double in seven to ten years, the money might be more profitable, safer, and more accessible in savings or some other form of investment.

Purposes of Investment

Perhaps the most important question to answer about any form of investment is, "Why are you investing?" The Wolfs are investing to finance the education of three children. They know that by the time Tim, 10 years old; Mary, 12; and Michael, almost 16; are ready for college tuition costs will be more than the parents can afford, even though both are working and saving all they possibly can in their education fund.

Although Andrea and Jerry are only 32 and 37, they have begun a retirement savings fund utilizing savings certificates at the highest rate of return offered by an insured savings institution. They plan on early retirement and need the retirement savings fund to supply living expenses before Social Security and civil service pensions begin.

Linda and Harry are retired and want their investments to return a high rate of interest to cover living costs to avoid reducing the principal of their investment for current expenses.

Thus, families save and invest for different purposes. These reasons generally fall into two main investment categories: the first is high interest return, and the second is capital appreciation—growth in value. In addition to safety, liquidity, yield, and convenience described and charted for savings institutions earlier in the chapter, investments may be compared on the basis of potential capital gain. Table 12.5 is a comparison of potential investment outlets for families or individuals. These ratings are general guidelines and, like the savings ratings, will vary with the economic conditions at the time, the alternatives open to the investor, the knowledge of investing strategies, the financial circumstances of the family, and the emotional stability of the persons to be affected by the investments.

Investment knowledge, financial circumstances, and emotional stability often direct *whether* to invest. Investing is risky. The degree of risk is usually, but not always, related to potential gain. Some people do not possess either the financial backing or the emotional stability to accept risk. Goals and needs will direct *where* to invest. It is advisable for each family to develop its own investment opportunity comparison table around facts gathered from the local financial environment.

There are many "ifs" involved in the above ratings. They apply to the situation at a particular time of economic history. The ratings may also differ according to the amount of money available for investing; for example, convenience of Treasury bills is rated "4" because they are sold in a minimum of $10,000 denominations. If a family had $50,000 to invest, the minimum investment of $10,000 would not be an inconvenience. Real estate is rated

Table 12.5 Comparing Investment Opportunities. Ratings are 1 (highest) to 4 (lowest).

Investment Opportunity	Safety	Liquidity	Yield	Conven- ience	Potential capital gain
Treasury bills	1	1	2	4	4
Treasury notes	1	2	2	3	4
Municipal bonds	2	2	2	3	3
Corporate bonds	2	2	1	3	3
Preferred stock	3	2	2	2	3
Common stock	4	2	3	2	1
Mutual funds	3	2	3	2	1
Real estate	3	4	4	4	1

with a potential capital gain of "1". In areas where the population is growing, this is a real potential if land is well chosen. In areas with negative population changes, the potential would be considerably lower.

ACQUIRING POSSESSIONS

As a result of management, wealth includes all the material goods that make up the level of living sought by individuals and families. These are material goods that have sentimental, economic, or functional value; they may have all three.

These material possessions that are so much a part of a person's life style are resources—assets—and are a part of wealth. They are acquired through inheritance, purchase, gifts or home production. Their worth varies with needs, with attitudes of appreciation, with uses, and with their relationship to other components of wealth. When material possessions outnumber other assets and savings are inadequate to even meet emergencies, these possessions may be constraints, not assets.

Home Ownership

The typical family occupies six apartments, one rented house, and two or three owned houses during its life cycle, a total of at least ten dwellings. The average family moves once every five years; the average homeowner moves once every 7 to 8 years. Thus, home ownership is not as permanent as a 30-year mortgage might indicate.

Housing needs vary with the stage of the family life cycle.[41] Stage I, the beginning family, is the period when a young couple usually rents a small apartment or house. Housing needs are for simplicity, compactness, convenience, privacy, and companionship. During this stage, the couple may acquire furnishings and accumulate funds for future purchases.

Stage II—the expanding family, from birth of first child to the time that child leaves home, is marked by the increased need for specialized space. If more children are born, additional space is needed for privacy and for family interaction. Safety is an important feature when there are small children or elderly people living in the unit. Storage areas to accommodate increased possessions required by developing families is important. At this time, families find apartment dwelling least satisfactory and consider buying their first home.

When children reach grade and high school age, the demand for space usually reaches its peak. At this time, flexible space, protection from undue noise and distraction, and privacy for thought or study for every member is desirable. Room for group hospitality for several age levels is often desirable. By this time, the family may be living in the second owned home.

Stage III—the contracting family, begins when the children leave home. Many parents remain in their homes as long as possible and find great satisfaction in having room for weekend and holiday visitors. As time passes, adjustments in living space may be necessary and desirable. Compactness, ease of maintenance, comfort in use, convenience, space for hobby equipment, and safety for uncertain balance and brittle bones are important housing standards late in this stage.

Nearly two-thirds of all American families own their own living units at some time during the family life cycle. People buy homes for many reasons— for security and stature, room for children to play, space to store and pursue hobbies, a place to have pets, and a means of building equity. The average American house increases in value by about 5 percent a year.[42] In more desirable communities, increases have recently ranged as high as 10 percent per year. The cost of housing is also increasing. The average price of a new house rose 14 percent in 1973 and has continued to rise since that time.[43] The ownership costs of a single-family house have risen more than the general consumer price index and more than rentals during the past ten years.

People usually believe that home ownership is more desirable and economical than renting. There are differences of opinion, depending on the situations and the location. "The homeowner is almost always better off than the renter, though not by as much as most salesmen suggest," wrote Main in "A Man's Home Is His Capital."[44] Main continued, "Scratch a tenant and underneath you will usually find a thwarted homeowner."[45] His practical examples comparing home ownership with renting indicate that nationally, the annual financial advantage of home ownership is less than 1 percent of the value of the house. One reason why a homeowner usually ends up dollars ahead of the tenant is because the owner is forced to build equity by making mortgage payments. People who are not committed to mortgage payments may not feel compelled to contribute regularly to savings when, for example, the desire for a new car enters the life-style pattern. Intentions for investing are often abandoned in favor of current spending. Housing is a living expense that cannot easily be ignored, and if the mortgage payment is not made, the family will still need a roof overhead.

The average house is a more expensive form for building equity than most families believe it is. The ability to borrow a large percentage of the cost of a house has increased the opportunity for home ownership, but interest is also a major cost. For example, when the mortgage interest rate is 8 percent, a 24 year mortgage on $25,000 *adds* $31,376 to the cost of the dwelling. When mortgage interest rates are 10 percent, the interest paid on a $25,000 mortgage adds $41,096 to the cost of the home. Closing costs and realtor's fees—transfer costs of home ownership—add a one-time payment of 8 to 10 percent to the price every 7 or 8 years when the homeowner moves.

How much house can the average family afford? The guideline that housing costs should not exceed $2\frac{1}{2}$ times the annual income was an actuality in 1971, when the Census Bureau reported the median family income of $10,285 and the median price of a new single family house was $25,200. But there are many circumstances that make this rule, at best, only a guide—increased building costs, housing needs, family living expenses, size and source of income, prior commitment of dollars, and other family assets are but a few of the considerations affecting housing investments. Families seeking home ownership may reduce the cost of the purchase by:

- shopping comparatively and considering alternate forms of housing before making a final selection

- resolving all unsatisfactory conditions before making an offer to purchase

- requesting an itemized bill for closing costs prior to date of closing

- shopping for lowest rate of interest and fewest points for establishing the mortgage

- making as large a down payment as possible without depleting other savings and investments

- financing for the shortest possible time period without making monthly payments burdensome.

Although costs inevitably rise, ownership of some form of housing may remain the most economically attractive and psychologically satisfying way to live. A home is more than a financial asset or liability. It is an environment for companionship where each member of the family can find room for relaxation, self-expression, intellectual growth, entertainment, work, composure, and group interaction.

Home Furnishings and Appliances

Furnishing a house or apartment is a major expense for many years. Although a family may move from one house to another, furnishings are usually moved with the family. Some small appliances purchased during the early years of marriage survive to the launching stage of the family life cycle and are passed on to second generations.

These two components of wealth represent a large expenditure over the years. Many families spend from 6 to 10 percent of their consumption expenditures for home furnishings each year. Annual expenditures for these items vary with the stage of family life, income, and location of residence.

There are several methods of accumulating furniture and appliances. Saving and paying cash for them is the most economical way, but not many families can save large sums to buy all needed furniture at one time. Many are not willing to part with savings for furnishings even though they may have sufficient funds to pay cash. Most families buy at least some of their home furnishings through use of credit, either by use of cash loans or installment plans. Revolving charge accounts and home-improvement purchase plans make it possible to buy more furnishings at one time and pay for them as they are used. It is estimated that next to the purchase of a home and cumulative expenditure for cars, money spent on home furnishings is, for many people, their largest expense. The initial cost of furnishing an average house with durable, moderately priced furniture may be close to one-half the cost of the house; this does not include expensive art objects or decorator items. If a house is completely refurnished once during the family's lifetime, the cost of furnishings could easily equal the cost of housing.[46]

Market studies indicate that spending increases for such items as home furnishings, furs, clothing, boats, movies, concerts, plays, and travel among the upper-middle-status families, especially those in the professions. They have more discretionary income for these items and may collect art objects that can be displayed in the home, such as ceramics, sculpture, or paintings. Collecting antiques is not only a hobby; it becomes a part of life style—a topic for conversation.

Planned spending results in effective use of home furnishing dollars. To make a home-furnishing plan, work from room to room listing first the most essential pieces desired. Spend adequate "looking time" before making decisions. A furnishing plan is usually a long-term plan that allows not only a longer period of time for saving to pay cash but gives family members a chance to express their preferences and to "live with" furnishings, piece by piece. This way a room, and eventually the entire house, reflects the personalities of the people living there.

Many possessions, particularly equipment and appliances, are purchased because of the time they save in performing household tasks. Others save energy. Some contribute primarily to satisfaction with living. Whatever the reason for acquiring them, such possessions contribute to wealth of the people who use them, care for them, and manage them effectively. When not used, they may be constraints, usurping space and money that could bring greater satisfaction if redirected to other uses.

PENSION PLANNING—CUSHION FOR RETIREMENT

Retirement is inevitable can be the most exciting years of a person's life. With time available for discretionary use and home and furnishings paid for, expenses may be less than in earlier years. Hobbies and travel may be pursued and friendships cultivated. These can be rewarding years if adequate financial preparation has been made. Yet the fact is that nearly 25 percent of retired people are living close to poverty.[47] Dreams of leisure time and travel cannot materialize when retirement incomes are inadequate for living essentials.

Social Security

The federal insurance system that includes compulsory contributions for most employed Americans is Social Security. Its retirement benefits are important as a regular, dependable income base during a person's nonworking years. The amount of the benefit is probably inadequate for most people's living expenses during retirement, but it is certain, and it forms a base on which to build other programs. Social security retirement benefits are paid to qualified persons regardless of other retirement programs. This fact is an important one in planning for retirement.

The amount of benefits a worker will draw on retirement depends on the age at which he or she retires (62 or 65), the number of quarters worked, and the average salary drawn over the last decade. At 62 or 65, wives who have not worked and are dependents of workers covered by Social Security will draw dependent benefits equal to a percentage of the husband's benefits. The percentage depends on whether the wife elects to begin payments at age 62 or 65 and the age at which the husband retired. Many women are covered by Social Security through employment but cannot draw both worker and dependent benefits at retirement. Thus, a wife who has worked and contributed to Social Security and whose husbands draws Social Security benefits must choose the plan that carries the higher benefits to her—either her own worker benefits or those due dependents of a covered worker. Dependent children under the age of 18 may also draw dependent benefits from Social Security.

Since the beginning of the program in 1935, changes have been made and the benefits upgraded. The system operates on a pay-as-you-go basis *similar* to Federal income taxes. Deductions are made from employees' wages and matched by the employer. Many self-employed persons contribute to Social Security. It is compulsory in most occupations and the rates of payment are regulated by law. It is important to keep abreast of changes in Social Security regulations and benefits that can be expected at various ages by each member of the family.

Persons may also contribute to a *private pension plan* through their employment. About one-third of the employed are eligible for pensions when they retire, but the typical pension benefits currently do not average one-third of the annual earnings received before retirement.[48]

Some private institutions purchase annuities for their employees. Public teachers and the school district contribute jointly to teacher retirement programs. Life insurance annuity policies are available for retirement, and an ordinary straight life insurance policy may be converted to a living insurance program when paid in full. Mutual funds have been discussed as a source of funds during retirement as have savings and other investments. Most people use a combination of pension, Social Security, and investments to make retirement incomes more adequate.

Managing Wealth

The primary focus of this chapter has been on managing the accumulation of wealth. Accumulation requires planning and decision-making. Judgments are difficult to make in financial matters because mistakes are costly, often affecting the quality of life and the family structure.

Wealth requires more than planning; continuous management is needed if it is to bring satisfaction to its owners. Too many people wait until they are out of money and then wish savings had been accumulated. It is when a person is out of a job or has just taken a cut in pay that the importance of wealth can be most evident. Security is not built on wishing; it is built on willpower. Building and maintaining wealth is managing dreams into realities. Wealth can be accumulated and controlled through application of management processes.

SET GOALS FOR BUILDING WEALTH

Establish target rates, returns for investments, and cut off dates when nonproducing strategies are channeled to an alternate investment. It can be helpful to set a specific rate of return expected from each investment. With fixed-rate, fixed-time savings accounts or bonds, exact targets can be identified.[49] The highest rates paid by insured savings and loan institutions and those of short-term Treasury bills that assure safety or principal may be used as yardsticks for the performance of other investments and as a standard for evaluating potential ventures.

CONTROL ACCUMULATION

Wealth should be planned for and evaluated to measure progress and to identify positions at a given time.[50]

Establish a Capital Fund—An Investment Budget

This is the basis for investing. Saving part of current income, allowing it to accumulate, and placing it in an investment is the process of *sparing* money. It is usually achieved through continued or more effective use of real income—appliances, cars, furnishings, clothing already on hand—plus the management ability to gain greater satisfaction from these material possessions. In other words, a capital fund is usually achieved by using the old car longer, maintaining appliances so they will last longer, and allowing savings to be funnelled into the capital fund. Whenever real income can be used instead of money, the money is spared for other uses, such as the capital fund.

Identify Risk Limits

No investment or savings medium is best for all purposes at all times. Some forms of investing and saving are liquid and can be converted into cash easily, and some are not so liquid—land, for example. Some involve risk of capital—such as common stocks; other do not—such as Treasury bills. Both loss of principal and loss of purchasing power need to be considered. Yields and returns differ. Usually the higher the yield, the greater the risk.

Determining how much risk will be accepted for potentially greater returns will help balance wealth accumulation. What is satisfactory for an elderly person requiring safety of principal and high interest return on which to live, may not be satisfactory for the person who desires compounding and growth of principal to compensate for the loss of purchasing power of a dollar in paying for the college education of children.

Develop Financial Managerial Skills

Purposefully developing financial managerial skills is a part of developing human resources. The ability to make decisions, knowledge of sources of information about investment potentials, understanding the elements of risk in investing, and the ability to compare savings institutions and their services to satisfy the personal needs of a family are all human resources to build wealth. As a homemaker's skills in managing meals and assuring nutritional quality of foods can increase satisfaction from living by improving health of each member, so can the skills that help a family build wealth contribute to the quality of living that the family can achieve throughout its life cycle.

Diversify Assets

"Don't put all your eggs in one basket" has been said many times in relation to investing. It is also true of saving. Liquidity is improved by having several smaller savings certificates of deposit rather than one large one. Choosing the lowest amount of savings that can be deposited and still receiving the maximum rate allows easier access to funds. When the accounts are established at different times with different maturity dates, it takes more planning to keep transferring the mature accounts to new, higher paying ones; but the funds are more accessible. There are interest penalties when a certificate of deposit is cashed before maturity. If money is needed unexpectedly, it is important to lose as little of the interest through penalty as possible. Thus, it may be possible to prematurely cash only one small certificate of deposit rather than a large one to minimize the loss.

Plan some safe investments. They serve as a buffer against losses from more risky investments. Include riskier investments if the potential return is worth the risk and if family assets are such that the loss would not impose a serious threat to living or to goal attainment. Assume risky investments only if undue strain and worry will not be created by the risky investment. Wealth is seldom worth loss of emotional health.

KNOW THE LOCATION AND EARNING VALUE OF ASSETS

No one can afford to buy stocks and forget about them. Price fluctuations need to be investigated regularly. Purchase price, date of purchase, number of stocks purchased, and the name of each company needs to be recorded. Sale prices, date, and net profit or losses must be reported to the Internal Revenue Service.

Frequent inventories of value of wealth are important if wealth is to grow. Knowing which assets are growing and which ones are not producing will help to evaluate when to sell or terminate some investments and switch into more productive forms of wealth.

Savings certificates with fixed rates of interest for specified time periods will either draw no interest after maturity, revert back to the passbook rate, or will begin again on a new certificate at the old rate for the same number of years or months as the original certificate if they are not renewed within ten days of their maturity. Some institutions notify the owners within the grace period; others do not. They are not required to do so by laws of most states. If these savings certificates and fixed-rate deposits are not inventoried and their maturity dates recorded, penalties and inconveniences could result. Money may not be available for planned objectives at specified times because the maturity date was forgotten.

For insurance purposes and as a means of analyzing financial resources for increasing satisfaction from wealth, each component needs to be inventoried and that list should be updated regularly. Income and capital gains produced by wealth appear on income tax statements but the wealth does not. An inventory of home furnishings, accessories, art objects, and stamp and coin collections is useful in establishing an accurate value of these items for a home owner's insurance policy.

Photographs are useful additions to an inventory in case of fire or theft. A person may include furnishings and accessories by standing in the middle of a room and taking a picture of each wall. These pictures should be filed, along with an inventory sheet, in a safe-deposit box. The serial numbers of all cameras, radios, stereo equipment, and similar items should be recorded along with the make, year of purchase, and price of each item. License numbers, motor and serial numbers of cars, motorcycles, and bicycles should be kept in a safe place at home, as well as in a safe deposit box.

It is impossible to do much wealth planning without up-to-date records. Most people will agree with that statement in general, but knowing the kinds of records that will produce results is management. If you own stocks, keep records of the dividend each stock earns. If you own bonds, be sure you know not only yield, but the current market value as well. Set up a system for recording the maturity dates of certificates of deposit in savings, and do not forget to determine net worth of all assets periodically. Compare past statements of net worth to determine the annual rate of total growth or loss of assets.

To calculate an investment's annual rate of return, start with the current value of the asset; subtract its value at the start of the year; add dividends for the year. Divide this sum by the value at the start of the year and multiply the result by 100 to get the percentage rate of return. This allows each security to be compared with others.[51] The formula for calculating annual investment rate may be written as follows:

$$\frac{CVA - V + D}{V} \times 100 = \%RR$$

$$CVA = \text{Current value of asset}$$
$$V = \text{Value at start of year}$$
$$D = \text{Cash dividends}$$
$$RR = \text{Rate of return}$$

Record keeping takes some effort—that is what separates dreamers from those who actively achieve wealth.

PROTECT ASSETS ADEQUATELY AND REASONABLY

Determining insurance needs is essential but difficult. A general guideline is to insure what one cannot afford to lose in a reasonable amount of time. Although a salesperson may call insurance an investment, its function is primarily *protection*. Whether or not a person needs insurance varies with what is to be protected. When there are small children and one earner, the earner's ability to provide a living for dependents needs to be insured against death, disability, or loss of job. Life carries uncertainties, and twentieth-century life has greatly increased some risks, particularly injury and medical expenses. Rising medical care costs make medical insurance important to financial security. Hospitalization and surgical coverage may no longer be adequate. An additional major medical policy can save people from bankruptcy caused by costly medical bills. It is not unusual for a family to have medical bills of $10,000 or more in a single year if there are several children and one has a broken arm, and another has an appendectomy, another has asthma and needs occasional emergency room treatment and one of the adults has pneumonia and is in the hospital for a week.

With all insurance policies, learn: who is protected, what the policy covers, what the policy excludes, to whom will benefits be paid, when will benefits be paid, and what conditions does the covered person have to meet? Perhaps the most important of these questions is, "What does the policy *exclude* and how much does it pay for what is included?"

People with any wealth or assets may not want to risk loss. Property liability insurance protects this wealth and future earnings if an accident should occur on the property or be caused by owned property.

Life insurance can assist in building an immediate estate in case of the untimely death of the head of a family. For the average person to build a $25,000 or $50,000 estate takes time, but, by means of annual life-insurance payments, an individual has a practical method for purchasing an estate to fit determined needs. That insurance estate may be planned as a living estate, a retirement estate, or a death benefit for the family.

The need for protection often comes at a time in the family life cycle when earnings are comparatively low. One effective and certain way to provide reasonable protection is through insurance. When insurance has been planned and arranged as a logical step to develop and protect wealth, the economic life of a family can progress even in the face of death.

Insurance is costly and takes away from current spending and saving. It should, therefore, be evaluated and weighed carefully before purchase. Rates differ drastically from one policy to another for the same coverage. Automobile insurance, for example, may vary as much as 25 to 30 percent from one company to another for the same car and driver. Not only do life insurance premiums differ from one company to another, but there are a variety of types of policies. The lowest-cost life insurance is a group term policy; it can offer excellent coverage. It can be a base on which to develop the size of essential life insurance protection. The same is true of medical policies available on a group basis through employment. These are usually the lowest cost forms of medical and surgical coverage. The group medical policy should be used as a base for the total medical coverage to protect the family against financial losses that cannot be afforded from earnings or accumulated wealth without undue hardship. When insurance is purchased as *protection* instead of an investment, it can perform its major function effectively. There are many other forms of investment that yield considerably higher interest or capital growth.

Consider Tax Structure

People in the middle- and upper-tax brackets may find it more beneficial to invest in tax-exempt bonds or equities with high expense write-offs, apartment or rental buildings, and stocks that reinvest earnings in the growth of the company rather than paying high dividends.

PLAN FOR TRANSFER OF WEALTH

It is a well-known fact that "you can't take wealth with you," but you can plan how wealth is to be distributed. With families, accumulation of wealth is a joint venture, and the death of one member of the group should cause as little disruption of the group's assets as possible. Estate planning can help to achieve that goal.[52]

Estate Planning

Everything a person owns at the time of death is legally a part of the deceased person's estate—savings and checking accounts, stocks and bonds, housing and real estate, and personal property. Estate planning includes more than accumulating assets to be left to survivors, although that is fundamental. It includes acquiring a knowledge and understanding of the legal involvements that come at the time of death and plannning for transfer of the estate in accordance with the wishes of the deceased.

The services of a competent and conscientious professional may be necessary. In fact, some estates require that a lawyer be engaged at the time of settlement. It is often customary for the lawyer who draws up a will—which should be drawn early in life and changed when necessary—to be engaged as legal adviser in settling the estate. Other qualified persons, such as the trust officer of a bank, can also be helpful in the development of estate plans and wealth management. In fact, recognizing when there is a need for professional financial advice and understanding certain legal procedures is important for every family, young and old.

Making a Will

A will is the planned distribution and disposition of a person's property after death. The will has no legal effect while the person lives, and it may be changed at any time as long as the person is legally competent. A will simplifies the distribution of an estate and allows the person making the will to specify how the estate is to be divided. A will may also specify who is to become guardian to care for children in case both parents are killed. When no will is made, an estate must be settled and distributed according to the laws of descent and distribution of the state in which the individual has lived and owned property. This may result in inequitable or unfortunate settlements.

A will is a legal document that specifies:

- who is to receive the property

- when property is to be received

- what proportions of the estate each person is to receive

- who shall settle the estate

- what particular conditions govern the distribution.

Any person of legal age and sound mind has the privilege of making a will and leaving property to one or more individuals. In most states the law provides that the person—male or female—be 18 years old or over and of sound mind.

There are two types of formal wills drawn up by attorneys for husbands and wives—a *joint will* made as a single document or a *mutual will* made as two separate documents containing identical instructions. A person may choose to make his own will but must sign and declare it to be his will in the presence of two or more witnesses. These witnesses must also sign the paper in the presence of each other and of the maker of the will. If a considerable amount of property is to be transferred or if complex situations are involved, it is advisable to seek advice of a competent lawyer.

The individual who dies with a will ordinarily names an executor or executrix to carry out the terms of the will. The person who dies without a will leaves his estate to be settled by an administrator appointed by the court. When a person dies *intestate*—without a will—the surviving husband or wife receives a dower or life estate of a percentage of all properties that the deceased owned during marriage.

Dower rights are not defeated by a will. The laws for distribution of property when no will is left are based on whether a man or woman is married or single and whether he or she has one or more children. In the event that there is no immediate family, the closest relatives are next in line of descent.

A will removes many causes of family jealousies and disputes that may arise when provisions for the survivors are made by the courts.

Joint Tenancy

Many couples hold property in *joint tenancy with right of survivorship*. If property is held in joint tenancy by a husband and wife, at the death of either party the property belongs to the other party without probate or court proceedings by right or survivorship. Neither party can divert such property by will. In addition to establishing joint tenancy as the form of ownership of assets in the deed or title, it is generally necessary that the following requirements be met in order to create joint tenancy:

- the interests of the joint tenants must be established in the same deed or conveyance

- the interests of the tenants must begin at the same time

- all the parties must have the same and similar interest in the property

- all tenants must be entitled to the entire possession of the property at all times.[53]

Some states have enacted laws to abolish the right of survivorship in property held in joint tenancy. However, if the deed states that the property title is vested in the joint tenants, then the right of survivorship is established. Joint tenancy is one form of estate planning that may save costs in the transfer of wealth at the death of one marriage partner; trusts are another.

Family Trust Funds

A trust provides a means of conserving funds or properties by transferring the management to a competent administrator, either a person or a financial institution. It is a legal arrangement whereby the funds or properties are placed in the safekeeping of a disinterested party, called a trustee, and the returns are paid to another party, called the beneficiary. The object of the trust is to supply more able management of properties than the person destined to receive the benefits possesses. Such an arrangement assures the originator of the trust that the person or persons for whom it is created will be more adequately provided for than by an outright bequest of the properties. There are two kinds of trusts: (1) the voluntary or living trust, set up by one person for another while both are living and (2) the testamentary trust, placed in a will to be received on death of the person arranging the trust.

A trust fund may be managed by an individual, by a local bank, or by a company organized primarily for handling such business. Usually the managing agency charges a retaining fee for its services.

The amount placed in trust may be large or small. Within recent years, trusts have grown more popular among people of moderate incomes. It was formerly a device used largely by the well-to-do for safeguarding and conserving family fortunes. The creator of the trust may specify the amount of income the beneficiary is to receive, the term of years the trust is to remain in force, and the disposition of the properties making up the trust at the end of the terms.

The establishment of a trust fund is a practical method for ensuring financial care of dependents; it is frequently used by a parent for a child or children, or by a husband for a wife. It is also used by wealthy people as a means of endowing a worthy cause, such as an educational project or institution, or of avoiding or reducing estate taxes.

Estate and Inheritance Taxes

During a person's lifetime local, state, and federal taxes are paid in the form of sales, property, and income taxes. If a person makes a gift of money or property, there is a federal, and sometimes a state, gift tax assessed against the giver—not the receiver—but a person may give up to $3,000 a year each, tax-free, to as many people as he wishes, or $30,000 total during his lifetime. When a person dies, there may be federal estate taxes and state inheritance or estate taxes to be paid.

In estate planning, it is important to understand the effect of inheritance and estate taxes on building and transferring of wealth. The terms inheritance tax and estate tax are sometimes confused. They are not synonomous, as is often supposed. The inheritance tax is levied on those who inherit property; the estate tax is levied on the estate itself. Thus, in the settling of an estate, both taxes may have to be paid.

The federal estate tax is levied on the *gross estate*, meaning the fair market value of all real and personal property making up the deceased's holdings except those situated outside the United States. The law allows certain exemptions and deductions that are taken into consideration in determining the *net estate*. From this net estate an exemption of $60,000 is allowed. The federal estate tax is payable 15 months after the death of the deceased, although in complicated cases the government may take much longer to compute and impose the tax. This delay may hold up an estate settlement for several years.

Estate planning entails a number of personal, social, and financial considerations. It may require the assistance of competent planners. The appropriate plan is one that will build and conserve wealth sufficient to meet the financial and personal needs of those to be supported by that wealth. A realistic estate plan will provide a fund to cover final expenses and costs of settling an estate, establish methods of avoiding unnecessary inheritance and estate taxes, and avoid misunderstandings and undue hardships among the estate's beneficiaries.

Summary

Wealth has been described in this chapter as a resource that can bring many comforts and satisfactions to those who achieve it. Wealth that is coveted beyond reason can bring disharmony and dissatisfaction to those who are unsuccessful in its management.

Wealth is accumulated slowly through purposeful management of economic, environmental, and human resources. It is seldom achieved quickly or easily. It requires continual planning, control, and reevaluation. It is both the product of and a purpose for management—both a resource and a goal in the lives of most people—and it is within the grasp of most families in today's society.

References

1. Galbraith, J. K., *The Affluent Society,* Hamish Hamilton, London, England, (1958), p. 1.

2. Galbraith, J. K., *The Affluent Society,* Penguin Books, Harmondsworth, Middlesex, (1962), p. 13.

3. *Ibid,* p. 14.

4. Katona, G., Mandell, L. and Schmiedeskamp, J., *1970 Survey of Consumer Finances,* Survey Research Center, The University of Michigan, Ann Arbor, Mich., (1971), pp. 35–49.

5. *Ibid,* p. 68.

6. *The American Almanac, Statistical Abstract of the U.S. for 1974,* Grosset and Dunlap, New York, (1973), p. 687 (Table 1163) and p. 692 (Table 1172); see also p. 693 (Table 1175).

7. *Statistical Abstract of the U.S.: 1974,* (95th ed.), U.S. Bureau of the Census, Washington, D.C., (1974), p. 397, (Table 648).

8. Katona, Mandell, and Schmiedeskamp, *op. cit.,* pp. 95–109.

9. *Ibid,* pp. 110–114.

10. *Ibid,* pp. 115–116.

11. *Shareownership 1970, Census of Shareowners,* New York Stock Exchange, New York, (1971).

12. Katona, Mandell and Schmiedeskamp, *op. cit.,* pp. 113–114.

13. *Statistical Abstract of the U.S.: 1974, op. cit.,* p. 468, (Table 762).

14. *The American Almanac for 1974, op. cit.,* p. 332 (Table 542).

15. *Ibid,* p. 332 (Table 542).

16. Montgomery, J. E., "Housing Technology: How Does It Affect the Energy Crisis?," *Journal of Home Economics,* 65: 9 (December 1973), pp. 16–22.

17. "Where People Are Putting Their Money Now," *U.S. News and World Report,* 78: 6 (Feb. 10, 1975), pp. 61–63.

18. *Ibid,* p. 62.

19. *Ibid,* p. 63.

20. Federal Reserve Board data reported in *U.S. News and World Report,* 78: 6 (February 10, 1975) p. 61.

21. "Value of a Life," *Wall Street Journal,* (August 1, 1967), pp. 1, 9.

22. Walker, K. E. and Gauger, W. H., *The Dollar Value of Household Work,* Social Sciences/ Consumer Economics and Public Policy No. 5 Information Bulletin, New York State College of Human Ecology, Cornell University, Ithaca, New York, (1973).

23. Williams, F. L. and Manning, S. L., "Net Worth Change of Selected Families," *Home Economics Research Journal,* 1: 2 (December 1972), p. 106.

24. Rice, A. S., *An Economic Life Cycle of Childless Families,* unpublished doctoral dissertation, Florida State University, Tallahassee, (1964), pp. 74–81; see also Katona, Mandell and Schmiedeskamp, *op. cit.,* pp. 95–97.

25. Williams and Manning, *op. cit.,* pp. 112–113.

26. *Ibid,* p. 113.

27. *Investments, Insurance, Wills Simplified,* Books by *U.S. News and World Report,* Washington, D. C., (1969).

28. Nelson, R. H., *Personal Money Management,* Addison–Wesley, Reading, Mass., (1973), p. 61.

29. Garman, E. T. and Eckert, S. W., *The Consumer's World* (Resource), McGraw-Hill, New York, (1974), pp. 340–343.

30. *Investments, Insurance, Wills Simplified, op. cit.,* p. 16.

31. Calculated from *Savings Deposit Growth Tables, Compounded Daily—*

360 Day Year, Pub. No. 1273, Delphi Information Sciences Corp., Santa Monica, Calif., (1973).

32. Calculated from *Savings Deposit Growth Tables, op. cit.*

33. "Can You Inflationproof Your Savings," *Changing Times,* 28: 10 (October 1974), pp. 7–12.

34. Moody's Investors Service, Inc., 99 Church Street, New York, 10007; see also Standard and Poor's Corp., 345 Hudson St., New York, 10014.

35. Additional information on buying stocks is available from such references as: Unger, M. A. and Wolf, H. A., *Personal Finance,* Allyn and Bacon, Boston, Mass., (1972); West, D. A., and Wood, G. L., *Personal Financial Management,* Houghton Mifflin, New York, (1972); and Nelson, R. H., *op. cit.*

36. Quint, B., "What Your Broker Doesn't Know Can Hurt You," *Money,* 2: 9 (September 1973), pp. 39–41.

37. "Mutual Funds: How to Find the Best Performers," *Changing Times,* 28: 7 (July 1974) pp. 6–10.

38. Madrick, J. G., "Finding a Mutual Fund That Fits," *Money,* 3: 8 (August 1974), pp. 41–46; "Mutual Funds: How to Find the Best Performers, *Changing Times,* 28: 7 (July 1974), pp. 6–10; see also the following advisory service publications: *Investment Companies, 1975 Edition,* Wiesenberger Services, New York, (1975); *Johnson's Investment Company Charts,* Johnson's Charts, Inc., Buffalo, N.Y., (1975); and *FundScope Magazine's Mutual Fund Guide,* (April issue of this monthly magazine carries mutual fund guide), Los Angeles; *Forbes Mutual Fund Survey* (August 15 issue of *Forbes* magazine), New York.

39. Nelson, R. H., *op. cit.,* p. 558.

40. *Ibid.,* p. 560.

41. Martin, M., Terrett, B., and Wheaton, W. L. C., *Housing, People and Cities,* McGraw-Hill, New York, (1962), pp. 92–94.

42. Main, J., "A Man's Home Is His Capital," *Money,* 1: 3 (December 1972), p. 31.

43. "If You Think Houses Are Costly Today—," *U.S. News and World Report,* 77: 20 (May 6, 1974), pp. 65, 70.

44. Main, J., *op. cit.,* p. 28.

45. *Ibid.,* p. 28, 31.

46. Nelson, R. H., *op. cit.,* pp. 288–302.

47. *Ibid.,* p. 399.

48. Phillips, E. B., and Lane, S. *Personal Finance Text and Case Problems,* (3rd ed.), John Wiley, New York, (1974); see also Nelson, R. H., *op. cit.,* p. 399.

49. "To Save or Invest Successfully, Make a Money Plan," *Changing Times,* 28: 5 (May 1974), pp. 15–18.

50. *Ibid,* p. 15.

51. *Ibid.,* pp. 16–17.

52. Newman, J., (ed.), *What Everyone Needs to Know About Law,* Books by *U.S. News and World Report,* Washington, D.C., (1973).

53. Donaldson, E. F., and Pfahl, J. M., *Personal Finance,* Ronald Press, New York, (1966), pp. 140, 356–357.

Part IV

MANAGEMENT IN ACTION

13

MANAGING ENVIRONMENTAL RESOURCES

In one of those rare books that awakens the national consciousness and changes history, Rachel Carson defined ecology as a "web of life—or death."[1] This was *Silent Spring*; a book that brought shocking awareness of pollution in this nation's rivers and lakes and the struggle between the social and physical environment. The editiors of *Consumer Reports* called it an exposé of pressures of chemical and agricultural interests against pesticide control and the contradictory policies of government agencies.[2]

Pesticides are only one of the countless environmental dangers that face this country and the world today. Man's survival depends on resources—oil, gas, coal, clean air, pure water, and many others. Survival depends on preservation of scarce life-sustaining resources for future generations. Survival also depends on adequate disposal of the wastes created by living in a mass-consumption society.

Population and Environmental Quality

The growing world population and high concentration in metropolitan areas make increased demands on the planet's fixed supply of air, water, and land. S. Fred Singer, Deputy Assistant Secretary of the Interior and Director of the Department's Research on Environmental Quality, calls America's problem one of "popullution."[3] Although the U.S. does not appear to have a population problem with a near "0" population growth rate and only fifty-five people per square mile (sixty-five excluding Alaska), the concentration of two-thirds of America's inhabitants into metropolitan areas and half of these people in central cities, with density averages of about 7,000 per square mile, *does* present a serious pollution problem.

POLLUTION

Population growth is closely related to pollution of natural resources and to adequacy of these environmental resources, some of which cannot be replaced. Must a clean environment be the casualty of a throw-away economy? People, especially in high density areas, produce waste—more than a million tons per day.[1] More than a billion pounds of solid wastes alone are discarded each day in this country.[5] That is ten pounds of waste per person daily; one ton per man, woman, and child each year.

What kind of waste is created in such masses by the ordinary process of living? Each year, 100 million rubber tires and 9 million automobiles become junk.[6] Many of them—150 cars a day in New York city alone—are simply abandoned on the street. The cost of hauling them away adds to the burden of city budgets. Hundreds of thousands of appliances, such as refrigerators, washing machines, television sets, electric toothbrushes, blenders, and toasters, become inoperable or obsolete and are discarded each year. Some 30 billion tons of paper, 4 million tons of plastics, 48 billion cans, and 26 billion bottles become trash.[7] Much of this trash lines the highways and camp-grounds of America's open spaces. This waste material also lines the curbs of city streets and hallways of public buildings; it is abandoned through an irresponsible attitude toward environmental quality and a throw-away lifestyle.

Food scraps and waste food constitute *garbage.* When garbage is combined with other household waste, residential refuse is generated, attracting flies and rats. Bodily discharges—human wastes—provide breeding grounds for insects, spread intestinal diseases, and threaten health.[8] Cattle waste—manure—has become more of a disposal problem than a fertilizer because of the practice of herding cattle into feed lots to fatten for butchering. This practice produces a pollution problem in the feed lots and a shortage of organic fertilizer in the fields.[9]

Increased world population—at a rate of about 200,000 persons a day—presents a growing demand for food.[10] At the same time, population growth diminishes land available for raising crops and increases the need for continuous money crops made possible through chemical fertilizers to boost the yield. Such fertilizers tend to leach into rivers and lakes. Sources of clean and treatable water supplies for home, industrial, and community use are becoming harder to locate. Problems of polluted waters, that Rachel Carson wrote about in 1962, continue.

The future outlook for rivers as a water supply is not encouraging unless their purity is enforced and updated and a more elaborate system of reservoirs is developed.[11] By the year 2000, daily withdrawals from lakes and streams "will be close to 900 billion gallons, or 80 percent of the average river flows." Only 150 billion gallons per day will be consumed through evaporation, but the remainder will be "returned to rivers, lakes, and estuaries, carrying a burden of pollutants from its contact with human beings and their farms and industries."[12] Soaps and detergents and the chemical and industrial by-products of manufacturing add their share of pollution to the nation's water supply.

Some waste is gaseous and may result from generating electric power, processing chemicals and petroleum, from industries, and from transportation. Transportation is responsible for a large proportion of the smog that shrouds large cities. About 25 percent of most city land areas in the industrialized Western world is devoted to roads and parking areas for automobiles. In Los Angeles, the figure is 55 percent.[13] In Tokyo, smog is so bad that cars are banned from more than 100 streets on certain busy shopping days; traffic policemen must pause regularly to breathe oxygen from a streetside station, and vending machines dispense air to pedestrians.[14]

Although it is difficult to measure air pollution damage in monetary terms, the U.S. Environmental Protection Agency reported their "best" estimate for measured effects of air pollution damage in the United States in 1970 was $12.3 billion. These estimates were based on: (1) a survey of literature and environmental economics; (2) extrapolation of studies that attempted to estimate air pollution damages and that passed critical review; and (3) prevailing air quality levels in 1970.[15] Air pollution damage to human health was estimated at $4.6 billion, damage to materials at $2.2 billion, and vegetation damage at $.2 billion; these totaled $7 billion for these areas alone. Lack of data prevented estimates of air pollution damage to domestic animals and wildlife.[16]

A certain amount of pollution is visual. Many cities resemble a jungle of distracting signs and on-premise advertising. Billboards, utility poles, junkyards, and automobile graveyards mar the roadsides of America. Many cities have enacted legislation to limit the size of business signs, and some states have laws that prohibit billboards within certain distances of freeways and highways. But, as yet, there is no federal legislation to control visual pollution.

Sound is a less tangible, physical resource that was once taken for granted. Now, its quality is also becoming polluted to a point where management becomes necessary if the population's hearing is to be preserved. Some cities have passed laws prohibiting jet flights over the city at speeds that break the sound barrier. Others do not allow planes to be scheduled into the city during certain hours of the night. Some cities require that night landings and takeoffs be made from runways that direct planes over low-density areas of the community, use ocean airways when feasible, and utilize areas that are not highly populated for building airports. Train and highway traffic also cause sound pollution.

Noise is generally defined as "unwanted sound," implying sounds that interfere with human communication, comfort, and health. Avoiding a noise problem is one way of controlling it. Design of quieter equipment and machinery, isolation of noisy equipment, changing the operation of a noise source, or construction of sound barriers and sound absorbers are other possibilities of controlling noise.

Mechanical vibrations and noise can cause hearing loss and produce other psychological and physical disturbances.[17] There are many such sources of noise distractions within living units. Sounds created by operation of time saving, temperature controlling, and entertainment equipment may create even more distraction within the home than external community noise. Small sounds within a home can be disturbing. The constant drip of a leaky faucet at night can cause as much distraction as traffic on a nearby highway. The vibration of an automatic furnace clicking on when the thermostat drops to a determined low can cause psychological tensions, especially if the furnace is located near the bedroom of a light sleeper. Television and radio can be educational and entertaining when controlled. Both can become noise when they interrupt communication between family members, impair hearing, or interrupt activities directed toward goal-attainment. Noise created by one family member may easily interfere with the work, the emotional tranquility, and often the health of another. There is also sound pollution and a disturbing effect of noise created by families living in close proximity—beside, beneath, and above another family's living unit.

As populations increase, more people crowd into cities seeking work and a life style in close proximity to other people. Along with the great sprawling suburban areas around America's cities have come increased demands on urban physical resources—sewers, roads, office buildings, apartments, and public facilities.

By the year 2000, the country may have to double its urban physical plants to take care of an estimated 60 million people. It is hoped that urban redevelopment will not continue to produce what *Business Week* calls "acres of downtown business districts scraped bare, then dotted with office towers, apartment slabs, stadiums, and civic centers, all isolated in enormous parking lots and looped with expressways, or housing projects of forbidding cruciform buildings, rising out of lifeless asphalt lots ringed with cyclone fences."[18]

"Suburban sprawl found wasteful and costly," was the headline on an Environmental Protection Agency *Citizen's Bulletin,* reporting findings of a community study. Planned communities, that employ a mixture of highrise and walk-up apartments, townhouses, and a few clustered one-family houses, were suggested as preferable to typical subdivisions of one-family houses if land use was to be improved in and around cities.[19] Emphasis on the environment, including the use of space, is making urban design one of today's community management challenges.

Just before World War II, the insecticidal properties of dichloro-diphenyl-trichloroethane—DDT—were recognized. It was used against mosquitoes and body lice with great success during the War. Thousands upon thousands of tons of DDT have been used since then to control household pests, rid swamps of malaria-carrying mosquitoes, and farms of insects that destroy crops. The fact that DDT remained active long after application was, at first, one of its most attractive features. But, in the past decade, it has become increasingly evident that creatures living in water, in air, and on land—including people—have built up concentrations of DDT in their bodies. It is toxic to many forms of animal and marine life and is transmitted when one fish is eaten by another or by man through the food chain.[20] Thus, even chemicals used to control the environment can also pollute it.

RESOURCE DEPLETION

As populations increase, they create more environmental problems and intensify those that already exist. Resources are depleted by high-ratio consumption. Through the prodding and planned product obsolescence of manufacturers and an upward trend in incomes, people have created a growing demand for household appliances, cars, throw-away packaging, and a variety of clothing and personal products. They expect to flip a switch and have instant light, to turn on a faucet and have hot or cold water, and to adjust a thermostat and control the temperature within an enclosure. The natural resources of this country and those of the world are being endangered by people's addiction to external rather than human energy as a way of life.

As technology has developed, more natural resources have been used for the sake of convenience. Natural resources were combined in new forms, such as iron, steel, and plastics. Coal, oil, natural gas, and uranium have been transformed into electricity to supply America's need for energy. The more than 68.5 million dwelling units in the United States are energy hungry, water hungry, waste-producing, and air-polluting units of an industrial, high-energy-consuming society, and the present sources of natural, tangible resources are running out. Predictions are that by 1980, this nation will be using 2.3 trillion kilowatts of electricity per year.[21] Imagine the chaos that would result if electricity throughout the nation was shut off for only one day. Computers, the data banks of economic institutions, would be crippled, payrolls would be delayed, and typewriters stilled. In the home, baths would be cold, food uncooked, televisions darkened, and air unheated. Continue this line of thinking, and the frightening effects of a national energy shortage become more meaningful. If the amount of electricity needed is not anticipated and its source assured, even years in advance, it may not be available in the future.

If forced to rely completely on its own oil resources, even at the current rate of five percent annual growth in oil consumption, our total reserve of oil would be exhausted in 20 years; our gas reserve would be depleted in two or three decades.[22] Coal could last longer—700 years at the 1970 level of consumption, 200 years at the projected year 2000 level.[23]

In a typical American home, energy is used to maintain comfortable temperatures—warm in winter and air-conditioned cool in summer. Energy is used to prepare, cook, store, preserve foods, and to wash dishes. Electrical energy is used to clean carpets, to power grooming and household appliances, and perform many landscaping chores.[24] Energy is used to clean, dry, and care for clothes and to remove waste from homes. At least 90 percent of all wired dwellings have radios, refrigerators, irons, televisions, vacuum cleaners, clothes washers, toasters, and coffee makers to aid in home-related work; all can be powered by electrical energy.[25] It is estimated that the average U.S. citizen spends one-eighth of his or her lifetime viewing television and as a society, Americans are spending some 2.6 billion more weekly man-hours before the TV set than they do in productive labor.[26]

Transportation is responsible for a large proportion of our natural resource depletion. In 1974, the average American car got 11.8 miles per gallon. At that time, about 7 million barrels of oil a day were going into the production of gasoline for autos. Doubling the mileage required for cars produced by the auto industry would, according to the Environmental Protection Agency, save about 40 percent of that oil.[27] Automobile production is costly in terms of natural resources. The U.S. auto industry consumes one-fifth of the nation's steel output, three-fifths of its rubber, and one-third of its glass.[28] Private automobiles use about 14.3 percent of the U.S. energy, more than the total residential energy consumption of 12.6 percent.[29]

Energy is expensive—both monetarily and environmentally. The average family spent $743 for energy in 1973, about 7 percent of the average income that year.[30] U.S. energy demands are doubling every 15 to 20 years, and America already uses 32 percent of the world's energy but constitutes only 6 percent of world population.[31]

Ecosystems

Ecosystems are life-support systems so ingenious that they are self-renewing; so massive that they can supply the needs of all living creatures. Air, water, and land are crucial elements of man's ecosystem. An ecosystem is a life-cycle relationship between elements of a natural environment. The fish in a pond feed on tiny plants and animals called plankton. Eventually, the fish die and their carcasses are broken down by micro-organisms into basic chemicals, consuming oxygen from the water in the process. Plant plankton, nourished by those chemicals, produce oxygen to replace that which was consumed by the micro-organisms. Animal plankton feed on the plant plankton, fish eat the animal plankton, and the cycle repeats itself.[32] The ecosystem is the relationship between the living organisms and their life-support environment throughout their life cycle.

On land, living things are nourished, grow old and die, then decompose to enrich the land again. People use the thin envelope of air, surrounding the planet, inhaling oxygen and exhaling carbon dioxide that vegetation absorbs. Plants photosynthesize the carbon, using it for growth and returning oxygen to the atmosphere. Each ecosystem is based on a delicate balance between its components. What happens to an ecosystem when people alter it, when the quality of one component becomes polluted, or when the supply of another resource is consumed out of proportion to its replacement in the system? The answer to this question is the reason why pollution and depletion of environmental resources is so disturbing.

Families are energy-driven ecosystems linked to the environment in which they exist through energy inputs and energy outputs, through the resources they consume in the pursuit of comfortable living, and the outputs of waste and pollutants. This increased use of energy-driven, energy-built "creature comforts" has diminished the human energy expended by most U.S. families and has diminished both the quality and quantity of natural environmental resources that supply these needs.

Most families are unaware of the extent to which their standard of living depends on availability of energy.[33] Energy is the ability to do work. Electricity is energy to produce heat for cooking or heating the air. Energy is also information that may be processed by family members in decision making.[34] Consider the energy usage in the following case vignette.

> *Karen Sue planned her dinner meal as she drove home from work. She had shopped for groceries on the way home but felt a little guilty at driving the extra two miles to pick up some of those special chocolate eclairs the Danish bakery makes. They are her son Danny's favorites, and he'll be leaving for his first ski weekend tomorrow.*
>
> *As the garage door swung open, tripped off by the electric eye, she thought, "Oh, good, I beat Jim home today." That meant she got the garage tonight and wouldn't have to scrape the windshield in the morning. She propped the groceries against her leg as she unlocked the back door and felt the warm air on her cold hands and face when the door opened. The air circulates so much better now that Jim wired the furnace fan to make it stay on continuously.*

Karen Sue put the groceries away hastily and went back out to the garage to see if there was a roast left in the freezer from the quarter beef they had bought last fall. The freezer was almost full of meat, strawberries, and vegetables from their summer garden. Back in the kitchen, Karen Sue put the roast in the microwave oven to thaw while she made Jim's favorite baked custard. She always mixed it in the blender, using the measurements on the side of the blender jar, leaving only the one container to wash.

With the custard in the oven and the roast buzzing away on the rotisserie, she opened a can of mushroom soup, mixed it with a package of frozen string beans, and placed them in the oven. At the last minute, she opened a can of French-fried onion rings that would top the green bean casserole and tasted one. The can opener worked so easily, now that she had replaced the plug on the end of the cord. Her compacter flattened the cans easily.

As she headed for the shower, Karen Sue put a load of clothes in the washing machine and vacuumed the lint that spilled out of Danny's pockets when she shook them.

The shower felt good. She always liked it extremely hot on the back of her neck. Dressing quickly, she lit a fire in the living room. It was easy with the gas jet behind the logs.

She curled up in a chair and dried her short hair with a new blow dryer. By the time Jim got home, she was watching television with dinner almost ready.

How many different ways did Karen Sue use energy in the course of one hour of her day? Which of the energy uses could have been eliminated without significantly changing the family's standard of living? What substitutes are available? What alternatives are possible?

PRINCIPLES OF ENERGY USE

To help answer these and other questions involved in home energy use, consider the following principles.[35]

1. *All processes require energy.* Some processes are human and, therefore, require human energy—motion, thought, and processing of information. Other processes are electrical, chemical, thermal, nuclear, or mechanical; these are collectively called physical energy.

2. *Energy is derived from many sources.* Human energy is derived from

food. Electric energy is derived from water power or from conversion of fuels—coal, oil, natural gas, and uranium. Chemical energy, stored in gas or oil is changed into useful energy through combustion or rapid movement of molecules in a combining process. Oil (petroleum) provides gasoline which is converted into chemical energy to power cars when the gasoline molecules react with the air molecules and combustion occurs, releasing energy.

3. *Sources of energy are limited.* Oil and gas reserves are in immediate danger. Other minerals are taken from the earth at an annual rate of approximately 25 tons per person to support each American's current lifestyle.[36] Demands for physical energy in the U.S. tax both fuel supplies and power-generating capacity. Brownouts, blackouts, and gasoline shortages already signal the danger of imminent depletion of energy sources; yet, consumption of most energy sources continues to increase at a rate of five percent or more per year.

4. *There are renewable energy inputs.* Human energy is renewable and tends to increase with use. Most physical energy—heat, chemical, electrical—is derived from fossil fuels that are not renewable by most standards. Trees, as a source of heat energy, are renewable, but it requires considerable time to regenerate a forest.

5. *The earth's capacity to absorb externalities is limited.* Pollution occurs when the air is not able to absorb the smoke that trails jet planes or carbons emitted from cars or when rivers and lakes are overwhelmed by man's wastes. Externalities are pollutants that cannot be accommodated by the earth's ecosystems.

6. *The total cost of inputs—energy and externalities—reveals the true cost of outputs.* Costs may be calculated in monetary terms, but they may also be considered in terms of other resources—time, effort, and energy to break down the waste or residue. Costs include those of converting, transporting, and removing waste produced when energy is used.

Ecosystems are trade-offs of inputs and outputs. When people consume, they gain utility, process it, use it, and discard it. What will it take for the by-products of consumption to be recycled as usable products again"? Is it American to continue consuming? When will preservation of the environment outweigh the desire for immediate satisfaction? Will the quality of environments become a primary factor in personal and family managerial practices?

The Search for Environmental Solutions

When Wilson Riles wrote the foreword to California's curriculum guide for consumer education, he said we are deciding now, by our very actions or failure to act, whether or not another generation will survive. "It will matter little to teach our children how to extract the last bit of oil from shale if we then use the oil to feed voracious engines that burn dry in the race for a faster life-style . . . It is no longer enough to ask the economic question: 'Can we afford it?' We must now ask the sociological question: 'Can our world afford for us to have it?'"[37]

What can be done about the energy crisis? How can environmental pollution and resource depletion be stopped without demanding more than people are willing to relinquish? Is there a choice? Can the natural ecosystem that supports human life, once damaged, ever be restored? How clean is clean air? Will it ever be reasonably pure again?

Solutions to environmental issues may be approached somewhat like crimes are approached by a trained detective. Everything that is known about the crime (or problem) forms the foundation of a triangle and is laid out for examination. By the processes of testing, reasoning, and isolating information, the points of the triangle focus inward on the logical solution. Recognition of interactions between physical and social environment is inevitable in the solution of energy crises, deteriorating cities, air and water contamination, or sound pollution.

Each solution will ultimately require individual cooperation, conservation, and decisions between the alternatives of environmental preservation or satisfaction of current demands. There are bound to be tradeoffs between high consumption and cost of cleaning up or preventing pollution of environmental resources. Management of environmental problems will mean control of human nature—control of wants that demand depletion of the physical resources that affect human survival.

Managing the natural resources and intangible surroundings may never be accomplished through individual effort. These are challenges that can be met by cooperative groups of people and the social institutions through which they operate. Additional restrictions may have to be placed on use of scarce resources as populations increase.

Some environmental problems may not be solved in ways that specific goal-oriented problems are because the emphasis is on values. In environmental management the specific goal is not always known, only that a solution to the problem must be found. Allocation and control of scarce national resources or management to assure quality of less tangible surroundings are problems that fit into the pattern of social decision making. Consequences of newly developed alternatives should be explored in advance if society is to manage environmental resources rather than to adapt to continual environmental crises.

For the immediate future, individuals, industry, and government may make concerted efforts to reduce the growth rate in energy demands. Because households are heavy energy users and because families are the principal environment in which attitudes, values, goals, and skills are developed, they are an important element in reduction of energy use. Conservation of energy could probably be the most important management consideration of this decade. A logical first step that may be taken by individuals is to eliminate all wasteful use of energy. "Don't be an energy hog," is a slogan that is growing in importance today. Sharing a ride, closing off the vents to unused rooms at home, adding weatherstripping to doors and windows in cold climates, keeping the thermostat a few degrees cooler in winter, and opening the windows instead of using the air conditioner can save on the electric or gas bill and also conserves precious energy fuel. Human power can also conserve energy. Using hand power instead of electrical power where possible—toothbrush, can opener, and mixers—is a beginning. These alternatives have an added benefit, because the resulting change contributes to health.

Becoming a "consumer ecologist" is another step in reducing energy usage and eliminating waste that is difficult to decompose. Choosing equipment on the basis of energy usage is becoming more a reality with increased understanding of energy efficiency labeling on some electrical appliances. If families are to become responsible consumer ecologists, they will need information about the energy costs of obsolescence and the recycling potential of goods. When shopping, favoring returnable bottles and aluminum cans over no-deposit bottles and cans is one way of reducing the problems of waste disposal. Aluminum foil, cellophane wrappings, and plastic and coated cardboard used to package supermarket products not only cost more but add to solid waste problems since they decompose slowly—or never—produce noxious gas when burned, and cannot be recycled. One solution is buying unpackaged products. Reducing the use of dangerous chemicals and cleaners such as hair spray, air fresheners, anti-perspirants, and paints in aerosol cans can reduce risk of inhaling harmful chemicals and of accidents from the aerosol cans.

Eliminating the "I want" philosophy of life by fighting needless consumption and purchasing only items that are needed is another way to save money *and* scarce environmental resources. Another double-duty saver is finding second uses for products. A new value base may be needed for decisions relating to consumption and home energy use. The nation's environmental crisis is also a family crisis, affecting and being affected by the values of families. People who care about environmental quality will direct actions against pollution. Adequate care, conservative use, and respectful attitudes for the environment as an important resource can bring greater satisfaction from living today and for future generations.

The ultimate solution to the energy crisis may be to develop new technology and to find new sources of energy for the future. Solar energy has potential. Other possibilities for heating homes and running automobiles may emerge. Part of the solution may come in group-owned rather than individually owned cars, appliances, and services. Future transportation may eliminate the need for individually owned cars, substituting mass-transit systems that are quiet, utilize little ground space, and operate quickly and efficiently. Bicycles that utilize human power are growing in popularity as a means of transportation and exercise.

Environmental health is a vital concern in today's society. Many government and citizens' groups have organized to improve forms of life, substances, and conditions in the surroundings that influence human health and welfare.

Management directed toward environmental quality goals may help people build more efficient dwellings with less need for the assortment of appliances and gadgetry that use electricity and fossil fuels. Housing designs could be made more functional—not only for convenience of human resources but for conservation of environmental resources. Control of sound pollution factors is within the management scope of the family. Acoustical tile, draperies, carpeting, exterior plantings, and sound insulation in the walls can improve the quality of sounds and remove some unwanted noise. Controlling the volume of television and radio can eliminate other noises. Use of earphones for private listening allows personal enjoyment of sounds without imposing them on others. Turning the television off when leaving a room reduces energy use, cost, and noise. Regular care of appliances can decrease the noise and increase the life of many household devices.

Little has been done to determine housing features necessary to reduce noise at its source and to understand the effect of spatial separation and screening to protect living quarters from urban noises. Must noise abatement be accomplished by blank walls, double windows, or air conditioning? What construction techniques can be used to screen out the noise of airplanes, trains, and car traffic?

The American uniform building codes have, until recently, given little consideration to insulation and design features to reduce noise and control reverberation. Following the lead of housing research in European countries to establish specific sound reduction characteristics of walls that separate two apartments, the United States Bureau of Standards has begun intensive study of housing design to reduce impact noises.[38] In certain cities, building codes include noise-control elements in design and location of noise-producing equipment like air conditioning and ventilating, valve-operated toilets, or garbage grinders.

Satisfaction derived from living environment is often dependent on the degree of control that can be exerted over household surroundings. The household environment is sure to affect the quality of living and often the health of the occupants. Perhaps this is why so many Americans seek home ownership—because they can more effectively control the less tangible as well as the tangible objects that surround them.

Knowledge—a human resource—can lead to alternatives for national as well as personal management. At present, electricity is largely dependent on fossil fuel for generation of power. Can this be changed? Can nuclear power be made safe? Can the movement of the ocean tides or geothermal energy be harnessed to provide power for electricity at reasonable cost? What are the untapped environmental resources that could be harnessed for man's future use?

The American Home Economics Association workbook for the Lake Placid Year Conference reported that if the present growth in world population, industrialization, pollution, food production, and resource depletion continues, growth on this planet would reach its limits within one hundred years. The conclusion was that a purposeful equilibrium could be designed to provide each person on earth with satisfying basic material needs and to provide each person an equal opportunity to "realize his individual human potential."[39] If the opportunity to realize individual human potential is chosen as the alternative, the sooner management is applied in that direction, the better; for human potential may satisfy basic lifestyle needs of individuals and societies of the present as well as of the future.

Resource shortages and environmental pollution offer each citizen and each family the opportunity to contribute to the solution of a major national and world-wide problem. Because the world faces resource shortages and pollution that can change lifestyles throughout the world, priorities for use of resources will become increasingly important as demands escalate. Attitudes affect these priorities for resource use. By conservation and purposeful management, new satisfactions may be derived and new technology developed to make life more challenging and rewarding for future generations. We can no longer afford to "wait and see" the results of these shortages and environmental degradation.

Social Components of the Environment

Some elements of a person's environment are important, not because they are becoming scarce or polluted, but because they are resources that influence the behavior of people. Interaction between the various environmental components is dynamic—changing. Managerial behavior usually functions in a complex of environments rather than in one single environment.[40] Not only do people use tangible and intangible natural environmental resources—air, land, water, sound, minerals, and energy sources—in the control of quality of life, but they have a series of social, political, and economic environments acting upon and, in turn, being affected by people.

POLITICAL INSTITUTIONS AS ENVIRONMENTAL RESOURCES

Political institutions are governmental structures and systems that influence a person's behavior—city, county, state, and national governments and their network of protective and enabling laws. As populations grow, political institutions become increasingly important.

Governments provide many resources that may be shared by citizens. Examples of these resources are police protection, water and sewage systems, libraries, roads and highways, mass transit, recreation centers, parks, and schools for the education of the population. These are valuable resources to a family, for they could scarcely be afforded on an individual basis. Facilities and services provided by the political institutions of a society are usually financed and their maintanence is supported by the public through taxation.

Personal and group values of political officials backed by those of constituents determine which services and facilities will be made available as well as their location. Lack of awareness of the variety of community facilities available and lack of purposeful use of them as resources, can turn these facilities and services into constraints on taxed family budgets. Since they will be supported regardless of personal use, awareness of community facilities and services should be cultivated as conscientiously as human resources.

Political institutions also provide a network of laws designed to bring order and leadership into the lives of the population. Many of these laws restrain the activities of individuals for the betterment of society as a whole. For example, when a city zoning board refuses to give a building permit to a landowner because of overtaxed water or sewage facilities, the landowner defers individual rights to group environmental benefits. Other laws are enacted for the protection of individuals as consumers in the marketplace against unfair treatment by business, or to protect business against monopolies.

Government agencies—the Food and Drug Administration, Federal Trade Commission, and the U.S. Department of Health, Education and Welfare—provide services for the population and require certain compliances as a measure of social environmental control. The establishment of an Environmental Protection Agency at a national level and similar agencies in a number of states recognized public concern over deterioration of the environment and a need for establishing trade-off levels between consumption and environmental preservation. According to Galbraith, "What counts is not the quantity of our goods, but the quality of life."[41] Government agencies are often charged with the task of improving the quality of goods and the quality of life. The primary function of most political institutions in democratic societies is to control the social, physical, and economic environments for the welfare of all residents within their jurisdiction. They exist to manage the environment.

Individuals and families have responsibilities to their political institutions. In democratic countries, people must obey the laws while they are in effect but have a voice in making the laws by participating in elections, studying the philosophies and platforms of people seeking office, expressing preferences through voting, and communicating with electing officials. Laws may also be changed when they do not appear to serve the population's best interests.

Management of the environment improves when people take a more active part in registering their preferences—supporting or denying support to proposed legislation, working for improved environmental legislation through channels designed for this purpose, and making the governmental institutions work by using them and managing them constructively, rather than being managed and controlled by them.

There are limits, however, to what laws and political institutions can do. If environmental concerns had highest priority in people's value systems, would there be a need for fines for industrial air pollution? Would there be a need for laws and price controls to limit use of scarce resources or to control the destruction of land in search of these resources? Would there be a need for control of pesticides used in agriculture or the amount of carbon produced by cars? Who demands the cars or the energy to operate home conveniences?

The issue of environmental quality is whether American society seeks solutions to environmental problems by: (1) depending on people's judgment and self control in resource use, (2) expecting business and the economic system to control the use of scarce resources and monitor its output of pollutants, or (3) relying on government agencies to clean up the environment and save national resources. The auto-emission air pollution problem is an example. Would consumers demand and producers develop engines with acceptable emission levels without government regulations? If the consumer-business market system cannot or does not solve the problem, should the political environment force acceptable emission standards through the Environmental Protection Agency or other governing bodies? What other alternatives are there to the trade-off between high-energy consumption and the cost of cleaning up or preventing pollution of man's life-support ecosystems?

ECONOMIC INSTITUTIONS AS ENVIRONMENTAL RESOURCES

Economic institutions have had more widespread effect on management of family living than almost any other enviromental resource. They have added creature comforts to life, made it possible to own and control cars, to "buy" houses before they can be paid for, and to accumulate a stockpile of possessions almost instantaneously with the formation of families.

Changes in standards produce changes in economic institutions. During the 15 years after World War II, two primary standards predominated family consumption—home ownership and the automobile. Traditional standards of marriage, children, and family responsibility created by a growing, home-oriented middle class, led to expansion of home-building industries and many home-related product markets. Financial success was exemplified by the automobile as the second highest symbol of advancement.[42] However, since the last decade, there has been a growing orientation toward individualism and personal fulfillment.[43]

According to Hoffman, there are presently three working definitions of success and the "good life." The first is defined in terms of money, position, and the accumulation of possessions. The second adds a belief in living a full, rich, exciting, and adventurous life. The third deemphasizes material possessions and stresses developing quality of life, self expression and self knowledge.[44] Such changes in values and definition of goals alter the demand for products and, thus, affect economic institutions.

Rapid changes in consumer standards and demand have caused expansion of plant facilities and acceleration of efforts to meet increased production demands. Business has equated progress with economic growth—a growing Gross National Product meant a better quality of life. Economic institutions linked themselves to progress through growth. Economic models assume that people act rationally—that competitive forces create socially responsible action through the profit mechanism. In actuality, even in a democratic society, that does not always happen.[45] Social responsibility in the form of environmental conservation is usually costly and erodes profits. Costs are transferred to the consumer, or economic development is traded for environmental protection.

What are the social responsibilities of corporations? Fabun calls corporations the dominant social institution that sets the pattern for the latter part of the 20th Century. He describes corporations as creative environments—energy-exchange systems "in which there is an input of energy from the environment, and a patterned internal activity that transforms the energy into output which, in turn, provokes a new energy input."[46] If this view of corporations as economic institutions is taken, they will be seen as open systems engaged in constant energy transactions with the environment. There are those who believe that if corporations are to fulfill their destiny as the dominant social institution of the century, they have grave responsibilities for developing the human potential of the people who make up the corporation and preserving the physical environmental quality of surroundings.

Consumption is closely related to pollution of natural resources and to the adequacy of those resources of the environment; some of these cannot be replaced. Some environmentalists advocate reducing standards of consumption as the ultimate solution to the degradation of quality and quantity of environmental resources. Others suggest that the sensible way to change present patterns of environmental deterioration is to make organizations and people pay the full costs of their activities. The costs of producing and distributing goods and services, according to this theory, should reflect the externalities. They argue that if business was forced to pay for all the pollution, waste disposal, and traffic congestion resulting from its activities and all the benefits it derives from airports, highways, and other public facilities, the condition of the environment would be far better.[47] But who, eventually, would pay for the externalities of business?

Is there an "Iron Law of Responsibility," as Davis contends, which stipulates that if business has the power to change the environment, it has equal responsibility to protect the environment?[48] Would an Environmental Protection Act have been needed if business had upheld the "Iron Law of Responsibility?" In fact, does business have the expertise and technology to solve environmental pollution and depletion problems?

Many businesses are making concerted efforts to solve environmental problems inherent in their industry. In 1971, Bylinsky reported that industry was cutting back on modernization and expansion plans to spend about $2 billion annually on air and water pollution control.[49] Lund reported an average expenditure of 10 percent of capital budgets in 1973 for air, water, and other pollution control facilities by 1,000 top American manufacturing companies.[50] In spite of these and other expenditures, more is needed if business is to meet future pollution control standards. Target dates of 1983 and 1985 are being set with specific goals and performance standards for high-polluting products and high energy-using systems.

Capability for U.S. energy independence by 1985 is being proposed by the Environmental Protection Agency but would mean compromises in environmental quality and special dispensation by the courts.[51] On the other hand, a 40 percent improvement in gas mileage of cars by 1983 could hasten the energy independence.[52] More stringent standards for hydrocarbon emissions of cars, proposed at the federal level, could reduce environmental pollution. Each compromise is a trade-off between environmental protection and economic growth. Will expenditures to control pollution take so many resources from expansion that economic development will be dangerously lessened? Will government regulators need defined guidelines and limited powers to prevent interference with free enterprise, or will industry need stronger motivation to protect the environment in the future? What is a reasonable cost of a "pure" environment? Is it unrealistic to expect the environment to become pure again? Will the standards that are being established for quality of the environment exact too high a lifestyle price from citizens? The real question is one of how clean an environment is desired, given the tradeoffs for material goods and services within the present American lifestyle, and what lifestyle compromises are essential for future generations.

Some analysts suggest that the social responsibility of business need not be unprofitable.[53] Markets for pollution-control devices are opening. Recycling can reduce costs, and trash reclamation could recycle waste. The idea that waste is raw material convertable into new and useful products by recycling is gaining support. It is one solution to two environmental problems—diminishing resources and pollution. In their *Special Reports on Major Business Problems,* the editors of *Business Week* tell how bottles, auto parts, and trash littering the landscape are being converted into rich resources.[54] Trash reclamation returns to the earth those things that have been removed. A great deal of recycling is already being done. Glass and aluminum companies are making new containers from waste cans and bottles. Recycled paper is used for a large percentage of the facial tissues that are being manufactured. Scrap iron, steel, aluminum, and copper are used in many industries. Techniques to capture and reprocess some of the more elusive wastes are developing, largely as a result of pollution controls and federal support of waste recovery research. As forests shrink, paper manufacturers become more willing to utilize wastepaper supplies.

There are still decisions to be made. Recycling newspaper to newsprint saves trees but it takes more fuel than converting newspaper into fertilizer. Burning garbage for power saves fossil fuel, but is the saving greater than when converting garbage to fuel oil? Industry is serving its social responsibility when it seeks these and other techniques for converting waste to resources, but there is only token recycling and reclamation presently in progress. Must there be laws to enforce recycling and to convert families to the routine practice of reclamation in large enough numbers to make a difference?

PEOPLE AS ENVIRONMENTAL RESOURCES

Not only do people and their environment interact, but people are a vital factor in the formation of their environment. Other people are part of a person's surroundings and influence level of wellbeing.[55]

The social components of the environment include nuclear families, extended families, friends and acquaintances, professional and business associates, neighborhood, community, and nation. This social environment is composed of all the cooperative human interaction systems that influence a person's values, standards, habits, and goals.

Nuclear Families

One's immediate family is a critical decision making, standard developing, habit instilling, and value-establishing unit. There is no question that the nuclear family determines not only the biological and physiological characteristics of a person but influences psychological and behavioral characteristics as well. The nuclear family provides the environment through which health practices are established, food preferences are developed, consumption patterns are formed, and values are learned. The nuclear family serves as a sounding board for hurt feelings of its members, establishes emotional patterns between husband and wife, parent and child, brother and sister, and supplies the setting for generating character and personality. The nuclear family is, therefore, a highly influential environment for generating resources.

Role expectations are first experienced in the nuclear family—roles that may limit or expand a person's ability to achieve full use of talents. Sex-stereotyped roles are inculcated almost from birth; many of them originate in the family. Can you honestly say that you believe it is appropriate for a man to assume the primary homemaker role while the woman assumes the primary earner role? Would a "yes" answer to that question have to be qualified by a condition such as, "If the husband is sick or disabled, in college, or if the situation is a temporary one because the husband has lost his job?" Is there something wrong with a man who enjoys sewing or arranging flowers? Is there something strange about a woman who prefers to work outside the home? What limiting conditions would you place on your answer? The nuclear family of the future must alter stereotyped cultural roles if the talents and capabilities of future generations are to be liberated.

Some people question the permanence of the family as a social unit. Broderick prophesied that the family will last as long as man survives, and in this continuity will be the fulfillment of certain functional requirements upon which survival depends—maintenance of a minimum level of order and morale among its members. No group can survive if it is unable to manage its resources well enough to support its material needs and keep the group operating.[56] For a newly married couple, the instrumental mechanics of living together become crucial—deciding where to live, who will handle the money, whether to attempt birth control, when to eat supper, how often to wash clothes and who will do the washing, or who prepares breakfast, fixes lamps, irons shirts, makes beds, and empties garbage. Until such issues are resolved, the family cannot function. Families may rely on tradition to guide them in the assignment of some tasks, taking advantage of a sort of standard division of labor developed over the centuries by society. In other cases, policy may be negotiated as expressive tasks to assure the accomplishment of work with the least conflict and risk of failure possible.[57]

Expressive tasks involve expression and control of human feelings. Most families operate on a much higher loyalty level than is necessary for the minimum—staying together. It is this family loyalty, commitment, and morale that transmits ideals and values that become a stabilizing influence and help in reconciling family conflict and conflicts between an individual and society. It is the nuclear family that may, eventually, hold the primary control over the quality of the environment for future generations. Nuclear families who value environmental quality and resource conservation will be highly instrumental in transmitting these values to future generations. When present families translate their environmental concerns into practices that restrict personal use of scarce resources, recycle all usable home waste, and choose appliances on the basis of energy consumption; future generations are more likely to do the same.

Extended Families

Extended family circles expand the pattern of morale-inducing, repetitive family activities that stabilize life. The extended family is particularly influential in expanding expressive family tasks, for it provides the social environment for transmission of cultural patterns and ethnic heritage.

Child-rearing practices, standards for moral conduct, and norms for managerial behavior are often passed from one generation to another, food recipes and meal patterns are copied by the younger generations, many instrumental, habitual, and daily tasks are subconsciously continued, and values are founded on parental and grandparental attitudes.[58]

The family, as a social component of the environment, is a powerful influence on behavior used to manage changing social, physical, and economic environments. The nuclear family and its extended circle of relatives is perhaps the most important source of managerial practices and goal attainment that a person encounters.

Associates

Peers probably have as much influence on the emancipation of teenagers as families do on the establishment of lifelong patterns of behavior. That is a generally accepted fact, but many people do not recognize the effect that associates have on adults. It takes a highly self-actualized person not to depend on the approval of friends for satisfaction from goal achievement. Vance Packard's *Pyramid Climbers* and *Status Seekers* and Whyte's *Organiza-*

tion Man illustrate how the goals of adults are influenced by their friends.[59] Peers—friends—provide acculturation into the ways of the social group, values, goals, and their management practices.

Peers and associates may be constraints as well as resources for goal attainment. Is it the effect of the group that causes all the members to look and act similarly? One junior-high student recently asked his teacher to send him to the office for detention and deliberately staged a scuffle with another student to justify the request. When the teacher asked why he was so anxious to have detention after school, he replied simply, "Because my friend has detention today."

The book, *I'm OK—You're OK,* has received widespread popularity. Questions such as, "Who are you?" "How do you feel about yourself—ok or not ok—and about other people?" are explored in the book.[60] People of all ages are concerned with these questions. According to Harris's philosophy, part of the relationship that binds people to others in the society outside the family circle is a reflection of self satisfaction or personal peace—an I'm ok feeling—and part is an acceptance of other people as they are—a you're ok feeling. If the quality of the relationship between friends and associates can be analyzed, people are more likely to find ways of managing their social environment. The manner in which people affect others may be a clue to managing the environment rather than requiring people to adapt to the environment.

The following poem written by Linda Kay Bishop, a fifteen year old girl, reflects the internal conflicts of accepting oneself and learning to function in the social environment of a teenager.

ME
Who am I?
Why am I here?
Is life to love
Or a thing to fear?

Why am I?
Why do I live?
Am I to take
Or am I to give?

What use am I?
What can I do?
Were you my friend
Or just one I knew?

Is there love?
Is it great?
May I love
Or must I wait?

What is love?
I really don't know?
Is it just there
Or does it grow?

Who are my friends:
Who are my foes?
Can I trust anyone?
Nobody knows.

Why am I happy?
Why do I cry?
Why am I living?
When will I die?[61]

Price questioned whether people can exert control, make decisions, and manage such problems as determining, "Who am I?" "Why am I living?" "How do I fit into the scheme of things?"[62] People of all ages seem to be asking similar questions. Social decision-making is, in part, answering the question, "Who am I?" and helping the person live his answer, changing roles to fit the person, *not* vice versa. If this is true, there may be some basis by which people select the role patterns they use to express themselves.

Value commitment, growth or self-actualization, and social decision making all exist within the social environment and can, in turn, affect all the environments chosen by an individual—economic, physical, as well as social. Value awareness and commitment to values are more likely to exist if an individual has lived in an environment that encourages rational value choice. Values can be selected within a permissive social environment according to individual preferences without fear of reprisal or rejection, without undue bias or prejudice, and with knowledge of a variety of different ways of life.[63] In social decisions, goals need to be relatively flexible, but clear and steadfast values are necessary if the person is to perceive the environment accurately and react to it in accordance with these values. This goal flexibility, value commitment relationship is a key factor in managing social decisions. The environment is also a key factor for control in social decisions—control that should be growth-oriented, leading to self actualization.

In some cultures, particularly those of the past, parents arranged the marriages of their children and attempted to control the social, physical, and economic environments in which these children would live as adults. Is the lesson to be learned from these cultures that one's environment cannot be chosen *for,* but must be selected *by,* a person if it is to bring satisfaction and personal growth? Certainly identification of the interrelationships within the social environment can make managerial control of other environments more feasible.

OTHER CULTURAL INSTITUTIONS AS SOCIAL RESOURCES

Employment appears to be the primary point of interaction between an individual and the intermediate environment.[64] Work environment affects the timing of managerial activities, the quantity of economic resources available and desired, and perhaps even the patterns of friendships developed in life.

Work status has, over the years, been the primary determinant in socioeconomic classification of families. The hours of work determine family routine—hour of rising, time schedule for eating, vacation patterns, and usually influence where the family will live.

For people who work, professional or trade organizations serve as a medium of interaction that influences the values, standards, and goals relating to the profession. How hard a person works depends not only on one's personal value system but on expectations of colleagues. Responsibility is imposed not only by labor bosses or administrators but also by other employees. Control is exerted by the employed to prevent anyone from "rocking the boat" by over- or under-exertion from the group norms. The group will delegate authority because their values are exemplified in the recipient. They provide information as to what the norms and values are and give control to the informal leaders. Thus managerial behavior occurs in the social environment.

Market studies conducted during the 1960's reported the "back fence conversations" between neighbors while hanging clothes on the line was the primary point of influence for brand-name purchases and in establishing lifestyle aspirations. The back fence was also the exchange arena for child-care practices, housekeeping tips, and the proverbial neighborhood gossip. Since clothes dryers have replaced the clothes line in about 40 percent of all households and nearly two-thirds of the families in the median income bracket, what common communication medium will replace the back fence in bridging the privacy barrier provided by single family dwellings?

With more wives working, will the office replace the back fence as a medium for exchanging management practices, environmental concerns, and acculturation of newcomers into the neighborhood? Community recreation centers provided in many housing developments and mobile home parks may serve the purpose; or television may supply the point of influence and medium for communication of community customs, happenings, and goal setting.

Will evolution of the clothes line and changing patterns of human involvement emphasize work instead of housing location as the focal point of social environment? With mobile corporation men, this has been the case for many years. Is it now becoming true of working women? Where contacts are made and what binds one person to another are critical questions in determining the scope of social environment.

Many social organizations provide information and services to assist people in adapting to their environment and in reaching common goals. Consumers are banding together to accomplish goals of maximizing satisfaction from the use of economic resources. Health and research organizations spread information to increase awareness of possible health hazards and adaptation when illness is present. Overweight people seek group approval in losing weight and find strength in sharing experiences with others who have similar goals. Other social organizations, such as the American Association of Retired Persons (AARP) and the National Retired Teachers Association (NRTA), provide information and services to assist their members in bridging the gap between work and retirement. The AARP and NRTA offer members numerous references, group gatherings, instructions, lobbying to influence protection, and companionship with others facing similar situations. Organizations such as these help in the management of change.

Managing Biological Components of the Environment

The biological components of the environment are human and nonhuman. The human component is concerned with the internal functioning of a person—the physiological, anatomical, and behavioral aspects of each individual.

Psychological functioning of people is closely related to working conditions, to attitudes and motivation. The "trapped feeling" homemakers sometimes experience with the coming of a second child is a psychological reaction to other humans.

Fatigue is often related as much to psychological reactions to a task as it is to the height or other characteristics of the work area. Psychological fatigue may be eliminated by changing the environment in which a task is performed, such as improving air circulation, doing disliked chores in front of a window where vision is focused outside instead of inside, or adding pleasant sounds, such as music to the environment.

Development of human resources (Chapter 7) and relationships between anatomical and physiological aspects of persons and the work environment

(Chapter 10) are discussed in previous chapters. Both a person's size and the space within a room are two determining factors in the consumer behavior of a person selecting furnishings such as a bed. Each component of the environment is, thus, interfaced in the management process of living.

The nonhuman biological elements of the environment may be resources or constraints. These nonhuman elements include animals, insects, microbes, viruses, and other nonhuman organisms.

When families have pets, there is an additional management factor introduced into the environment. Some households treat their pets as though they were human. Families may spend as much or more on the health care of their pets as on family members. Pets may dominate the time patterns of people who must return home from work at noon to walk the pet and those who cannot take vacations because "Baby" doesn't like to be left with the veterinarian or at a "pet motel." The cost of dog food may equal that of a child's. But pets bring companionship to many people. For the old and the lonely, a pet can bring many moments of happiness. For people who need to be depended upon to achieve satisfaction, pets may provide that dependence.

For some families, animals provide a source of income. The livelihood of a rodeo calf roper depends on his horse. An animal trainer has no job without his animals. Horse and dog racing is big business in some parts of the country and provides occupations for many people.

The degree to which pets and animals contribute to their owner's satisfaction will determine whether they are resources or constraints to a particular person. But there is no question that pets inject an additional element into management. They must be fed, groomed, taught to follow instructions and commands, and they require companionship. They often bring insects into the house, they carry microbes, and they may infect family members with viruses. Children who live with pets often learn many things about life from their pets and may learn to respect and care for others through their experiences with pets.

For the blind, a "seeing-eye dog" may provide mobility. Such a dog is not only a pet; it is a resource for managing the surroundings of a physically disabled person.

Summary

The environment is composed of many resources—natural, tangible resources such as earth, rain, minerals, and nontangible resources such as air, light, sound, temperature, humidity and space. The world has changed since the days of cave dwellers. The very different environment in which citizens exist is creating unceasing demands on the natural resources of the world. Increasing populations and concentration in small areas have magnified the pollution problems in cities and placed heavy demands on scarce resources to supply energy and improved lifestyles. This chapter has explored population and environmental quality, pollution, and resource depletion. Some possible solutions have been proposed, but more questions have been raised than answers, for natural elements of the environment are not yet controllable. Life-support ecosystems, once forced out of balance by pollution and waste, heal slowly.

Social components of the environment were examined for their effect on personal values, standards, habits, and goals. Effective management includes recognizing and developing ways to use environmental resources in such a way that their supply will be balanced over time and their quality assured for future generations.

References

1. Carson, R., *Silent Spring,* Crest, New York, (1962).

2. Editors of *Consumer Reports,* "Foreword," in Graham, F., Jr., *Since Silent Spring,* Houghton Mifflin, Boston, Mass., (1970), p. v.

3. Mayer, L. A., "W. S. Population Growth: Would Slower Be Better?" in B. Q. Hafen, (ed.), *Man, Health and Environment,* Burgess, Minneapolis, Minn., (1972), pp. 215–229.

4. Purdom, P. W., (ed.), *Environmental Health,* Academic Press, New York, (1971), pp. 7–8.

5. Cailliet, G., Setzer, P., and Love, M., *Everyman's Guide to Ecological Living,* Macmillan, New York, (1971), p. 1.

6. Young, G., "Pollution, Threat to Man's Only Home," *National Geographic,* 138: 6 (December 1970), p. 781.

7. Cailliet, G., *et. al, op. cit.* p. 2.

8. Purdom, P. W., *op. cit.,* p. 8.

9. Billard, J. B., "The Revolution in American Agriculture," *National Geographic,* 137: 2 (February 1970), pp. 147–185.

10. Faulkner, D. H., "Who Will Feed the Hungry Millions?" *Plain Truth,* 36: 2 (February 8, 1971) p. 2.

11. Zemaitis, W. L., "Water and Waste Water," in Purdom, P. W., (ed.), *op. cit.,* pp. 149–187.

12. Revelle, R., Khosla, A., and Vinovskis, M., (eds.), *The Survival Equation: Man, Resources, and His Environment,* Houghton Mifflin, Boston, Mass., (1971), p. 394.

13. Whikehart, W. R., "Our Energy Crisis—And the One Real Solution," *Plain Truth,* 39: 4 (April 1974), pp. 26–29.

14. Young, G., *op. cit.,* pp. 739, 747.

15. Waddell, T. E., *The Economic Damages of Air Pollution,* 600/5-74-012, U.S. Environmental Protection Agency, Office of Research and Development, Washington, D.C., (May 1974), pp. 1–4.

16. *Ibid,* pp. 2, 117–123.

17. Jackson, W. E., "Environmental Control," in Purdom, P. W., (ed.), *op. cit.,* pp. 414–428.

18. "Making Cities Better Places to Live," *Business Week,* (August 22, 1970), p. 36.

19. *EPA Citizen's Bulletin,* (October 1974), Environmental Protection Agency, Washington, D.C., p. 1.

20. Young, G., *op. cit.,* p. 765.

21. "Electricity, the Individual and the Energy Crisis," *Insights Into Consumerism,* (Spring/Summer 1974), J. C. Penney, New York, p. 1.

22. Montgomery, J. E., "Housing Technology: How Does It Affect the Energy Crisis?," *Journal of Home Economics,* 65: 9 (December 1973), pp. 16–22.

23. Rocks, L., and Runyon, R. P., *The Energy Crisis,* Crown, New York, (1972), p. 8.

24. Field, A., "Energy Conservation: A Challenge for Home Economists," *Journal of Home Economics,* 65: 9 (December 1973), pp. 23–26.

25. Montgomery, J. E. *op. cit.,* p. 17.

26. Whikehart, W. R., *op. cit.,* p. 27.

27. "Must Clean Environment Be A Casualty?" *U.S. News and World Report, 77,* (March 11, 1974), pp. 39–43.

28. Whikehart, W. R., *op. cit.,* p. 26.

29. MacGillivray, W. D., "Saving Energy Can Ease Shortage and Save Money," *Capitol Report,* (Spring 1974), p. 5.

30. *Ibid.*, p. 5.

31. "The Energy Crisis and Home Economics," *Journal of Home Economics, 65:* 9 (December 1973), p. 6.

32. Amos, W. H., "Teeming Life of a Pond," *National Geographic, 138:* 2 (August 2, 1970), p. 147.

33. Field, A., *op. cit.,* p. 23.

34. Paolucci, B., and Hogan, M. J., "The Energy Crisis and the Family," *Journal of Home Economics, 65:* 9 (December 1973), pp. 12–15.

35. *Ibid*, 13–15; see also Berg, C. A., "Energy Conservation Through Effective Utilization," *Science, 181,* 4095, (July 13, 1973), pp. 128–138.

36. "Turning Junk and Trash into a Resource," in *Special Reports on Major Business Problems,* (*Business Week* Reprints compiled by the editors), McGraw-Hill, New York, (1973).

37. Riles, W., "Foreword," in *Curriculum Design for Consumer Education: Kindergarten Through Grade Fourteen,* California State Dept. of Education, Sacramento, Calif., (1974), p. iii.

38. Senn, C. L., "Housing and the Residential Environment," in Purdom, P. W., *op. cit.,* pp. 483–514.

39. *Workbook for a Lake Placid Year Conference,* American Home Economics Association, Washington, D. C., (1973), p. 7.

40. Steidl, R. E., "An Ecological Approach to the Study of Family Managerial Behavior," in *The Family: Focus on Management,* Proceedings of a National Conference, American Home Economics Assn., Washington, D.C., (1970), pp. 22–33.

41. Galbraith, J. K., *The New Industrial State,* McGraw-Hill, New York, (1967), pp. 7–8.

42. "Values and Consumers' Changing Spending Patterns," *Forum: Consumers in a Changing Economy,* J. C. Penney Co., New York, (Spring/ Summer 1975), pp. 18–19.

43. *Ibid,* p. 18.

44. *Ibid,* pp. 18–19.

45. Meyer, D., "Business and the Environment," in Bahr, G., and Bangs, F. K., (eds.), *Foundations of Education for Business,* Yearbook No. 13, National Business Education Assn., Reston, Virginia, (1975).

46. Fabun, D., *The Corporation as a Creative Environment,* Glenco Press for Kaiser Aluminum and Chemical Corp., Beverly Hills, Calif., (1972), pp. 2, 12.

47. Mayer, L. A., *op. cit.,* p. 221.

48. Davis, K., *The Social Responsibility of Business.* Tape Recording. McGraw-Hill, New York, (1969).

49. Bylinsky, G., "The Mounting Bill for Pollution Control," *Fortune, 84* (July 1971), pp. 86–89, 130–132.

50. Lund, L., "Pollution Abatement Proceeds—Unabated," *Conference Board Record, 10* (1973), pp. 9–11.

51. "Must Clean Environment Be a Casualty?" *op. cit.,* p. 43.

52. *Ibid,* p. 40.

53. Mayer, D., *op. cit.,* p. 217.

54. "Turning Junk and Trash into a Resource," *op. cit.*

55. Purdom, P. W., *op. cit.,* p. 2.

56. Broderick, C. B., "The Interrelationships of Family Functions," in *The Family, Focus on Management, op. cit.,* pp. 1–4.

57. *Ibid.,* pp. 1–3.

58. Duvall, E. M., Hill, R. H., and Duvall, S. M., "Being Married." Association Press, New York, (1960); see also, Duvall, E. M., *Family Development,* Lippincott, New York, (1971).

59. Packard, V., *The Pyramid Climbers,* McGraw-Hill, New York, (1962);
     Packard, V., *The Status Seekers,* McKay, New York, (1959): Whyte, W.
     H., *Organization Man,* Simon and Schuster, New York, (1956).

60. Harris, T. A., *I'm OK—You're OK,* Avon Books, New York, (1969).

61. Bishop, L. K., "Me," Unpublished poem, printed by permission of Linda
     Kay Bishop, (1975).

62. Price, D. Z., "Social Decision-Making," *The Family: Focus on Manage-
     ment, op. cit.,* pp. 14–21.

63. *Ibid,* p. 16.

64. Steidl, R. E., *op. cit.,* pp. 22–33.

14

LIVING IN A WORLD OF MANY PEOPLE

Families and larger social groups are interdependent. The quality of personal and family life is influenced by the social setting—the community, state, and nation in which people live. Families, in turn, influence the quality of community life. This chapter focuses on family-community interaction and on the adjustments made to changes in family or in community life.

Family-Community Interaction

Although families produce goods and services for their own use, a variety of goods and services is also available through public agencies and businesses. This provision of goods and services both expands and limits the freedom of individual and families, as illustrated in the following example.

A family may decide to build its own living unit. To reach this goal, specialized goods and services are available to the family through membership in a community. Parts of the building process—such as digging a foundation or laying concrete—can be purchased, donated by others, or traded for work done by the family. Tools and equipment—saws, sanders, or concrete mixers—can be borrowed, traded, rented, or purchased.

Freedom to design and build a living unit is limited, not only by family preferences, but by the rights of others in the community. Zoning regulations and local building codes affect the location of the living unit on the land, the selection of construction materials, the size, and the arrangement of rooms. These regulations are enforced by local officials who inspect the plans and the construction for conformity with existing standards. These regulations, however, can be altered by family action. Zoning decisions can be appealed by the individuals, and through group efforts building codes can be changed. Local governments also influence the nature of the housing indirectly through property-tax assessments.

Lending agencies may also influence the building process. If the family needs to borrow money, lending agencies will evaluate both the family's ability to repay the loan and the potential value of the planned unit. If the location seems unsuitable or if the lender believes the cost of the house will be more than its resale value, the money may not be made available, or changes may have to be made in the building's design. Lenders make these decisions because they are responsible for the money provided by other community members.

The availability of goods and services also affects the family's housing decisions. The availability of utilities to a specific location influences the feasibility of construction. Utilities, such as water or electricity, may be secured through family action, such as drilling a well or purchasing an electrical generator. In some states, however, even water rights on personal property may be regulated by law. Telephone service may be unavailable because of equipment shortages or may be costly if the location is remote. Similar shortages of a specific material may require substitutions or delays in the construction process.

Informal community pressures and previous land owners may also affect the construction by imposing specific limitations on land use. These limitations may be enforceable after the sale of the land. Neighbors' comments on colors and material selections during the construction process can affect subsequent decisions made by the family.

This example illustrates only a few family and community interactions. While the interdependence of families restricts some courses of action, it also produces alternatives that would be impossible if each family had to be completely self-sufficient.

The reader may want to consider which responsibilities should be delegated to institutions and which should be retained by individuals and families. In the case of an illness should a person be able to reject treatment because of religious beliefs? Some activities, such as traffic control, education, or land use, are judged to be community, rather than personal, responsibilities. Consideration should also be given to the level of government and specific agency that will be carrying out these responsibilities. What skills and abilities should these decision makers possess if they are to represent the entire community? If a conflict of individual and community rights occurs, how will such conflict be handled? How much impact should funding agencies have on the policies of more specialized groups? How much impact should small, but vocal groups have on the welfare of the entire community? These questions are of importance to home managers because decisions made by communities affect the quality of individual and family life.

QUESTIONS OF COMMUNITY RIGHTS AND RESPONSIBILITIES

As members of society, individuals possess rights and responsibilities that vary with the person's civil, family, and contract status.[1]

Civil Rights

The Constitution and its Amendments list the basic rights of citizens. Because this document is the "supreme law of the land," action taken at all other levels of government should be consistent with this document. Traditional values of privacy and freedom are emphasized in Constitutional rights.

These rights also include obligations, such as paying taxes, supporting the government, serving on juries, and avoiding infringing upon the civil rights of others. If a person does not accept these responsibilities, he or she may, by law, lose civil rights.

Family Status

State more than federal law affects the specific rights and responsibilities occurring with family status. Responsibilities for debts and for financial support, rights to income and ownership, and survivors' rights are among those specified by the state.[2] Because an increasing proportion of society is either too young or too old to work, the responsibilities for financial support of non-working family members is of current concern. If children are financially able to support their parents, should these children or the state do so? If a brother or sister is able, should that person be responsible to provide income for a sibling who is unable to work?

Marriage is a unique form of contract in that it can be broken only by the state. Certain details can be specified in the contract—rights to property and possessions belonging to individuals before marriage. Thus far, the courts have limited, if not invalidated, the rights of individuals to specify in a marriage contract, conditions or consequences for dissolution of a marriage.[3]

Parental rights and responsibilities for children is another special concern because the welfare of these children determines the future of society. For this reason, states have enacted protective legislation for children's welfare. Child-neglect or abuse legislation, for example, is intended to protect the physical and emotional health of minors. Parental duties are also specified in criminal and civil statutes, social service agency regulations, and in court actions. Katz stated that these regulations are based on middle-class standards and have been enforced more with low-income families than with those of middle- or upper-income groups.[4] In situations where parents are not meeting the basic needs of their children, laws and regulations may be oriented toward rehabilitation of the parents, protection of the children, or some combination of the two concerns. In cases where children break the law, these children may have some rights that adults do not, but concern has been expressed that in the legal processes, children may lose Constitutional rights.[5]

Contract

Enforceable by law, *contracts* are written or oral agreements between two or more parties to do or to not do something.[6] Contract law is important to both business and families. Opening a savings account, purchasing health insurance, leasing an apartment, co-signing a loan, or buying toys are examples of exchanges that involve contractual rights and obligations.

To be legally binding, certain contractual standards must be met. Contract law describes, for example, the qualifications of people who can take part in legal contracts. Although partnerships and corporations are valid parties in a contract, people who are insane or intoxicated at the time of making a contract are not legally responsible to fulfill contractual obligations.[7] *Minors,* those under legal age, have limited responsibilities to keep promises made in contracts; and parental obligations for children's contracts vary with the situation. In common law, married women's debts and property belong to their husbands; therefore, women in these states cannot be parties in a contract. Statutes in other states have revised these trends to allow married women to make at least some legal contractual agreements.[8]

There are required standards that must be met in the *offer,* the acceptance, and the items, services, or *basis of exchange*.[9] Written contracts usually seem difficult to read because the specific wording affects the rights and responsibilities of the parties but are more dependable than oral contracts. For these reasons, consumer educators recommend that people read, know, and understand what they sign. All parts of the contract should be filled in before signing, and any oral promises made to the consumer should be added to the contract in writing before signing. Contracts serve to expand and limit individual rights and responsibilities; knowledge of contract law or legal advice can insure fairness in these exchanges.

Laws should encourage people to carry out their responsibilities, but there are limitations in possible legislative or court action. In the case of divorce, for example, courts may assign support payments for children or a former spouse, but these assignments might be difficult to enforce.

Legal rights and responsibilities are based upon civil, family, and contract status; and they vary with the location and time. For this reason, a specific universal list of rights and responsibilities cannot be written. People concerned about the quality of individual and family life may want to study local, state, and national policies and legislation that influence qualities of life. Professionals working with families can have impact on revision or development of policies and legislation to promote the quality of individual and family life.[11]

LIVING IN A CULTURAL MIX

In communities, families live near others whose religious, economic, and cultural backgrounds may differ from their own. Although segregation by social class and race exists, news media, employment, or school attendance promote an awareness of, if not an interaction with, people whose life style is different from that of the family. To function in a community, family standards must be consistent, to some degree, with those of the larger community.[12] If personal or family standards are too different from those of the community, the person or group may be shunned or ostracized. If some family members adopt new standards of which other family members disapprove, internal family conflict can result.

Minority-group families, facing prejudice and discrimination—no matter how subtle it is—have special problems to manage. If a Black or Chinese American parent teaches his or her child pride in cultural heritage but cannot find employment, how will that child feel about community standards and cultural origins? If this child grows up to find the same limited choices, will he or she feel inferior? If people believe that they are inferior, is the stability of their lives minimized? If people are fighting for survival, might they exploit others to survive? Under these circumstances, can crime and family breakdown be frequent problems? If problems result because of unequal opportunity, should these problems be managed by the individual, by the community, or by the entire society?[13]

Should people in a community be responsible for the welfare of friends, neighbors, or others in the community who are strangers to them? From previous discussions, it can be assumed that community decisions and interpersonal actions affect the lives of others who may be ignored in the decision-making process. Should the consequences for these individuals be considered by decision makers? If so, what size of a social group should be considered, and should long range, as well as shorter range consequences be evaluated? If one person's actions harm the lives of others, does the entire community lose some of its potential?

In theory, this concept of mutual or *social responsibility* is a positive notion, but families and communities differ in their application of the concept.[14] In accepting responsibility for the welfare of others, can actions be taken that do not abridge individual rights?

For example, some community groups, because of religious orientation or personal values, are opposed to birth control. If a community finances family planning services, is the community imposing on these people's values? If a community does not finance family-planning services, is the community limiting the rights and the potentials of those who want to limit family size and cannot afford to purchase these services? If families have more children than they can support or bring unwanted children into the world, will the welfare of the children be in jeopardy?

If costs are incurred to promote community welfare, how should support for these services be obtained? Should the contributions be voluntary? Should the costs be equally shared by all tax payers or by only the citizens who use the services? Should those in need be required to accept help or should participation be voluntary? Should the services be provided directly by the community or through existing private agencies? If corrective action—further or better education, income subsidies, health services, or other options—does not have the desired effects or promotes negative consequences, what changes should be made? Answers to questions like these help individuals and families to better understand their views of social responsibilities in community life.

Changes in Family Life

Major changes inevitably occur in the lives of families. Changes made through individual and family choice can be managed, and at least some of the consequences of uncontrollable events, such as death, illness, or unemployment, can also be managed. These events precipitating family change can originate in the larger environment or in the family group.[15]

The adaptations to change can have either positive and exciting or bothersome and negative consequences for people, depending on how the situation is managed. If the negative consequences outweigh the positive, the change is called a *crisis.*

INTERNAL FAMILY CHANGE

Changes in roles or responsibilities of family members warrant adjustments in household management. Death of a marriage partner has long been identified as a major family change, as has divorce or marital separation.[16] Even the changes usually considered positive, such as marriage or pregnancy, necessitate adjustments in family life. Although this discussion of internal family change is not exhaustive, an exploration of some adjustments made because of marriage, birth of a child, disability, divorce, or death should help the reader to consider the application of management concepts to family change.

Family Formation

Marriage brings new relationships and new responsibilities to each partner's life. Relationships with inlaws, patterns of mutual responsibilities, and family goals evolve across time, and each couple finds unique adaptations to these and other changes. The resources brought to a marriage affect these adaptations. Human resources such as judgment, attitudes, empathy, patience, communication skills, and the sharing of material possessions, can be applied to this change. The degree of success in this adaptation and the development of additional resources help to effect future changes.

Children

Pregnancy and the birth of the first child in a family can be considered major changes requiring adjustment in roles and responsibilities. Researchers have identified both positive and negative consequences for first-time parents. In one study, wives generally identified personal—physical and emotional—problems during the first year of parenthood, such as tiredness or frustration with interruptions. However, husbands reported broader problem areas, such as adjustments in the use of time or money. Parents who evaluated this change positively tended to plan for the birth, to be relatively free from other problems, and to demonstrate positive adjustment to marriage. Conceiving a child before marriage, however, was positively related to feelings of crisis. The researcher concluded that parenthood created only minor stress for most respondents, and that the stress was accompanied by rewards. Among the rewards were reduced boredom, pride in the child's development, and increased feelings of family unity.[17]

Disability

Physical or mental *disability* also requires personal and family adaptation. Although limitations accompany disabilities, people also possess capabilities for adaptation that can be developed. Because families mediate between individuals and society, families have impact on success in adaptation.[18]

As children, people develop basic human resources in their family setting. If parents cannot communicate or if their husband-wife relationship is disorganized, the child's development can be hampered. In a study of schizophrenia, for example, researchers observed serious disorganization in patients' families.[19] If the patient is to learn to adapt to life, other family members may also need to change their behavior.

Adaptability is an influential human resource in this management of change. It involves the use of intellectual powers, planning for the future, and the knowledge that personal identity need not be lost in the process of change.[20]

Expectations of accomplishing goals affect how diligently a person will work to reach goals.[21] If a disturbed person believes he or she can adjust to life, the chance of reaching this goal is increased. If a physically disabled person believes he can learn to live an independent life, he will be motivated to learn the needed adaptations. Conversely, fear of failure or negative self-evaluations can inhibit the adaptation process.

People who feel needed are more likely to adapt than those who feel they can contribute nothing to their family or to society. In this adaptation, too much or too little anxiety can interfere. If a person is satisfied to let others take over responsibilities, or if too rapid an adaptation is planned by a disabled person, either the lack of motivation or the resulting anxiety can inhibit learning and adjustment.[22]

Divorce

Marital separation or divorce also involves adjustments in roles and in responsibilities of family members. If children are part of the family group, the adjustments are somewhat different than if the couple is childless; parental responsibilities usually continue even after marital responsibilities have ended.

If community standards oppose divorce as a solution to marital problems, the couple may find adjustment more difficult. If the other partner suggests divorce or if only a short time is allowed for consideration, the likelihood of a crisis is increased. Because clear societal expectations are absent in the relationships between a formerly married couple, personal adjustments are made more difficult.[23]

Adjustments to divorce are both economic and social. To reallocate household work, some skills may need to be learned and others updated because of their nonuse. Extended family and friendship bonds as well as family leadership may be revised in this process of change.

Reductions in household income often accompany divorce.[24] Style of living, including housing and recreation, may need to be adjusted to meet a lowered income. Financial assistance and understanding from extended family may help to make this adjustment workable.

Parents and children can manipulate, rather than manage, the adjustment process. Time with children, for example, can be used as bargaining power to provide adequate income, to continue the attachment, or to cause guilt feelings in the absent parent. Children can also manipulate their divorced parents by bargaining for affection or by being disobedient.[25] Although short-range goals can be reached through manipulation, the longer-ranged consequences might not be pleasant—lack of trust, hurt feelings, and incomplete adjustment to change.

Typically, one parent retains custody of minor children, and the other parent has visiting rights. If the child prefers to live with one parent, this opinion is considered by the courts. Because children's preferences can be based on parental leniency in discipline or a number of other factors, the courts rather than the children, make the decision. These decisions are especially difficult for children who may want to live with both or neither parent.[26]

The nature of a child's adjustment to life with one parent rather than with two also varies with the child's age. Mothering an infant, for example, may be difficult for a parent who is adjusting to divorce. The use of extended family or paid help as a temporary mother substitute can aid in this adjustment.

Older children, however, face the adjustment to less frequent contact with one parent. A preschooler, for example, was overheard to say, ". . . when Daddy lived with us." Because children might feel guilt or blame for the divorce, honest communication between both parents and the children about the divorce has been recommended.[27] Talking about the other parent in a negative way does not improve the family's or the child's adjustment.

Some divorced parents remarry; in fact, general societal expectations are that divorce is a temporary adjustment. Families also face adjustments with remarriage. Among the issues in remarriage are the following: Will the stepparent's role be that of a father or mother, or will it be more like that of an aunt or uncle? If the former spouse has visiting rights, will only that parent spend time with the child; or will the new couple interact with the child? If children need discipline, can either member of the couple provide it, and will one parent support the other's decisions? Will the new marriage partner adopt the child or children? Answers to these questions vary with the people in the situation. There is no universally "best" alternative in adjusting to change in family life.

Death

Although most people recognize that death is inevitable, people fear the limited control they have over the length of their own lives.[28] Scientists have developed medicines, procedures for organ transplants, and other methods to prolong life, and in the process, individuals have had fewer experiences with death of friends or family members. Because of this less frequent exposure, death has been identified in affluent societies as a crisis in family life.

In a case study of 20 dying patients, Cappon concluded that people die as they live. People who held religious beliefs were more accepting of death than those who held no such belief. There was little psychological difference in terminally ill patients in comparison to other ill people. These dying people did not want to continue life as it was; however, most did not want to die.[29]

Death is a phase of life for which people have no previous experience; therefore, what help can professionals, friends, or family offer to the dying person? Cappon recommended that peoply try to listen to the dying—to their thoughts, fears, and memories. He suggested that conversation about death should only be in response to the person's questions.[30]

A sense of loss or *grief* is a normal reaction to the death of a close friend or a family member. Feelings of anger, bitterness, and sorrow can be mixed in grief.[31] Unexpected or untimely death evokes more traumatic feelings of crisis than it does after a long life or an extended illness.[32] People whose personal identities are tied to one relationship can feel a tremendous loss, tension, and feelings of deprivation.[33] Consider the female who has had 15 years of a relatively happy marriage. Her husband's death, after a short illness, leaves her without his financial help, human resources, and companionship. She, alone, is responsible for their children. In such a situation, people may withdraw from others while trying to reorganize their lives. Because a widow or widower's role is more clearly defined in society, financial assistance and other forms of aid may be more readily available to facilitate the adjustment than in the case of divorce.

These changes in the number or capabilities of family members bring with them the need for the family group to adjust. Although professionals can identify alternatives that might be appropriate for the family, each family will seek solutions that will work for its unique situation.

EXTERNAL FAMILY CHANGE

Change in other than the capabilities and number of family members also motivates adjustment in household management. Mobility, for example, brings a family in contact with new people and with differing economic, political, social, and community resources.

Those moving to a new community or wanting to expand their awareness of local resources have access to a variety of sources of information. Community newspapers, telephone directories, local Chambers of Commerce, newcomers' groups, church groups, friends, and neighbors are examples of some of the possible sources of information.

Those planning to move to another community may find it advantageous to subscribe to the future community's newspaper beforehand. The availability and cost of housing and other goods and services can be estimated through attention to advertising. Current activities of community organizations and some issues in local government can be determined through reading news articles, letters to the editor, and editorials. Although all aspects of community resources will not be featured at one time, a subscription to a local newspaper can serve as one introduction to a new community.

The study of a local telephone directory can help community members identify previously unrecognized resources. County, local, state, and federal offices in the community are listed in the white pages under the name of the government level. Nonprofit organizations that have telephones will also be listed in the white pages. Advertising in the yellow pages lists businesses alphabetically by the types of goods or services produced or distributed. Hours of church services, libraries, and other organizations may also be included.

Chambers of Commerce and other local groups may have printed information on local businesses, climate, schools, and other community services. Although this information is written with a positive bias, it is another source of knowledge about community resources. Membership in community organizations and informal contact with community members can also alert families to available resources.

Knowledge of these resources may not lead to their immediate use, because some resources are infrequently used; others have eligibility requirements, while still others may require fees not currently available. The important skill is to know how to find community resources when they are needed for goal-attainment.

Some of these resources are *publically supported* through tax dollars or voluntary contributions; others are privately owned. Some public resources are used by only a part of the community, but the presence and quality of these resources affect the qualities of community life. Libraries, museums, theaters, and parks may not interest all citizens, but many are owned by the community. Roads, community lighting, police and fire departments, schools, or medical services can be provided by the family or the neighborhood but are often provided or supported by local, state, or national government.

Public ownership permits these resources to be used by many individuals and families. Public libraries, for example, allow a number of people access to the same publication. This shared use of resources reduces the cost per use, in comparison to private ownership. Communities also provide some goods and services to families who cannot do so for themselves; food stamp programs, income or housing subsidies, and health-care services are examples. To utilize some of these services, individuals and families must prove that they meet eligibility requirements. Other services are available to the entire community, but the cost to the individual may vary with the person's financial status. The quality and quantity of community services, whether publicly or privately provided, affect the quality of individual and family life.

A new job, unemployment, increases or decreases in work hours, a court appearance, or any change in the location, methods, or duration of a person's activities can lead to adjustments in household management. The next section of the chapter explores general guidelines for the management of change.

Managing Change

Change is part of life; without it growth is prevented. However, most people fear new experiences, ideas, or activities. In managing, people can direct the change positively and at a realistic pace, while minimizing the negative consequences of events that are not completely controllable.[34]

IMPACT OF ATTITUDES

Although some people fear change, others consider it an opportunity, a new challenge to be mastered. There are always risks in making change; but its complete absence is stagnation, not stability. For example, the success of a change of employment depends, in part, on the attitude of the new employee.

If the person is afraid to make a mistake, how willing will he or she be to implement a new procedure, to use a new type of equipment, or to develop a new skill? If the employee considers the new job to be a positive challenge, problems may arise, but they can be handled without the immobilizing fear of failure.

The important attitudinal concept is the ability to separate realistic from unrealistic fears. A person who wants to repair a television set but knows nothing about working with high voltage electricity faces a realistic fear for personal safety. However, a person who wants to learn a new craft or sport but is afraid of not doing it well enough may want to evaluate the importance or validity of this fear. Parents naturally fear for their children's future life and safety, but excessive fear can cause parents to inhibit their children's growth producing experiences and to transfer this fear of new experience to the children.

ANTICIPATING CHANGE

People who recognize the possibility of a specific change occurring at some time in the future can prepare for it. Those who are surprised by change may panic or cause themselves additional problems. As stated earlier in the chapter, adjustment to divorce, the death of a friend or family member, or the birth of a child is less of a crisis if the event is anticipated by those in the situation. Knowledge of a potential change such as an impending lay-off, a possible shortage of materials, or the marriage of a son or daughter helps to manage both desirable and less desirable outcomes and consequences of the change.

PACE OF CHANGE

People can control the pace of some changes in their lives. Studies have indicated that the pace of change is related to physical health. Too much change in a one-year period can be associated with a high chance of illness during the next two years.[35]

If a family has had a baby, moved to a new living unit, experienced decreased income, and a family member is simultaneously considering a change of employment, the pace of change can be slowed by not accepting the new job. If the new employment is evaluated to be an exciting opportunity, can the family cope with the additional change? Although some physical illness can be related to a fast pace of change, should people postpone desired activities because they might get sick? The amount of risk people are willing to take will influence individual answers to this question.

FINDING STABILITY

Toffler recommends that people identify points or zones of stability in their lives—aspects of life that will remain constant.[36] These zones of stability are familiar objects or relationships that a person can depend on even though many other aspects of life change. A specific car, a style of clothing, family relationships, a specific job, a living unit, religious tradition, or patterned use of time are examples of objects or relationships that can be retained in the face of constant change. These stability zones differ for each person but can provide continuity in change.

GROUP MEMBERSHIP

Social interaction with those who are making or have made similar adjustments can help to identify alternatives and to implement change. Organizations such as Weight Watchers, Alcoholics Anonymous, Newcomers' Clubs, Parents without Partners, or Crisis Centers are based on the idea that people can help others to make a successful transition to a new situation or way of life. The moral support, information, and feelings of others can facilitate adaptation that an individual might not be able to control completely. Peer pressure can stimulate motivation to alter habits that are undesirable but difficult to change.

SELECTIVE USE

With technological change such as the introduction of television, computers, or medical advances, limited or selective use is also a possible way to manage change. Although some people might condemn technology because it brings about some undesirable repercussions, individuals can be selective in their uses of the products, equipment, or services and, therefore, minimize the undesirable results.

For example, must a person continue to watch a television program that he or she dislikes? Letters of complaint or, if the program is good, compliments to the station or network are part of a citizen's rights and responsibilities. People who consider their goals, values, and standards when selecting television programs will be more satisfied with their viewing than will those who watch indiscriminantly and then complain about time waste.

Similarly, recent Congressional hearings have investigated the impact of computerized information on individual rights to privacy.[37] People are beginning to question the kinds of information that should be gathered and the limitations that should be imposed on access to this data. Questions related to the use of technological innovations help people to consider the results and consequences of the specific changes.

Advances in medical technology have brought about unexpected legal and moral questions. For example, should doctors prolong the life of a person who is no longer responsible for his actions, no longer able to take care of himself, to communicate, or to move? If this action will put other family members into severe debt, should death be postponed? The legal answer is usually "yes," but what should the moral answer be?

If a couple can only have children through artificial insemination and decide to do so, would that child be stigmatized by the courts as illegitimate? If science was able to control genetic factors, who has the right to decide the amount and kinds of intelligence that should be given to unborn children? Would parents decide? Would a panel of peers or professionals make such a decision? The question of the uses to be made of technological innovations are truly important to the quality of personal and family life as well as to the general society.

These guidelines for the management of change can alert the reader to adaptations possible in a variety of situations. Personal characteristics helpful to such management include courage to be current, honest self-evaluation, a problem solving attitude, recognition of the need for change, and awareness of goals.[38] These personal awareness characteristics can lead to evaluation of the meaning of proposed change. Although some changes can lead to an improvement in the quality of personal or family life, other changes can decrease quality of life and these should be avoided.

Professionals as Agents of Change

Professionals working with individuals and families promote and support change in the lives of clients, patients, or students. Social workers, authors, teachers, interior decorators, extension agents, counselors, ministers, nutritionists, and others working with families all advocate change.

CHARACTERISTICS OF THE PROFESSIONAL

Research has identifed characteristics of a successful agent of change. They influence the likelihood of success in promoting change. Awareness of the following characteristics can aid change agents in reaching their goals.

Goals

If goals of the professional and the client population are similar, the change agent is likely to influence behavior in the desired way.[39] Students, families, or community members who recognize that the professional's knowledge and skills can benefit their lives will be more able to accept help. If the professional is insensitive to the goals of those in the community, even his practical, easily understood information may not be trusted.

Communication

Professionals who communicate frequently with client populations are more likely to promote change than those who do not.[40] Communication can lead to mutual acceptance, can create a climate for growth, and can promote empathy.[41] An extension agent, teacher, or dietician who fulfills a responsible role in community life will be sensitive to community interests and needs and will be known and respected by other community members.

Patience

Patience is another characteristic of a successful change agent.[42] People accept new ideas at their own pace.[43] Community leaders, for example, may need to be convinced of the value of parent education or day care for the elderly before the remainder of the community will support such a program.

CHARACTERISTICS OF THE CHANGE

In addition to the human characteristics of the change agent, the specific features of the change influence its acceptance. Change that is easily understood, can be experimented with on a limited basis, and achieves observable and measurable results is more likely to be accepted than that which lacks these characteristics.[44]

Difficulty

An idea, plan, or proposed innovation that is easily understood is more appealing than a complex change. Also, if the people can appreciate the worth of the change for their lives, it will be more easily implemented. Products, for example, that are difficult to store or use may not be as easily introduced as those that are more convenient.

If a consumer can appreciate the personal worth of comparative shopping for an expensive household appliance, that consumer will be more willing to seek information about the specific appliance. If the information is presented in an understandable format and if unfamiliar terms are explained, the information will be more easily used than will an extremely technical, publication.

Experimentation

Change that can be experimented with is more easily accepted than is permanent change. A person who wants to complete a high school equivalency program, to obtain further education, or to return to work may be more willing to do so on a part-time, rather than full-time basis. Success in the part-time activity may or may not lead to full-time acceptance of the new role. However, risk of failure is not as great in a limited trial as it is in a full-time commitment.

Measurability

Change that leads to observable, desired results is more quickly accepted than that which does not lead to improvement or which results in negative repercussions. People in one community, for example, established a telephone referral service for senior citizens needing help. Although the idea was exciting, most of the callers did not receive the requested help, so the number of calls decreased and the program was disbanded. The problem in this situation was the lack of measurable, desired results. Changes in personal satisfaction, attitudes, feelings of self respect, or other changes in human resources are not as easily measurable by an outsider; but does this fact lessen the importance of these changes?

Timeliness

If positive results occur rapidly, people will be more motivated toward a change than if the results are expected to occur at an indefinite future time. If a person can quickly modify a habit or develop a skill through participation in a program, he or she will be motivated by the timely results. If, however, a person calls a professional to seek some information but is told that it will take at least a month to get the material, the person may become discouraged.

Alternatives that are workable in one situation may not apply to another. Because each person's and family's life is unique, knowledge of the managerial concepts can guide people to develop their own workable adaptations to change. Professionals can sensitize their clients, patients, coworkers, or students to potential changes, to possible outcomes or consequences, and to feasible alternatives for managing the change. The specific course of action however, can only be selected and implemented by the individual or family. Professionals who offer only one alternative while recognizing other equally workable ones may be simplifying their work but deprive their clients of choice—of the right to decide for themselves. Although clients, patients, students, coworkers, or friends may want and need assistance, they also need to decide about their own future.

Summary

This chapter has focused on management in a changing world. The interaction of individual and community rights and responsibilities was explored. Widely available sources of information about community resources were discussed. Some research findings on adaptations made by families to internal family change were summarized. Guidelines for managing change and guiding others through it were outlined. People who understand management and apply the concepts to their lives will anticipate and meet the challenges of life in a changing world. Unpredictable events may alter people's lives, but application of the managerial concepts helps to deal constructively with the risks and fears associated with change.

References

1. Kirk, H., *The Family in the American Economy,* University of Chicago, Chicago, Ill., (1953), p. 15.

2. Creamer, J. S., *A Citizen's Guide to Legal Rights,* Holt, Rinehart & Winston, New York, (1971).

3. Clark, H. H., *The Law of Domestic Relations in the United States,* West, St. Paul, Minn., (1968), pp. 28–31.

4. Katz, S. N., *When Parents Fail: The Law's Response to Family Breakdowns,* Beacon, Boston, Mass., (1971), p. 42.

5. Creamer, J. S., *op. cit.,* pp. 267–275.

6. Farmer, R. A., *et. al., What You Should Know About Contracts,* Arco, New York, (1969), p. 9.

7. *Ibid.,* pp. 17, 24–25.

8. *Ibid.,* pp. 22–24.

9. *Ibid.,* pp. 37–55.

10. Brandwein, R. A., Brown, C. A., and Fox, E. M., "Women and Children Last: The Social Situation of Divorced Mothers and Their Families." *Journal of Marriage and the Family, 36:*3 (August 1974), p. 501.

11. Morse, R. L. D., "The Lengthening Distance Between the Haves and the Have–Nots," *Journal of Home Economics, 59:*8 (October 1967), pp. 636–640; Marshall, W. H., "Home Economists and Legislation Affecting Families," *Journal of Home Economics, 59:*8 (October 1967), pp. 641–643.

12. Le Masters, E. E., *Parents in Modern America,* Dorsey, Homewood, Ill., (1970), p. 206.

13. *Report of the National Advisory Commission on Civil Disorders,* Bantam, New York, (1968).

14. Augenstein, L. G., "Social Responsibility," *Journal of Home Economics, 59:*8 (October 1967), pp. 629–635.

15. Glasser, P. H., and Glasser L. N., (ed.), *Families in Crisis,* Harper & Row, New York, (1970), p. 6.

16. Lidz, T., *The Family and Human Adaptation,* International Universities, New York, (1963), p. 4.

17. Russell, C. S., "Transition to Parenthood: Problems and Gratification, *Journal of Marriage and the Family, 36:*2 (May 1974), pp. 294–301.

18. Lidz, T., *op. cit.*

19. *Ibid.,* p. 39–78.

20. McDaniel, J. W., *Physical Disabilities and Human Behavior,* Pergamon, New York, (1969), pp. 137–167.

21. *Ibid.*

22. *Ibid.*

23. Rose, V. L., and Price–Bonham, S., "Divorce Adjustment: A Woman's Problem?" *The Family Coordinator, 22:*3 (July 1973), pp. 291–297.

24. Brandwein, R. A., Brown, C. A., and Fox, E. M., *op. cit.,* pp. 498–515.

25. Stuart, I. R., and Abel, L. E., (ed.), *Children of Separation and Divorce,* Grossman, New York, (1972), pp. 13–15.

26. Golomb, I. L., "The Scope of Legal Responsibility," in Stuart, I. R., and Abt, L. E., *op. cit.,* pp. 56–61.

27. *Ibid.,* p. 23.

28. Chadwick, M., "Notes Upon the Fear of Death," in Ruitenbeck, H. M., (ed.), *Death: Interpretations,* Delta, New York, (1969).

29. Cappon, D., "The Psychology of Dying," in Ruitenbeck, H. M., *op. cit.,* pp. 61–72.

30. *Ibid.*

31. Becker, H., "The Sorrow of Bereavement," in Ruitenbeck, H. M., *op. cit.,* p. 210.

32. Leheman, S. R., "Reactions to Untimely Death," in Ruitenbeck, H. M., *op. cit.,* pp. 231–233.

33. Putney, S. and Putney, G. J., *The Adjusted American: Normal Neuroses in the Individual and Society,* Harper & Row, New York, (1964), pp. 104–105.

34. Rockefeller, J. D., *The Second American Revolution,* Harper & Row, New York, (1973), p. 4.

35. Wolfe, S. W., "Avoid Sickness—How Life Changes Affect Your Health," *Family Circle,* (May 1972), pp. 30, 166–170.

36. Toffler, A., *Future Shock,* Harper & Row, New York, (1971).

37. *Federal Data Banks, Computers and the Bill of Rights,* Hearings before Senate Subcommittee on Constitutional Rights, 92nd Congress, 1st Session, (February 23–March 17, 1971), U.S. Government Printing Office, Washington, D.C., (1971).

38. Hall, O. A., "Facilitating Change," *The Adventure of Change: Selected Speeches from the 57th Annual Meeting,* American Home Economics Association, Washington, D.C., (1966), pp. 32–36.

39. Nielson, J., *The Change Agent and the Process of Change,* Michigan Agricultural Experiment Station, Research Bulletin 17, (1967), p. 69.

40. Rogers, E. M., with Shoemaker, F. F., *Communication of Innovations: A Cross-Cultural Approach,* Free Press, New York, (1971), p. 234.

41. Hall, O. A., *op. cit.,* pp. 37–38.

42. *Ibid.,* p. 39.

43. Rogers, E. M., with Shoemaker, F. F., *op. cit.,* p. 175.

44. *Ibid.,* p. 22.

15

MANAGING CHANGE

The story of processionary caterpillars has gone the rounds of management circles for so long that the origin of the story has been lost, but it is said to be true . . .

Processionary caterpillars feed on pine needles. They move through the pine trees in long processions with one caterpillar leading and all the rest following, each with eyes half closed and head snugly fitted against the rear extremity of the predecessor.

Jean-Henri Fabre, the French naturalist, became interested in the unusual habits of these creatures. After patiently experimenting with a group of processionary caterpillars, Fabre finally enticed them to the rim of a large flowerpot where he succeeded in getting the first one connected with the last one. They formed a complete circle that started moving around in a procession with neither beginning nor end.

The naturalist expected that they would get tired of their useless march and begin a new direction. After all, they had to eat and an ample supply of their favorite food filled the center of the pot, was close at hand and plainly visible, but outside the range of the circle.

Yet, alas, through sheer force of habit, the living, creeping circle kept moving around the rim of the pot . . . around and around, keeping the same relentless pace for seven days and seven nights . . . and would have continued had it not been for sheer exhaustion and ultimate starvation. The caterpillars were blindly following instinct, habit, tradition, past experience, or standard practice, unaware of a life or death crisis. Habitual activity was stronger than starvation to these caterpillars. They meant well, but they got no place! They made no decisions for themselves, set no goals, had no interaction with the environment beyond the immediate path of movement, and used no resources except those required for constant activity.

Are there people whose lives have become like those of Fabre's processionary caterpillars? Activity is not progress and does not necessarily lead to change. Management may occur to some degree in daily lives, but the big questions are, "What is the quality of the management activities, and are these processes helping people reach the life they desire?" If the need for change is ignored, will crisis become the consequence? Fabre's processionary caterpillars had so much "order" in their lives that they died from lack of direction in change.

This chapter identifies five social situations that could create crises if change were not managed effectively and explores avenues for change through management. Case vignettes and readings are utilized as decision-making experiences for individual thought or group discussion.

Crisis or Change?

During a lifetime each individual and each family faces a number of stress situations and will inevitably face at least one of the four main types of crises. Ignoring change signals is some people's method of handling impending crises. Others approach changes aggresively and cause them to occur in accordance with planned outcomes. Some use crisis situations as an opportunity for improving their quality of living. An individual's mobility for improved job opportunity may be such an opportunity.

The fact that one out of every five persons in the U.S. moves in a given year would indicate that, if even half of these moves are to improve a job, housing conditions, social relations, or environmental satisfaction, many thousands of people have learned to utilize mobility as a positive way of managing dissatisfying situations. This management uses change for personal improvement, but are there changes one person can design to improve a society's quality of living?

Some impending crises and stress situations are the result of internal conflict; others result from social trends that alter a person's chosen pattern of living, endanger health, or threaten the mental balance and stability of family life. When Lederer and Burdick wrote *The Ugly American,* they provided an example of how one woman, Emma Atkins, could change an ageless cultural pattern that was causing great pain to the old people of Chang 'Dong.[1] As you read the following story, notice the subtlety of the change, the lack of force, and the patience to find the acceptable avenue toward change for the people of Chang 'Dong.

THE BENT BACKS OF CHANG 'DONG

Emma Atkins was a simple and straightforward person. She was not a busybody; but she had learned that when she wanted to know something the best way to find out was to ask a direct question. She had been in Chang 'Dong only two weeks when she asked an unanswerable question.

She was working in her kitchen with two of her Sarkhanese neighbors, trying to make a small guava which grew in the jungle into a jam. The glowing charcoal stove and the sweet aroma of the bubbling fruit gave the kitchen a cozy and homey atmosphere. Emma felt good. She had just finished telling her neighbors about how a kitchen was equipped in America; then through the open window, she saw an old lady of Chang 'Dong hobble by, and the question flashed across her mind. She turned to the two women and spoke slowly, for the Sarkhanese language was new to her.

"Why is it that all the old people of Chang 'Dong are bent over?" Emma asked. "Every older person I have seen is bent over and walks as if his back is hurting."

The two neighbor women shrugged.

"It is just that old people become bent," one of them answered. "That's the natural thing which happens to older people."

Emma was not satisfied, but she did not pursue the problem any further then. Instead, she kept her eyes open. By the time the rainy season was over, she had observed that every person over sixty in the village walked with a perpetual stoop. And from the way they grimaced when they had to hurry, she realized that the stoop was extremely painful. The older people accepted their backaches as their fate, and when Emma asked them why they walked bent over, they only smiled.

Three weeks after the monsoon ended, the older people in the village began to sweep out their own homes, the paths leading from their houses to the road, and finally the road itself. This sweeping was inevitably done by older people. They used a broom made of palm fronds. It had a short handle, maybe two feet long, and naturally they bent over as they swept.

One day, as Emma was watching the wrinkled and stooped woman from the next house sweep the road, things fell into place. She went out to talk to the woman.

"Grandmother, I know why your back is twisted forward," she said. "It's because you do so much sweeping bent over that short broom. Sweeping in that position several hours a day gradually moulds you into a bent position. When people become old their muscles and bones are not as flexible as when they were young."

"Wife of the engineer, I do not think it is so," the old lady answered softly. "The old people of Southern Sarkhan have always had bent backs."

"Yes, and I'll bet that they all got them from sweeping several

hours a day with a short-handled broom," Emma said. "Why don't you put a long handle on the broom and see how it works?"

However, Emma found that it was difficult to get longer handles. Wood of any kind was scarce in that area, and expensive. The handles the Sarkhanese used for their brooms came from a reed with a short strong stem about two feet long. For centuries this reed had been used; and, centuries ago people had given up looking for anything better. It was traditional for brooms to have short handles, and for the brooms to be used exclusively by people too old to work in the rice fields. But Emma wasn't bound by centuries of tradition, and she began to look for a substitute for the short broom handle.

It would have been simple, of course, to have imported wooden poles, but long ago Homer had taught her that only things that people did for themselves would really change their behavior. With midwestern practicality, Emma set about researching her problem. It was

The old woman looked puzzled. Emma realized that in her excitement she had spoken in English. She put the question to the woman in Sarkhanese.

"Brooms are not meant to have long handles," the old lady said matter-of-factly. "It has never been that way. I have never seen a broom with a long handle, and even if the wood were available, I do not think we would waste it on long handles for brooms. Wood is a very scarce thing in Chang 'Dong."

Emma knew when to drop a conversation. She had long ago discovered that people don't stop doing traditional things merely because they're irrational. She also knew that when people are criticized for an action, they stubbornly persist in continuing it. That evening Emma had to talk with Homer.

"Homer, have you noticed the bent backs of the old people in this village?" Emma asked.

"Nope, I haven't," Homer said, washing down a bowl of rice with a bottle of beer. "But if you say they're bent, I'll believe it. What about it?"

"Well, just don't say 'what about it'," Emma said angrily. "I'm getting to the age where when my bones get stiff, it hurts. Imagine the agony those old people go through with their backs perpetually bent. It's worse than lumbago. I've asked them, and they tell me it's excruciating."

"All right, all right, Emma," Atkins said. "What are we going to do about it?"

"Well, the first thing we're going to do is get longer broom handles," Emma said with heat.

a frustrating task. She tried to join several of the short reeds together to make a long broomstick. This failed. Every kind of local material she used to try to lengthen the broomstick handles failed.

Emma refused to be defeated. She widened the scope of her search, until one day she found what she was after. She was driving the jeep down a steep mountain road about forty miles from Chang 'Dong. Suddenly she jammed on the brakes. Lining one side of the road for perhaps twenty feet was a reed very similar to the short reed that grew in Chang 'Dong—except that this reed had a strong stalk that rose five feet into the air before it thinned out.

"Homer," she ordered her husband, "climb out and dig me up a half-dozen of those reeds. But don't disturb the roots."

When she got back to Chang 'Dong, she planted the reeds beside her house and tended them carefully. Then, one day, when several of her neighbors were in her house she casually cut a tall reed, bound the usual coconut fronds to it, and began to sweep. The women were aware that something was unusual, but for several minutes they could not figure out what was wrong. Then one of the women spoke.

"She sweeps with her back straight," the woman said in surprise. "I have never seen such a thing."

Emma did not say a word. She continued to sweep right past them, out on the front porch, and then down the walk. The dust and debris flew in clouds; and everyone watching was aware of the greater efficiency of being able to sweep while standing up.

Emma, having finished her sweeping, returned to her house and began to prepare tea for her guests. She did not speak to them about the broom, but when they left, it was on the front porch, and all of her guests eyed it carefully as they departed.

The next day when Emma swept off her porch, there were three old grandmothers who watched from a distance. When she was finished Emma leaned her long-handled broom against the clump of reeds which she had brought down from the hills. The lesson was clear.

The next day, perhaps ten older people, including a number of men, watched Emma as she swept. This time, when she was finished, an old man, his back bent so that he scurried with a crab-like motion, came over to Emma.

"Wife of the engineer, I would like to know where I might get a broom handle like the one you have," the man said. "I am not sure that our shorthandled brooms have bent our backs like this but I am sure that your way of sweeping is a more powerful way."

Emma told him to help himself to one of the reeds growing beside the house. The old man hesitated.

"I will take one and thank you; but if I take one, others may also ask, and soon your reeds will be gone."

"It is nothing to worry about, old man," Emma said. "There are many such reeds in the hills. I found these by the stream at Nanghsa. Your people could walk up there and bring back as many as the village could use in a year on the back of one water buffalo." The old man did not cut one of Emma's reeds. Instead he turned and hurried back to the group of older people. They talked rapidly, and several hours later Emma saw them heading for the hills with a water buffalo in front of them.

Soon after, Homer completed his work in Chang 'Dong, and they moved to Rhotok, a small village about seventy miles to the east. And it was not until four years later, when Emma was back in Pittsburgh, that she learned the final results of her broomhandle project. One day she got a letter in a large handsome yellow-bamboo paper envelope. Inside, written in an exquisite script, was a letter from the headman of Chang 'Dong.

Wife of the engineer:

I am writing you to thank you for a thing that you did for the old people of Chang 'Dong. For many centuries, longer than any man can remember, we have always had old people with bent backs in this village. And in every village that we know of the old people have always had bent backs.

We had always thought this was a part of growing old, and it was one of the reasons that we dreaded old age. But, wife of the engineer, you have changed all that. By the lucky accident of your long-handled broom you showed us a new way to sweep. It is a small thing, but it has changed the lives of our old people. For four years, ever since you have left, we have been using the long reeds for broom handles. You will be happy to know that today there are few bent backs in the village of Chang 'Dong. Today the backs of our old people are straight and firm. No longer are their bodies painful during the months of the monsoon.

This is a small thing, I know, but for our people it is an important thing.

I know you are not of our religion, wife of the engineer, but perhaps you will be pleased to know that on the outskirts of the village we have constructed a small shrine in your memory. It is a simple affair; at the foot of the altar are these words: "In memory of the woman who unbent the backs of our people." And in front of the shrine there is a stack of the old short reeds which we used to use.

Again, wife of the engineer, we thank you and we think of you.
"*What does he mean, 'lucky accident'?*" *Emma said to Homer.*
"*Why I looked all over for three months before I found those long
reeds. That was no accident.*"
*Homer did not look up at her from the letter. He knew that the in-
dignation in her voice was false. He knew that if he looked now he
would see tears glittering in the corners of her eyes. He waited a
decent amount of time; when he raised his head she was just pushing
her handkerchief back into the pocket of her apron.*[2]

Crisis or Creative Opportunity?

Crises affect people in different ways. What one family defines as a crisis may
not be recognized by another as a serious problem. The definition of a crisis
depends not only on the nature of the problem, but on the values and
management practices of the affected group. Any negative situation for which
a person's resources and usual pattern of living are inadequate could be
considered a crisis. A crisis is, thus, any major change in which the negative
consequences outweigh the positive ones.

According to the nature of the problem, crises may be classified as those
resulting from: *dismemberment* (loss of a member of the group), *demoralization* (loss of status and self esteem), *accession* (the addition of a member), or
deterioration (degeneration of character, values, or environment).[3] Identifying
the kind of trouble that is to be confronted can help families manage the
crisis. Such theoretical classifications sometimes help people view their crises
with greater clarity and achieve workable solutions.[4]

Skills needed to handle a crisis vary with the following factors: planning;
the crisis situation; the pace of change; previous experience in dealing with
crisis-level problems; attitude toward the problem's magnitude; number of supportive relatives, neighbors, and friends; social expectations of peers; community and family customs; and the personal maturity and resourcefulness of
the persons involved.[5]

Sudden crises have been known to be unifying factors in family relations.
Slow, degenerative changes are often more demoralizing to family relationships than unexpected disasters.

Most family researchers agree that the well-organized family or individual
has defined goals and is steadily working toward them. Those whose management practices are stable are more likely to survive crises successfully and
respond more rapidly. A person's success at handling a crisis depends on the
resources he has developed and how he plans to use them.

The word "crisis" comes from a Greek word meaning "decisiveness," or "point of decision." Maltz calls crisis a fork in the road where one fork leads to a more positive condition, the other path leads to a worse condition.[6] A medical crisis is a turning point where a person either gets better and lives, or gets worse and dies. It may not always be that easy to label crisis level alternatives. In a personal crisis, however, an individual's happiness and welfare may hang in balance, and he may survive the crisis, scarred but strong; or he may be emotionally and physically defeated by the experience. A crisis can either make or break a person; it can provide bursts of strength, power, and wisdom not ordinarily possible, or it can completely overwhelm a person. The difference may not be in the person's personality trait but is sometimes in the way a person learns to react to crisis. This is management—exercising control mechanisms. Reaction to crisis situations may be taught and learned, as in fire drills that teach people how to react and where to exit in case of fire.

The process of learning to react to crisis is outlined by Maltz as: (1) learn related skills and processes during relaxed periods, (2) practice without pressure, (3) react positively and agressively, rather than defensively, to crisis, (4) evaluate crisis situations realistically.[7] The effective course is not to make mountains out of molehills, nor is it to ignore the situation until it is beyond the person's control.

The way a person survives a mistake, rather than the number of mistakes, is the true measure of a manager. Crisis recovery is similar. Cavan identifies a number of indicators of successful recovery from a crisis. Among them are: acceptance of the situational elements that are clearly beyond control with a minimum of self-deception or self-pity, relaxation of tensions, and a return to close to normal "living" patterns, ability to use one's experiences as fully as before the crisis, understanding one's feelings, and reorganizing economic and social life.[8]

Typical crises that families and individuals face were discussed in Chapter 14. A few examples are: death (a dismemberment type), unemployment (deterioration), marriage (accession), divorce (demoralization) and illegitimacy (a combination of demoralization and accession). These are internal crises that must be faced by individuals within a family group. But there are many crises that are faced collectively by societies because these crises are broad in scope, impinge on the environment, and are interpreted in different ways by different people. They effect family life but are beyond the control of any one family.

Change, the Control Mechanism

Change is often the solution to crisis. It is the result of management—the process of sensing problems and making successful steps into the unknown, getting away from the processionary track, breaking the mold, and finding satisfying solutions or compromises to crises and stress situations. Change can produce a satisfying life and build constructive order out of chaos.

Management is the vehicle of change that provides access to meeting the needs of the situation and people. Management can facilitate solution of crisis-level internal family problems, and it can resolve contemporary stress situations that threaten to, if they have not already, become crises. Changing values, family upheaval, resource abuse, world food shortages, role reidentification, and economic uncertainty are but a few of these external changes that must be resolved if life is to have future quality and direction.

CHANGING VALUES

In previous chapters it has been pointed out that values are those deep convictions that establish direction for action and cause choices among alternatives. Much of the needed adjustment in marriage is due to a combination of values and preconceived role expectations about marital and family life. Managerial values are clearly visible in the following *Changing Times* article, "What Does She Do All Day?"[9]

These are normal people with everyday living problems, joys, and satisfactions. These vignettes represent typical activities of many women and the people who share their lives at various stages of the family life cycle. As you read the vignettes, consider the following questions as exercises for decision making.

The lives of the homemakers reveal a great deal about the values of each family. Which values are common among all three families? Most people have an individual way of putting their values together into a hierarchy-order. Do the women's values appear in the same order of importance? Which ones are reversed?

To some people, management means order as a form of control. What control mechanisms could be introduced into the lives of each wife? Would your recommendations be compatible with the values that seem evident in each family?

People differ in their ability to handle crises, but surviving a crisis may depend as much on the kind of help a person gets as on inner strength of character. The kind of help people need during a crisis includes: assistance with daily tasks, avoidance of false assurances, help in confronting the crisis, elimination of blame, encouragement to seek and accept help, and guidance in finding facts.[10] Using each family setting as a case situation, introduce a demoralizing crisis (such as alcoholism, drug abuse, or infidelity) into each family setting. Which family would be most disrupted by this type of crisis? What personal characteristics of the wife would cause the other families to weather the crisis more effectively? Which families would be more likely to receive useful help from others in facing a demoralizing crisis?

Which of the families would be most disrupted by a dismemberment crisis (untimely death or serious injury of a family member)? What management qualities would tend to hold the family together and cushion them against such a crisis? Maltz said that crisis management could be learned through the four steps outlined earlier (p. 428). How might any one of the families described use the four steps to practice crisis management?

What Does She Do All Day?

Even the nicest and most understanding, most admiring husband asks the question now and then. Not out of rancor, mind you, but in honest wonder. She has an automatic washer and dryer, doesn't she? The oven turns itself off. It doesn't take that long to make a few beds and wash the dishes. What in the world does she do all day?

Wives, on the other hand, are seldom in doubt about what he does all day. For example: "Men have an easier time of it than women. They go to the office every day. They have coffee breaks and talk to people and meet well-dressed women who get their hair done at the beauty shop. They send out for doughnuts and eat their lunch out, while their poor wives ..."

While their poor wives what?

A harassed, overworked, pressured, happy mother-of-five submitted this appraisal to Changing Times. *She wrote it on a day when the washer sprang a leak, a disembodied rabbit head appeared in the backyard and two strange children took up occupancy of her bedroom. That's the kind of day that makes any wife and mother feel unpaid, unsung, unappreciated and on the short end of the matrimonial contract.*

She is one of three wives who were invited to explain—in detail— what they do all day. The objective: to enlighten the men and reassure the ladies by revealing the unvarnished truth about those pleasant, leisurely hours a husband's fantasy tells him SHE is enjoying while HE keeps nose to grindstone and shoulder to wheel.

Meet the Girls

Two problems appeared at the outset. No woman, thank heaven, is the same as any other woman—therefore, no woman's day can be exactly the same as her sisters'. Nor is each day (despite claims to the contrary) like every other day. The task was to strike a norm, or as close to a norm as possible.

The editors attacked the first problem by concluding that there are three stages in the life of most married women, and securing a volunteer for each stage, all very real and very willing to keep a record of a typical day provided anonymity was preserved.

First stage—the early years, *without children, without house. Just an apartment and a husband to worry over.*

Representing this stage is Anne, in her late twenties. She lives in a middle-sized Virginia city, where her husband has a government job. She has been married just over a year, lives in a one-bedroom apartment and does her own cooking, cleaning, laundry and other chores.

Her comment, after keeping a minute-by-minute diary of one day at home:

"Before this exercise, I would have ended my day with a nagging sense of chores undone and time wasted. At last I am a free woman! Not only do I no longer feel guilty, but am overwhelmed with a sense of accomplishment! Have doubled my respect for the mothers of America—how in the world do they do it?"

Second stage—the middle years, *with children, house and husband.*

The mothers-in-midstream have as their spokeswoman the afore-mentioned mother-of-five, whom we shall call Ellen. A piano teacher in spare minutes, she lives in a dignified shambles of a house (7 rooms, 2½ baths), on a tree-lined, big-city street in the Midwest with her artist–husband. He has a studio at home and is in and out of the house during the day.

In addition to the four children at home, there are two large dogs, one small dog and one cat. The two large dogs spend much of their time outside. The small dog is strictly a homebody. So is the cat. The children—girl of 9 and boys of 12, 14 and 17—go to public school. The oldest boy, age 22, lives a few blocks away with his wife and year-old son.

Ellen is in her forties, has been wed 24 years.

After a day eventful enough to shatter the equanimity of the strongest of men, she wrote:

"I don't want my life different. Years ago I studied the piano and practiced 6 hours a day and loved it. I was ambitious, anxious and stupid, so I would not want to relive that. I have a husband, kids, a dress, dogs, cat, car of my own, two pianos and my cup runneth over . . ."

Third stage—the later years, *with children gone from the nest and only a husband to care for.*

Enjoying her dessert years is Sylvia, a young grandmother, married to a corporation official who commutes daily from their New Jersey home. She has three married daughters, none of them living close by, three grandchildren (3, 1½ and 3 months) and two dogs. Her home is a big, comfortable house remodeled from an old stable, with flower and vegetable gardens.

"I can truthfully say this is the best period of married life," she says. "You miss your children and become nostalgic at times, but you also have a feeling of accomplishment and satisfaction that they are independent... I can remember contemplating this phase of my life with quite some trepdiation but now, though I would not trade the earlier years for anything, I can only say I hope this lasts forever."

Anne, Ellen and Sylvia agreed to keep a simple minute-by-minute diary of a single day's activities. They were given forms divided into 15-minute time segments and instructed to identify such activities as child care, kitchen work, shopping, personal care, husband care.

Finally, to solve the problem of making the day as representative as possible, it was decided to pick one at random and without advanced warning. The chosen day was a Thursday for Anne and Ellen, a Friday for Sylvia. They got the go-signal the night before.

Off and Running

When does a housewife's day begin? Anne, the newlywed, was "Up!" at 7 A.M. Ellen rose at 6:30 ("Help! Another day. Turned light off somebody left on all night"). Sylvia's day began 15 minutes later ("Arise and dress").

Day's end came at a respectable 11 for Sylvia and Anne. Ellen's 18-hour day ended sometime after 12:30 on a somewhat frantic note: "Went downstairs for cheese and crackers for husband-me. Going to take a shower. Took it. Washed hair. Scrubbed bathroom. Don't know what for. If a burglar comes in, at least he'll see one clean bathroom." Husband said: "What in the world are you doing?" I said: "Nothing, you want the light off? Another hard day tomorrow. Good night."

What Happened in Between?

Consider Anne in her one-bedroom apartment, with roughly 14 hours of activity in front of her. When she put it all down, it was neat and uncluttered with detail:

7:15 Personal care.

7:30 Kitchen work.

7:45 Breakfast and leisure (newspaper).

8–9 Husband care–driving to work.

9–9:30 Kitchen work.

9:30–9:45 Meal planning–grocery list.

9:45–10 Leisure (second cup of coffee plus newspaper).

10–11 Housecleaning.

11–11:15 Sorting laundry.

11:15–1:45 Errands and shopping.

1:45–2:15 Kitchen work–put groceries away.

2:15–2:30 Husband care (talk on the phone with him).

2:30–2:45 lunch.

And so goes the day. Anne spent an hour and a half at the dentist's that Thursday. It took her an hour to pick up her husband at work and bring him home. She needed a half hour to prepare dinner, enjoyed a half hour of cocktails and conversation with her husband, spent a half hour at dinner and another half hour cleaning up. At 8:30 that evening, she took 15 minutes to work on household accounts, another 15 minutes on the phone and writing letters, another 15 for folding laundry. By 9:15 Anne had 45 minutes to read the paper, read a book, talk to husband. By 10 she was in a "luxurious steamy tub," and at 10:30 she was getting things set for the next morning's breakfast.

If she recapitulated her day—this particular day—she would find she spent about 3½ hours in the kitchen, an hour and 45 minutes on housecleaning and laundry, 3 hours and 45 minutes on leisure and personal health and care, and about 2½ hours shopping and running errands. As days go, it was orderly, efficient, well-planned.

Jump on the Merry-Go-Round

Almost every minute of Ellen's day, on the other hand, is a wild merry-go-round. Take those morning hours when Anne briskly but smoothly went through her chores. Here's what Ellen was up to:

  6:45 Let dog out. Let dog in. Drank coffee. Lost pen, found it on stove.

  7:00 Argument with dog. She'd rather use our bathroom.

  7:15 Looked upstairs, downstairs, basement for my glasses. Will look in car when dressed.

  7:30 Let cat in. Took beef kidneys out of freezer to defrost for cat.

  7:45 Went upstairs to wake four kids. Only one would budge. Put bacon on.

  8:00 Looked for glasses again. Looked for pocketbook. Went up again to wake kids.

  8:15 Gave two other dogs snacks. Went down basement. Forgot what for.

  8:30 Kids all around. Put dog out. In.

  8:45 Looking for homework and other stuff.

  9:00–9:30 Forgot to write it down.

  9:30 Went out to car, upstairs, down basement and found glasses in laundry basket.

  9:45 Put 1812 Overture on record player, so cleaning would be more fun. Dusted tables, piano, turned record player off.

  10:00 Practiced piano. Went upstairs, made one bed. Came down. Got vacuum cleaner, but husband wants to talk to me. Talks. (He's wrong, I'm right.)

And so the day went—full of crisis, challenge and conquest.

 At 10:45, she "saw a rabbit with no body" in the back yard (dogs had bagged it). This produced trauma and resulted in the laundry being hung in the basement that day. The boys had "dirty and clean clothes all mixed up, so put all in washing machine." She polished some silver, fed the cat and discovered she had forgotten to put soap *in the washing machine." At 11:30 she ate (fruit and a chocolate bar) then rushed down to the basement to find the wax. "Waxed one table, finished cleaning powder room, found a small can of paint in the medicine cabinet. The phone rang. Wrong number."*

The daughter-in-law called at noon in a frantic state: "Baby won't eat."

The afternoon went fast. She painted furniture, got the fireplace halfway cleaned, talked to a friend on the phone, concluded: "House was a mess. Couldn't think where to start. Drank coffee."

There came a break while she drove her husband downtown. By 3:45, "Kids drifting in. Looked in freezer, pantry, refrigerator. Must go to store for food." But first she had to finish the bed-making and by that time: "Other people's kids all over house. Spilled milk. Cleaned up. Somebody spilled sugar. Cleaned up. Went upstairs to say no TV. Went out front to stop fight. Down basement to get clothes. Still wet."

At 5:00, this doleful comment: "Kids all over the place. Two strange ones in my bedroom. Fed cat again. All the dogs are barking. Told 14-year-old to cut grass. Have to get to store."

Ellen made it to the store by 5:30, got dinner started, and helped her daughter with a music lesson. Just about the time she discovered a leak in the pantry ceiling. "Mopped the floor." At 6:45, phone calls. One was from mother. "She told me to rest and I looked awful yesterday."

At 7:00, there were reminders to the boys to do their homework, get rid of the rabbit head and throw out the garbage. There was also a leak in the "dumb washing machine." An hour or so of relative peace descended as dinner was eaten, kitchen detail finished, dogs fed. By 10:00, things were humming in the house again.

"Went upstairs to tell kids to stop fighting and get on with homework. Down basement to get things to iron. Husband said come watch TV—world-shaking news coming soon. I made a note of things I musn't forget to do tomorrow. Told kids to get to bed this instant. Went downstairs for pen and apple juice. Went in bedroom to watch TV with husband. Did crossword puzzle instead.

"11 P.M.: Heard boys out front playing football. Told husband can't go on like this. Got boys in. Boys said won't do it again. I said BED."

When Ellen sent in her report on what she did, she added a few comments about what she doesn't do:

"I don't gad about. I don't go to the hairdresser. Two years ago I did and I had my hair color changed and I looked sharp and chic and all that, but the kids didn't like it."

"Today I did not go to a luncheon or tea or shopping for clothes. If I need a dress, I dash to the store and look at the Reduced Rack."

"I don't do any good works. I stay home mostly. I don't belong to anything. Only the Music Federation, and I'm not what they'd like to call active."

The Great Time Coming

Ellen can take heart. Her day will come—when the kids are all grownup and the grandchildren are too distant to be a real responsibility. Sylvia, now enjoying her later years, has discovered this.

Between 7 and 11 A.M. she spent a leisurely morning, preparing breakfast, taking her husband to the station, having a second cup of coffee with her paper, clearing the table, putting laundry in the washer, talking on the phone, straightening the house, hanging out the wash, going marketing and putting away the groceries.

By 11 she was performing "good works" as a hospital volunteer, followed by time for gardening and personal care, besides sorting and putting away the wash and feeding the dogs. By 5:30, she was ready to set the table and prepare dinner, leaving enough time to meet the 6:15 at the station to pick up her husband. Friends dropped by for a while before dinner, then a quiet meal for two and cleanup. By 8:15 there was time to read the paper, watch TV, make some phone calls, sew and enjoy an hour of reading in bed.

The bounty of this stage in her life is the leisurely pace—the almost five hours for gardening and sewing and reading, and the relaxed ease with which she could perform her housework, get the laundry done, go shopping, cook.

Sylvia calls this her "wonderful" stage of life, for with this new freedom every day can be different. The pressure is off. Of course, there are the grandchildren. "When they are visiting, my entire time is devoted to them. And there are still times when the children need you. And then you feel ten feet high . . ."

And so she completes a cycle.

Newlywed Anne still has stars in her eyes: "Housework, with its tedious routines and constant maintenance, is no fun, at least for me. But flowers on a polished table and candlelight on silver make it all worthwhile. I enjoy being a woman and a wife, and while I may not enjoy every minute, I do enjoy every day."

Ahead of Anne lies the kinds of days that Ellen scrambles frantically through. Perhaps they'll be a little less hectic, perhaps a bit more so. But they'll undoubtedly fit this description that Ellen gives: "This busi-

*ness of being a housewife is no joke. It's serious, friend. All my days
are like this."*

*And just over Ellen's horizon, in turn, is the Sylvia stage—responsi-
bilities and housework, yes, but new freedoms and satisfactions as
well. That's the stage, remember, of which Sylvia said: "Though I
would not trade the earlier years for anything, I can only say I hope
this lasts forever."* [11]

These are typical, middle-class, middle-income, white, Anglo-Saxon
families. Do they represent typical patterns of living for all families in the nation? How different are the days of the women of the Appalachian region?
How different are their values?

Society is changing and traditional values are also changing with it. How
can a generation that has experienced the first domestic use of electricity,
heard the first scratchy sounds of radio, followed the development of airplanes
to the superjets of common transportation, experienced flights to the moon
through television, and watched other forms of communication and transportation grow from pony express days to a mechanized era where even a tax return
is audited by a computer, be expected *not* to change? The technological history
that the senior citizens of this nation have lived is phenomenal. It is bound to
have caused changes in the values that direct life. Yet, few of that generation
suffered shock from these revolutionary developments in technology. Kanopka
says, "The shock—and the resulting fear—comes from changing human relations involving value confrontations." [12]

Henry Fairlie, an eloquent champion of the middle class, wrote in 1970,
"Our Values are Being Challenged." [13] He spoke of an erosion of his mother's
values, first in himself and still further in his nineteen-year-old son, and viewed
that erosion as general, widespread, and somewhat desperate.

Fairlie wrote about the traditional middle-class values that are being
profitably scorned by newspapers, magazines, films, and the younger generation. He concluded that the upsetting thing about the scorners and mockers is
that in private "they are desperately anxious to inculcate into their own
children, lo and behold, the traditional middle-class values" that they so
profitably scorn. [14]

In describing the values that enable people to control their environment
and their lives, Fairlie included:

Promptness—the system of intricate arrangements and timing that demands daily and hourly attention,

Education—belief that the better and more advanced the education a
child receives, the wider the choices that will be open to him,

Hygiene and Health—insistence that a child must not sacrifice his future health and close his future options through a sickly frame that restricts choices not only in physical but also in mental activity,

Thrift—to provide for the future and to exert a degree of control over life,

Honesty—because honorable transactions make life both more predictable and more pleasant, and

Work—for its own sake, not just to earn a living, for work shapes a day and so shapes a life that it helps give the individual control over his own.[15]

Is it erosion of strongly felt, traditional middle-class values that has led to sexual freedom, tolerance of drug abuse and alcoholism, questioning of truth and morality, branding the symbols of control and success as "pigs" and "the establishment," and blanket distrust in government officials? Some would return to "the good old days" and feel that only then could the values that are being eroded by a "surfeit of honey" and an overabundance of riches be recaptured.

Need the riches of a technological society erode traditional values? Are these middle-class values, so eloquently described by Fairlie, appealing enough to the young that they will be reinstated in generations to come? What values are replacing them? What do the trends of drifting youth on the city street, sexual promiscuity, and the growing number of drug addicts say about the value conflicts that face people in today's world?

In a recent television interview, ambassador and former child movie star Shirley Temple Black said, "We cannot live in the past, but we can learn from the past." Today's youth are in a stage of unrest, as were those of other ages. Abuse of drugs and sex, aimlessness and rebelliousness may be the mark of a small minority, but they permeate many lives. This generation of youth has been reared in an almost unbroken era of prosperity. They are uninterested in the limited material world their parents knew as children. The "good old days" are *now*, and "the depression" was when they didn't get the job they counted on last summer.[16] But some of today's youth who have lived on the rim of affluence wonder with anguish why their lot was cast with "the other America." Poverty hurts more in an affluent society. In a time when the "haves" have so much, to the "have nots" money represents power and is apt to be valued out of proportion.

Lee wrote that the thing most needed by individuals in a changing society is a compass, a "knowledge of how to find their way in the unknown, a sense of inquiry which will make this exploration inviting, an ability to see and draw conclusions from what they see; and, if possible, the courage to go forth."[17] The value content of everyday life and the value of personal uniqueness—of self actualization—can serve as that compass that prepares a person to retain meaning in the midst of change.

Cultural value patterns were described in Chapter 3. Lee stresses the stabilizing effect of cultural value patterns in a changing society. When she was studying the culture of the Tikopia of the South Pacific, she became conscious of the frequent exchange of handmade mats at special ceremonial occasions—hundreds of mats representing long hours of work by the women of the household were given and received. There was nothing utilitarian in this practice, for each woman was probably equally proficient with the rest at mat-making. These people were sharing their work, their time, their creativity with others and were giving a piece of their lives to the households of their friends and relations.[18]

In comparison to the Tikopia of South Pacific, even the poor in America have many possessions. In wealthy countries does the mediation value of social warmth and the sharing of one's time and self still have meaning? Has the sharing of gifts become so commercialized in our own society that a gift no longer infuses an individual's life into that of another? Is the joy of sharing that can give special meaning to life becoming lost in the tinsel and glitter of profit-making? What values are associated with Christmas in today's families?

Today's teens are the brightest generation ever known; they question, experiment, and are committed to causes. Their commitments reach beyond themselves. They are concerned with humanitarianism, and they will defend the underdog to the end. They translate the value of honesty into a "tell it like it is," why-hide-it attitude. This new generation is struggling to clarify values and to reconcile them with the actions of society. What will they and their children write about the values of their middle-America?

Konopka refers to positive self-assertion of young people as a transitional value. She says, "This can be beautiful; those with inner security who know their own value are less prone to drag down others; they do not have to carry the ugly bitterness of frustration that eats on the inside and breaks out in reactions to it—in hurting others, slander, drug abuse, possibly suicide."[19]

In *Doctor Zhivago,* Pasternak wrote about the misfortune of losing confidence in the value of personal opinions, the danger of imagining that moral responsibility is out of date and that each person must live by the notions of others. Pasternak was writing, not about our own modern civilization, but about a similar era of change and chaos that followed the Russian Revolution.[20]

Order to life and direction for change might well begin with appreciating differences and seeing positive meaning from acculturation of racial, national, religious, and cultural backgrounds and with accepting diversity in life styles as exciting, not threatening, as long as they do not harm others. Seeing egalitarianism as equal opportunity between sexes, races, cultures, and religions as well as marriage partners is another value of prime importance in this transitional stage. Accepting responsibility as social citizens is another step toward resolution of changing values and identifying controlled direction for change.

FAMILY UPHEAVAL

Marriage, as the foundation of family life, has become a serious social question. The nuclear family is being challenged by a high divorce rate. At least 50 percent of teenage marriages, and there is also a disturbing increase in divorces among people married over ten years. Divorce is a dismemberment crisis causing separation of the family unit. It brings associated feelings of dissapointment, anger, heartache, and recriminations, and many pressing economic problems. Although two could never live as cheaply as one when the marriage was intact, it is certain that two households cannot be supported with the same number of dollars that supported one household. Divorce has a high price tag in human as well as economic resources.

The traditional nuclear family is being challenged by an increase in alternate forms of family life. There are several alternate living patterns that are on the increase and tend to challenge marriage as the predominant form of family pattern. One is *out-of-wedlock partnerships.* Karlen estimated that about five percent of the nation's young people live together in an out-of-wedlock, male-female partnership arrangement.[21] These are not simple "trial marriages;" they are open partnerships. But the partners behave as husbands and wives; they become jealous of each other, they disagree, argue and make up, and they share many happy moments of companionship. Theirs is a temporary arrangement in the sense that the door is left open to dissolution without legal complications. They also leave the question of responsibility unresolved—economic responsibility such as who will bring up the children or pay the rent and how, if one leaves the other.

Another alternate life style has been called the Gay Liberation Movement. A growing tendency of society to accept the rights of people to make their own choices and to live in the way they see fit brings some people to accept *homosexual partnerships.*

People who are dissatisfied with their present way of life are inventing new family patterns. *Communes* are one of these. They are increasing in number and popularity. There are many kinds of communes—some go back to the land with stick hoes, some are religious and of high order, others are simply an arrangement for pooling resources to gain better living in an era of inflation and unemployment. There are also more marriages today than at any other time in history, and when marriages fail, eighty percent of the people who divorce eventually remarry.

According to Lane, "Alternate life style is simply a convenient, modern sociological term" for similar deviations that have existed throughout history.[22] She also points out the qualitative difference between one family and another and cautions that there are grave risks when people talk about *the* family, since each family is as different as each individual. Her view is that family life will survive because men and women depend on the universal functions of nurturing of the young and fulfillment of economic and emotional needs among family members for their survival. Others view companionship and the mutual interdependence as the bonding feature of family life.

Betty Yorburg, author of *The Future of the American Family,* predicts that homosexual marriages, group marriages, and single-parent households will probably become more prevalent in years to come because of increased tolerance of individual choice and cultural pluralism in less ethnocentric, more educated, and more permissively reared citizens. But she does not predict this in lieu of the nuclear family. She concludes that the American husband-wife, parent-child, individualistic nuclear family will also survive but not without a struggle.[23]

Revolution in family life is not new. Platt describes the great 1920's revolt in American families as one expressed through music with jazz; "in dance with the Charleston; in drugs with the hip flask, which was illegal; in sex with so-called free love and trial marriage; in dress with short skirts and rolled stockings; in hair length with bobbed hair."[24] He refers to the 1960's revolt and points out the similarities existing between this latter period's forms of rebellion and those of the 1920's.

Platt also points to some of the limitations of the nuclear family: the psychological stress and loss of many satisfactions of living. He says the nuclear family is not built for children who must grow up in homogenous apartment buildings with parents the same age and children the same age "boxed in with their peer group and the TV set." The nuclear family has limitations for parents, also—too many demands that once were shared in extended families with a brother who took care of financial problems, an uncle who gave advice, and a sister who you laughed and played with. He added that in the nuclear family all these demands are on one spouse, "who has to manage all these different roles in succession: financial wizard, therapist, cook, wagon driver, good partner in bed, and an absolutely charming guest at the company dinner."[25]

The answers Platt suggests are for "Child-Care Communities" in buildings in which 10 or 15 families might live with community dining facilities and community child day-care centers, for lawyers to help design a system of rights and privileges in a well-understood contract for mutual support, as well as for mutual and personal protection. Platt calls for new family patterns that would be socially acceptable and more psychologically rewarding than the nuclear family patterns of today. The management system is valuable in helping people confront family upheaval crises.

WORLD FOOD SHORTAGE

Illinois' Senator Charles H. Percy expresses grave concern that the worldwide food crisis threatens to seriously exceed the impact of the energy crisis. Nobel Prize Winner and agronomist Norman Borlaug feels that we have come to the crucial stage where at least 50 million people could perish from famine. The soaring demand for food has begun to exceed the production capacity of the world's farmers and fishermen.

Population growth is adding an annual 70 to 75 million more mouths to be fed on this earth, about 200,000 each day,[26] creating a demand for millions of extra tons of grain each year. American agriculture plays a major role in feeding the hungry millions. In recent years, American farmers have produced about one-fourth of the world's wheat and corn crops and three-fourths of the world's soybeans. According to Faulkner, the United States has been the largest cash exporter of grains and other farm products and the world's largest single source of food aid.[27]

In spite of the fact that the U.S. population growth *rate* is practically at a standstill, our population grows in numbers each year because of better health and sanitation conditions that make more live births possible and extends life. In other countries, the population rate continues to increase. India's rate has risen from 2.3 percent a decade ago, to 2.6 percent in the mid seventies. Other nations have similar growth patterns.

"Who will feed the hungry millions," is a legitimate and crucial question. Population is usurping farm lands, weather is unpredictable, farming is not always profitable, and the world has become dangerously over-dependent on the United States and a few other nations for food. There are many hungry mouths to feed in the United States as well. While America complains of high food costs and struggles with very real problems of supermarket survival, the Eastern world is starving.

How can management relieve the world food shortage? What can a technological nation offer the hunger-driven Bangladesh or the drought-struck African nations? More efficient use can be made of the food we have. Less waste, improved diets among our own people, careful evaluation of nutritional value, as well as economic buys in food, and more effective means of sharing our surplus with other nations of the world are partial answers. Increased nutritional education here and abroad is another. Population control may have a positive impact, also.

ROLE IDENTIFICATION

Another external change that must be resolved if families are to have future quality and direction is role identification of its members. Amy Bowman wrote, "Between the black-hat image of the militant, man-hating feminist and the white-hat image of female gentility is the more balanced outlook" of woman as an intelligent human being with a desire for freedom to unfold such powers as were given to her.[28] Can roles be balanced without becoming neutralized?

Roles are changing. The increasing number of working wives has caused many of these changes. Increased education of women has led to other role changes. Women are preparing themselves for positions beyond those occupied by women since World War II. More are remaining single; more continue to work as consistently and for as many years as men. Women are realizing that it is not necessary to choose *between* work and family life and are discovering management can make it possible to successfully accomplish both. Roles are changing within the family, and these new roles may be equally or more satisfying to all who are affected.

Women as heads of households are changing role identification and many laws along with it. These women face economic, social, and psychological problems that families headed by men do not face. They are becoming more numerous and more militant. Patterson reports a number of discriminations against employed women who head households. Group life insurance policies sometimes provide larger benefits for male than for female workers, women's disability income has had unreasonably low limits regardless of the earnings, and nearly one-third of the sex complaints to the Equal Employment Opportunity Commission in one year alleged sex bias in benefits. There are sex-biased disability, pension, and job-training programs. In addition to the continuing pay discrimination (the average woman worker earned only 62 percent as much as the average man in 1972), there are credit and loan discriminations, and finding housing at affordable prices poses serious problems for families headed by women.[29]

More than one out of every ten families in the United States is headed by a woman, and about 20 million people live in these families. Heading such families are single women supporting parents; widowed, separated, divorced, or deserted women; unwed mothers, wives of unemployed or unemployable men, and are, in general, urban dwellers, members of minority races, and often poorly educated.

Not only does role reorientation affect women but more children are now living with fathers, and more men are running households. Many assume this role as a result of the wife's death. Children of parents without partners are maturing earlier, sometimes increasing the generation gap.

Development of self awareness (see Chapter 7) is a prerequisite to understanding role identification and reorientation. Learning to cope with male and female role expectations in both conventional and non-conventional ways and reconciling personal feelings with those prevelant in society is high on the priority list for adjustment in marriage.[30]

Many of the solutions to the problems of sex-related role identification will be found through research, education, and social policy. Many will result from more effective management—through identifying objectives and desired outcomes, mobilizing efforts, establishing control, and following through with evaluation and reorientation of external and internal forces of conflict.[31]

A role change is often the consequence of crisis. It is a form of adjustment, a compromise between what *was* and what *will be*. To accomplish effectively a change in role, people of any sex and any age will find the road smoother if they set their priorities carefully, assume responsibility for the reorientation, consider the effects on others, and build an inner sense of self reliance. Not only is individual development extremely important but in an active, surging world, the strength of one individual is of less consequence than if linked with others in causing change.

According to Bowman, "Women have an awesome and vitally important opportunity, through their individual and collective uniqueness, to improve the quality of life."[32] Men have, for centuries, contributed to the economic support that is the basis of improved quality of life. Are these roles now to be exchanged, combined, or interchanged? What will be the long-range effect of role changes? Will men live longer and women have shorter lives if the stress of being a wage earner is transferred to women?

ECONOMIC UNCERTAINTY

In the face of starvation and resource depletion, how can economic uncertainty be classed as an impending crisis? More marriages are threatened and more suicides caused by economic uncertainty than any other single factor. America is facing a life of luxury, a massive collective of facts and data, a tradition of technology, and, at the same time, is groping for the solutions to the pressing problems of inflation and recession.

Economic uncertainty is a combination of many factors: poverty and affluence, spiraling welfare, vascillating interest rates, increasing tolerance of personal bankruptcy, mounting national debt load, consumer revolt against a *caveat emptor* business philosophy, strikes and union negotiations, a changing stock market, and a cost of living that is rising at an unpredictably high rate while unemployment is also mounting.

There is no other sane method of approaching economic uncertainty than through more purposeful management.

Five families are described on the following pages, each representing a stage in the family life cycle. The characteristics and economic circumstances are based on statistical medians for the head of the family at particular ages. The buying practices, expectations, and expenditures are based on market studies and national surveys of consumer expenditures and income. The table on which the information in the vignettes was based is presented in Chapter 12, entitled Probable Expenditure Patterns of Families At Different Stages in the Life Cycle. The families are described in terms of the predominant theme of the life style at that particular stage. As you read, consider how a family crisis would affect not only its economic picture but the management of human resources as well.

The first stage is usually one of adapting—of learning to think in terms of "we" as well as "I," of communicating wants and values that are not yet crystallized, of reducing dependence on parents for support, and of establishing a satisfying life style. This is usually a period of higher expenditures for transportation, recreation, equipment, and clothing per person. It is also a stage when credit can be abused, and a small unexpected expenditure can become a crisis. It is likely that a couple's first argument will be over the expenditure of money.

Age of Adaptation

Willie was fuming mad when he heard that Leola bought a new pair of shoes just when they almost had the budget to where they could handle it—and to have charged them was inexcusable! How could she do a thing like that to him?

Willie is 23; his wife, Leola, is 21. His college expenses are being financed through a football scholarship, a government loan, and his wife's earnings as a secretary—in all, about $6,130. The Smiths live in a one-bedroom apartment in Alumni Village, crowded and noisy with children but convenient to class and fairly inexpensive ($65 a month rent plus about $40 a month for telephone, utilities, and household operation).

Willie rides his bicycle to class so Leola can take their four-year-old car to work. The car has been "acting up" lately and needed repairs last month. Because it was convenient, they took it to a neighborhood service station that would make the repairs and let them pay the bill weekly. The Smiths spend about $100 a week, with the car taking the largest portion—about $19 a week for insurance and operation. The additional $6 a week for the repair bill will have to come from someplace, and Willie had thought it would be from the clothing allotment—until Leola bought the shoes.

They are eating on about $15 a week, and Leola usually takes a sack lunch to work. Willie eats his meals in the cafeteria with the team during football season but eats at home the rest of the year.

They are pretty careful about the clothes budget most of the time, but neither of them can resist a special on ski clothes and are consequently paying off a charge account at the ski shop. They are buying a TV on credit; this costs them $8.50 a week.

They have been healthy during their first year of marriage, but Leola had to have her glasses changed last month, and that cost them $50. Since the weekly medical budget is only $5.80 and insurance takes $4.60 of that, they had to use all their savings to pay for the glasses. They had been saving the $50 for a trip to visit Willie's parents during the Easter holidays. Now they will have to ask Willie's parents to pay for the trip or stay home.

In spite of their money problems, they usually spend about $11 a week on recreation and restaurant food. Willie's parents pay the premiums on his small life insurance policy. Leola doesn't have any. They save some of their recreation money occasionally, but Willie usually needs extra money for books at the beginning of each semester, and that uses almost all of the savings. They give each other record albums for birthdays. Leola has a beautiful stereo set she bought before they were married.

The Smiths have been adapting their resources to meet their current needs and desires and, through the use of credit, have kept their heads above water during their first year of marriage. Theirs is a kind of precarious brinksmanship. Soon they will be forced to consider more urgent priorities and long-range goals for they are expecting a baby in August, two months after Willie graduates.

Leola will have to stop work in July because of company rules. Willie had expected to stay in school another year to get his master's degree. Now, even if Willie can find a coaching or teaching job in September, their first pay check won't come until October 1, and they have no health insurance for doctor and hospital bills associated with pregnancy.

Leola and Willie have been adapting their resources to meet their immediate wants and needs and to prepare Willie for a teaching-coaching job. Now they will have to adapt to a change in family size and to another stage in their life cycle.

Age of Anticipation

Bob Livingston is 27 and beginning his management training program with a large department store chain. He'll be stationed in Chicago for the next two years. His net pay is $8,000 which Betty works hard to stretch as far as it will go. They chose an unimpressive apartment in a good neighborhood because their daughter, Lee Ann, will be starting to school next year, and they like the schools in that neighborhood. The rent, utilities, and household operation bills take about 25 percent of Bob's $666 a month check.

The Livingstons spend about $100 a month for transportation including a car payment, insurance, and operation. They bought a TV-stereo component unit for the living room soon after they arrived. Using his employee discount, Bob will be paying $40 a month for 18 months for the unit. That leaves them only $5 a month for other furnishings and equipment since their total furniture and equipment budget is $45 (6½ percent of Bob's income). Betty hunts for specials on accessories, and she has repainted the bedroom furniture since they moved.

Betty shops carefully for the food they eat at home. She studies the Wednesday night ads in the newspaper and plans the week's menus around the specials. She likes to shop on Thursday morning with a neighbor in their apartment building. They make a morning of it and usually have lunch together at some out-of-the-way place on the way home. Betty spends about $115 a month for groceries, and the family eats out together on weekends. They spend about $35 a month on food away from home including Bob's lunches. Tobacco and alcoholic beverages take 3½ percent of expenditures, $22 a month in the Livingston's case.

Betty dresses carefully and makes sure that Bob's perma-pressed shirts and slacks are hung up as soon as they come out of the dryer. She's learning to sew so she can make Lee Ann's clothes. The Livingstons have budgeted between $65 and $70 a month for clothes but are spending slightly more now because they need heavier winter clothes than they did in Virginia. By using the store employees' discount for most of their purchases, they are able to get more clothes of better quality, but Betty sometimes prefers to buy her things in a specialty shop.

The Livingston's play bridge every other Tuesday with some of the trainees and their wives and have joined a newcomer's Gourmet Dinner Club which meets in the homes of local townspeople one night a month. Bob plays poker occasionally and has joined the Lion's Club and a professional management association. Betty is active in their Presbyterian Church affairs and belongs to a sorority alumni group in town. They have high hopes for Lee Ann and have already started her on an allowance.

The Livingstons anticipate the time when Bob finishes his training and can manage a store of his own within the chain. They are looking forward to the time when they can afford a better life in part of the country closer to home.

Age of Acquisition

Karl Swenson has just turned 43. He is an assistant professor in the language department at State College. He started working on his Ph.D. five summers ago but just can't afford to take time off from work to complete his residence time. The Swensons will have about $17,500 income this year, including the $2,600 that Olsa makes doing part-time bookkeeping for a law firm.

Last year the Swensons bought a seven-year-old house for $38,000. This was a bargain, but with mortgage interest of 9 percent, payments take about one-fourth of Karl's salary. Olsa has been redecorating the house with a mixture of antiques, which she refinishes, and some good-quality pieces of furniture from The Decorator's Shop.

Olsa works hard at shopping, studies the newspaper ads, and reads *Consumer Reports* before she shops for new equipment. She does comparative shopping when she needs large items and usually buys the household appliances at discount stores, but she doesn't like their furniture or clothes.

The Swensons are spending about 32 percent of total consumption for housing, about 20 percent for food, 15 percent on transportation, 12 percent on clothing, 6 percent on medical care, and 5 percent on recreation. They devote about 3 percent to personal care, 2 percent to education, and 1 percent to reading material.

Their son, Tom, will be graduating from high school this year and insists that he must have his own car next year. He would pay part of the down payment and could sell his cycle if Dad would keep up the car payments. He's going to live at home his first two years of college. Their daughter, Mary, will begin high school next year and needs new clothes. The braces will finally be coming off her teeth, and with new clothes she should make a good impression in high school. She and her mother have been watching the local specialty shops for their annual sales.

Karl worries that his $30,000 worth of life insurance is not enough. The college pays his medical insurance, and he pays the additional $30 a month for a group family medical policy. It is withheld from his monthly check so it doesn't hurt as much as the $620 he pays for insurance on the two cars. Karl has been buying $50 worth of mutual funds per month for about 10 years, but with Tom in college and the additional car, he will have to figure some other way to cut costs if he is to continue the investment plan. Perhaps Olsa will decide to take the full-time office job after all—just for a few years, until the children are through college.

The Swensons are caught up in a whirlwind of acquisition. During some months, their expenditures exceed their income, and the end is not yet in sight. . .

Age of Achievement

At 53, Barney is doing much better than he expected. He is making $19,500 as regional sales manager for a wholesale manufacturer. He dreads the traveling sometimes because he is away from Nancy and the boys so much, but it's his job and it is paying for their home in Rolling Hills, swimming pool, cars, and the comfortable life they share.

Nancy and Barney play golf on weekends and do a little jogging to keep in shape. Nancy is a Gray Lady at the hospital on Wednesdays, and she works hard on the community drive every Fall. Tim, their oldest son, is in graduate school and his new bride, Ann, is working to pay expenses. The Clancys and Ann's parents each contribute $100 a month to the newlyweds to help them through school. Tim's younger brothers are still at home, but they are very different from Tim. Tim was an outstanding student, a champion swimmer, and a cleancut young man, very much like his father. Sonny and Mark are a different breed. Sonny has been floundering in Junior College for five semesters and still hasn't completed his Associate Degree. Mark dropped out and works occasionally at odd jobs but doesn't commit himself to anything, in spite of the fact that he has the highest IQ of the three boys. Neither Mark nor Sonny are the least bit interested in smart clothes. They say, "It's not what a man has that counts, it's what he believes." They wear their hair long; Mark has a beard. They bring home every stray dog that wanders by. They often just sit and think, and they make Barney uncomfortable when they ask him why he spends so much time away from home just to buy things that don't really matter in life.

The Clancys spend a lot on entertainment, but that's part of Barney's job. He'd like to do more home entertaining, but there's no telling when Sonny or Mark might show up, and clients wouldn't understand the "youth rebellion." So Barney takes Nancy along as often as he can when he entertains for the company. She's very friendly and puts people at ease immediately. Nancy has been a big help to Barney. When he had his first heart attack 10 years ago, she took evening classes at the university to update her teaching credentials. She was fortunate to find a job in a school only 5 miles from home. Nancy enjoyed working with elementary children, and she continued teaching for five years after Barney returned to work. Nancy still substitutes. She says it's "good insurance", and it relieves Barney's worries about what would happen to the family if he had another heart attack.

This is the Clancy's *age of achievement*. Barney has a good job, his wife can work if she chooses, the boys are growing up, and the Clancys are proud of them (most of the time).

In spite of some hard luck when Barney was sick, they have managed to put away some money for the boys' education. But because of inflation, it is hard to be certain the money will be enough. If Barney can just continue working until he is 65, things should work out pretty well for them.

Age of Adjustment

Retirement takes some "getting used to." Roal Gonzales had to retire last year when he was 62 because of back trouble. If he could have worked three more years his retirement would have been more, but he was sick so often, he was afraid of being fired—not for himself, but for Maria. Her doctor and hospital bills keep mounting up.

Before Maria became sick they had always paid cash for everything, or if they charged, they never defaulted on a bill. They didn't buy at all if they weren't sure they could afford it.

Raol had been a carpenter and had earned plenty of money in his day—some years as much as $12,000. He worked hard and was proud of his trade. His wife never had to work away from home. She looked after the house and the four children, and she kept their children clean and respectable. She was an efficient housekeeper and loved the "whir" of the vacuum cleaner. But now she has to rest as much as possible and conserve her energy. She has multiple sclerosis. She gets around slowly with the help of a cane, enough to supervise the cooking, but Raol does most of the house work now.

The children come as often as they can to visit Maria and Raol and do what they can to help, but they have their own families to care for—all except Juan, who never married. Juan lives with his parents and does most of the shopping and much of the work around the big house on weekends. Raol wonders if they should sell the house now that they don't need all the bedrooms, but Maria loves the old house. It has so many memories, and it is near their friends. She says, "Chicanos need to live near their friends; they stick together in time of trouble."

With the money Juan pays them for his room (he insists) and Raol's retirement and a small Social Security check, Raol and Maria have an annual income of a little over $6,000. Their income taxes are about $570, nothing like they used to pay when Raol was working, but he'll be glad when he and Maria are over 65 and can take an additional exclusion on their taxes.

They would be quite comfortable if it weren't for the medical bills. If only Raol's medical insurance had included major medical coverage or they had been able to save more, but, like most large families, it just took all he made for ordinary living.

The Gonzales' have a tight budget and spend about 23 percent of consumption expenditures on medical services and prescriptions, 20 percent on food, 12 percent on household operation, upkeep, and utilities, 10 percent on transportation, and 7 percent or less on clothing. They often save from their money for clothing and household operations to spend on gifts for the children.

Raol and Maria are facing many adjustments—to ill health and added medical expenses, to having more time than energy to do the things they wish to do, to deciding what to do with the big house, and to live on a retirement income that is less than half the normal family income. Now with the increase in cost of food and fuel, how will they manage?

These are people—ordinary, American people with hopes and dreams as well as fears for the uncertainty of their economic future. Like Fabre's processionary caterpillars, they are following tradition and patterns of activity that are a part of their heritage; but unlike the processionary caterpillars, they are adjusting, seeking alternatives, and learning to manage crisis level changes in their lives.

References

1. Lederer, W. J. and Burdick, E., *The Ugly American,* W. W. Norton, Co., New York, (1958), pp. 232–238.

2. Reprinted from *The Ugly American* by William J. Lederer and Eugene Burdick. By permission of W. W. Norton & Company, Inc. Copyright © 1958 by William J. Lederer and Eugene Burdick, pp. 232–238.

3. Duvall, E. M., *Family Development,* Lippincott, New York, (1971), pp. 505–507; Duvall, E. M., Hill, R. H., and Duvall, S. M., *Being Married,* Association Press, New York, (1960), pp. 298–299.

4. Klemer, R. H., *Marriage and Family Relationships,* Harper and Row, New York, (1970).

5. Cavan, R. S., (ed.), *Marriage and Family in the Modern World, (3rd Ed.),* Thomas Crowell, (1969), pp. 390–420.

6. Maltz, M., *Psycho-Cybernetics,* Pocket Books, New York, (1969), pp. 204–222.

7. *Ibid,* p. 206.

8. Cavan, R. S., *op. cit.,* pp. 416–420.

9. "What Does She Do All Day?" *Changing Times,* 19: 1 (January 1965), pp. 24–28.

10. Wench, D. A., "Coping With Crisis," *Today's Homemaker,* (March 1970), pp. 1–2. (Agricultural Extension Service, University of California and Orange County, Anaheim, Calif.).

11. "What Does She Do All Day?" pp. 24–28. Reprinted by permission from *Changing Times,* the Kiplinger Magazine, (January 1965 issue). Copyright 1964 by The Kiplinger Washington Editors, Inc., 1729 H. Street, N. W., Washington, D. C. 20006.

12. Konopka, G., "Social Change and Human Values," *Journal of Home Economics, 66:* 6 (September 1974), pp. 12–14.

13. Fairlie, H., "Our Values are Being Scorned and Mocked," *McCalls,* 97: 10 (July 1970), pp. 42–3, 100, 102–3.

14. *Ibid.,* p. 100.

15. *Ibid,* pp. 100–103.

16. Rice, A. S., "Where Are We in Consumer Education?" *What's New in Home Economics, 35:* 2 (February 1971), pp. 34–36, 92.

17. Lee, D., "The Individual in a Changing Society," *Journal of Home Economics, 52:* 2 (February 1960), 79–82.

18. *Ibid,* pp. 79–80.

19. Konopka, G., *op. cit.,* p. 13.

20. Pasternak, B., *Doctor Zhivago,* Signet Books, New York, (1958), p. 336.

21. Karlen, A., *Sexuality and Homosexuality—A New View,* W. W. Norton, New York, (1971).

22. Lane, B., "The Challenge of Shaping Future Families," *Journal of Home Economics,* 65: 2 (February 1973), pp. 25–27.

23. Yorburg, B., "The Future of the American Family," *Intellect,* 101: 2346 (January 1973), pp. 253–260.

24. Platt, J., "A Fearful and Wonderful World for Living," in College of Home Economics, Iowa State University, *Families of the Future,* Iowa State University Press, Ames, Iowa, (1972), pp. 3–13.

25. *Ibid,* p. 9.

26. Low, P. F., "Realities of the Population Explosion," in B. Q. Hafen, (ed.), *Man, Health, and Environment,* Burgess, Minneapolis, Minn., (1972), pp. 201–214.

27. Faulkner, D. H., "Who Will Feed the Hungry Millions?" *Plain Truth,* 40: 2 (February 1975), p. 2.

28. Bowman, A., "How Liberated Can you Get?" *Plain Truth,* 40: 2 (February 1975), p. 7.

29. Patterson, J., "If You're a Woman and Head a Family," *Journal of Home Economics,* 65: 1 (January 1973), pp. 20–22.

30. Ryder, V., "Family Life Education: Helping Students to Know Themselves," *Journal of Home Economics,* 67: 1 (January 1975), pp. 8–14.

31. *Ibid,* p. 14.

32. Bowman, A., *op. cit.,* p. 7.

GLOSSARY

Affective resources   traits and feelings pertaining to or resulting from emotions, such as interests, attitudes, motivation, or enthusiasm.

Alternatives   possible courses of action.

Annual income profile   a graph representing the pattern of money, fringe benefits, and other economic resources received by an organization or an individual over a twelve month period.

Assets   any worthwhile possessions, personal qualities, traits, or characteristics of the environment that can be used for goal achievement.

Attitude   a viewpoint or predisposed feeling sufficiently definite to influence activity in a certain direction.

Authority   power allotted to one person or to part of the group because the remainder of the group believes this delegation of power to be desirable.

Autonomic decision making   shared decision making achieved by delegating separate authority for specific types of decisions to individuals within the group.

Biological time   cyclical occurrence of certain bodily functions such as hunger.

Bond   a certificate of debt issued by a corporation, municipality, or government guaranteeing payment of the original investment plus interest by a specified future date.

Budget   a financial plan based on goals, expected income, current wealth, and other economic resources as well as expenditures.

Capacity   ability to receive, hold, and absorb information and ideas. In credit, the ability to repay a loan evidenced by income or wealth.

Capital   any form of material wealth (cash, securities, property, or equipment) or personal characteristic used or available for use in the production of more wealth.

Center   an area designed for the completion of a specific activity.

Channel   medium through which a message is sent.

Cognitive dissonance   inconsistent information gathered in or after decision making.

Cognitive resources   mental traits or characteristics that relate to knowledge acquired by reasoning and perception such as intelligence, understanding, or adaptability.

Collateral   assets pledged as security for a loan or credit sale.

Communication   the process of human interaction, the sending and receiving of messages.

Conflict   internal or interpersonal differences of opinion.

Constraint   a potential resource that is functioning as a liability instead of an asset.

Consumption   selection and use of goods and services.

Control   to exercise authority over, to direct, command, regulate, check, or verify by comparison with a standard or goal.

Conventional standards   measures of comparisons that originate from social groups.

Conversion   transformation of one resource into another, accompanied by a delay in benefits.

Credit   current purchasing power expanded through deferred payments.

Crisis   a major change in which the negative consequences outweigh the positive ones.

Decision making   the process of selecting from alternative courses of action.

Decision-making style   procedure unique to an individual or group used to select from alternatives.

Democratic decision making a process in which those affected by decisions have influence in the selection of alternatives.

Dominance a power relationship in which one person or part of a group has relatively more influence than others.

Economic decisions selection from alternate goals.

Economic resources assets pertaining to production, distribution, or consumption and having use in goal attainment.

Ecosystem relationship between living organisms and their life-support environment throughout their life cycle.

Egalitarian equal relationship and power structure.

Energy power to work, to carry on physical or mental activities.

Environment a combination of physical, cultural, and social conditions that surround and affect the nature and quality of living of an individual or group.

Environmental resources qualities, characteristics, or components of one's surroundings that may be used to achieve goals.

Equalitarian decision making shared power.

Evaluating the managerial process that assesses progress toward goals and proposes changes in goals, standards, or resource allocation.

Explicit values consciously held concepts of the desirable.

Family an identifiable unit of interacting personalities sharing resources, especially living space, and committed to common goals.

Family functions purposes served by the family for the individual, the family group, or society.

Family life cycle a theoretical concept of the developmental stages of life of a modal or typical family.

Fatigue feelings of exertion accompanied by reduced performance.

Feedback   the process of returning information to the sender of communication.

Fixed expenses   stable costs that recur in a predictable time pattern.

Flexible expenses   costs that vary from time period to time period such as monthly clothing expenditures.

Free time   time that is not devoted to work or sleep.

Fringe benefits   nonmonetary assets usually derived from employment.

Goals   ends toward which people work.

Habit   established pattern of activity requiring little conscious thought.

Heuristics   use of general policies or principles to select from alternatives.

Home-related work   goods or services provided by family members to keep a functioning household.

Human capital   personal assets or qualities that have power to increase other resources.

Human ecology   study of spatial and temporal interrelationships between people and their economic, social, political, and physical environments.

Human needs   stages in the development of a fully functioning personality.

Human resources   traits or qualities within people that are instrumental to reach goals. Human resources include cognitive, affective, psychomotor, and temporal traits or characteristics of people and other resources that cannot be used independently of individuals.

Immediate goals   ends toward which people work that can be accomplished in less than one year.

Implementing   the managerial process that activates the planning and organizing processes.

Implicit values   concepts of the desirable demonstrated in repeated behavior but not verbalized.

Inflexible activities events that occur only at specific times.

Input a resource introduced into a system to effect change.

Installment credit ability to purchase with a contractual credit arrangement with a series of repayments of specified amounts to be paid at a given time each month or week for a certain length of time.

Instrumental value a concept of the desirable serving as a means to demonstrate higher level values.

Insure to protect against loss or to underwrite by contracting with an agency for payment upon loss.

Interference anything that interrupts or alters the intended meaning of communication.

Intermediate goals ends toward which people work that can be achieved in approximately two to five years.

Interval level planning scheduling when items in an ordered list will be accomplished and estimating the duration of activities.

Intrinsic value a concept of the desirable sought for itself.

Invest to use money with the intent to earn income or increase capital.

Irrational decision selection from alternatives based on impulse or emotions.

Leadership the process of influencing others.

Leisure use of uncommitted time that is rewarding for its own sake.

Lend to grant temporary use of money with the condition that the amount borrowed will be repaid, often with interest.

Liability an obligation or debt.

Life style patterns of role combinations shared by groups of people in a society.

Lifetime income profile a graph representing the shape of actual or expected income over the lifetime of an individual or group.

Liquid assets   wealth that can be readily converted into cash.

Liquidity   sufficient cash to cover debts without utilizing fixed assets; ease and speed of converting investments into cash when desired.

Long-range goals   ends toward which people work that require more than five years to accomplish.

Management   the process of planning, organizing, implementing, and evaluating the use of resources to accomplish goals and satisfy wants. Management is controlling the direction of change, making things happen rather than letting them happen.

Meta-communication   evaluation of the effectiveness of interpersonal interaction with the intent to strengthen the relationship.

Models   simplifications of life situations used to explain or understand complex operations.

Money income   gross receipts of monetary gain derived from labor, transfer payments, or capital.

Mortgage   A conditional pledge of property to a lender as security for payment of a debt.

Motivation   reasons sufficient to cause action or behavior.

Net worth   difference between monetary worth of assets and liabilities.

Nominal level planning   listing, by name only, the tasks to be accomplished.

Nonrational decision   selection from alternatives based on intuition and a blending of facts and emotions.

Opportunity cost   loss of resources attributable to choice of one alternative compared with another.

Optimum decision making   the process of selecting the best single alternative.

Ordinal level planning   organizing a list of accomplishments to be achieved into priorities of importance or into a sequence of time.

Organizing   the managerial process emphasizing the ordering of activities and resources to reach goals.

Output   the product of a system, such as the impact of a system on the environment.

Perception   meaning assigned to an object, situation, or experience.

Performance standards   measures of comparison that specify the quality or quantity of results in goal attainment.

Person-centered organization   division of labor emphasizing learning possibilities for the worker in task completion.

Plan   any scheme, program, or method developed prior to and for the purpose of goal accomplishment.

Planning   the future-oriented managerial process emphasizing setting of goals and standards.

Power   the potential influence of one person or part of the group over others.

Procedural standards   measures of comparison that reflect values and specify how goals are to be reached.

Process   a particular method involving a number of steps or operations in task performance usually contributing to a system. The verb form means to use in a particular way.

Production   creation of goods and services.

Psychological time   awareness of the passage of time, making scientific time seem to pass either slowly or swiftly.

Psychomotor resources   human assets that combine muscular activity with associated mental processes; ability and proficiency in carrying out activities.

Quality of life   satisfaction derived from material and nonmaterial accomplishment.

Ratio-level planning   synchronizing plans with persons assigned to carry out the plans.

Rational decision   selection from alternatives based on objective analyses of facts.

Resources   assets that can be used to reach goals.

Safety   freedom from danger or risk. In investments, it is the degree of assurance of reacquiring at least the same number of dollars invested.

Satisficing   the process of selecting a reasonable, but not necessarily best, alternative.

Save   to defer; conserve for future use.

Scientific standards   measures of comparison originating from fact or research.

Scientific time   clock and calendar time based on movements of the earth in relation to the sun and moon counted in minutes, hours, days, weeks, months, seasons, and years.

Self-actualization   to realize maximum personal potential.

Self concept   attitude of worth and awareness of personal image.

Self discipline   the power to control personal behavior to complete an activity.

Self disclosure   sharing information about one's self.

Sequence   the order in which activities are carried out.

Skill   ability and proficiency; expertise and dexterity in carrying out an act in such a way as to achieve dependable, consistent results.

Social decision   selection from alternate values or roles.

Standards   judgments used to measure progress toward and attainment of goals.

Substitution   replacement of one resource for another.

Success   satisfying achievement of specified goals and life style.

Supervision   overseeing the goal-directed activity of others which may include transmittal of what is to be done, instruction and guidance in task performance, and motivation to act.

Synchronization   meshing events, people, and nonhuman resources in time.

Syncratic decision making   shared decision making in which each decision is made by the group.

System   a set or arrangement of interacting, interdependent processes forming a unity or performing a specific function.

Task-centered organization   division of responsibility based on quality and efficiency in task accomplishment.

Technical decision   selection from alternate procedures to reach a single goal.

Temporal resources   assets relating to time, including scientific, biological, and psychological time.

Time sense   an individual's awareness and perception of time.

Trade-off   exchange of input and output; to barter one desirable quality or good for another.

Utility   the want-satisfying power of an alternative or resource.

Values   concepts of the desirable that are strong enough to motivate action and serve as guidelines for goal orientation; describe why people act as they do.

Wealth   composite holdings of real property — monetary assets, durables and personal possessions, as well as the characteristic pattern of such holdings.

Work   activities producing measurable results for one's self or others.

Work habits   established routine of activities directed toward measurable results.

Yield   profit or loss usually expressed as interest or dividends and customarily calculated as a percentage of the invested amount.

INDEX

Adaptability, 14, 169, 254
to disability, 405-406
Age, 100-101, 124-128
and cost of living, 124-125, 126-128
influence on decision making, 100-101
and resource use, 125, 221
Allowance, 312
Alternatives, 186-187, 317-318, 440-442
in change, 414, 427-428
definition of, 457
to nuclear families, 7-8, 440-442
in purchases, 317-318
Assets, 34, 109-110, 281-283, 351-353
definition of, 34, 109
diversification of, 329, 351-352
earning value of, 352-353
fixed dollar, 325, 329
human, 34-36, 110
liquid, 326-328, 462
pattern of holdings, 326-329
protection of, 353
Attitudes, 163-164
definition of, 457
regarding household tasks, 241
regarding money, 311-314, 316
regarding wife's working, 261
Authority, 101, 457

Balance, 119, 124, 187
Bankruptcy, 274-275
Beginning families, 19-20, 123, 309
Benefits, fringe, 36, 146, 148, 280-281, 288-290, 460
Body:
alignment, 243
efficiency in use of, 243-244, 251-254
language, 199-200, 209-210
mechanics, 244
Bonds, 340-341, 457
corporate and municipal, 340-341
government, 340

quality ratings of, 340
yield from, 340-341
Boredom, 405
Brinksmanship, 274
Budgetism, 274
Budgets, 300-308
costs of, 306
definition of, 457
establishing, 300-308
flexibility of, 302-305
realistic, 301-302
standard, 306
workable, 305-308

Capacity, 457
Capital, 457
human, 110, 183-184, 298, 330, 460
Case situations:
Age of Achievement, 448-449
Age of Acquisition, 447-448
Age of Adaptation, 445-446
Age of Adjustment, 449-451
Age of Anticipation, 446-447
Bent Backs of Chang 'Dong, 422-427
Hitchhiker, 118-119
Karen Sue and her energy-driven family, 373-374
Processionary Caterpillars, 421
What Does She Do All Day? 430-437
Center:
definition of, 458
financial record-keeping, 314-315
of gravity and work performance, 243-244
work, 251, 254-255, 314-315
Change, 3-4, 404-414, 421-451
and quality of life, 18, 399, 409-412, 414, 421-422
anticipating, 410
as goal of management, 39
attitude toward, 409-410
characteristics of, 413-414, 427-429

classes of, Mundel's, 116-118
crises causing, 404-408, 427-428, 440-445
death, 407-408, 427-428
divorce, 406-407, 427-428
external, 408-409
in family life, 404-408, 445-451. *See also*
    Family, changes in; Family, life styles;
    and Life styles.
group support in, 411
in income, 17, 290-294
life cycle, 19-25, 124-125, 289, 308-311, 331,
    445-451, 459
managing, 409-412, 421-451
measurability of, 414
pace of, 410
professionals as agents of, 412-414
in roles, 9, 159, 160, 246, 385, 404, 443-444
stability in, 411
steps in, 427-428
technological, 224, 411-412
Channel, 458
Childless families, 22-25
Children:
    absence of, 6, 22-25
    adjustment to divorce, 406-407
    by artificial insemination, 412
    care of, 441
    consequences of, 405
    cost of rearing, 125
    effect of, on homekeeping, 129-130, 223,
        242, 246, 345
    household work of, 129-130, 250-251
    time perception of, 220
    training of, 250
    of working wives, 129-130, 261-262
Circadian rhythm, 35, 147, 220
Civil rights, 401
Clustering, 229-230
Cognitive dissonance, 88, 458
Collateral, 458
Commitment, 174, 176
Communes, 7, 440
Communication, 39, 195-211
    between professionals and clients, 413
    changing nature of, 203-204
    channels of, 197
    components of, 196-201
    decoding of, 198
    definition of, 195, 458
    evaluation of, 210-211
    feedback in, 199-201

listening rate in, 198
management and, 171-172, 206-211
nonverbal, 197, 200, 209-210
patterns of, 202-206
perceptions in, 196-197
purpose of, 195-196
screening in, 199
self disclosure in, 201-202
speaking rate in, 198
strengthening of, 195-211, 316
word meanings in, 208-209
Communicativeness, 171-172
Community:
    facilities, 110, 139, 140, 143, 147, 149-150
    property laws, 11
    restrictions on housing, 399-400
    rights and responsibilities, 400-402
    welfare, 403
Conceptual framework of management process,
    45-48
Conflict, 458
    resolution of, 206-208
Conservation of resources, 122, 376-379, 383-
    384
Constraint, 112, 158-159, 299, 458
Consumers, 16-18, 306-307, 389-390
    families as, 11, 16-18, 306-307, 382-383
    low-income, 17, 262, 306-307
    teenage, 16, 125
Consumer technology, 184, 316-318
    analyzing information, 184, 318
    comparative shopping, 317
    eliminating waste, 316, 377
    reading warranties, 318
    timing purchases, 316-317
Consumption, 458
Contract law, 401-402
Controlling, 120, 234-235
    definition of, 458
    financial activities, 315-318
Conversion, 119, 458
Costs:
    of child rearing, 125
    of environmental pollution, 368-371, 376-
        379, 382-384
    of food, 124, 126-127, 306, 317
    of goals, 280-281
    of goods and services in relation to income,
        18
    of living, 124-125, 128-129, 306-307
    opportunity, 462

Creativity, 176-178
  environment for developing, 178
Credit, 273, 293-299, 458
  cost of, 298-299
  definition of, 293
  installment, 294, 461
  laws, 297, 299
  management of, 293, 297-299
  ratio to income, 295, 299
  reputation, 296-297
  types of, 294
  vulnerability to, 299
Crisis, 404, 427-429, 458
  as opportunity, 427-429
  classification of, 427
  definitions of, 404, 427-428
  learning to manage, 428
  recovery from, 428-430
Culture, 64, 123, 388-389, 439-440
  effect on quality of life, 402-404
  effect on values, 64, 439-440
Cybernetics, 275

Debt, personal, 274-275, 287, 295-296, 299
Decision making, 85-103
  autonomic, 102, 457
  definition of, 85-458
  democratic, 9-10, 102, 459
  equalitarian, 102, 459
  and family composition, 100-101
  heuristic, 89-90
  influence in, 9, 101-102
  and management, 39, 85-86
  mode, 97
  models, 91-96
  process of, 40, 86-91
  rule, 97
  social class differences in, 102
  steps, 86-91
  strategies, 99-101
  style, 96-98, 458
  syncratic, 465
  technical, 91, 95-96, 465
Decisions:
  central-satellite, 98-99
  economic, 91, 93-95, 459
  examples of managerial, 12-14
  heuristic, 89-90
  irrational, 96, 461
  nonrational, 96, 462
  optimal, 89, 462

rational, 96, 464
satisficing, 89, 464
social, 91-93, 464
technical, 91, 95-96
types of, 91-96
Disability, 405-406
Dishwashing, 243, 246, 250, 255
Dispersion of family members, 14-15, 406-407
Divorce, 7, 406-407, 440
Dominance, 101-102, 459
Durable goods as components of wealth, 326, 328, 347-348

Economic resources, 145-146, 148-149, 280-300, 459
Economic uncertainty, 444-445
Ecosystems, 372-375, 459
Education:
  as human capital investment, 119-120, 184, 298
  and income, 289, 291
  as a value, 437
Employment:
  earnings of women, 289
  habits and routines, 173
  as medium for exchange of management practices, 389-390
  as social environmental resource, 37, 389-390
  of wives, and contribution to family income, 130
    and household operation time, 6, 261-262
    and power structure, 6, 102-103
  of women and resource use, 129-130
  time used in, 222-223
Energy:
  conservation of, 371, 383-384
  costs of household tasks, 242-243
  definition of, 373, 459
  depletion of, 371-375
  expenditures of disabled homemakers, 260
  forms of, 373, 374-375
  principles in using, 374-375
  as resource, 373-375
Enthusiasm, 169-170
Environment:
  biological components of, 390-391
  conservation of, 122, 367, 376-379, 383-384
  definition of, 459
  economic, 382-384
  far, 142
  intermediate, 142

near, 142
physical, 37
quality of, 110, 368, 372, 376-379, 381
social, 37, 379-390
Equipment, 258, 372, 377
Equity, 326, 346
Estates, 355-358
  joint tenancy, 357
  planning of, 355
  taxes on, 358
  transfer of, 355
  trust funds, 357-358
Evaluating, 42, 210-211, 234-235, 278, 319-320
  definition of, 42, 459
  progress toward financial success, 319-320
Expenditures, 301-308
  balancing income and, 307-308
  estimating, for budget purposes, 301-308
  fixed, 302-303, 460
  of low-income families, 306-307
  patterns of, 306-307
Expenses, 302-305
  fixed, 302, 303
  flexible, 302, 304, 305
Externalities and environmental control, 368-371, 375

Failure, fear of, 168, 260
Fair Credit Reporting Act, 297
Families:
  beginning, 19, 20, 275, 309-310
  childless, 22-25, 123
  contracting, 19, 21-22, 309-311
  corporation, 127-128
  definition of, 5, 459
  economic functions of, 10-11, 12
  expanding, 19, 20-21, 309-311
  extended, 6, 7, 101, 386
  functions of, 8-14, 384-386, 459
  low-income, 17, 262, 306-307
  as managerial units, 385-389
  middle-income, 17, 395
  nuclear, 6, 7, 385-386, 440-442
  as resources, 384-389
  single-parent, 6, 296, 443
  social functions of, 10-14, 384-386
  socio-economic status, 12, 389
  see also Family
Family:
  changes in, 404-408

communication, 201-202
definition of, 5-6, 459
dispersion, 14-16
dissolution, 406-408
formation, 404
heritage, 10, 23
integration, 10
interaction with community, 11-14, 399-400
life cycle, 19-25, 68, 124-125, 289, 308-311, 331, 445-451, 459
life styles, 5-7, 21-25, 440-442, 445-451
status, 13, 401
upheaval, 440-442
see also Families
Fatigue, 242, 258, 459
  alleviation of, 244, 390
  definition of, 459
  frustration, 258-259
  of homemakers with young children, 242
  posture and, 243
  and rest, 244-245
  work heights and, 251-258
Feedback, 199-201, 460
Financial management, 273-320, 324-359
  allowance system, 312
  equal salary system, 312-313
  family finance system, 311-312
  fifty-fifty system, 313
  handout or dole system, 313-314
  ten steps to more successful, 277-278, 279-320
Food:
  costs, 124, 126-127, 306, 317
  shortages, 442
  waste, 368
Fringe benefits, 36, 280-281, 288-290

Goal-orientation, 170, 273-275, 283, 300-301, 316, 378
Goals, 39, 46, 66-69, 125, 128, 167-168
  change in, 67-69
  classification of, 66
  definition of, 57, 66, 460
  financial, 279-281
  immediate, 66, 69, 279, 281, 460
  intermediate, 66-67, 69, 280-281, 461
  long term, 66-67, 69, 280-281, 462
  means-ends, 66, 67
  mindedness, 67-68
  national, 4
  orientation of, 67-68

relationship to values and standards, 66, 74-76

setting priorities in, 66-68

short-term, 66

Gross National Product, 4, 157, 241, 330-331, 382

and home-related work, 4, 241

as measure of progress, 4

Guidance, 42

Habit, 157, 172-174, 460

and management, 50

and personal development, 157, 172-174

work, 172-175

Handicapped persons, 259-261, 262, 405-406

Heritage, 10, 123

Heuristics, 89-90, 460

Home furnishings and appliances, 347-348, 372

expenditure for, 348

methods of accumulating, 348

purchases of upper-middle status families, 348

Homemaker, 241, 242-245

preferences in household tasks, 247

Home ownership, 345-347, 382

costs of, 346-347

and family life cycle, 345-346

as form of wealth, 345-347

reasons for, 346

reducing costs of, 347

Home-related work, 241-263

activities involved in, 223-224, 228-230, 430-437

of disabled homemakers, 259-261

division of labor in, 250-251

efficiency and, 243-244

human resources used in, 241-246

posture and energy in, 243-244

principles of, 243-258

role of homemaker in, 245-247

tasks, 241-243, 258

time spent in, 9, 223-224, 245-247

value of, 241, 330

Homestead rights, 11

Homosexual partnerships, 440

Honesty, 166-167, 438

Housing, 372, 378-379, 382

characteristics of, 372-375

effect of community facilities and restrictions on, 399-400

expenditures for, 273, 294-295, 462

influence on time used in household work, 251-258

Human:

capital, 110, 119-120, 183-184, 298, 330, 460

development, 31-33, 157-188

ecology, 460

needs, 58-60, 78-79, 163-164

resources, 34-36, 139-140, 141, 144-148, 157-188, 460

Implementing, 41, 47, 48-49, 232-234

definition of, 41, 460

direction in, 41

guidance in, 41

process of, 41

self discipline in, 41, 233, 464

supervision in, 41, 233

Impulse buying, 302, 305, 307, 316-317

Income:

annual, profile, 284-288, 457

average lifetime, 289, 291

elastic, 36, 293-295

families with low, 17, 306-307, 317

lifetime, profiles, 289, 291-293, 309-311, 461

occupational effect on, 285, 288, 289, 291-294

real, 287

Industrialization, effect on family life, 14, 368-372

Initiative, 170

Input, 46, 197, 461

Insurance, 307, 326-327, 329, 352, 353-355

Integration of family, 10

Intelligence, 168-169

Interdependence, 42, 119-120

Interference, 205, 461

Interrelatedness, 48-50, 115-120

of management functions, 48-50

model of, 49

of resources, 115-120

Invest, 275-276, 461

Investments, 339-345

annual rate of return from, 352-353

budgeting for, 332-333, 338, 351

in common and preferred stocks, 341, 344-345

comparison of, 334, 340-345

in corporate and municipal bonds, 340-341, 344-345

forms of, 340-343

in government securities, 340, 344-345
in mutual funds, 342, 344-345
purpose of, 343-344
in real estate, 342-343, 344-345
risk elements in, 339, 351
variable income, 325

Joint tenancy, 357
Judgment, 169

Kitchen arrangement, 254-257

Labor, division of, 9, 164-165, 250-251, 258
Leadership, 9-10, 461
Leisure time, 13, 15, 224-225, 461
Lend, 275-276, 461
Liability, 282-283, 461
Life cycle, 19-25, 68, 124-125, 289, 308-311,
     331, 445-451, 459
Life styles, 4-8, 367-372, 373-374, 382-384,
     439-440, 461
  alternate, 7-8, 440-442
  definition of, 5
  economic, 445-451
  family, 6-7
  influence of employment on, 389-390
  lower-status, 306-307
  middle-status, 306-307
  upper-stratus, 306
  of working wife families, 6, 129-130
Lifetime:
  income, 289, 291
  income profiles, 289, 291-293, 461
Liquid assets, 326-328, 462
Lists, 39-40

Management, 31-53, 57, 74-76, 85, 219-235,
     241-263, 273-320, 367-392, 409-415,
     421-451, 462
  as behavioral interaction process, 32-33, 37-
     42
  challenge of, 52-53
  change and, 11-14, 404-414, 421-451
  components of, 37-42
  definition of, 31, 37
  financial, 273-320
  over the life cycle, 308-311
  by objectives, 273-275
  purpose of, 39
  quality of, 50-51
Meta-communication, 211, 462

Minority groups, 403
Minors, 402
Mismanagement, 50-51
Mobility, 15-16, 202, 260, 408, 422
Models:
  annual income profiles, 284-288
  for communication, 199
  of decision making components, 90-95
  definition of, 462
  of economic decision making, 93
  for financial success, 275-276
  for identifying personal values, 62
  for planning, 42-43
  of interrelatedness of management functions,
     49
  lifetime income profiles, 289, 291-293
  of management process, 45-48
  management success pyramid, 179, 180
  for organizing time, 230-231
  of relationships between decisions, 98-99
  of restrictions in time use, 228
  of social decision making, 91-93, 464
  of technical decision making, 91, 95-96
Money:
  attitudes toward, 311-314, 316
  income, 3, 283, 462
  management, 273-320, 324-359
Mortgage, 273, 294-295, 462
Motions in home-keeping tasks, 242-244, 251-
     259
Motivation, 57-79, 158, 247, 258-259, 462
  definition of, 57, 462
  goals and, 57, 66-69
  management and, 57-59
  standards and, 57, 69-74
  values and, 60-66

Needs, 33, 58-60
  comparison with values, 59-60
  levels of, 58-59, 163-164
  maintenance, 78
  motivational, 78-79
  psychological, 58
  safety, 58-59, 163
  social, 58, 164-165
Net worth, 281-283, 462
Noise, 370
Norms:
  energy costs, 342-343
  time costs for household work, 9, 245-
     247

Opportunity cost, 275, 462
Organization, 40-41, 463, 465
  person centered, 40, 463
  task centered, 40, 465
Organizing, 38, 40-41, 462
  definition of, 40
  financial resources, 311-315
  levels of complexity in, 41
  process of, 40-41, 47, 49
Output, 375, 463
Overmanagement, dangers of, 51-52

Pace, 33-34, 229
Parkinson's Law, 124, 130
Pattern maintenance, 10, 439-440
Pension planning, 349-350
  through Social Security, 349
  private, 349-350
Perception, 196-197, 463
Perseverance, 170-171
Personality development, 8
Philosophy, 121-122, 314
  of life, 6, 19, 374, 377
  relation to values, 64
Planning, 38-40, 42-45
  definition of, 39, 463
  of income use, 300-315
  inflexible activities, 227, 461
  interval level, 43-44, 461
  levels of, 42-45, 461, 462, 463
  long-term financial, 308-315
  nominal level, 42, 462
  ordinal level, 43-44, 462
  ratio level, 43-45, 463
  time use, 227-228, 231-232
Plans, 40, 463
  annual financial, 300-308
  intermediate, 40
  long range, 40, 308-315
  related to organization, 44-45
  short term, 40
Policies, family, 3
Political institutions, 380-381
Pollution, 368-371
  and population growth, 367-371
  remedies for, 376-379, 383-384
Population, 15-16, 367, 442
  distribution, 16, 367
  and environmental quality, 367-372
  mobility, 15-16, 202, 260, 408, 422
  and world food shortage, 442

Power, 9-10, 101-103, 463
  cultural aspects of, 102
  definition of, 463
  dominance of, 101-102
  egalitarian, 459
Process, 32-33, 37-39, 463
Procrastination, 234
Production, 184, 223, 463
Psychic capital, 141

Quality of living, 3, 4-8, 14, 17, 31, 37, 42, 50,
    283, 316, 444
  culture and, 402-404
  definition of, 4, 463
  improvement of, 5, 376-379
  influence of social setting on, 399-404
  motivators and, 65, 74
  and population distribution, 15, 367-371

Real estate, 326, 327, 335, 342-343
Record keeping, 353
  center, 314-315
  for taxes, 318-319
Resources, 34-37, 109-131, 137-151, 157-188
  accessibility of, 114-115
  affective, 35, 144-145, 242
  alternate uses of, 119, 186-187
  assessment of, 137-151
  balance of, 124, 187
  characteristics of, 112-120
  classification of, 137-150
  clusters of, 185-186
  cognitive, 35, 144-145, 242, 458
  community, 110, 150, 408-409
  conservation of, 122, 376-379, 383-384
  conversion of, 119
  creation of, 119-120
  definition of, 109-110, 464
  depletion of, 371-372
  diminishing utility of, 113
  development of management, 168-172
  ecological classification of, 141-142
  economic, 36, 145-146, 148-149, 280-300,
    459
  environmental, 37, 110, 122, 146-147, 149-
    150
  factors affecting use of, 121-131
  human, 34-36, 110, 139-140, 141, 144-145,
    157, 180-183, 367-391, 459
  interchangeability of, 112-115, 116-120
  interdependency of, 119

limited, 115
manageability of, 120
national, 139-140
people as, 384-390
place utility of, 114
psychomotor, 35, 144-145, 147, 242, 463
quality and quantity of, 15, 124-125, 374-375, 442
relation to goals, 109, 111, 125, 128, 129, 138-140
scarcity of, 115
social-linkage classification of, 142-143
specific versus general, 140-141
substitution of, 116
temporal, 35-36, 145, 147-148, 465
timing input of, 185-186
use of, 110-111
utility of, 111, 113
Rights and responsibilities:
civil, 401
community, 400-402
contract, 401-402
family economic, 10-11, 12
parental, 401
social, 403-404
Risk:
in decision making, 94-95
identifying acceptable limits of, 351
in investments, 35, 339, 344
of limited resources, 262
in self development, 167-168
Role, 6, 9-11, 68, 241
changes, 404, 443-444
expectations, 246, 385
identification, 8-14, 443-444
reversal, 6
selection, 91
sex, 9, 160, 443-444
Routine:
clustering of activities, 229
habit, 172-174
procedural, 229

Safety, 163-164, 464
Satisficing, 89, 464
Saving, 275-276, 280, 295, 329, 332-339, 351-352, 464
reasons for, 280, 332-333
regularity and, 335
Savings institutions, 333-338
comparison of, 333-335

criteria for comparing, 334
growth of monthly deposits in, 337
liquidity of, 334
monthly deposit needed to reach goals in, 338
safety of, 334
time required for money to double in, 335, 336
yield of accounts in, 334
Schedule, 44
Sequence, 229, 245, 464
Self-actualization, 31, 58-59, 162-167, 388, 438-439
characteristics of, 165-166
definition of, 464
Self concept, 159-162, 444, 464
Self discipline, 41, 233, 464
Self improvement, 58
Services, 4, 129, 223-224, 241, 330
as a form of income, 4, 241, 287
money value of, 4, 129-130, 241, 330
Skill, 241, 351, 464
Sleep, 176, 224
Social Security, 349
Social functions of families, 10-14, 384-386
Solidarity, 10, 385-386
Spending patterns, 306-307
of low-income families, 17, 306-307
Standard budgets, 306
Standard of living, 71-74, 121-122, 272, 382-384
energy-driven, 373-374
and financial planning, 301, 325
Standards, 66, 69-74
classification of, 71-74
of consumption, 383-384
conventional, 70-71, 458
definition of, 57, 69, 464
examples of, 75-76
flexible, 71-73
for home-related work, 245-247
importance of, 70-71
performance, 76-78, 463
procedural, 76-78, 463
qualitative, 71, 73
scientific, 71, 464
sources of, 70-71
Status, 386-389
financial, 281-283
social, 12
Stocks, 329, 341-342, 351
common and preferred, 341

mutual funds, 342
  qualifications of brokers of, 341
Storage, 256-257
Strategies:
  conflict decision, 99
  cooperative decisions, 99
  for eliminating financial waste, 316-318
Substitution of resources, 116-119, 464
Success, 382-384
  definition of, 277-279, 464
Supervision, 41, 229, 233, 241, 465
Synchronization, 230-232, 465
System, 37-39, 311-314
  definition of, 465
  of financial management, 311-314

Time:
  as a resource, 35-36, 138-140, 145, 147-148
  biological, 35, 220, 457
  clock, 35, 36, 220, 235
  continuity of, 221
  evaluating use of, 226, 234-235
  free, 224, 460
  historical, 220-221
  leisure, 224-225
  management of, 219-235
  measurement of, 221-222
  norms for household work, 9, 246, 250
  pace of, 229-230
  patterns of using, 221-226, 246
  planning of, 227-228, 231-232
  psychological, 35, 145, 147, 463
  sense of, 147, 219, 465
  sequence of, 229
  scientific, 35, 145, 464
Trade-off, 15-16, 375-376, 465

Utility, 93, 111, 113-114, 375, 465
  diminishing, 113
  place, 114
  time, 114

Values, 46, 60-66, 389
  changes in American, 437-440
  characteristics of, 60-63
  clarification of, 61-63, 74-76
  classification of, 64-65, 91
  compared with motivators, 59-60, 74-76
  definition of, 60, 63, 465
  explicit, 61, 459
  implicit, 61, 460

  instrumental, 64-65, 461
  patterns of, 63-64
  traditional middle-class, 437-438

Wants, 33, 111, 317
Warranties, 318
Wealth, 36, 300, 325-359
  accumulation of, 331-352
  components of, 325-326
  control of, 350-352
  definition of, 325, 465
  inherited, 291-292, 331-332, 345
  management of, 330-331, 350-359
  as resource, 325, 345
  tax structure in, 355
  transfer of, 355-359
Wills, 355-357
  and dower rights, 356
  making of, 355-356
  types of, 356
Women:
  changing roles of, 9, 159, 160, 246, 385, 404, 443-444
  credibility of, 296
  with debt troubles, 296
  heading households, 6, 443
Work:
  areas, 257
  as a value, 438
  centers, 251, 254-255, 314-315
  definition of, 465
  habits, 172-175, 465
  heights, 251, 255
  methods of improving, 247-251
  time used in home-keeping, 9, 129-130, 223-224, 245-246
  triangle in kitchen, 255
  volunteer, 224
Working wife, 9, 102-103, 129-130, 222-223, 261-262, 389-390
Work simplification, 41, 247-259
  operation chart in, 250
  pathway chart in, 247
  process chart in, 248-250

Yield:
  definition of, 334, 465
  on investments, 327, 329, 344, 352-353
  from savings, 334